After the Clockwork Universe

The Emerging Science and Culture of Integral Society

S. J. Goerner

Floris Books

First published in 1999 by Floris Books

British Library CIP Data available

ISBN 0-86315-290-2

Printed in Great Britain
by Page Brothers (Norwich) Ltd, Norwich.

Contents

III THE HUMAN PREDICAMENT

Foreword

*We are at a watershed in history, a time of a 'Great
Divide,' as U.S. society shifts away from the dominant force
of Modernism ... Periods of transition, however, are
inherently uncertain. On the crest of the Great Divide,
history may slide either way.*   Paul Ray

A few years ago I wrote a nice academic book which described an
immense subterranean change taking place across science, from anthropology to physics. I explained too that this scientific change was
emerging in parallel with an even broader social transformation which
was somehow of the same nature. Then, after that book came out, a
strange thing happened. People involved in the social transformation
started calling, wanting to know more about how the science spoke to
their work and their concerns. These people were quite literally from
all walks of life. They were business people, youth groups, political
reform groups, educators, religious groups, physicists, media consultants, urban planners, retired people, economists and a host of others
too numerous to mention. Now I too stand amazed. I've been arguing
intellectually that an immense social change is in progress, but now I
realize that it is real.

So, I am going to try to tell the story again in more human terms.
Here is the gist. A great turning is going on. It covers all spheres of
life. It is beginning to come together and it is beginning to develop a
voice. If you look closely you will see it all around. However, what
you will *not* see is how the pieces connect. In a specialist world, no
one has time for integration. As a result, we are in the midst of a
major change which is both obvious, and yet still largely invisible and
hard to understand.

I have also discovered a study which explains why I found all those
people and why they found me. So, let us start with a dose of reality.
In 1996 sociologist Paul Ray conducted a survey which revealed a

remarkable trend. Until ten years ago the U.S. population was composed of two main cultural groups, Modernists and Traditionalists. Ray
found that one quarter of the population — *44 million adults* — now
fit a third group which he calls Cultural Creatives. Modernists ground
themselves in science, technology, and industry. They tend to disdain
older traditions. Traditionalists find their solidity in church and community and have doubts about the course that Modernists set. Creatives
hear the call of both older traditions. They seek a new society in which
science and spirit, technology and community work together for the
salvation of all. They represent a landmark change.

Creatives are found in every endeavour: medicine, art, science, business, education, religion, and so on. Furthermore, these numbers are
American, but the phenomenon is not. All over the world, people are
trying to build a new society which works in ways that the old one
does not. Using a loose amalgam of science and social activism, the
Creatives constitute a powerful movement whose great desire is to
bring about an *Integral Society* — one whose head, heart and soul are
no longer at odds.

This movement is already larger than those which ignited any previous historical shift. Yet, there is a problem. Most of the people involved do not realize they are part of a movement, especially one of
this size. Rather individuals and small groups rally around specific
issues and work at rethinking in specific fields. As a result, they talk
in the language and concerns of a hundred different fields. This makes
them unintelligible to one another and invisible to the outside world.
It also makes their power diffuse. We see only a few heretics pounding
their heads against the walls of various complacent establishments. We
hear only a Tower of Babel. Yet, world civilization is now filled with
millions upon millions of such voices, all aimed in the same direction.

For civilization to save itself, Creatives must come together and
realize their commonality in a more concrete way. They already have
a sense that their efforts are of a piece. The cry, 'Save the Planet,' for
instance, is heard by all and there is a common affinity for nature,
spirituality and holistic alternatives in medicine. Yet, Creatives need
to broaden their understanding of themselves and their reason for
being. They also need better science to ground their social and economic theory. These are the kinds of gaps which the new science can fill.
It is already beginning to step in.

Creatives have always been interested in cutting edge science, but for years they have had to work with snatches of new science whose connections to sustainable community were often hazy at best. This no longer needs to be the case. Over the last thirty years a host of mini-revolutions have been going on in scientific field after field. These too are of a piece. Beneath a bewildering variety of names and specialist jargon lies a single, common and quite comprehensive scientific shift. Putting these pieces together creates a powerful, embracing and yet remarkably concrete new view of the world, life and society.

It is this solid and increasingly well-synthesized picture that the Creatives need to bring about their new world. Many intuit that this is so. The need now is to make the new science clear and comprehensive, while keeping it honest, so that it does not go astray. That is what I am going to try to do in this book. My goal is to create a clear, well-connected understanding of the new science so people in the social transformation can use it to remake their world.

What view is being born? For about four hundred years Western civilization has been dominated by a way of thinking popularly known as the machine age or the clockwork universe. Today we are witnessing the rise of the Web view of the world. It is rising in both science and society for utterly practical reasons. It is rising in society because clockwork ways are failing — in education, economics, politics, and so on. It is rising in science because scientists finally have tools to explore how interwoven systems work. Thus, scientists have known that the world is deeply entwined for a very long time, but twentieth century electronics has finally provided tools which help them see what this really means. The result is a sudden jolt. Science's view as a whole — and that of virtually every field within it — is on the verge of a transformation. Many different words are emerging but the basic principles of change are all the same.

Thus, all those heretics speaking all those languages are actually giving birth to a very coherent new view. As pieces from across the spectrum come together, our view of life and the world is transformed. Yet, this new picture is also ancient. In it we rediscover secular and spiritual insights that are as old as the hills. Old and new, scientific and spiritual, practical and transformative — all our pieces begin to fit in a wondrously seamless whole.

I, like others, call this change the rise of *Integral Society* and its attending *Integral Science* because both have everything to do with connectivity. I call it 'Web World' because, where for four hundred

years we tried to describe everything as a machine, we are suddenly
realizing that most things are better described as webs. Furthermore,
webs don't work like simple machines. We are beginning to understand what this might mean — from biology and economics to social
sustainability and spirituality.

Let me leave you with one more thought. The change we are facing
can be described as 'Big Change' because it occurs in all spheres at
once — social, political, economic, spiritual, and scientific. Every once
in a while a crescendo of change surges forth. Like a seventh wave
swollen with streams from many directions, Big Change sweeps away
the social reality that was, leaving a new one in its wake. That is what
is happening today. It has happened before.

The object of this book is to make today's Big Change soundly
visible so you can judge. It is important to see clearly because, on the
crest of a Great Divide, history can slide either way. The better we see,
the better our chances of birthing a safe, sane and sustainable
civilization.

Preface

Today we live according to the latest version of how the universe functions. This view affects our behaviour and thought, just as previous versions affected those who lived with them. Like the people of the past, we disregard phenomena which do not fit our view because they are 'wrong' or 'outdated.' Like our ancestors, we know the real truth.   James Burke, *The Day The Universe Changed*

Big Change has happened before. Thus, about four hundred years ago, western civilization underwent a remarkable transformation: the medieval world of knights, priests, and commoners unraveled and the modern world of capitalists, scientists and laymen emerged. At that time seemingly immutable beliefs about science, politics, economics, social relations and religion broke from their bindings, shifted, intertwined and moved out again, producing a whole new tapestry of life. Western civilization changed from top to bottom and the world we call the clockwork universe emerged.

Since science as we know it also emerged at this time, we tend to dismiss the seventeenth-century transformation as a one time event, the end of superstition. But apparently it was not. Now we of the modern world are facing a similar transformation. Seemingly immutable beliefs have already broken from their bindings and are shifting. If we are lucky, and if we take care, they will intertwine and move out again, producing yet another new — and hopefully improved — tapestry of life. This book is about those shifting threads in science, politics, economics, social relations and spirituality and the possibility that they are all part of one great movement, the reweaving of Western and perhaps world civilization. The clockwork version of the world is unraveling and the tapestry of the world as a dynamic interwoven web is taking form. This is the story of that new tapestry and the what, why and how that go with it.

Personally, I believe the transformation is underway. I see my main task as making that clear and explaining why a sweeping change could take place. I use three threads — history, science and society at large — to do so. Each is necessary to the overall picture.

History is relevant because it shows how our current story of the world came into being and how societies change. We are the product of a previous reweaving. To see the parallels between then and now, we must see how the past too is a web.

Science is relevant because it is the main reason modern people feel their tapestry reflects 'real truth' (no credulity, just facts) and because science too is undergoing a broad and encompassing transformation. Watching this profound change move across science and understanding the reasons for it helps make the social change vastly more understandable. Four hundred years ago a Polish priest named Copernicus changed the earth's place in the solar system and with it people's perception of how they fit in the universe. Today, despite our sophistication, we are facing an equally radical rethinking.

But for all the fascinating aspects of history and science, what draws me to this subject is the final thread, society at large and the potential for change there as well. Clockwork assumptions now permeate everything we do, from how we educate our children and run a business to how we imagine God. Most people have no idea that this is the case. Few realize how different the world seemed before the clockwork world and fewer still imagine that something much different could come after. On the other hand, many of those same people believe that something is wrong. Whether it is governmental absurdity, economic malaise, increasingly horrific violence, or religions that do more to create bigotry than love — our world seems to have gone awry and a sense of disquiet haunts most people. The only thing that keeps most of us running in our usual treadmills is that no one seems to know what else to do.

This is where my story begins, a civilization on the cusp of change. Many people sense it, but little in our philosophy prepares us for this change. Or does it? I've thought about the change we are facing for a long time, particularly with an eye as to how to explain it. Is science about to change our view of the world? Is this a spiritual resurgence, brought about by a realization that there is something more to life than can be put on a data sheet? Is this a social rethinking brought on by economic fragility, loss of community, and rage at power structures that seem to have gone profoundly astray? My answer is that it is *all of these*. These issues are interwoven, not separate. What is interesting is that whenever I give talks about this change I find that most people know this. They know our crisis is multi-faceted and that the facets are related. I show how the facets connect, but in doing so I am mainly giving coherence to an already deeply felt belief. Apparently the average lay person's philosophy is quite prepared, even eager, for this change. Thus, though in theory the ideas expressed in this book are radical, my experience is that most people do not experience them as such. They experience them as a clarification of something already suspected and deeply desired.

So let me make a distinction. I am not going to describe the unraveling of western civilization nor the end of science. What we are facing is the unraveling of our culture's dominant philosophies, a tightly-woven mutually-reinforcing web of beliefs that got their start four hundred years ago and are highly institutionalized today. Because they are institutionalized, these beliefs dominate public discussion and exert political, economic and social influence. They are so intertwined, that they form a monolithic, seemingly immutable complex — which oddly enough is exactly how the medieval complex of Catholic Church, medieval nobility and the theory of God's design seemed before them. As before, the dominant complex is giving way.

Still, though this dominant web forms the prism through which most of us have been taught to view the world, it should not be mistaken for all that people know or believe. Rather, as Burke says, it is merely the latest model of how the universe functions, replete with benefits and shortcomings. If you probe a little bit, you will find that many people have been waiting for and working toward a better model for a long time. It is now coming together.

The shock is the degree of change. Modern ideas, despite their sophistication, are not an almost perfect picture of the world, but merely another latest version of how the world works — one that is about to go away.

What lies on the other side? Much that is expected and much that is not. The core of the change centers on the image of webs and uses terms like interdependence and connectivity. Most people already know this. Global village, eco-systems and planetary consciousness: images of connectivity already abound. Yet, current images of connectivity barely scratch the surface. The new science will add a specificity and profundity not yet popularized. New understandings, for instance, play out rigorously in places not previously imagined. Societies, economies, and your body, for example, are all webs which follow similar rules and patterns of change. Many seemingly immutable scientific images will also melt away. For example, many of the dreadful images of Darwinian evolution will go away. A lot of equally dreadful beliefs about human beings will go with them.

The metaphoric shift from clock to web is thus but the tip of a very large iceberg. A lot of important specifics go with the new metaphor and these have profound implications for all that we believe. To help handle these specifics, I'm going to introduce the book by giving a brief summary of the whole story — a little gestalt to hold on to as the details of the story unfold throughout the body of the book. The next few pages provide a condensed picture with pointers to chapters where the discussions take place.

Web World

There are no separate problems anymore.
John Lovejoy, CBS Morning News, 4/20/92

How could a profound change sweep the modern world? Let me start by describing how the change is actually taking place — in a way that includes society and science.

For a long time now a very large number of people all over the world have been working, driven by a sense that something is not right — scientifically, socially, economically, spiritually — and that a new way is needed. The picture I'll describe is the result of work being done in an endless number of places all over the globe. Some of it was done recently and some long ago. No one person or group commissioned all this work. Each particular effort started as a result of someone facing a thorny problem — in public policy, in business, in religion, in biology, in human relationships and even in physics. But the result is striking and odd. Individuals, driven by problems in their disparate fields, are coming up with remarkably common insights. They find themselves in unexpected harmony with a vast common effort. Now transformations in business, government, science, spirituality, and health (to mention a few) are going on in parallel and writers like myself can come along and say 'a vast movement is afoot.' A complex tissue of work now all seems to push in the same direction.

Thus, the social explanation of why a change is happening is that the great hive mind we call humanity has been at work. It is reaching critical mass on a new common view. This view was not invented by one great person, but by many great people, some famous and most obscure. It is an act of the great 'we' or, as the Chinese would say, of 'the web that has no weaver.' Furthermore, though this explanation is unusual, it should not be too surprising. After thirty years of the ecology movement, most of us are already conditioned to think in terms of complex webs with subtle connections and invisible order. Even schoolchildren think in terms of global connections. A hive mind is already easy to imagine. This ease of imagining is, in fact, an indication of the change.

Still, it is hard to imagine why people working on incredibly different problems should come up with common insights. What could be common between physics, public policy and religion? Oddly enough, science provides the easiest and most concrete path to answering this question. The answer, however, requires that we go back in history to see why we view the world as a machine whereas our ancestors did not.

Thus, five hundred years ago most educated people still saw the world of the Middle Ages, a world in which rocks were alive, angels were real and everything's place in nature was fixed by God's design. But the medieval world was crumbling as cynicism grew about who benefited from fixed positions.

Then, four hundred years ago, the Scientific Revolution came to the rescue, pulling western civilization out of the era of credulity and abusive authority into the modern world of Reason and Scientific Laws. Science and western society have been inseparable ever since. Virtually every aspect of western civilization — from family relationships and economics to God sitting 'outside the system' — has been coloured by the sweep of reason and science. In Burke's terms, science defines our 'latest version of how the universe functions.' This tacit colouring of everything we do explains why commonalties lie hidden in physics, public policy and religion. (Chapter 1 explains why this happened and outlines the history of how it took place.)

So, nowadays, it goes without saying that when you say 'modern,' you also mean 'scientific.' Similarly, if you say a view is different from the modern view, you also seem to be saying it will be different from the scientific view — or at least currently dominant scientific views. This last is a problem for a book like this one. Science has been so brilliant, powerful, and demonstrable that it often seems essentially complete, which is why its latest theories are often taught as if they were Truth (with a capital T). Doubting these seems to mark one as a doubter of Reason, a throwback to the age of credulity. Besides, everywhere one looks one part of science reinforces another giving a wonderful consistency to the whole system. Certainly science will keep on improving itself, but it is now almost impossible to imagine a Copernican-type change to science as a whole. What change of heart could possibly sweep through all of science, altering a wide range of scientific theories and with them social assumptions? The system seems too tight.

Traditionally people have assumed that the only way to change science would be to overthrow the one view that dominates the whole of modern science. People call this dominant view the Newtonian view or the mechanistic view and they use nineteenth-century physics as the pinnacle example. I call it the clockwork view.

People inside and outside of science have been pushing for mechanism's end for centuries for fairly obvious reasons. Mechanism brought humankind power and a shroud of emptiness. Because it was powerful, we couldn't put it down. Because it spread callousness, sterility and soullessness on everything it touched, philosophers have been decrying its use for over two hundred years. Popular media echoes the dilemma. Science and technology have made the world ugly and yet we cannot and will not turn away from them.

Concern about callous machine attitudes toward human beings and the environment is at an all time high. Cynicism is also growing about who benefits from controlling the machines of industry and government. Unfortunately, machine-science seems ever so solid and overthrow seems unlikely. The two big exceptions to its rule, quantum mechanics and relativity, make a knowable difference only at incredibly small sizes or at near-light speeds. The regular world still belongs to Newton.

This is where my story becomes a bit unconventional. Overthrow is not necessary because science is about to shed the machine mantle all by itself. You see, there is a core flaw woven throughout the fabric of dominant scientific views. It is nobody's fault really, and it has little to do with Newton or mechanism *per se*. So, let me redirect you. The other name for the dominant scientific view is 'analytic.' Analysis means 'studying things by breaking them apart.' Hence, four hundred years ago, when science as we know it was beginning, its great thinkers founded their endeavour on a seemingly indispensable set of strategies: control, isolate, break down. These are core scientific methods even today and, given the state of the art in the 1600s, they were indeed indispensable. Unfortunately they did shape scientific and hence social beliefs. Analytic assumptions now play out in an unbelievably diverse array of social and scientific beliefs. I explore some of this array in Chapter 2, including effects on beliefs about weight loss and whether we can predict the future. (Chapters 3–8 follow how analytic assumptions play out in beliefs about what makes a business run well to how life evolved).

Meanwhile let us concentrate on the idea that there is a relatively simple reason why all sorts of people are coming up with common insights and why science as a whole is about to change. The simple reason is that our culture is riddled with assumptions based on separation, separability, and *non*-dependence. These assumptions are now crumbling under the sheer weight of evidence that 'separating' often creates false impressions. Ironically, analytic thinking is breaking down, killed by the sins of its own omissions.

Today the great realization is that breaking apart and controlling *radically underestimates the role that connectedness (interdependence) plays in the world*. Thus, the change of heart that is about to sweep through science as a whole, is a new and profound appreciation of interdependent dynamics, or in my terms, 'the way webs work.' This change of heart will alter perceptions up and down the scientific and cultural ladder because a lot of what we think we know is invisibly distorted by analytic assumptions.

The magnitude of this change is also understandable. Interdependence is the one thing that *is* everywhere. Interdependence is found between atoms in a molecule, planets in the solar system, ants in their colonies, cells in your body and agents in economies. I will be discussing how it plays out in urban planning, anthropology and subatomic physics, to mention a few. It is also hidden under a vast range of terms including networks, teamwork, eco-systems, systems theory, communities, feedback loops, societies, etc. Interdependence is also an everyday occurrence. Thus, when you go to the grocery store you are experiencing an incredibly dynamic web of connections between farmers, packagers, distributors, delivery men, grocers, advertisers, banks, tractor makers, etc.

The reasons for a wholesale shift are, thus, neither mystical nor obscure. You don't need a theory of quantum realities to understand.

Interdependence is the one thing that applies to science and society as a whole. Indeed, once you strip away the differing words, it becomes easy to see that a massive change is already in progress. The hive mind has been at work. Over the last thirty or more years a remarkable parallel development has been taking place. Mini-revolutions in physics, brain research, economics and archaeology are of a piece. Underneath a bewildering variety of specialist concerns is one great common movement — the shift to a type of science that concentrates on how complex interwoven webs work. What is surprising is how long the switch has been going on, how well pieces from different fields fit and how much quality work exists that most laymen and classical academics do not know about. And all of it, every single stitch, is a result of analytic assumptions being overthrown because their inadequacies have reached the level of absurdity and dysfunction.

So, five hundred years ago Copernicus rocked the medieval world by showing that the sun was the center of the solar system. Now we can see that the center of science as a whole is shifting from a view based on *in*dependence (studying separate things) to one based on *inter*dependence (studying how things are woven together). It is this shift that is about to make a huge difference — while still being perfectly scientific and utterly commonsensical.

Order and Rigour — the Roots of a New Age

Still, this explanation for the change does not tell you enough. Science is beginning to develop a web view that will replace the machine view, but how much could really change? Web-thinking has been growing in- and outside of science for years now. It has already made tremendous inroads in world civilization through the ecology movement. But it has not broken analytic dominance in either science or society and there is a growing sense of so what? The world may be interwoven, but knowing this does not help much with daily dilemmas or large-scale problems.

So web-thinking needs a boost, something to make it more useful and more compelling. What could give web-thinking the boost it needs to come of age? The two-stage answer is: (1) new tools and, (2) the discovery of pervasive order.

The first boost is easy to understand. You can't have a decent science of interdependent dynamics without appropriate tools. Computers and other electronics allow scientists to develop tools which, for the first time, can handle the complexity of interwoven systems. This means today's scientists can explore *how* connections (bumps, encounters, feedback loops, etc.) work using simulations, computer graphics, etc. In short, computers make it possible to study webs rigorously. Like the microscope and the printing press, computers open up a whole new world of science.

So, people have been trying to understand how our interwoven world works for two thousand years but now we have the beginnings — just the bare beginnings — of a set of tools that are more appropriate for the job. Already a glittering parade of insights about how webs work have begun to alter scientific perceptions. Scientists, especially the young ones, are now flocking to these tools and insights in a movement that is huge, obvious, completely understandable but still largely hidden in a fog of scientific jargon. For example, the terms Chaos and Complexity are both pop labels for a new science emerging around the expanded understanding of *interdependent dynamics*. (Chapter 2 explores these.)

The second boost is harder to understand, but much more important because it speaks to the nature of the world in which we live. When scientists began using their wondrous new tools they made a startling discovery. Systems which appeared to be a tangled mess, housed an unexpected type of order. Order in chaos! — as the catch phrase goes. Furthermore, this extraordinary and alluring order is everywhere. Every corner of our world is sewn tight with beautiful, delicate, dancing order of a kind clockwork science never imagined. The implication is profound. Ours is not an empty, disorderly world, but an exquisitely structured web whose design embraces and affects all things.

So let me give you a new catch phrase. *Webs produce pattern, structure and organization — we just couldn't see it before.* You can say this phrase over and over to yourself because it lies behind every scientific change that will be discussed in this book — from city planning to planetary motion. It is the one over-arching insight that binds all fields together. It is the reason web-thinking is becoming more approachable and more useful. How does a brain with its web of neurons work? Why do fire-flies flash and tree-toads croak in synchrony? What are the patterns by which epidemics spread? New answers are cropping up everywhere. Web science comes of age because we have tools to explore the order which rises from interwoven exchange.

There is one last important piece to the new view. This new ability to see the order which pervades the universe is naturally spurring a re-thinking of the origins of that order, from the earliest beginnings down to our daily lives. A host of new insights about how organizations emerge and evolve are also popping up. Here we begin to understand the pressures that drive webs and the cycles they follow.

As we begin to understand these ideas in a rigorous way, we suddenly find that one huge thing wrong with our current views is that we have but the barest comprehension of why organizations emerge and evolve as they do. Why did life emerge? Was it an accident? Why do great societies rise only to crumble? Are these accidents too? We also find that the science that we have been using — and which we thought was nearly complete — is, in fact, crude and naive. We realize this most poignantly because we discover that we have misconstrued human nature, particularly how we came into the world and what we must do to survive and thrive.

The most important implication of the new science, therefore, is a radical rethinking of evolution itself. No longer a crude outcome of accidents and selfish genes, evolution now appears to be a massively interwoven ordering process which runs from molecules to man. Neurophysiologist Roger Sperry put the idea this way:

> In the eyes of science ... man's creator becomes the vast
> interwoven fabric of all evolving nature ... A cosmic scheme that
> renders most others simplistic in comparison.

If we add energy, therefore, we find that life and the intricate world in all its wondrous forms is a result of web dynamics and energy flow. It is not so hard to imagine. What makes a tornado rise up and what makes a whirlpool organize into a funnel? Energy flow gives webs shape and pushes them to move. (I describe energy's role in Chapter 3.)

But there is more. What made the cauldron of chemical soup on early earth coalesce into the first living cells? Life itself was born of energy and intertwining. The swirl and flow then continued. Early life breathed out, breathed in and the atmosphere, oceans and land shifted, linked and structured themselves into webs and cycles both large and small. All that 'is' on this earth — grass, trees, air, oceans, animals, and human beings — is linked, bound in a design whose intricacy we are just now coming to comprehend. We will probably never fully fathom it.

Life's own intricacy then grew. What made early cells band together into little collectives whose members took on special tasks — blood, nerve, lung, and feet — to make a better whole? Groups survive better and can do more than individuals alone. Indeed, collaboration seems to be a main source of evolutionary leaps. Underneath, however, energy flow and web dynamics still set the beat and pushed the pattern. The pulse continues today. For four billion years life has become more intricate, and better flowing — until today, when we can see in the phosphorescent glow of computer-graphics exactly how interwoven systems bend and twist to give rise to brains, eyes and feet. (I describe the new view of evolution in Chapter 4.)

Increasing intricacy also did not stop with living organisms. Rather there is strong evidence that similar pressures and patterns play out in social evolution (see Chapter 7). Even economics is beginning to be rethought as a web, or rather, an ecology. Here new insights about organization and evolution make it easier to see why human beings often destroy their own socio-economic systems (see Chapter 8). Failure to nurture fine-grained connections creates economic instability. The collapse of complex civilizations and the struggle to make a sustainable world today are the stories here.

Now you might think that this is where the story ends. But the more daring among us have not stopped. These people carry the story on into the evolution of minds and consciousness. These mysteries too appear to be part of the design, a most delicate part of the weave. Clockwork thinkers did not dare say such things because, in their world, everything is material and essentially dead. But in a web world these ideas are not so strange. The world is itself flowing and creative. That the Great Ordering Oneness in which we are embedded created consciousness is no more or less miraculous than that it created life and its increasing intricacy. (Chapter 5 outlines some of the new thinking on mind and consciousness.)

The new understanding of evolution, thus creates a cascade of paradigm shifts which produces one vastly changed whole. Darwinian images soften and dissolve while a new sense of how the world works and how human beings fit within an entwined design rise to take their place. Three recurrent themes run throughout the new vision:

- *Learning* is a universal process at work in the world. It is behind the evolution of mind and also behind humanity's central survival strategy — collaborative learning.

- *Collaboration* is the central path of evolution and the best way to survive and thrive.

- *Energy* — the rules of energy and interwoven change play out at all
  levels. We must learn the rules which govern change in an interwoven world because apparently we too are affected by its invisible
  motion.

There is also one last bit more. When you put the pieces of the science
together, the result is a picture of the world that matches rather closely
the one described by the great spiritual traditions (see Appendix C).
Harmony, for instance, begins to make sense again. Secular philosophies too seem less disjointed. Indeed, a lot of pieces begin to fit
together and our sense of humankind's place in the world changes
abruptly. The Integral dream of head, heart and soul rejoined becomes
completely reasonable.

The Integral World — or What Analysis Missed

Understanding how the world goes about ordering itself — dynamically and interdependently — creates a very big change. In it we are
radically reborn. And as odd as this may sound, it is largely the result
of hundreds of scientific pieces beginning to fall into place.

The result is exactly like what happened with Copernicus and the
sun-centered model of the solar system, only on a much larger scale.
Like an optical illusion that can be seen two ways, we've been looking
at the world one way only to realize suddenly that there is another —
better — way to see the world hidden in the same set of spots. All the
facets of the world that you know remain, but they now trace out a
profoundly different form.

The contrast in vision is easy to see. Machine science created an image
of the world which was sterile at best. The physical world was a billiard
ball universe of colliding particles going nowhere. Life was an accident
that proceeded through a nature red in tooth and claw. Human history was
a sound and fury signifying nothing and the events which populate the
world were mostly random. Humankind was alone and part of nothing
much larger than itself. None of these images will survive the change.

In their place is emerging the picture of a subtly structured world. This
world is at once old, new, and vastly more appealing. Where current
science promotes the image of randomly-bumping particles, the new
science sees a self-organizing universe. Where the old believed economies
could be planned and controlled, the new believes economies must be
grown, particularly at a grass-roots level. Where the old saw nature as red

in tooth and claw, the new finds nature a subtle seamstress who sews Beings great and small into chains and circles which make the world flow. Life was not an accident (at least not completely), nor is it separate. Life and its push toward increasing complexity appears to be the result of an interwoven process involving the whole biosphere. We are part of something larger than ourselves and creation is still with us. This cosmos weaves order into the finest corner of the world.

The change we face is immense and beautiful. We are witnessing the end of the analytic era and the beginning of the synthetic, integrative, interwoven era in science. What is ending is the belief that *analytic* science was all that science could, should, or need be. What is unexpected is the magnitude of the perceptual change. Once upon a time humankind imagined itself embraced by an invisible web, a natural part of an awesome and creative cosmos. We believed this 10,000 years ago in the dawn of time. We believed it a thousand years ago in the age of God's Design. We are about to believe this again, now for well-grounded scientific reasons.

* * *

And so we return to the original thesis now in a much changed form. We live in an interwoven world, a 'web that has no weaver,' as the Chinese say. This web, woven at once by all of us, is reaching a point of self-transformation. It is not just political man or economic man or even scientific and spiritual man, but all these elements of humankind that are changing. Like a caterpillar that has woven itself a cocoon, western civilization and perhaps world civilization is on the cusp of a metamorphosis. And perhaps, just perhaps, the civilization that will emerge will be not only more beautiful, but also more rigorous and more sane than any that has preceded it. That is the hope and the movement afoot.

How to read this book

> *Upon this gifted age, in its dark hour, falls from the sky a*
> *meteoric shower of facts ...*
> *They lie unquestioned, uncombined.*
> *Wisdom enough to leech us of our ill is daily spun;*
> *but there exists no loom to weave it into fabric ...*
>
> Edna St Vincent Millay

Today there is a new loom and we can weave a new fabric. We need
to see whole cloth, because uncombined pieces give us no vision. We
need better vision because our times are precarious. What I am going
to do is integrate at least some of the meteoric shower of science,
history and social change that fills our world.

Synthesis, however, can be daunting. Connecting threads requires I
touch on a lot of subjects. Because some topics will interest some
readers more than others, I have written each chapter as something of
a stand alone and ended each with a brief summary of its main ideas.
Thus, though there is a general building of concepts, it is also possible
to read about the topic that interests one first, to see how it may be
affected by the tide of new thinking. I hope these arrangements
help provide a balance between the need to see the whole, and the
need to include the specific. I strongly recommend you explore areas
that interest you first, if tackling the whole spectrum seems too
overwhelming.

The book itself is divided into four sections. The first section, 'A
Bit of History,' explores the last Big Change and sets the stage for the
current one. The second section, 'Web World' outlines the scientific
change from math to mind. The third, 'The Human Predicament' looks
at how the new view helps reframe history, economics and human
nature. The fourth, 'Integral Society' looks at reform efforts bubbling
up today. It also explores the reconciliation of head, heart and soul
looming on the horizon.

Part I: A Bit of History
Chapter 1: Big Change, Past and Present
This explores the rise and fall of the medieval world and the rise and
exhaustion of the clockwork view. It shows how Big Change works as
an interwoven process.

Part II: Web World
Chapter 2: Crumbling and Emerging
This explains why scientific views are changing in mundane and exotic
ways, from diets and ant trails to chaos and fractals. It also begins to
explain why there is a larger design at work in the world.

Chapter 3: Energy and Basic Principles of Change
This describes energy's under-reported role in evolution and organization. It outlines basic patterns of change using simple systems and summarizes the main principles of the new dynamics.

Chapter 4: The Creative Cosmos
This describes how web dynamics play out in the creation of life and the evolution of all things on earth. It explains how Dynamic Evolution differs from Darwinian Evolution and why Darwinism has tended to corrupt our view of life.

Chapter 5: The Mind of God, Many and One
This explores the evolution of brains, minds and consciousness. It develops a deep understanding of why human societies are a collaborative learning system.

Part III: The Human Predicament
Chapter 6: The Nature of Humanity and the World
This summarizes how Integral Science changes our view of the world and ourselves.

Chapter 7: The Cycles of Civilization
Thanks to the way our brain evolved, human beings are predisposed to two cultural patterns, one collaborative and one domineering. Dominator culture dominates today, but it is also unstable. This chapter outlines the standard cycle of dominator civilization and explores the causes of regression and collapse in terms of the new science.

Chapter 8: The Economic Debate
This looks at why clockwork thinking is failing in economics and what some of the alternatives might be.

Part IV: Integral Society
Chapter 9: Seeds of a New Way
In the end, the quest to create a safe, sane, sustainable civilization must be the quest to build an intricate and robust human ecology. This chapter looks at some of the efforts afoot to reweave social fabrics and reinvigorate human ecologies.

Chapter 10: The Awakening
This looks at why our head, heart and soul might reasonably come back together.

Appendix A: Copernicus Again!
A summary of some of today's Copernican changes — that is, seemingly indisputable beliefs which undergo radical revision. Reductionism and materialism, for example, will both disappear.

Appendix B: Contrasts in Scientific and Cultural Visions
A summary in tabular form of the contrasts between clockwork and web science and culture.

Appendix C: Oneness and the Perennial Philosophy
A summary of the perennial philosophy and some of the parallels between it and the new scientific vision of the physical world.

PART 1

A BIT OF HISTORY

Throughout the centuries there have been the accepted facts,
the conventional wisdom ... and often much of it turned out
to be totally wrong. Then the visionaries stepped in,
expanded our vision and changed the picture.

James Burke

CHAPTER 1

BIG CHANGE, PAST AND PRESENT

Alas, all is Newtonian. Magic is gone from the world.
Character in television program, *Northern Exposure*

In the beginning God created reality. Shortly thereafter people began creating models to explain how that reality worked. In the late 1500s, scientists struck upon a particularly productive model — the world as a machine. This model — also called the clockwork universe, the modern world, mechanism, and Newtonian science — is, of course, exquisitely powerful. It has sent men to the moon, it has put computers on our desks and it is now mapping the human genome. It is frequently taken to *be* science and it is closely associated with physics, past and present. Our everyday existence is so cluttered with the wonders of this science that most of us find it hard to imagine what life was like without it. Indeed, the power of the machine view is so obvious that mentioning it is trite.

On the other hand, the machine sense of the world has been decried almost as often as it has been praised. Machine science is commonly associated with dissection, control, manipulation, cruelty, sterility and the oppressive kind of future envisioned in George Orwell's *1984* or Aldous Huxley's *Brave New World*. It is regularly characterized as either hostile to, inappropriate for, or completely baffled by certain things, particularly human things. Movies habitually portray scientists as socially inept, having technical facts and know-how, but out of place with illogical things like emotion (remember Mr Spock in television's *Star Trek*). In fact, the image of scientists discounting human concerns like warmth, caring, consciousness and spirituality — calling them illusion, epiphenomena, or superstition — is formula. And this formula is based on fact. Thus, the distinguished twentieth-century psychologist, John Watson, gave the following machine-age advice:

There is a sensible way of treating children. Never hug or kiss
them, never let them sit in your lap. If you must, kiss them
once on the forehead when you say goodnight and shake hands
with them in the morning.

But it is not just emotive areas like caring and spirituality that elude
machine science, complex things like economies and societies are also
problematic. The disciplines that study these topics use machine
science techniques, but the results are soft. The so-called soft sciences
can't predict, they can't control and they seem to have but a poor
understanding of what makes their systems change. Whether it is the
cliché of economists giving contradictory advice or the specter of political experts failing to predict such major events as the collapse of the
Soviet Union — you don't have to look far for examples of the
machine view's poor relationship to the human world.

Everyone knows these images. In fact, they are so common, that
few of us ever stop to think how odd it is that our culture's single
greatest knowledge-making machine is commonly portrayed as antithetical to the human world. The people who do think about such
things have largely been stumped. Machine science's conflicting faces
— brilliant, beneficial, powerful, ugly, oppressive, and inadequate —
defines a dilemma that has plagued philosophers for the last two
hundred years. How is it that a model this powerful could be other
than fact and yet if this model is fact how is it that it is so poor at
almost all questions concerning human beings from what gives meaning to life to why economies and civilizations collapse?

So philosophers decry but, when push comes to shove, machine
science usually wins. It simply seems too true. The modern version of
the real truth is that science is very good at physical things, very poor
at human subtlety and its tendency to produce alienation and amorality
is simply part of the high cost of looking objectively at the facts of the
real world. Many people wish it were otherwise, but few really believe
these characteristics of science will ever change.

On the other hand, there is now a very reputable and rapidly
growing group that does believe science will change and that it will
change in a wholesale fashion in the relatively near future. This group
is composed of scientists in disciplines ranging from mathematics and
biology to economics, and anthropology and it is being joined by
philosophers, social activists, artists, mystics and humanists of many

stripes. This book is an attempt to make it clear why they believe science — and society — will change and what they imagine the universe will look like on the other side of the change. The machine view, the clockwork universe, is ending in both science and society. This ending constitutes a huge change with implications for all that we know — or think we know.

Still, in order to understand why we may be facing Big Change, we need more than a fairy-tale understanding of how and why societies reinvent themselves. Thus, I begin my story with a tour of two earlier Big Changes, the birth of the medieval world and the birth of the clockwork world. These are not simple stories of the triumph of science, of course, but complex stories of civilizations in change. Let us begin with the idea that our ancestors saw the world very differently than we do.

Once upon a Time

Once upon a time, the world was a very different place. It was full of angels and kings. And then suddenly, in a relatively short period of time, it wasn't. In roughly the seventeenth century, Western civilization underwent a remarkable change. A large number of people in all walks of life began to agree that their world worked like a machine and they began to reconstruct their world in this image. Machine themes — a focus on material reality, lawfulness, rationality and logic — emerged in all areas of human endeavour from the Enlightenment's belief in a lawful, controllable universe to the industrial revolution's remaking of economics. All of these elements were part of a general shift whose various parts fed each other.

Machine science was born during this period but it wasn't just science that changed, it was the entire structure of western civilization including the way everyday people lived their lives and experienced their world. In fact, you could say without exaggeration that what changed was people's core experience of the world. In the year 1600 most educated people living in Western Europe still looked out on the world of the Middle Ages. In this world, all creatures were part of a Great Chain of Being, with man between the angels and the lower animals. The universe was experienced as alive, imbued with purpose and infused with spirit. The world was enchanted, there was ample place for miracles and Divine intervention. Kings were instituted by God for the protection of their people.

Yet, by 1700 most educated people perceived a very different world. They saw a rational universe, constructed and set in motion by the Creator but with subsequent events accounted for by mechanical forces and lawful behaviors. Man was separate from nature and had the potential to control nature through scientific knowledge and technological prowess. Angels and the Great Chain of Being were part of religion, not the physical world. Kings were political beings with personal interests that were often given precedence over the needs of their people.

This core shift spread out from Europe and eventually transformed every institution and much of the way of life in most of the world. It marked the transition from the medieval to the modern era. It marked the birth of the now infamous clockwork universe.

Historians looking at such a switch are pressed to explain why it happened. One standard story has emerged. Why did the modern world arise? Our children are usually told that the scientific revolution produced a non-superstitious, correct view of the world and the medieval view crumbled before the terrible clarity of its logic.

There is some truth to this view. Yet, if it were completely true, a major scientific transformation would no longer be possible. Our current version of how the universe works would indeed be, in Burke's terms, 'the real truth' and its grim implications would be inevitable. But this is *not* so. As the bulk of this book makes clear, there is ample evidence that science is again in the midst of a Copernican revolution of epic proportions. The current scientific view is not a final truth, but an ageing one about to succumb.

So, let me suggest that the standard story of why the modern world arose is incomplete, not so much wrong as woefully simplistic. The real story is a tangled web — which, in fact, is the whole point. Big Change involves political, economic, social, scientific, and spiritual issues all at the same time. To avoid naiveté, then, we must understand why a whole social fabric rises and falls as a piece. To avoid chagrin later on, we must also start with respect. So note: the people of the Middle Ages also thought their beliefs were built on unshakable science which had stood the test of time. I start therefore with a more accurate view of this science.

Ordinary Observers and Cultural Weaving

Ordinary observers gazing at the night sky, see stars roll past in a long slow sweep. Stars near the Pole circle around the North Star and never disappear. Somewhere around 330 BC, Aristotle explained this celestial motion using a model of the universe made up of eight crystalline spheres upon which the sun, moon, planets and stars were embedded. The earth sat at the center, encased within. The sun circled past each day and the stars followed each night because the spheres revolved gently around their central core, the earth. The universe was closed and the heavens were perfect and unchanging in their circular orbits. And, as the ordinary observer could see, the earth was stationary and the stars moved around it.

Now Aristotle's model was scientific, it was based on observation and logic. It even evolved like a good scientific model should. Thus, ordinary observers also noted that there were times when the planets seemed to change course. Mars, for instance, would sometimes stop and go backwards. Clausidus Ptolemy, an Alexandrian astronomer, put forth the first convincing explanation of this anomaly in the second century AD. He suggested that each planet sat on a smaller crystal sphere which was itself turning within the main one. This meant that there would be times when a minisphere turning within its larger sphere would make a planet appear to move backwards. Backward motion came from epicycles within the larger whole.

Elegant indeed! This modified Aristotelian view, fitting observation and appearing to be common sense, held sway virtually unchanged for over a thousand years.

Then, starting in the 1400s common sense began to change. By 1700 the average educated person viewed the Crystal Spheres as a symbol of superstition and an affront to reason. How did this happen? If you read modern accounts you will hear about the scientific revolution starting with Copernicus. The simple version of the story is that the poor pre-scientific people of the sixteenth century thought that the earth was stationary and sun revolved around it. Copernicus demolished this primitive view by showing that the earth actually moved around the stationary sun. On the other hand, the earth-centered view fits what ordinary observers see and no one can call Aristotle, one of the founders of Greek science, a fuzzy-headed thinker. Why then would his model be considered an affront to reason? There must be more to the story.

Figure 1. Aristotle's crystal spheres sitting on Atlas' shoulders.

The key to the larger story has to do with the way science and a society's story of itself become entwined over the years such that beliefs in one bolster beliefs in the other. The Crystal Spheres is a case in point. The people of the Middle Ages cared about the Crystal Spheres, not because of its science, but because it symbolized their important place in God's Design. Thus, medieval clerics had told their flocks that God had put them on earth because it was the center of universe and because they were the apple of His eye. This simple extrapolation explains the rest of the now famous story of those times. In setting the record right, Copernicus destroyed people's sense of having significance and of being embraced in an ordered and loving universe.

The first step in freeing ourselves from today's brave, yet tragic story, is to see that we are like our ancestors. We believe our story of the world will never change because we assume it is based on science which will never change. But science *is* about change. The Crystal Spheres, therefore, teach us an important lesson. To understand history, one must realize that it is the *human* story which is most important. Then, as now, most people don't care much about science *per se*. What people care about are the stories which experts tell about what a scientific idea *means* for them in their daily life.

History thus suggests that science and society evolve together in a two-way push-pull with stories leading the way. Furthermore, over time the interlacing between the two becomes massive. So, let me state the obvious. Copernicus is not famous because of planetary motion, but because his model challenged the social fabric of the times. Somehow, over many years, the Crystal Spheres had been converted from a model of celestial motion to a mainstay of the whole society, with far-flung political, economic and spiritual connections. Indeed, by 1514, when Copernicus began his work, Crystal Sphere images extended to every nook and cranny of medieval life. Hence, it wasn't just man's place in the universe which was at stake, it was an entire conceptualization of how the world worked including social relationships, economic relationships, politics, government, art, and even how cannonballs flew.

The Crystal Spheres became a mainstay of medieval social fabric by a process I call 'cultural weaving.' Hence, by 1500 — after a thousand years of acceptance and refinement — the Crystal Spheres had come to seem like an unchangeable pillar of fact. And, just as we tie our pillars of fact into many aspects of our world, so this model had been woven into many things. Clerics, for example, used the Crystal Spheres' perfect unchanging motion as an example of the unchanging perfection of God's plan for the world. In God's plan each object had a fixed place in an unchanging hierarchy from rocks, plants and man to heavenly beings, and, finally, God, the Prime Mover (another Aristotelian invention). It wasn't just theology, however. Medieval theorists also applied crystal images to social theory. Hence, according to feudal theorists of the times, just as the stars were fixed in their orbs, so it was obvious that people were meant to be fixed in their social positions. God put people where they were and that is where they should stay.

This process of tying pillar of fact to other areas went on for centuries and, even in the Middle Ages, the connections were often quite logical. A case in point is the way the Crystal Spheres supported cannonball theory. Thus, one reason Crystal Sphere experts knew the earth stood still was because when you dropped something it fell straight down. Aristotle had said that all natural movement was straight down, toward the center of the earth. He had further reasoned that one could tell whether the earth was moving or not by how objects fell. Hence, if the earth were moving, then when you dropped something, it should fall down *and* sideways in the direction the earth was moving — as, for example, a rock dropped from a moving wagon would do. The earth must be stationary because dropped rocks didn't move sideways. The logic was impeccable. As a result, the stationary earth, and the naturalness of downward motion became one tightly bound complex which people applied to everyday problems such as cannonball theory. Thus, according to sixteenth-century theory, cannonballs flew out in the angle the cannon was pointed and then fell straight back down to earth as befit natural motion on a stationary earth.

It all seemed very reasonable — at the time. And, by the 1500s when Copernicus came around, Crystal Sphere logic and images were woven throughout the entirety of sixteenth-century reality. King Arthur's table was round, for example, because roundness symbolized perfection in heavenly orbits and chivalry's sacred place in God's Design. Furthermore, so many connections had been made, some metaphoric and some logical, that the resulting picture seemed incredibly unlikely to change. Thus, to the sixteenth-century person on the street the existing social pattern seemed as pre-ordained and unavoidable as the stars moving in the skies. Whether they liked it or not, this was the way the world worked — or so they thought. Science, life and religion all agreed!

Hence, without anyone planning the result or engaging in grossly irrational thinking, cultural weaving produced a tight, consistent web which connected incredibly divergent phenomena — literally the gamut of society. People started with some observable facts, created a story to explain them and then wove an entire society in its image. The result was a *knowledge web*, a self-reinforcing picture of the world woven out of what seemed to be solid knowledge.

Let me also emphasize that this web is more than just a mental image. When people live according to the latest version of how the universe works, they build everything in kind. Hence, as Burke puts it, fifteenth-century Europeans 'knew' that the sky was made of closed concentric crystal spheres, rotating around a central earth. It was supported by observation and science that had stood the test of time. *Knowing then led to doing!* Literature, music, art, politics, economics — soon everything began to mirror what people 'knew.' Threads from all over began to reinforce each other. The system eventually began to seem impervious precisely because everywhere one looked, everyone and every thing agreed!

Cultural weaving is, of course, also alive and well today. Whether it is the Pope asking Stephen Hawking to explain how his theories support religion or social Darwinists using survival of the fittest to explain why the poor deserve their plight, human beings are always on the lookout for a heavy-duty idea that they can use to strengthen their own beliefs. Knowing has also led to doing. Social structure, religion, economics — everything inside our society now reflects clockwork beliefs. By the 1700s, for instance, feudalism was ending and the industrial world beginning. The world was alive with Enlightenment beliefs about man's ability to order his world and the rational being's need to create a fair and harmonious society. It was an era of optimism and unlimited faith in progress. It was the century of the American and French revolutions — liberty, equality, fraternity! All of this was part of the new social system being built around a new pillar of fact — Newton and his model of the solar system.

We are like our ancestors. We just use Newton and Darwin instead of Aristotle and Ptolemy. We don't believe the earth is at the center of the universe. We don't believe cannonballs fly up and fall straight back down and we don't believe that God fixes peoples' places in the social order (at least not most of us). We look back at Aristotle's once illustrious Crystal Spheres with contempt. We know better because we now have the 'real truth.'

Unfortunately, the arrogance of this last belief is dangerous. The usual result of looking back on an unraveled web is retrospective absurdity. Hence, after the medieval view ended it began to seem like a self-reinforcing rat's nest that no sophisticated person would believe. This thought, however, applies to our times too. Thus, if Big Change sweeps our world, then future generations will assume web-thinking is obvious and find machine-thinking absurd. Because knowing leads to doing, post-modern society will probably also be as different from modern society as modern is from medieval.

Root Metaphors

> *A new metaphor must channel needs of the present, dreams*
> *for the future and memories of the past into one workable*
> *whole.*   J.S. May

Knowledge webs also usually reflect a root metaphor, such as 'world as machine' or 'world as a living organism.' The reasons for this too are understandable. Metaphors are easily communicated and give coherence to what seems to be a jumble of unrelated facts. They provide a conceptual framework that can be shared not only by a community of scientists but also by a community of human beings engaged in all forms of endeavour.

Cultural weaving does the rest. The metaphor shapes the logic used and becomes part and parcel of a hidden consistency that connects incredibly divergent phenomena. As a result, social fabrics are also *tapestries which trace out a design.* We find these designs at work in the perspectives that shape the institutions and daily life of cultural groups from the ancient Mesopotamians to the Amazonian Indians, from Hottentots to the nation states of our own time.

The mainstay model serves as a great and concrete example of the root metaphor, a kind of keystone, and the two build themselves up together. Stephen Pepper, a philosopher-historian who studies such things, calls the result a world hypothesis, a tacit theory of 'how the world works' that unites a long thread of thinking and is invariably tied to a root metaphor. Thus, a culture's knowledge web is woven around a metaphor and exemplified by a mainstay model.

Here is the rub. Societies assume that their metaphor is equivalent to the facts, but this is not true. Metaphors are a way to organize facts. People use them because without them observations form only a meaningless heap. Yet many metaphors will work. The one which rises at a given time is shaped by memories, dreams, hatreds and a host of other cultural artifacts too numerous to mention.

Facts (observations) do not change, but the way people organize them, the lens they choose, does. History is a game of trying to find metaphors which fit the facts while also making the society work better. The concept of 'working better' is key. History shows that, when societies reorganize themselves around a new metaphor, they are driven partly by new facts, but mostly by *human needs*. I cannot emphasize this last enough. To understand Big Change, therefore, we must understand how and why real people with real needs leave their old ways. The next section explores how this worked in the birth of medieval society.

The Tapestry of God's Design

The medieval world also had a root metaphor. It was not the Crystal Spheres. No, the medieval metaphor was of a hidden organizing master plan, the world laid out according to God's Design. God's Design was a palpable real truth for our ancestors, just as the clockwork universe is to us. Why did they choose it? Clockwork thinkers dismiss God's Design as superstition. In fact, it was a necessary and powerful metaphor which spoke to the needs of the time. This is how it happened.

At the height of the Roman Empire, Europe (or rather Rome's western provinces) had been secure under an efficient government and connected by roads along which commerce and social exchange flowed freely. But then Rome crumbled and the long barbarian nightmare began. Commerce and exchange fell apart rather rapidly after the fall. Rome was gone and security had gone with it. Invasions by Muslims, Vikings, and Magyars in the eight, ninth and tenth centuries set the tone of the age — Christian kingdoms surrounded and harassed by foes. The medieval tapestry was a product of these times — a world which hacked out survival in dangerous times and clung longingly to memories of a more civilized era long since shrouded in the mists of time.

In the beginning, people receded into human pockets which eventually became so isolated that dialects developed barring communication between people even fifty miles apart. Dense forests, impassable roads, wild animals, raiders and bandits — small wonder inhabitants turned inward and looked backward, clinging to increasingly shrouded images of a golden Roman past. Eventually, a patchwork of bastions grew up reflecting, as one historian put it, their owners' 'ever-present expectation of violence and attack.' Memory and danger, thus, set the tone for the medieval world which rose from the dust of an older order. Emerging slowly with barbarian conversions to Christianity from 400 AD on, a distinctive Christian European society evolved out of what was once a motley collection of tribal provinces.

Christian missionaries spreading the word of their God during and after the fall of Rome brought the metaphor of God's Design around which the new society began to form. This metaphor came most clearly from one of Christianity's greatest philosophers, St Augustine. But metaphor is too light a word. Augustine's vision of God's Design was a concrete and elegant theory which was completely appropriate to the times. Writing after the sack of Rome in 410 AD, Augustine's vision of God's Design was an exquisitely reasoned basis for hope and a description of how a new civilization should be built. He argued that, through all the ups and downs of transient human empires, God's saving grace of was working in the hearts of men. A struggle was being met. Two societies, he said, were competing through the centuries for the allegiance of men. One society, the community of those who loved God, would find their final home in heaven. These people formed the City of God. The other society, the City of the World, was formed by those whose minds and hearts were set only on worldly things. God's Design called those who loved God to build God's City on earth and join the struggle by which this must be done.

Augustine's theory was, thus, not a vague vision of God's Design but an integrated theory of history, life and state. It advocated mutual support and care for the weak and called for a righteous struggle against injustice. It rejected money and worldly things as an evil because these had been behind Rome's fall. It offered personal salvation in the afterlife but it also sought a new world which would be built through commitment to the City of God on earth. This powerful vision of history, life and state still stirs people today. Back then it provided a metaphoric core that spoke to the times and gave direction to an emerging social fabric. Knowing led to doing! Across Europe an embryonic cultural web took hold which blended spirituality and reality into a functional whole.

Threads from the old were used to build the new. Christian, Roman, and tribal elements all contributed to the weave. First came the Church. Survivalist times had made life an arduous and usually brief struggle. 'Life,' wrote Petrarch in the fourteenth century, 'was nothing but a hard and weary journey toward the eternal home for which we look; or, if we neglect our salvation, an equally pleasureless way to eternal death.' It was a dark mood that fit dark times. Stressing the inscrutability of God's Design and the superiority of life in the afterworld, the Church spoke to the dark times and offered hope. All was orderly, a plan lay underneath earthly flux, it was just beyond human ken. Eventually, the Church provided an embracing matrix of life for the new society. It gave rules for how to proceed and a reason for existence, effort and all that was.

The remnants of Rome also left their trace. Monasteries preserved what was left of classical culture. Hence it is not surprising that priests used Aristotle's model to illustrate their God's Design. It fit. People believed in God's Design because it helped bring order to the chaos of their lives. The perfect motion of the Crystal Spheres illustrated the ineffable workings of that order in a palpable way.

Finally, tribal elements also fed the fusion. At the time of the fall, Europe was inhabited by an array of semi-tribal societies most of whom still believed that the people were an organic whole. These societies, for example, believed that law ought to be a natural outgrowth of the whole life of the people, not merely a set of rules imposed from above as it had been with Rome. Their kings were not so much rulers, as chieftains who led the people. Furthermore, in tribal society warriors voluntarily pledged their life and skill to their leader. Honour-bound warriors, allied to a chieftain, protected the tribe and ravaged their enemies. In converting them to Christianity, clerics taught these warriors to fight not for booty but for glory and for God's City on earth. This blend of Christian and tribal beliefs eventually produced the concept of chivalry — honour-bound knights fighting for God, for justice and for the good of the community.

All of these threads fit the times and the new design served in unexpected ways. For example, the new Christianity argued that faith in worldly things destroyed civilizations as well as individual souls and the Church cast an anathema against money. But since extensive trade did not exist, lack of currency served to keep people focused on home and the organic whole. Christian lords who were honour-bound to protect the community, completed the fabric. The result was feudalism, a system based on the need for self-sufficiency and held together by honour and the vision of God's Design.

And a beautiful vision it was. In the theory of God's Design, the whole community was part of a great mystery that bore the breath of the Divine. Human beings great and small were interwoven with each other and the world in the hidden design. God had established three Estates, each with a given task for the good of the whole. The first Estate, the clerics, served as guides to faith, upholders of justice and champions of the oppressed. The second Estate, the nobles, governed but they also gave their lives to protect the community. Chivalry bound them by honour to protect the weak, fight for the right against injustice and to practice courtesy and humility. The third Estate, the commoners or serfs, belonged to the land owned by their lord protectors and worked it for the benefit of all. The lord was bound to maintain them in sickness and in health and right their oppressions as directed by the Church. Thus, in the beginning, serfs were viewed as stewards of the land, not slaves as Rome had used. The tribe was still One, despite different functions. Together God's three Estates formed an organically-whole community whose various parts worked together in a design that served the needs of the times. In historian Barbara Tuchman's words: 'the clergy was to pray for all men, the knights to fight for them and the commoner worked that all might eat.'

Rising Times

The medieval tapestry of God's Design was functional and palpable. And for a time it seemed to be working well. The new society was well-established by the eighth century and seemed pre-ordained by the tenth. By this time feudal society, with everyone playing their role, seemed to be surviving the invaders, opening up the world and expanding the economy. By the eleventh century the tide was turning. Barbarian raids began to trail off and as they did European contact with the rest of the world grew. As European bastions and their protectors became more powerful they moved to take back land from the Moors in Spain and Italy and to seek conquest as far as the holy lands in the Crusades.

The seas became safer and overland routes opened. As they did, commerce expanded starting in Italy around 950 AD and spreading through Europe with the first crusade in 1096. As an exchange economy returned, specialized craftsmanship was revived and guilds emerged. Money became more common. Christian theory cursed money and it hadn't been very important in early medieval life, but now money helped improve things. Commoners often used money to buy privileges from their lords. These included freedom from the serf's bond to the land. Free towns and free men emerged as nobles granted charters for liberties as free communes to towns — in exchange for money, of course.

Secure in its theory and basking in an expanding economy with novelties and luxuries provided by imports, the medieval view flowered into perfection in the twelfth and thirteenth centuries. Commerce stimulated a surge in art, technology, guilding, learning, and exploration by land and sea. Leaders of church reform movements tried to reshape human society into an ordered unity that would reflect the universal government of God. Religion was expressed equally in the gentle preaching of St Francis and in the soaring cathedrals rising arch upon arch. These High Middle Ages brought the compass, the spinning wheel, the windmill, watermill and treadle loom. Universities were established at Paris, Bologna, Padua, Naples, Oxford, Cambridge, Salamanca, Montpelier, Valladolid, and Toulouse to teach the new ideas coming in with expanded contact. Giotto painted human feeling, Dante framed his great design of human fate and Roger Bacon delved into experimental science declaring that the progress of human knowledge was being impeded by philosophers' reluctance to admit their own ignorance.

Creativity, technology, and faith flowered. In Tierney's words: 'In 1275 a medieval man might reasonably hope that his society was on the way to creating a serene civilization that could endure for centuries.' But it didn't. So let us explore the other side of Big Change, the downward roll.

The Unraveling of God's Design

The medieval tapestry of God's Design symbolized by the perfect motion of the Aristotelian Crystal Spheres, held sway from about 500 AD to 1600 AD. God's Design was not a superstition, it was a social reality. So, what happened to it?

In the simple version of the story, the scientific revolution created a crisis. Somewhere between Copernicus' model of the solar system (1543) and Galileo's trial for heresy (1632), a new view of the world began to take root. In 1687 Newton showed that the solar system operated in according to mathematically-precise physical laws. A new mainstay emerged. By the early 1700s everyone 'knew' the universe was infinite and worked like a giant clock. Social institutions and human endeavours from art to politics soon came to reflect this new knowledge. Now, the mechanics of a physical universe sets our place in the universe, not God's Design.

But is that it? Did the medieval world end because scientists discovered the 'real truth'? No, the story is still simplistic. So I'm going to suggest a different answer. The medieval world did not end because Copernicus challenged the Crystal Spheres, nor even because of the scientific revolution *per se*. Rather, both Copernicus and the scientific revolution emerged *because the medieval web failed.*

The theory of God's Design stopped working. It ceased bringing order and started creating chaos instead. As it did, the social fabric that its creators had so beautifully woven, began to unravel. And a great unraveling it was. Social relations, economics, religion, science, politics — all of these threads began to fail. Failure created crises and a need for a new foundation. Human needs eventually drove a new social web into being (in this case, the clockwork one).

The next step in understanding Big Change, then, requires we understand why the medieval world failed. This failure created pressure for a new way. This is not a simple story of science, of course, but a complicated story of how a social system becomes corrupt and entrenched. Let us therefore, return to Copernicus and how his work fit into a real world of practical problems and power structures now anchored in habits and fears of their own.

New Thinking

By the early 1500s Aristotle's Crystal Spheres were the official model of the now universal Catholic Church. Unfortunately, by 1500 the Julian calendar based on those spheres and used by the Church was in urgent need of revision. Setting the dates of important religious days often required calculating the phase of the moon and other heavenly conjunctions, but by 1500 the Julian calendar was eleven days wrong on the moon's cycles.

This situation was visible and of great concern to the average believer. Since the Church provided the matrix of medieval life, holy days were much more than holidays, they had an effect on a wide range of spiritual and legal issues. Inheritance, for example, was affected by whether a child was born on a holy day, as was pardoning of certain crimes. Worse, missing holy days lessened a person's chance of salvation and salvation meant the difference between the golden afterlife and endless torture in hell. Something had to be done!

In 1514, under pressure from a wide range of constituents, the Pope gave the urgent task of calendar reform to a Polish priest/mathematician named Nicklaus Kopernig, better known as Copernicus. Copernicus said that the task would require resolving anomalies in the relative motions of the sun, moon and earth and that this might mean a model with the earth moving around a central stationary sun. But the Church's hesitation was brief, the problem was urgent. Two years after its publication in 1543, Church authorities accepted Copernicus' model without apparent reaction and by 1582 it had been used to reform the calendar just as originally intended.

Valued for its mathematical elegance and its ability to make the heavens available to accurate observation, Gemma Frisius, a Dutch astronomer, expressed the official view at the time:

> It hardly matters to me whether he claims that the Earth moves or that it is immobile, so long as we get an absolutely exact knowledge of the movements of the stars ...

So, Copernicus created the heliocentric model on behalf of the Church and his work was accepted as a convenient mathematical fiction. The moon's cycles began to match the calendar which supported the idea that Copernicus' model was in some way better than Aristotle's.

On the other hand, this was the start of the scientific revolution!

Hindsight says that the Church should have reacted with horror and one might suppose that its unruffled acceptance reflected complacency, arrogance or naiveté. Indeed, these were present. John of Jandun articulated the complacent view succinctly: 'No one will ever believe it is actually physical.'

Yet, there was more to this lack of fluster than naiveté or complacency. You see, the idea wasn't exactly new. Copernicus hadn't invented the heliocentric idea any more than Columbus had invented the idea that the world was round. Both men were actually demonstrating the validity of ancient ideas which were already circulating in underground circles. Both represent eruptions in a pot slowly beginning to boil. Thus, by 1500 the times had been changing for a very long time and, under a surface that seemed impervious to change, the medieval status quo was already beginning to bubble and break.

One reason for simmering change was the rediscovery of the broader world all but forgotten in the long centuries of darkness. The universities of the High Middle Ages were built primarily to teach the logic, science and law coming from new translations of Greek, Roman and Arab works which had been brought in by trade, fleeing refugees and captured Moorish libraries. Not surprisingly, the medieval belief system began to bubble and churn as startling new ideas began to flow in. Rediscovering the world produced a powerful interest in the study of classical literature. The study of such classics, called humane studies, flourished from the twelfth century on. This lead to an age of humanism pre-dating the Renaissance but echoing the same 'discovery of the world and of man' that would mark the later age.

In a curious quirk of fate, first hand knowledge of Aristotle's full range of thinking stimulated an intellectual renaissance that would eventually end the Aristotelian Crystal Spheres system which had become calcified during centuries of isolation. 'Calcified' is the word, of course. By the 1200s, the Catholic Church had become the well-institutionalized arbiter of truth and it took this role seriously. Furthermore, Church authorities held that knowledge came through divine revelation and they were skeptical about sense data which they thought could mislead. Their main approach to knowledge was to explain all things in terms of their place in the Design. It was the world of Scholasticism! Thus, though it shocks the modern mind, there was no observation, analysis or search for causes. Rather, to find the nature of a thing, medieval scholars invariably looked heavenward where, in the words of one historian they 'would lose themselves from the very start in moral generalities and Scriptural cases.' Aristotle, on the other hand, held that the human mind could attain truth about the natural universe by logic and reflection on sense experience. He emphasized natural law, curiosity and a openness to thought — all of which stood in stark contrast with the increasingly rigidified modes of medieval thought.

The new thinking was hard to suppress, however, because so much of it was so very useful. By the 1440s the rediscovery of Aristotelian maps of the earth helped generate the revolution in cartography that would lead to Columbus' expedition to the New World. A new way of thinking about the world and its place in the universe began to take form. Writing during this period, thinkers such as the German mathematician Nicolas had pondered what a more open universe would be like:

> If the universe is infinite, then the Earth is not necessarily, or
> even possibly at its center. And if that is so, the Earth may
> well be circling the Sun. It is only the viewpoint of the
> observer as he stands on the Earth that makes him think it the
> center of the universe.

Greek science emphasized logical thinking and observation and exalted the power of the reasoning and creative inquisitiveness over dogma and unchallenged authority. These were heady and dangerous ideas in a time when institutionalization had led to entrenched authority that was less and less appreciative of challenge. By 1500 the intellectual expansion which had been growing in small circles met up with the printing press (invented in the late 1400s) and paper imported from China to create a boom in thinking. The change that started in the universities and small intellectual circles spread to an ever wider public as books became affordable and literacy spread.

From Feudalism to Capitalism

Intellectual empowerment gained way partly because it helped solve practical problems like calendars and cannonball flight. Still, Big Change was also aided by a growing push toward social empowerment coming from a completely different direction.

Feudal theory was breaking under the strain of an increasingly complex society. Feudalism had been meant for the time of bastions when survival depended on mutual support in the organic community and bond to the liege lord. In that time Christian hatred of money and laws against interest and banking worked well because money was not necessary. Increasing trade went against all this. Nobles, clergy and finally even commoners began to develop a taste for something better than could be made by local peasants. This created an incentive to produce surplus goods that could be used in exchange. It also created an incentive for the return of money which had been all but absent in feudal society. As specialized products became more valuable, a more complicated commoner class began to emerge. The simple world of priests, knights and peasants became complicated with merchants, specialized craftsmen in guilds and new professionals such as doctors and lawyers coming out of the universities. None of this fit in the original plan.

But, then, the plan had changed too. Feudal society was no longer a mutual support system based on social contracts and organic wholes, but a simple classist society, fixed by birth and with conflicting interests among the classes. The golden theory of God's Design was now tarnished and dark.

The theory still guided institutions, however, so the money-exchange economy grew like a tumor hidden inside the still-dominant feudal pattern of life. It was the incubation of baby capitalism! In the beginning enterprising peasants used money from surpluses and specialties to purchase freedoms from their lords. Nobles who wanted to make money sold them charters for liberties for free communes. Freemen living in free towns emerged.

By the 1300s, however, baby capitalism was beginning to reveal all the ugly sides that we think of today. Nobles often sold mills and other means of production to get more money for war. Bourgeois owners who controlled the tools of production emerged and began to exploit their brethren. The guild of masters, journeymen and apprentices, once united by a common craft, slowly spread apart into owners and hired hands divided by class hatred. Owners developed into a patrician class which took control of town government. They then used their positions to further their own interests. They favored each other in governing groups and set taxes that fell most heavily on the poor.

The Birth of the Nation-State

According to medieval theory the lord should have responded to such oppressions by ordering the necessary reform, for in Aquinas' words: 'Princes are instituted by God, not to seek their own gain, but the common good of the people.' But this princely theory, too, corresponded less and less to reality. The ruling class was built on what Tuchman calls 'the habit of violence.' The knight's reason for existence was the glory of combat. Unfortunately, the nobility of combat justified endless private wars between nobles in- and outside a monarchy long after the waves of infidels and invaders tailed off.

Chivalry, however, made an odd kind of war. Chivalry bound all Christian knights into a transnational brotherhood. Hence the goal of fighting each other was not killing *per se* or even the acquisition of land, but demonstration of prowess and superiority. Thus, the best way to conduct a Christian-against-Christian war was to capture opposing nobles and then allow their subjects to ransom them back. (Remember the legends of Robin Hood where King John bleeds the peasants for King Richard's ransom?) The other way to conduct campaigns was to ruin one's opponent by destroying his means which largely meant killing or maiming his peasants. Either way, the cost of war fell more and more disproportionately on the peasants and appeared less and less a service to them.

The growing taste for finer things plus the increasing cost of war (horses, retainers, bastions, armaments, etc.) also meant that nobles felt an increasing need for money. Selling charters to serfs and raising their taxes helped some, but despite the Christian anathema against money, war became more and more of a business. Ransoms produced income. So did pillage. By the time of the flowering, knights who had lost their fiefs or who had gained a taste for plunder began to form bands, called free companies, which ravaged lands for profit.

The land's noble was supposed to stop such brigandage and they often tried. But, since brigands were usually knights and part of the chivalric brotherhood, they were usually captured and held for ransom. Since most were unlanded, however, many had to work their way out of ransom by service to the capturing noble. Thus, brigand knights shifted between banditry and service to a lord as fortune suggested. The results were devastating. As Tuchman put it, 'Where knights had once wielded the swords that brought order out of chaos, by the fourteenth century the violence and lawlessness of men of the sword had become a major cause of disorder.'

Chivalry had become dysfunctional. In the original feudal chivalric view, a knight served in voluntary allegiance bound by honour. There were no standing armies before the fourteenth century and the amount of time owed to a liege might be but thirty or forty days a year. Unfortunately, as social complexity grew, the nobles' interests moved farther and farther away from both their liege and the peasantry of their land. Noble families formed alliances by marriage and these began to criss-cross national boundaries. Vassals often had complicated interests spread throughout the continent and they often took up arms against their own nominal monarch. The Hundred Years War which devastated Europe in the fourteenth century was the natural fruition of this complicated web of interests which vastly overshadowed any sense of obligation to the peasants of the land. Three claimants to the French throne took turns ravaging the French countryside with the net effect of massive famine and the near ruination of the peasant economy. Peasants paid in blood for claimants' self-interest in a system which was less and less mutual.

The failure of the fealty system began the end of feudalism and the incubation of the modern nation. With commitment crumbling and more money available, kings naturally moved to stabilize their power by paying for the services of their fighting men. Hired soldiers were always available and had no mixed allegiances. As kings bought armies, however, the decentralized world of bastions connected by honour to a king began to unravel. The long slow movement toward strong central monarchical control and the modern nation state began.

Church and the Politics of Heresy

Still, the nobles were not the only ones to cause unraveling. The rediscovery of the world had given the clergy an increasing taste for wealth and luxury too. From the late 1200s on the Pope's guests dined off gold and silver plates in halls lined with imported tapestries. Lower prelates and priests began dressing in beautiful fashion with silk and fur-lined sleeves, jeweled girdles and gilt purses — some even going abroad with honour guards. Even the Franciscans — those who St Francis called to walk barefoot among the poor and beg for the necessities of life — acquired riches, lands and, in Tuchman's words, 'wore good leather boots and were not loved.'

The clergy had long lived on taxing the peasants and these taxes increased. But new means of income were also developed. Simony, the practice of selling clerical offices with their accompanying revenues, became scandalously common and led to increasing unfitness among the clergy. Pardoners sold pardons for sins from gluttony to homicide. Priests and friars sold fake relics and prelates sold dispensations for sins ranging from trading with infidels to having illegitimate children (many of which were their own, for clerics were also notorious seducers).

The clergy also turned their role as guides to salvation into a means of oppression through their authority to define the 'true path' — or, in other words, by their authority to say who was a heretic. Early Christian missionaries had held a multiplicity of beliefs. To expedite conversion of the pagan peoples, these had often been blended with local customs and myths. However, as Christianity became dominant, success bred institutionalization, particularly in Rome. As various Popes struggled to centralize clerical power in Rome, pluralism became less tolerable, even among Christians. Control became a major issue and the term 'Catholic' meaning 'one, true, universal' belief, emerged to distinguish the increasingly centralized and tightly controlled version of Christianity from the many variants that still existed.

So, not too surprisingly, the righteous killing of heretics became a complex blend of cleric and political purposes — as in the case of the burning of Joan of Arc. Thus, though many clerics tried to reform the Church, eventually the main Roman strategy was to classify objectors as heretics and invoke their extermination in the name of righteousness. The most horrific example of this took place in the ruthless extermination of the Cathar Christians in the south of France. The Cathars (meaning 'the pure') preached a back-to-basics kind of Christianity which took root readily in places where abuses of power among the Catholic clergy were common. After several attempts to restore Catholic control, Pope Innocent III declared the Cathars heretics and called a crusade against them which drenched the south of France in bloodshed, essentially depopulating the province of Languedoc. During the massacre of the citizens of Béziers, when a soldier suggested that many good Catholics lived within, the bishop is said to have replied, 'Kill them all. God will know his own.'

The killing of heretics also became more and more of a business. Since purification often required investigating large numbers, an efficient ecclesiastical organization was needed. So the mass destruction of the Cathars, the Waldensians and other rebellious Christian groups also led to the development of the Inquisition. Often fully believing in the honour of their task, Inquisitors produced a fanaticism toward heretics that led them to violate the Church's own rules about torture, voluntary confession and surrender to the secular government. The torture and burning of heretics, common throughout the Middle Ages, reached new levels by the late fourteenth century. Fanaticism combined with political and even personal motives led to a weakening sense of religious shepherds guiding men to salvation and a clearer image of enforcers of absolute authority who destroyed anyone who dissented.

'Whether,' as Tuchman put it, 'their pretensions to be men of God made their sins more disturbing or because playing on their parishioners' fear of hell made their treachery particularly vicious, the peasant's sense of betrayal by the clergy was particularly sharp.' By the mid-1300s anti-clericalism was rising and sporadic attacks on clerics burst out. Scorned yet feared because as Tuchman says, 'they might, after all, have the key to salvation,' the relationship between priest and peasant class changed.

Crumbling and Emerging

Theory and fabric were both beginning to fail. Peasant revolts against the betrayal of the nobles and clergy occurred sporadically throughout the late Middle Ages. But the fourteenth century added the ultimate insult to the now well tarnished theory of an organic whole under God's Design. The Hundred Year War occurred in this century as did several devastating famines. Carnage produced by brigandage was at an all-time high. Then human destruction met its match. In 1347–50 and 1368–70, two outbreaks of the Black Death killed half the population. Young, old, rich, poor, righteous and wicked — all died and the second outburst seemed particularly aimed at children.

As one historian put it: 'Survivors of the plague, finding themselves neither destroyed nor improved could discover no Divine purpose in the pain they had suffered. This scourge had been too terrible to be accepted without questioning.' Faltering under the burden of plague, famine and war, the flowering of the previous two centuries crumbled and Europe fell into a profound stupor.

The medieval world view shifted with a jolt. Among other things, God changed. Before the Black Death, God was mysterious but largely benevolent; after the Black Death, He was increasingly pictured as a judgmental vengeful God. This shift began the move to the idea that God stood outside, set the world in motion and then left humanity alone to figure it out. People became more and more preoccupied with how to avoid His wrath by learning what is right. As a result, they became more interested in education and in the control of themselves and their world. A small current began.

On the other hand, so many peasants had died that the value of laborers increased. Peasants gained some status. By the early 1400s, the plague's survivors were savoring the joy of having survived using money inherited from those who had died. By the late 1400s towns and commerce were reviving and a new sense of the world was emerging. These people were much less likely to view the material world as a soulful sojourn to the next. Life was to be lived. The time was ripe for a Renaissance which emphasized learning, life in the here-and-now, and control of the world though rational understanding.

Rebirth

Whether the people of the Renaissance (roughly 1450–1600) were actually different from medieval man is an issue historians debate endlessly. But regardless of what historians think, it is clear that Renaissance people saw themselves as different. It was Renaissance Italians who invented the term 'Dark Ages' and the idea that the barbarian invasions and the end of Rome brought on a trance of a thousand years. Occupying the most central hub in the flourishing East/West trade routes, Renaissance Italians felt it was both a joy and a duty to end that trance. They turned the humanism that started in the twelfth century into a new view of life.

'Humanism' came to mean a view of life that, while devoutly accepting the existence of God, shared many of the intellectual attitudes of the ancient Greek/Roman world. Humanists were interested in esthetics, saw the usefulness of history and science, and were convinced that man's chief duty was to enjoy his life soberly and serve his community actively. Humanists deplored ignorance. They believed that man was essentially good and that if men were educated, the standards of ethics would rise. Renaissance thinkers also turned their backs on medieval idealization of poverty, celibacy and seclusion. Thus, where medieval scholars had tended to be monastic recluses, the Renaissance scholar was much more likely to be a public figure — a teacher, a propagandist, a diplomat.

Following the Greek lead, a new awareness of individuality and self emerged. The medievalists saw man lost in the organic whole of the communal design and waiting passively on the will of God. In contrast, Humanists emphasized man's ability to think and act and to guide the destiny of others — a conception articulated best in Machiavelli's *The Prince*. Human accomplishments, once seen as a reflection of divine will, increasingly reflected human ability in its own right.

Roman theories of power deriving from the consent of the governed became fashionable — despite the fact that monarchs with money had become increasingly powerful. Consent of the governed appealed to the increasingly wealthy bourgeoisie and it never hurt to please those with money. Then too the theory was bolstered with some practice from earlier days. From the English barons at Runnymede in 1215 to the first meeting of the French Estates General in 1302, representative assemblies that participated in shaping governmental decisions had become common practice in the high Middle Ages. The consent theory also helped salve the discontent over involuntary subjugation to the now rarely-protective nobles of the openly crumbling feudal theory. Hence, paradoxically, the theory of consent helped transfer power to kings who increasingly symbolized a larger whole to which allegiance might be more reliably given. The nation-state with kings, hired armies and voluntary citizens was being born.

Thus, in ways both great and small, Renaissance Humanism fed the yearning for change which had now blanketed the medieval world. People sensed that things were not going as they should — in either church or state. They longed for some sort of regeneration, some sort of revival. Renaissance Humanism laid the seeds of a new theory of life. Rome, the spiritual capital of the world and the long lost imperial capital, became the focus of this great change.

Yet, the Renaissance would not be enough. Renaissance men did not see themselves as starting something new but as recovering what was lost. 'Renaissance' or 'rebirth' stood specifically for the rebirth of the classical world's past glories. More importantly, the Renaissance came largely from the birth of refined tastes and the desire for intellectual freedom among the wealthy (noble, cleric, and bourgeoisie), but a deeper problem was brewing. Medieval theory still held sway but its function, the mutual support system, had fallen apart. Nobles and clerics, the traditional champions of justice, were too preoccupied with personal concerns to work much on poverty. Worse, increasing wealth meant increasing ability to concentrate power — political, and economic. As a result Europe, as never before, was splitting into two worlds: a tiny world of privilege and wealth, and a huge world of poverty and suffering.

The Renaissance did not speak to these issues. Real social change, therefore, would have to come from another source — and it would begin with the other great product of the 1500–1600 period, the Reformation. Where the Renaissance was part of the flowering of capitalism, the Reformation emerged as a response to the economic and social betrayal that capitalism produced. This betrayal was epitomized by the now gluttonously wealthy Catholic Church which, in complete opposition to its original principles, was increasingly a source of suffering, not a remedy to it.

The Fire Built by Betrayal

Feudal theory still reigned in the 1500s and most serfs were still bound to the land. Early peddlers and traders who left their lord's fief were scorned as vagrants. But many of these were now proud merchants who could pay for educations that would make their sons rich doctors or lawyers. Hans Luther, a peasant turned entrepreneur, thus envisioned a career in law for his young son Martin. Cheerful and lively but also stubborn, introspective, and fearful of the wrath of God, Martin became a monk instead. In 1510, the serious young friar Martin Luther accompanied a senior friar on a diplomatic mission to Rome. There he saw first hand the state of Holy Rome, the capital of Christendom. Offended by the ostentatiousness of clerical palaces and scandalized by the blasé attitude with which clerical corruption was viewed, this young friar from the rough Germanic provinces was left in a state of upheaval — a state he would eventually spread to others.

The Church was not blind to its shortcomings and there were already several types of reform efforts present. There were spiritualists who advocated a return to piety, concilliarists who advocated institutional reform by an ecumenical council, and humanists who emphasized reason versus revelation as the path to reform. The Pope himself was a humanist. Yet, Luther's resolution to his own personal upheaval hit a very emotional issue. In a close study of the early prophets and apostles he found evidence of a God of mercy, a God who gave salvation through a 'change of heart.' Salvation came from faith, not through purchases of indulgences! Faith was at once merciful and accessible to all, even the poor. It was personal. As Luther once wrote: 'He who wants to be saved should be so minded as if there were no human being but he alone, and that the consolation and promise of God through all the Scriptures concerned him only.'

This loving God was the God of the early Church, but the Catholic hierarchy, with its concern for wealth and emphasis on absolute authority, could no longer envisage it. Too much now rested on Papal and Council infallibility and this conflicted with Luther's other idea: 'Christian man must examine and judge for himself.' In 1517 Luther posted his famous articles on the door of the Wittenburg Church and debate on all manner of issues against the Church exploded. The Protestant Reformation was on.

Other reformers had preached similar ideas for one hundred years, but somehow Luther's challenge sparked the resentment that had long been smoldering. Europe ignited. No doubt Luther himself was part of the difference but so too were the times and his political situation. Had his German sovereign Frederick been less hostile to the Italian Popes it is quite likely Luther would have been burned early in his career, like many reform-minded heretics before him. But increasing monarchical powers and complicated political arrangements were now rampant and would continue to complexify this ending of Catholic universality.

Was the Reformation political or clerical? Its hard to say. England's Henry VIII severed the English Church for personal and political reasons. Calvinism with its appeal to those who prospered through self-exertion fell on fertile ground among the entrepreneurial Dutch in the Netherlands. It helped kindled the Dutch revolt against their Catholic Spanish ruler, Philip. But then Philip also despised the banking and commercial enterprise that made the heart of the Dutch character. Whatever the reasons, for the next hundred years Europe would be consumed with wars wound up one way or the other with the Protestant-Catholic split.

The Turning Point

And so we reach the turning point century, 1600–1700. Perhaps, we see why the medieval web failed and how that its failure set the context for all that happened next. It was a very complex and interwoven event. The Renaissance, the Reformation, humanism, education, the birth of the nation-state, the birth of the individual, capitalism with its belief in achievement by individual initiative versus classes set by birth — all these attended the collapsing facade of medieval theory. These threads met and in the seventeenth century a variety of thinkers and coalescing movements began to weave them together into a new pattern.

It was a time that begged for a new tapestry of life. The medieval view had emphasized a plan beyond human knowing unveiled only through divine revelation. But Divine revelation had often been used to promote élite good at the expense of justice and integrity. Now the Greek view of a world following natural laws began to replace it. Critical of authority, the new thinkers emphasized *natural laws* that could be explored by *reason*. Most men believed in God, the question was how to uncover his plan given that clerics were not always reliable. Small wonder science mushroomed. Since revelation could be manipulated, it seemed obvious that the only reliable road to knowledge of God's plans in the natural world was through logic, reason, observation and experiment. Science should guide man's thinking, not dogma and revelation.

It is also not surprising that the metaphor that took root was the machine. In the words of historian Peter Gay, the philosophers who came to characterize this century 'did not believe in miracles, and, if they believed in God at all, they thought of Him as the mechanic of the universe — a sort of cosmic watchmaker.' He had built a superb machine, given it laws to run by and then withdrawn. Now human beings could wrest its operating rules from nature by observation, experiment and reason. Rational Man, no longer a child spoon-fed by corrupt authority, was capable of understanding the workings of a clockwork universe.

The clockwork metaphor was also à propos because, more than any other device of its day, the clock symbolized precision. Mathematical precision was the key to Copernicus' challenge to the Crystal Spheres and mathematical precision provided by a variety of new approaches and tools was at the core of the emerging scientific revolution. By the 1600s almost every major philosopher was trying to introduce the rigour and clarity of mathematics into all departments of knowledge. By 1700, in the words of one historian, 'it became customary to think of scientific inquiries as mathematical in nature and of scientific laws as mathematical in form.' If a new religion was being born at the time, it was the religion of Mathematics. Even the great skeptic David Hume who doubted Reason itself, did not doubt Mathematics.

So, Copernicus was not alone in producing convenient mathematical fictions that challenged the status quo. Starting with the Renaissance, a rash of new mathematics and newly thinking men produced an increasing threat to the medieval world's symbolic keystone, the Crystal Spheres. In 1543 Italian artillery expert Niccolo Tartaglia used geometric techniques to show that the trajectory of a cannonball was curved. This challenged the Aristotelian theory that natural motion went straight down. In 1577, the Danish astronomer Tycho Brahe, proclaimed the existence of a new star traveling in an oval orbit. New stars challenged the belief that the universe was unchanging and an oval orbit challenged the belief that stars traveled in perfect circles reflecting heaven's perfection. In 1610, using the recently invented looker-telescope the Italian astronomer Galileo Galilei challenged heavenly perfection by suggesting that sun spots were imperfections on the sun!

Finally, in 1632 Galileo published a book called *Dialogue on the Two Chief Systems of the World* which suggested in rather clear terms that the opponents of the heliocentric model were simpletons. Things had gone too far! The Church had accepted Copernicus' work as a convenient mathematical fiction, but there was now danger that the more credulous of God's flock might actually believe it was true. Galileo was condemned to house arrest for the rest of his life and his book was placed on the Index of Prohibited Books. Scientific work in Italy ceased abruptly.

Luckily, as the Reformation attests, Rome's control was not absolute everywhere and the scientific revolution was not limited to its Italian Renaissance roots. In 1600, after eighteen years of studying why a compass works, Queen Elizabeth's personal physician, William Gilbert surmised that the earth was a giant magnet and that it was magnetic attraction that led things to fall toward and remain on earth.

Aristotle's natural downward motion was a product of natural laws! In 1602, Johannes Kepler was able to show that Mars' orbit was both elliptical and regular. Using Gilbert's ideas, Kepler argued that this elliptical orbit was the result of the sun's influence — the closer to the sun the stronger the influence, the farther away the weaker the influence.

Kepler's laws gave foundation to the still embryonic movement toward a clockwork metaphor embodied elegantly in mathematics. Still, despite various advances, calculating mathematical relationships remained tremendously time-consuming. It had taken Kepler nine-hundred pages of calculations to show that Mars' orbit was elliptical!

Then, in 1687 an Englishman named Isaac Newton published a book entitled *Philosophae Naturalis Principia Mathematica*. The world, as the saying goes, would never be the same again. Newton laid out such an all-encompassing theory of celestial mechanics and motion that, in the words of one historian, 'it stunned science into virtual inactivity for nearly a century.' Ladened with equations this little book laid out, in systematic form, the basic principles of the theory now known as *classical mechanics*, the study of moving bodies regardless of their nature.

Newton occupies a singular place in the history of science. The poet Alexander Pope put it succinctly:

> Nature and Nature's laws lay hid in night;
> God said, Let Newton BE! and all was light.

How did Newton achieve this status? The simple rules he laid out have been used without alteration to generate explanations for a tremendous variety of physical phenomena from the trajectory of a baseball to tidal forces and the diffraction of light. They have been so productive and so correct that virtually all else pales in comparison. They still stand as unchanging pillars of fact and quite justify the clockwork view using Newtonian mechanics as its keystone. No longer in dribs and drabs, the clarity and comprehensiveness of Newton's mechanics destroyed the Crystal Spheres model as if in one fell swoop.

And, of course, Newton was not all theory. Like Copernicus, Newton sealed his place in history through mathematical implementation. In Newton's case implementation was most powerfully accomplished through his invention of calculus. Calculus made it possible to

rapidly convert little bits of data into precise mathematical relationships — equations of motion! — and this regardless of whether the
motion was of a cannonball or light. Valued for its precision and
mathematical elegance, Newton used calculus to produce the ultimate
equations of motion for the planets themselves. More than any other
single tool, calculus made physics as we know it possible.

A Brave New World

And so the world changed. The theory of God's Design had failed
politically, socially, economically, spiritually and scientifically. It was
a long slow unraveling followed by a rather abrupt demise. The clockwork metaphor and the new science stepped in to fill the void. Slowly
but surely the new version of how the universe works grew in strength
and spread logically and insidiously much as its predecessor had done
before. By mid-century scientific societies had been established all
over Europe. Cultural reweaving began.

There were plenty of people to do cultural weaving because, in the
beginning, science was open to all educated people. Thus, early science
was done not only by philosophers, mathematicians, astronomers and
doctors, but also by navigators, merchants, bankers, farmers and
princes. England's George III took up botany, Portugal's John V
studied astronomy, and Voltaire's mistress wrote on gravitation.

Thanks to Newton's mathematics and other advances, the new science made way because it helped solve problems far beyond calendar
reform. Take cannonball theory, for example. Military engineers
imported the new mathematical methods and by the late-1600s they
had become very successful at getting cannon balls to hit their targets.
By the early 1700s mathematics and the scientific itch were improving
machinery and starting the industrial revolution. Jethro Tull invented
the seed-planting drill in 1701, Thomas Newcomen invented the steam
pump in 1712, John Kay invented flying shuttle weaving in 1733 and
Michael Menzies invented the threshing machine in 1732 ... etc., etc.

Nor was it just physical things that were being rethought in the
machine's image. In 1747 a doctor, Julien Offroy de la Mettrie, wrote
a notorious little book entitled *Man a Machine* that held that all mental
activity derived from physical activity. Scottish philosopher David
Hume published his finest work, *A Treatise of Human Nature* and sub-
titled it 'An Attempt to Introduce the Experimental Method of

Reasoning into Moral Subjects.' The moral subjects to which he was referring were the passions, ethics and politics of man. The experimental method was Newtonian science. Our world was beginning.

Enlightenment!

Still, there is more to a civilization than science. A new tapestry needs political, social, economic and even spiritual threads. Following close on Newton's heals, a diverse collection of philosophers began articulating new ideas on society, ethics, politics, economics, and so on, to replace the old. By the early 1700s the Enlightenment and a new tapestry of life were beginning to emerge.

The Renaissance and Reformation supported the idea that human beings were becoming mature enough to think for themselves, to find their way without paternal authority. Man was emerging from immaturity, his 'nonage' as Immanuel Kant would later put it. This century would start a critical attitude toward any sort of orthodoxy, and especially toward orthodox religion.

Enlightenment philosophers were therefore not a uniform movement but a tremendously diverse set of radical intellectual thinkers. The only thing they completely agreed upon was criticism, primarily of what went before — scholastic thought, religious dogmatism, subjugation of the common man, etc. — but also of anything in their path. As one might expect, their criticisms did not always go in the same direction. Still, in Gay's words 'destructive criticism cleared the ground for construction' and the pressures of their times apparently acted like an invisible hand directing their pens. Thus, diverse thinkers such as the skeptic David Hume, the romantic Jean Jacques Rousseau and the satirical Voltaire, nevertheless produced a relatively coherent and strikingly brave new sense of the world. The ideas that gave unity to their diversity were freedom, individualism, critical thought, and life in a grounded practical here-and-now world. All this fit post-medieval thinking.

The new scientific view also gave them unity. Newton had urged men to observe and then analyze their observations to discover the laws of the physical world. Hence, in the beginning science was really another name for critical reason applied to all things. To Enlightenment thinkers, therefore, it seemed reasonable that the laws that governed the human world might also be unveiled by applying a critical process. Small wonder Newton served as a pillar. The philosophers of the Enlightenment sought nothing less than a Science of Man built in the image of Newton's Science of Motion.

Critical thinking applied to all things! Early thinkers also saw society as a fabric of interacting parts, so progress in one sphere would lead to progress in others! Voltaire and Hume for instance, believed that freedom of trade, freedom of religion and freedom of political opinion were all linked. Voltaire said: 'Where there is not liberty of conscience, there is seldom liberty of trade, the same tyranny encroaching upon the commerce as upon Relligion.'

Religious tolerance even appeared to be linked to commercial prosperity and the greatness of the state! As Voltaire penned, 'In a republic, toleration is the fruit of liberty and the basis of happiness and abundance.' After 150 years of persecutions and religious wars (Reformation to early 1700s), religious fanaticism began to decline. The Huguenots in France and the Roman Catholics in England who had survived terrible persecutions in the 1600s found themselves tolerated and even permitted to practice in the 1700s. An absolute monarch in every other way, Frederick the Great of Prussia declared: 'In this country every man must go to heaven his own way.'

Freer thought and a freer economy made for rising expectations and the beginnings of a faith in progress. As the exchange economy replaced the feudal one, the traditional Christian hostility to money softened. The picture of a universe divided between a City of God and a City of the World blurred. Indeed, the material world and life in the here-and-now became fashionable. The once despised peddlers had become freemen and eventually wealthy men. These men became symbols of personal freedom gained through individual effort. Economic man, the industrious entrepreneurial maker of wealth, prosperity and personal freedom began to take form.

Connections also extended to the spheres of morality and caring. From the High Middle Ages on money had made men free. It quite literally freed the serfs. But without the Church championing justice and the organic community to catch them, freedom had also left crippled and starving peasants to fend for themselves — a plight too common to be ignored in the new Reason. Thus, concepts of justice and decency soon became attached to the concepts of rational thinking and scientific improvement. The idea was simple. Reason should make men free *and* happy.

Civilization was to be made more just and humane. In Gay's words,

'Moral science meant making morality scientific and using science for moral purposes.' The effects of this kind of thinking became visible in changing attitudes toward human relations everywhere. Voltaire made the cruelty of criminal trials notorious, and torture and mutilation became rare. In Massachusetts, in 1700, Robert Calef raised an angry voice in the name of 'reason and true Christianity' against witch trials. Humanism took on its other great connotation: 'humane.'

Freedom was also at the core of much of this social change. The concept of equality became fashionable. The old clean-cut social hierarchies retained much of their prestige, but faced with powerful social aspirations in the bourgeoisie, they were under attack. All men were capable of thought and education and industry would free men from bondage making society as a whole prosper. A society of free and equal men made a nation strong. Even the world of the family was changing in the direction of freedom. The extended patriarchal family, still the pattern in the seventeenth century, was giving way to the nuclear family, with its growing equality, intimacy and well-defined boundaries against the community. A father's power over his children and a husband's power over his wife declined markedly.

Economics and the real world were also part of the mesh. Underneath the new science and the new decency was not philosophic man but practical man. Enlightenment thinkers rejected airy fantasies about first causes, concentrating their intellectual energies instead on practical problems like improving man's lot in this world. Thinking, they said, must bear useful fruit; talk must be to some practical purpose. Following the individualist spirit of the times, Enlightenment thinkers also argued that self-interest would spur industriousness. Adam Smith, the most celebrated economist of his day, argued that if each man is free to improve his own economic position and if economic systems are free to utilize the best skills of all, then everyone, manufacturer, laborer and society will benefit.

The concept of competition as the creator of wealth was not far behind. By the 1700s wealth garnered through conquest was being overtaken by prosperity created by trade. Bold merchants, wanting untrammeled profits, sought freedom to buy and sell as they chose. They abhorred the dominant economic theory, Mercantilism, which believed in state control of precious metals, skilled workers and trade.[1] For these new men, free trade was at the heart of a free and prosperous nation. Freedom allowed men to compete and competition benefited all. Hence, as David Hume wrote: 'Not only as a man but as a British subject I pray for the flourishing commerce of Germany, Spain, Italy, and even France itself.' In France, a group called the Physiocrates championed that idea that lifting trade restrictions would encourage agricultural production. Their phrase, *laissez faire,* came to define the new belief in a free economic world.

Naturally, rational men pursuing free trade also needed political freedom. This too had a voice, heard most clearly in England's John Locke. Like Renaissance humanists before him, Locke held that political institutions arose as a result of social contracts between men. The ideal society was a tolerant secular society. Citizens of a state should obey its laws for political and legal reasons, not on religious or tribal grounds. There should be the right to dissent, the right to free speech for all reasonable men. There should be an end to arbitrary government and an end to cruel treatment of accused persons. Locke, of course, inspired many of America's founding fathers and, as a result, the American Constitution reads like an Enlightenment manifesto.

From Theory to Reality

There was, however, a long way to go to a new social and political reality. The Age of Enlightenment was an age of ferment, but until the end of the 1700s most of the ferment was expressed more in words than in radical political action. There were many reasons for this. First, the ranks of the Enlightenment intelligentsia were filled primarily by bourgeois gentry — people who already enjoyed good education along with material, social and even political progress. Thus, most Enlightenment thinkers had fine thoughts, but a lot to lose and mixed feelings about losing it.

Then too destruction was also decreasing, at least near home, and this too lessened the drive for change. Most aggressive energy was focused on empire building far from home. Even domestic European wars in the late 1600s and early 1700s were mild compared with the late medieval and early Reformation wars, with their wholesale massacres and widespread ravaging of the land. The two great empires of England and France fought each other sporadically over the century but their encounters were contained military actions over fixed terrains for the purpose of imperial expansion.

Complacency was also somewhat justified because some political and intellectual progress was being made. For example, in 1688, the year after Newton published his *Principia,* his fellow Englishmen had their Glorious Revolution. They expelled their Catholic King James II, imported Protestant William and Mary to fill his place and enacted laws strengthening Parliament and curbing the power of the king. This had made England the first model of Enlightenment thought. Furthermore, though monarchical rule was more absolute outside England, many monarchs were also Enlightenment thinkers. Monarchs even in harshly absolutist states — such as Prussia, Russia, and Austria — made some effort to better the lot of the peasant, to modernize state administration, and to become more tolerant, at least religiously, as in the case of Frederick in Prussia. Thus, through the early and middle parts of the century middle class prosperity, relative stability and relative lack of disruption meant most of Europe remained quiet under absolutist monarchical control.

Still dissatisfaction simmered and action came eventually. In 1751, the intellectual crisis of the Enlightenment reached its climax when a veritable who's who of liberal French thinkers dared to publish the first volume of the *Encyclopedia.* Much more than a collection of facts, the *Encyclopedia* crystallized the radical Enlightenment credo that man could improve his lot if he used reason as his guiding principle instead of faith. The critical spirit erupted. The *Encyclopedia* challenged authority in every field from religion to government.

Enlightenment thinkers had finally gone too far. The *Encyclopedia* was suppressed. But, though its editor Denis Diderot had to go underground, he continued to publish new volumes with effective results. Beginning in the 1760s, the absolutist serenity of country after country began to be studded with political unrest. Everywhere the basic demands were the same: the right to participate in politics, the right to vote and the right to greater freedom of expression.

Then came 1776. Europe had been watching developments in Britain's colonies in America with considerable interest for a decade or more. There had been constant controversy between the colonies and the mother country for years and the issues were heavily wound up with Enlightenment beliefs. Here were free men resisting, first by argument and then by arms, what Enlightenment philosophers enthusiastically called tyranny. These were their men — rational yet passionately concerned about equality, peaceful yet ready to go to war for their freedom. The success of the American Revolutionary war was a vindication of Enlightenment thought, enshrined in the Declaration of

Independence. In wresting freedom from a major power Americans demonstrated that Enlightenment ideas could work politically.

Despite the American success, however, Europe remained the fief of its monarchs. The American Revolution had been started by the American bourgeois class, but in Europe the bourgeoisie was still too complacent for revolution. Crumbling occurred instead from another direction. The costs of the monarchical extravagance were taking their toll and in the 1770s and 1780s it became increasingly clear that the French government was on the verge of bankruptcy. In 1787, Louis XVI attempted to deal with the state's financial crisis by calling a meeting of the Estates General, a national assembly composed of the three traditional classes — clergy, nobility, and commoner. It was the first such meeting in 175 years and the idea was for consensus to be reached with each class getting one vote. The commoners however wanted one vote to each man, a condition that would give them 50% of the total votes. The King refused and the commoners broke away and formed their own National Assembly. The rest is history. No longer able to keep control, on July 14, 1789, an enraged Parisian crowd stormed the Bastille. By the end of August many aristocrats had been killed and a bold 'Declaration of the Rights of Man and of the Citizen' was passed into law.

And so the Age of Enlightenment became the Age of Revolution. In the brief ten years before the century ended, France formed a republic, executed a king, established an effective if faction-ridden revolutionary régime and passed through a period of confusion which ended with a *coup d'état* and Napoleon's accession to power in 1799. When the nineteenth century dawned, some gains had been made and others scuttled. But two things were clear: the old Europe was dead, and the Enlightenment had survived. One observer foresaw both conclusions in 1792 when the Revolution was still young. Consoling German soldiers after their monarch's failed attempt to rout the French Revolution, a German poet named Goethe soothed:

> Here and today begins a new age in the history of the world.
> Some day you will all be able to say — I was present at its
> birth.

This completes my story of Big Change past. By 1800, the clockwork world had begun to produce a new political and social reality (at least in various places and to varying extents). Critical thinking and humanism, had been resurrected from antiquity and reinvented in a way that fit the times. Metaphor led again! — though social pressure also pushed. Knowing that the world was a machine (which human beings could understand — led to doing and a human world reflecting that knowledge's image. Economics, politics, literature, music, art — everything came to mirror the view created by the knowledge.'

The new science and technology would produce more and more amazing inventions and better standards of living throughout the 1800s. Belief in political freedom would eventually lead most European countries to become republics and most monarchs (if they survived) to shrivel into figureheads. Enlightenment thinkers struggled to make societies more just and more open. They succeeded in various arenas, in this place and that. The belief that all citizens should be educated and that — at least in theory — societies should be egalitarian and humane became the norm.

The Cycle of Big Change

The summary of why Big Change happens is actually quite simple. All societies start with observable facts of the world, like stars moving across the sky at night. They also start with a need to be functional and whole, usually in a way that previous times were not. New societies are usually driven into being by crises caused by a failing fabric. When pressures in the human world link up with a better story of the physical world, then a new society begins. Weavers in search of a better way build a new society out of what they now 'know.' The new metaphor will appear in all things.

Societies and their metaphors, therefore, seem to go through a standard cycle (see Figure 2):

Coming together for Common Cause. A sense of struggle, pressure and danger defines beginning times. There is a struggle to understand why a once great society is failing. There is a struggle to find new ways and a struggle to remain afloat in what is often a hostile sea. Still, somehow pressures and ideas coalesce into a new way. A sense of common cause is usually the binding force.

Building. A sense of joy defines the building phase. Even if there is much to overcome, energy is flowing and the path seems clear. If

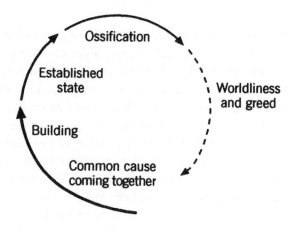

Figure 2. The cycle of Big Change.

cultural weavers succeed, threads are woven into a society which works in ways which the old one did not.

Establishment. A sense of fulfilment defines the phase of establishment. Social success is witnessed on all sides, from art to politics. Old demons are vanquished and power is now moving out. People at all levels take pride in their society. Most assume it will remain noble forever.

Ossification. A sense of habit which no longer serves defines the ossification phase. Once upon a time, the society's beliefs were tools which its people used to build a world which worked. Institutions, however, tend to convert good ideas into immutable truths which cannot be questioned. Interpretations become dogmas used regardless of whether they work. The dream of making a better world is replaced by devotion to institutional control.

Worldliness and Greed. A sense of social dysfunction which cannot be stopped defines the worldliness phase. It is a short step from ossification to corruption. Self-serving people use cherished icons and institutional power to amass personal power regardless of its effect on the society at large. Social tension rises along with confusion and malaise. If the self-serving gain enough power, they will thrive while the rest of the society sinks into greater despair.

The social system which once brought hope, now brings pain.

Habits which used to bring order, now bring chaos. The great social web begins to unravel. Eventually, it begins to seem like a rat's nest that no sophisticated person would believe. Unfortunately, conditioned by centuries of habit, people will find it hard to imagine anything else.

Today we hope that we are not like our ancestors, but there is strong evidence that we are. If we are, then times will change because our cultural web failed (despite its brilliance and good intentions). Not us? As long as we are looking at cycles, let us explore the already visible downside of the clockwork universe.

The Dark Side of the Enlightenment Dream

The Enlightenment dream has worked wonders, but it also did not work out as neatly as the new thinkers hoped. Threads of the next round of unraveling could be seen early on.

The first problem was that humanity had a dark side that rationality could not control. Entering with the Enlightenment belief in rationality's ability to create a just and humane society, the French Revolution produced the reign of terror. The rest of the world watched aghast as inherited civilized values that had held from the time of Rome were ravaged. Blood flowed in the name of humanitarian purpose and Utopian scheme — as it would again in the Russian Revolution's conversion to communism.

But, of course by the time of the Russian Revolution, the image of another machine-age icon had also been severely tarnished. Capitalism had a very dark side. Those pragmatic competitive entrepreneurs who were supposed to free the world, actually spent a lot of time exploiting others in the name of that new greatest of all Goods — making money! The prosperity built by self-interest was often (perhaps usually) prosperity of self at the cost of others.

Capitalism's dark side, in turn, had a tendency to link up with a political dark side. Noble capitalism joined with Noble Conquest — the Age of Enlightenment being also the Age of European Empires — and the connotation of 'imperialism' as being the conquest of other countries with the purpose of exploiting their people and resources came into being. Little brown, yellow, red and black brothers the world over became the exploited economic slaves of European powers.

Abuse also happened at home as well as abroad. Early feudal theory had bound everyone from prince to serf into an organic whole. Everyone served God's Design and the clergy was specifically charged with opposing injustice. But now that theory was gone, replaced by visions of self-interest which would automatically benefit everyone. No institution in the new society actively opposed injustice. Hence, despite its assuring rhetoric, abuse became common practice.

The problem, as Karl Marx pointed out, was that when one person owned the means of production they could: (1) command a disproportionate share of the profits, (2) cease actually working themselves, and (3) abuse those who worked for wages because of their dependence on the means. This problem had been evident in the fourteenth century, but the burgeoning industrial society brought it to new levels. As economies became industrial, 'means' became more and more complex and workers became more and more dependent. As this happened, workers could work or starve — and owners often kept them at a close balance between the two.

Enlightenment economic and social theory provided a rationale for all this. Noble money, self-interest and capitalism would automatically produced the best of all possible worlds! (No matter how many people in the lower classes starved to death.) Nor was this rationale accidental. The sense of mutuality in this new society was very thin from early on. Hence, despite their role in humanistic reform, many Enlightenment thinkers had mixed feelings about exploitation. Enlightenment theory was formulated primarily by the bourgeoisie and the one subject most of them wavered on was the treatment of the masses. The lower orders of society were definitely *not* enlightened. For the most part they were illiterate, filthy and lived in the extreme want and disease that comes with economic exploitation. Voltaire called them 'a ferocious and blind monster' and claimed that he had 'never intended to enlighten shoemakers and servants; that was the job of the apostles.' Many Enlightenment thinkers argued that religious fear of hell and damnation was justified as a means of social control because the lower orders were too irrational to govern themselves. Thus, echoing Gibbon's words on Rome, Voltaire wrote: 'The various modes of worship ... [are] considered by the people as equally true; by the philosophers as equally false; and by the magistrates as equally useful.'

Voltaire's words expose the ugly side of the bourgeois Enlightenment — élitism, particularly capitalist élitism. Clockwork economics rationalized the nobility of capitalist greed. Religions such as Calvinism converted money directly into a mark of election. Those who had money were better — no matter how they earned their money or even *if* they earned their money. The wealthy formed a meritocracy, the new elect.

Unfortunately, Enlightenment theory didn't require these new élites to be champions of the oppressed. Quite the contrary! Capitalist theory argued that self-interest, competition and money would *automatically* make men free and happy! Unbridled faith in these three, however, created a system designed for social betrayal. The Enlightenment produced a trickle-down theory of economics based on the idea that an invisible hand would make selfish endeavours benefit all. In practice, the benefit was not very mutual. Wealth tended to become concentrated in the hands of a very few and the trickle from these tended to be small. Money makes money, so moneyed interests tended to form mutual-support brotherhoods that made the wealth of those involved multiply at tremendous rates. Concentrated money created concentrated power and a new cycle of abuse was born on the heels of the old. The net result was that the medieval aristocracy of war blended with the modern aristocracy of money creating a new élite that was just as exclusive, self-absorbed and abusive as its predecessor. Social betrayal didn't take long. From the early nineteenth century on, abuse of power by moneyed interests became an on-going source of suffering and social instability.

But it all seemed reasonable. In the new theory, wealth indicated superiority which, in turn, justified using coercive power created by concentrated money. Freedom, equality, and justice were really only for an elect few who — by reason of their Enlightenment and Election — were justified in applying their intelligence to control the world and manipulate the unenlightened.

Science was also used to support the cause. No longer God's will or the divine right of kings, abusive power was now justified by mechanistic efficiency principles. The new vision of natural laws, converted by Newton into the magic of precise prediction, had been quickly converted by others into the belief that science's primary purpose was to allow men to control and exploit the world. This, in turn, was quickly converted into rationales for élite control and exploitation. Even today élites charged with operating the machinery of government and business are likely to be taught that their job is to control that machinery through whatever manipulations are needed. Their use of power over others is justified in the name of an efficient machine and the merit that placed them where they are.

Thus, the Republican spirit which, at least in principle, held those with power to be servants of their people before themselves, was subverted with startling rapidity — as exemplified by Napoleon, one minute the hero of the common man and the next, a self-appointed absolutist Emperor. The notion which actually took root was a darkly mechanistic one. Those with money and power are the operators. They stand outside, planning and controlling the machinery of nation and economy. By 1832 Hegel would write, 'The Few assume to be the *Deputies,* but they are often only the *Despoilers* of the Many.'

Even in America, where the Enlightenment's theory of capitalism has produced an incredible standard of living, capitalist élitism — and its belief in deputies who stand outside and exert mechanistic control — still produces seething class resentments. Yet when corporate raiders kill companies for the profits of a few and CEOs give themselves huge bonuses in years when they lay off thousands, this resentment hangs like a malaise without direction because, after all, science says (or so it seems) that capitalistic self-centeredness and manipulation provides the best path to prosperity — though whose prosperity is always a question.

The machine world rediscovered Augustine's City of the World and made it noble. Ah, how the pendulum does swing!

Materialism and the Death of God

The machine world's dark side also brought an ever-shrinking sense of spirituality and meaning. Enlightenment men agreed that wherever science advanced, authoritarian religion must retreat. In the beginning, however, it was dogma and corrupt authority they were attacking, not religion. Most early Enlightenment thinkers, including Rousseau, Voltaire, and Benjamin Franklin, were Deists who argued that the astounding intricacy of nature was sufficient to demonstrate God's existence. Then too, most Christian sects including Catholicism attempted to include reason. Clerics such as the Cambridge Platonists in England said that true Christianity was the practice of reason and the exercise of virtue. They too complained about the hypocrisy of doctrinal disputes among power-hungry self-serving clerics. Thus, in the beginning God was not dead.

But atheists, skeptics and agnostics also emerged partly in reaction to religious dogmatism and partly because, if science could explain how the universe worked, God seemed to be superfluous. Thus, when Napoleon received a copy of Pierre Laplace's *Mécanique Céleste*, he remarked to the author: 'You have written this huge book on the system of the world without once mentioning the author of the universe.' Laplace is said to have replied: 'Sire, I have no need of that hypothesis.'

But Laplace's response was mild. Attacks on the superfluous hypothesis of God turned more dogmatic and more alienated with time and another thread, materialism. The rediscovery of Greek science included the rediscovery of the idea that the basic unit of the universe was the atom. The idea that all things are composed of masses of atoms gained momentum in the 1600s and by the 1700s it was incorporated into a materialist philosophy that held, not only that there was no need for God, but that *nothing existed except matter*. You will perhaps recognize this philosophy today in the depressing remark: 'You are nothing but a bunch of chemicals.' Materialist atheists *knew* that God did not exist. They believed that the progress of science would eventually demolish superstitions such as God because in their view anything that was super-*material* simply did not exist. The term *super*natural thus became synonymous with 'non-real.'

Science became increasingly associated with this materialism and also its other side, reductionism. If breaking things down makes a problem simpler and if atoms are at the bottom of everything, then the best, and perhaps only, way of doing science is by breaking things down into their smallest bits. This seemed reasonable, but as this idea took root, it moved from reasonable to indisputable and science became locked into a reductionist requirement. (I will have more to say about this in later chapters.)

As science became reductionist and materialist, what it meant to be rational followed accordingly. Rationalism is the view that, to be valid, all human thinking on all subjects should be similar to scientific thinking. Hence, in the beginning rationalism had been extremely broad because science had been virtually synonymous with critical thinking. Unfortunately, this breadth did not continue. As materialism and reductionism grew, what it meant to be rational shrank. Eventually, materialism's grip made being rational and scientific synonymous with disdaining anything beyond measurable configurations of matter. This created a disdain, not only toward God, but toward caring, warmth, love and many other aspects of our daily experience.

Thus, as science turned materialist, the terms Humanism, Rationalism and Secularism took on their final and most hated connotation — a snobbish disdain for belief in anything beyond the material world. Deism stopped being enlightened or scientific. Materialism and money — the City of the World — became the guiding belief and the one true reality. Frederick Nietzsche said it best when, in surveying the wreckage wrought by materialist science, he commented: 'God is dead. God remains dead. And we have killed him.' The year was 1882.

The Race to Fill the Void

Materialism did indeed change the game. Not only did it kill God but under its reign the universe grew ever more starkly mechanical, pointless and dead. Machine science's justification of economic and social control were also taking their toll. The universe began looking less like Newton's lawful well-oiled clock and more like the infamous system of purposeless particles that would preoccupy early twentieth century philosophers.

The backlash soon began. By the early 1800s many intellectuals were already decrying scientific rationality as soulless, a tool of élites and establishments for maintaining uniformity, control, dehumanization and oppression. Thinkers such as Goethe and Schiller in Germany and Wordsworth and Coleridge in England, began to lament the lack of foundations on which to base one's life. Money and material, was that all there was?

By the early 1830s a race was on to fill the void left by the loss of meaning and the sense of purpose to life — both of which medieval man had found in God's Design. Nature, the beautiful, harmonious, soulful nature epitomized by Rousseau, was the first to step forward to fill the Void. The Romantic revolt, emphasizing nature, intuition, emotion and an organic world — in stark contrast to the materialist, mechanical world — was in full sway. Breaking the stultifying convention of the eighteenth century, the new poetry of the Romantic soul poured from pens in every major European country. Transcendentalists such as Emerson and Thoreau also made their mark on American thinking.

Yet this soulful Romantic challenge to mechanism did not last as a social spur. It found no real source of power in economics, politics or science. It eventually died of despair in the abyss of nineteenth-century poverty and political abuse, leaving us the image of the starving poet isolated in his garret while the materialistic sweep of science and the modern world went relentlessly, uncaringly by.

Two darker Gods came next and they did find power using theories of History and the Human Will. Each was extolled as a replacement for God. Each provided an answer for what gave direction to the world and meaning to life and each was an extrapolation of an original Enlightenment thrust. The two replacement Gods are better known as the State and the Individual.

The State

First came the theory of History. Germany's great philosopher, Georg Wilhelm Friedrich Hegel wrote specifically against materialist mechanist excesses. Like Augustine a thousand years before, he too sought a foundation for hope in what seemed to be a crumbling world. But Hegel placed hope, not in God, but in the heroic German State — built by the people and for the people — that was emerging in front of his eyes. Thus, Hegel's view was historical, but with a very different guiding force than Augustine's. The abuse of clerical power was still too close. Hegel instead said that through the ups and downs of transient human empires, history was unfolding toward a higher more enlightened society through a dialectical process of thesis-antithesis-synthesis. With each swing of the pendulum, humankind rose above itself into a new more integrated state.

Hegel's theory of History transformed the Enlightenment's theory of 'progress toward an enlightened society' into the movement of an Absolute Mind unfolding inexorably toward the final perfect society embodied in the final perfect state. The vision struck home and for many years Germans referred to Hegel as simply 'The Philosopher.' Marx would use Hegel's Evolution of the Absolute as the driving force behind the class struggle, the reason why the proletariat masses would inevitably rise against their oppressors. Fueled by rampant discontentment with the bitter realities of industrial life, Marx's ideas quickly ignited a growing revolutionary labor movement across Europe. The ultimate result would be the Russian Revolution and a world-wide rise of socialism and communism.

Unfortunately Hegel had left a grand logic in which the impersonal movement of History (the Dialectic) was the only thing that really mattered. Individuals didn't matter and neither did what was done in the name of movement toward the perfect society. Shortly after the Russian masses rose to establish their new society, their communist government began killing its own citizens with startling thoroughness. In the largest single case of genocide in history, the government of the USSR killed an estimated 66 million of its citizens between 1917 and 1959. Josef Stalin's personal contribution is estimated at close to 23 million. All of it was justified in the name of the perfect society and historical necessity.

The Individual

The theory of Human Will evolved in parallel with the theory of History. Renaissance and Enlightenment philosophers had both extolled virtues of the individual. The Romantics had emphasized the genius of individual creativity, and the heroic potential of the unique individual. Nor was this belief in the individual at all surprising. Medieval Man had been the passive and often abused child of God. Individual Will had freed the serfs, spawned the Renaissance and Reformation, overthrown despots and made society prosper.

Renaissance individuals, however, had become Enlightenment individuals and these had become rich and soft. As middle-class Enlightenment society became conventionalized, 'bourgeoisie' became a term of derision. Bourgeoisie no longer meant upwardly-mobile entrepreneurial peasants, it meant middle-class conformists interested only in maintaining their comfort and privilege. As Nietzsche put it:

> Liberal institutions straightway cease from being liberal the moment they are soundly established: once this is attained no more grievous and more thorough enemies of freedom exist than liberal institutions.

The individualist situation was, thus, extremely confused. Élites often inflated individualism into narcissism, extolling its virtue among those in power and then using their virtue to justify their power. On the other hand, many philosophers who decried narcissism among élites, invoked the power of the individual as the means of extraction. Thus, in the late 1800s, the individualism took a new turn. Nietzsche redefined it as the Human Will which defied bourgeois conventionality, conquered 'the herd' and gave direction to the world. Ironically, his vision of Human Will produced two radically different thrusts: (1) Fascism, expressing the dominant Ego and Will, and (2) Nihilism/ Existentialism, expressing the alienated, solitary Ego and Will.

By the late nineteenth century, the economic abuses of capitalism was producing a powerful revulsion all over Europe. The shallowness of the now conventional, bourgeois society was also producing a sense of betrayal among the oppressed classes. The deep depression before World War I and the profound disenchantment among those who experienced the War then produced large numbers of bitter cynical people yearning for a better way. Some of these looked to charismatic individuals who they hoped could bring new order and meaning.

Human Will blended with rabid nationalism offered the hope of a Triumph of Will, a new world forged for the people by powerful leaders. This hope founded fascism — the People, the Homeland, the Élite and the Leader. The repressive and genocidal results of twentieth-century fascism need no further description, Hitler's personal contribution being roughly eleven million Jews, Poles, Slavs and invalids. Genocide again, but this time directed against anyone alien or imperfect.

Meaninglessness

Ironically, fascism and communism were both attempts to fill the Void. Both tried to reverse the betrayal brought by machine-age economic abuse. Both used materialistic science as a rationale and both applied rationality in the name of some Good. At their core, both were also attempts to recover the deep humanist dream — blessed individual, blessed freedom, blessed people ... end the oppression. In the face of mechanist betrayal some chose communism and some chose fascism, but both choices ended in ruthless authoritarian regimes which abhorred liberalism, suppressed human rights and democratic institutions and killed in the name of the new Gods: History and the Human Will.

Standing behind watching all this is the Alienated, Solitary Ego and Will, the lost soul of this century's twin terrors of Existentialism and Nihilism. Alone in a material world, having no God but one's self and no direction or meaning to give one comfort, this self seeks desperately for a basis of meaning and none is forth-coming. One can deconstruct reality and find its groundlessness, for we are very clever now. One can say that all is mind and that materialism is nothing ... but then we wake up in the everyday world with materialist reality still cranking away. Ours is a complicated century.

Under The Reign of Science

And so we reach today. Science, which began as an attempt to understand the world at large, became the precise objective study of the physical world. Machines began to cover the landscape and information began to float through the air. Disease began to be conquered and life-span expanded. The green revolution made fruits ripen into flawless perfection and by mid-century fertilizers, pesticides and mechanized farming made it possible to feed the worlds millions (never mind that we don't). As science's miracles multiplied, it simply became too amazing not to believe.

Four hundred years of cultural weaving are reaching completion. Where the Church provided the matrix of medieval life, science now provides the matrix of modern life. It gives rules for how to proceed and a reason for all that is. Science is now the purveyor of absolute truth about the real — that is, material — world and it has replaced religion as society's arbiter of truth. When one has to decide what to do, one asks science.

Unfortunately, science resembles the medieval Church in other ways as well. By the early nineteenth-century science was already being called a religion, *scientism*. Like religion, it cast anathema's such as 'superstition' and 'non-scientific' on that which it deemed heretical. High priests emerged and gave infallible Truth to laymen. Where in the beginning science was done by educated people at large, it became increasingly the domain of specialists. Specialists created their own language and soon their own in-crowds which sought control of their scientific field. This often involved pressure to conform and suppression of differing views. It all seemed reasonable and much was unconscious. Still, as various schools became dominant, they also sought to consolidate their social, financial, and political power. Science became a complex blend of social, scientific and political purposes. By the mid-twentieth century, various commanding schools of thought began to look like new entrenched establishments bent as much on keeping control of thought as they were on advancing the faith.

Hence, as strange as it seems, western science has acquired its own reputation for hostility to reason. Modern commoners now nod disdainfully at the arrogance, close-mindedness and self-absorption often found in science — particularly soft sciences like economics, psychology, and sociology. But they also give scientists respect because 'they might, after all, have the key to salvation.'

Besides, machine science has long been too convincing, powerful and pervasive to stop. In this century it has come into full bloom. Ninety percent of all scientists who have ever lived are alive today and the last two generations have performed feats more incredible than anything the founding fathers ever imagined. Science seems ever more essentially complete, *essentially fact*. Physicists speak with confidence about nearing completion of the TOTE, 'Total Theory of Everything.' Just a little detail work and science will be history — a thesis stated explicitly by a wide variety of scientific authorities from the turn of the century to the present day. Thus, on taking up the Cambridge professorship once held by Newton, Stephen Hawkings entitled his inaugural address: 'Is the end in sight for theoretical physics?' Leon Lederman, director of the Fermi National Accelerator Laboratory, put it more succinctly: 'We hope to explain the entire universe in a single, simple formula that you can wear on your T-shirt.'

We have woven our cultural web and it is very tight.

Once upon a Time Revisited

Big Change has happened before and it may happen again. So let us review. Before Copernicus and the rest of the scientific revolution, everyday Western Europeans imagined themselves embraced in a cosmos designed for their elucidation. Mysterious and awesome, this world was alive and harmonious. Rocks, plants, animals and human beings great and small were all bound together in God's plan. Science, spirituality and palpable social reality all agreed.

But that view unraveled and a new one emerged. The machine world sprang forth with a burst of optimism on human rationality and progress. Step by step it has justified its beliefs with unbelievable scientific achievements from curing diseases to sending pictures through the air. It has educated the world, made it rational and, at least in certain places and to certain degrees, it has made people free and societies prosperous and humane. It has been a beautiful and amazing transformation!

But the machine world also has a dark side. We now live in a universe where most things are assumed to be either dead, unconscious or unfeeling. Science is associated with control, manipulation, dissection and often with the end of the world. Competition drives evolution and anomalies like altruism are explained as complicated epicycles of selfish genes. The world is no longer enchanted and it is no longer loving. Human beings are alive but going nowhere in a universe without design.

We have woven our cultural web and it is tight, but it is also failing. What does this failure mean in everyday life? It means that the modern landscape has become a place where absurdity is common, often because the machines of government, education, and business have been carefully planned by people who see themselves as outside the system and who see those in the system as pawns to be manipulated or cogs to be disposed of after using. Corruption in public figures is expected as is self-absorbed callousness among the rich and a sense of stupor in the middle class. We are taught that unfettered self-interest will produce the Good, that ugliness is genetically unavoidable and that money and material are at the heart of the way the world works. Genocide erupts again in Europe, Africa and the Middle East and the so-called advanced countries stand helpless. Communism and Fascism have failed but increasing poverty and senseless violence now haunts America, the richest, most enlightened country in the world. Historian Morris Berman put it this way:

> The alienation and futility that characterized ... a handful of intellectuals at the beginning of the century have come to characterize the consciousness of the common man at its end. Jobs are stupefying, relationships vapid and transient, the arena of politics absurd. In the vacuum created by the collapse of traditional values, we have hysterical evangelical revivals, mass

conversions to the Church of the Reverend Moon, and a
general retreat into the oblivion provided by drugs, television,
and tranquilizers.

And even if you don't think things are quite this bad, it is likely
that you have a strange sense that something is not right — but exactly
what is wrong and what one should do seems unclear. It all seems so
complicated and beyond our ability to change.

We now stand at the close of the twentieth century with little
exhilaration. So many beautiful theories have turned into ugly realities
that the idea of Utopia seems ludicrous. Progress to a humane, rational
society? No, human cruelty is fixed in our genes. So many fine
theories have turned to ugliness that the concept of truth itself is
tarnished. It is difficult to say anything with confidence anymore. What
exists of post-modern philosophy seems little more than a reiteration
that no such thing as Truth (with a capital T) exists. Unfortunately this
leaves the great perennial questions unanswered: what undergirds the
world, what can we believe and which way should we go?

What could possibly change this state of things? Believe it or not,
a new Big Change is already underway.

PART II

WEB WORLD

Regard with silent wonder
the Eternal Weaver's masterpiece.
A single movement sends the shuttle
Over, under, till the myriad threads
Meet and interlace, creating
Countless unions at one stroke!
The warp, not mounted thread by thread
But laid down in the timeless past,
Awaits the casting of the weft,
Forever waits the Master's will.

Goethe (1749–1832)

CHAPTER 2

CRUMBLING AND EMERGING

We have awoken to find ourselves in a dark woods.
Dante, *The Divine Comedy*

Ours is an odd century. There is no doubt that we have witnessed the flowering of the original Enlightenment view that human reason allied to freedom should govern human endeavours. Science, the instrument of reason, is the triumph and miracle of the world. As the events in Eastern Europe from 1989 onwards attest, the rule of democracy and the push toward fundamental human rights continues to struggle forward in country after country. 'The West' is now a catch phrase for freedom, belief in a humane society and a government 'of the people, by the people and for the people.' The western alliance stands triumphant over the ruins of communism, validating the truth and strength of liberal, free-market capitalist beliefs. The Enlightenment seems to be coming to full bloom!

Yet, our century has also been compared to what Tuchman calls the Calamitous Fourteenth Century, a period when mayhem tore at the very fabric of society. The comparison hits on every count: two ruinous World Wars, with devastating economic depressions preceding each of these; the rise and fall of both fascism and communism; massive populations undergoing starvation and migration; the use of genocide as a means of political and ethnic control; a resurgence of religious fundamentalism spawning intolerance, terrorism, and holy wars; the AIDS pandemic and the rise of killer viruses. The struggle is also not over. Now, at the end of the calamitous twentieth century, we experience a profound sense of instability in the world economy. Millions upon millions live in poverty, or under oppressive or exploitative social, economic and political systems — and the gap between haves and have nots is again steadily increasing even in so-called advanced nations. Pressure for a more workable way grows with all these trends.

The crumbling of the medieval view was marked by the Hundred Years War, the Black Death, famines and the ruination of the peasant economy through brigandage. Crumbling came on the heels of flowering. Many people believe our century marks the same exhaustion, this time of the modern view. Thus, upon receiving the Philadelphia Liberty Medal, Vaclav Havel, president of the newly liberated Czech Republic, had this to say:

> There are good reasons for suggesting that the modern age has
> ended. Many things indicate that we are going though a
> transitional period ... It is as if something were crumbling,
> decaying and exhausting itself, while something else, still
> indistinct, were arising from the rubble ... (1994)

Havel is not alone in believing that the modern view has run its course and something new is emerging. But perhaps he and the others are wrong. After all Havel is the president of a country whose people have experienced all the calamities of this century first-hand. They have but recently overcome Soviet Communist oppression and this at a very high cost. So perhaps he is sensing only crumbling and emerging in his own domain. Why should Americans, for example, think that their world is decaying and exhausting itself? Hasn't everything that the Enlightenment held out been delivered triumphantly by modern science and technology? What is wrong? Besides, what else could there be?

This will bring me back to science, in both its light and dark forms. We believe our scientific view will never change because it is too well demonstrated. At the same time, we also realize at some level that this same science is killing us. It is powerful but empty and cold. Havel, thus, continues:

> The dizzying development of science, with its unconditional
> faith in objective reality ... led to the birth of modern
> technological civilization. It is the first civilization that spans
> the entire globe and binds together all societies, submitting
> them to a common global destiny ...
>
> At the same time, the relationship to the world that modern

science fostered ... appears to have exhausted its potential. This relationship is missing something. It fails to connect with the most intrinsic nature of reality and with natural human experience ... We may know immeasurably more about the universe than our ancestors did, and yet it increasingly seems they knew something more essential about it than we do.

Havel also notes that the gap between scientific beliefs and human realities creates dangerous pressures. As he says:

The fewer answers ... rational knowledge provides to the basic questions of human being, the more deeply it would seem that people — behind its back as it were — cling to the ancient certainties of their tribe. Because of this ... cultural conflicts are increasing and are more dangerous today than at any other time in history.

Many people sense profound change afoot in the world, but right now most sense only crumbling. We know that the human world is not working, but it is hard to say what we could or should do differently. The transformation in science will rectify this situation. We have built our society around clockwork beliefs, but these are simplistic and inadequate. We believe so strongly that our science is immune to Big Change, that we have a terrible time imagining how any other view could be valid — much less more powerful. We are like our ancestors. We need a new story, but we have a hard time seeing past the one which dominates now. This is why making the new science clear and relevant is so important.

Few people realize the magnitude of the change facing the scientific world. Beneath a calm, confident exterior, classical scientific images based on simple causality are crumbling. In their place a new science based on web dynamics (interdependence) and its organizing tendencies is emerging. In this completely understandable shift, all things change.

How Much could Change?

*When we try to pick out anything by itself, we find it hitched
to everything else in the universe.*   John Muir

In 1997 as in 1700 most educated people look out on a clockwork
universe, a passive, essentially dead universe in which events are
accounted for by mechanical forces. Throughout this century people
have looked to scientific breakthroughs to end this view. Yet, despite
many prophesies, none of the major scientific revolutions of this
century — quantum mechanics, relativity, origins of the universe —
have budged this core machine view. Some, like genetics, have tended
to intensify it. Today more than ever the machine worldview seems
unchallengeable and unchangeable.

The machine view will end, however, because of a fatal flaw that
is so simple that it is invisible. The ensuing change will be huge
because machine science and its flaw now colour every nook and
cranny of our reality. Hence, right now, the belief that things are
fundamentally non-dependent (separate, separable and not connected)
permeates our reality. At the bottom of the world are fundamental
particles, little separate pieces of matter. At the top of the world are
ruling élites that are separate from the governed and managers that are
distinct from 'employees' (a common if appalling twist of words). God
is separate from the world, your mind is separate from your body and,
if you develop correctly, you will have a strong autonomous ego, fit
to compete with other egos. Wherever one looks the same logic plays
out — in unbelievably different ways. Even genes are described as
completely insular, immune to all pressures in their surroundings.

We take almost all of the ideas listed above for granted. Yet, in
some relatively short period all of the images listed above will take
their place along side such retrospectively unimaginable ideas as
believing the sun revolves around the earth. They will all go away
because they are all based on assumptions of 'how the world works'
in separate disconnected pieces — and not together.

This chapter begins exploring the new science with four examples:
one mundane, one radical, one awe-inspiring and one completely

general. How much difference could a little more interdependence make? Because cultural weaving is subtle, the answer is 'a lot.' On the other hand, because we have always lived in webs, most people already have a feel for how they work. Thus, most people experience the change as a new appreciation of the long-suspected and unconsciously known.

There is an old Korean story that is apropos here. A small fish said to the wise fish, 'what is all this stuff called water that I'm hearing about?' So, it is with today's Big Change. We are about to discover that we are swimming in a fluid web of interdependence, but didn't see it. We are also about to discover that this fluid makes a big difference. Let us see why, using the utterly mundane example.

The Persuasive Insanity of Modern Science

A woman in gray sweat pants and a cutoff top strides back and forth on the stage urging the audience to 'Stop the Insanity!' It is Susan Powters, one of a new breed of diet gurus preaching an interesting message: if you want to lose weight stop counting calories. Like the other new gurus, she teaches that the object of the weight loss game is to speed up metabolism so that your body burns accumulated fat rapidly. A combination of exercise and a well-balanced low-fat diet will turn your body into a high-metabolizing fat-burning machine. It will also make you more healthy.

What insanity is she stopping? A belief taught by the old diet industry, supported by old scientific research and followed by millions of hapless consumers — the belief that the fewer calories you eat the thinner you will become. Why is this insane? Herein lies the first clues to why our current worldview might change.

To ordinary observers eating is related to weight gain. We all know this. It has been explained by a well-known scientific story. The body breaks food down to get energy. It uses the energy to think, run, breathe and otherwise keep going. Unfortunately unused energy is stored as fat and, since fat no longer symbolizes wealth, modern people want to get rid of it. But how? In the 1950s scientists began suggesting that fat could be controlled using a simple prescription: count calories. Scientists had determined the energy content of different foods by burning them under controlled laboratory conditions and reported the results in heat units called *calories*. Using the food burning story, they told people that if one knew how many calories one took in and how many one used, one could determine how much fat would be put on (other things being equal, of course). Hence, count your calories! More calories equals more fat, and less calories equals less fat. This simple idea was a sensation fifty years ago and a whole science-supported diet industry sprang up to help a fat-conscious public count their calories.

What could be wrong with this? One answer has to do with one of machine science's sacred forms of revelation, the controlled experiment. Thus, if you take grade-school science they will tell you about *the* experimental method and describe it as one of the hallmarks of science. The idea is simple: isolate what you are studying; vary one variable while holding everything else constant. Isolation and control lets you make precise statements about what causes what. It produces repeatable results and gives confidence that variable X produces result Y. It is all very reasonable. It is central to the process of creating certain and objective truth. It has been very successful. What is wrong? See if you can guess why the controlled experimental method produces misleading results as we take a brief tour of the diet débâcle and its unexpected insanity.

The Wonder of Interwoven Systems

The human body is one of those very interwoven things that is not easy to break down. Certain industries seeking profit, however, are willing to put a lot of money into understanding how the body works, and money plus concern for accuracy has attracted a lot of high quality scientists. Consequently, medicine and other body-related fields like physiology and neurophysiology have served as major incubators of an unexpected change.

Scientists doing rigorous research on body-weight questions started with the classical approach: isolate, control, vary some variable and use statistics to get a handle on the results. In the case of weight loss, the process was simple. They knew the story about more calories equaling more fat — other things being equal. Their job is to find the 'other things' which is exactly what they did. One researcher noted that if you ate *only* protein, you could eat huge numbers of calories and still lose weight at an alarming rate. Odd, many calories, no fat! The body didn't store these calories as fat because it couldn't break all that protein down without chemicals from other foods being present so the protein passed right through the body. Another researcher noted that the acid in grapefruit made metabolism speed up which meant more calories were burned and fewer stored as fat. If you ate a lot of grapefruit, you could eat more and still lose weight. The list goes on: more water, more fiber, more vitamins, more exercise, more unprocessed foods, better combinations of food, and, of course, fewer calories from fat. Yet despite these variations on other things not being equal the simple idea that more calories equaled more fat lived on. By and large, it still lives on.

It has only been in the last few years that the real clincher has stepped in: fewer calories frequently leads to more fat! Yes, if you want to gain weight, one of the best ways to do this is by reducing calories below a certain point or not eating for a while. Thus, hospitals treating concentration camp victims of starvation discovered (quite by accident) that they could speed the return to normal weight by adding periods of fasting. Sumo wrestlers trying to put on weight starve during the day and eat a big meal at night.

The newest revelation (though it is actually quite old) is that when you reduce calorie intake below a certain level, the body shifts into a special and very slow type of metabolism called keto-metabolism. Apparently over many years of evolution, the body got smart. If you take away its food, it battens down its hatches and prepares to stave off starvation any way it can. One of the ways it does this is to burn calories very slowly. Once you start consuming calories again, there is a terrible rebound effect. The same number of calories that used to cause weight loss now causes weight gain.

And so the diet industry débâcle. If you have used diets off and on over long periods, your metabolism may be primed to gain weight. As if by magic, people are beginning to realize that virtually no one who loses weight the fifty-year-old scientific way keeps the weight off. The American government is beginning to investigate certain large diet chains for fraud and a new round of weight-loss gurus preach 'Stop the Insanity!' Fewer calories do not equal less fat! In fact, if you don't keep your calories above a certain level, you are almost certain to gain weight in the long run. How could science have been so wrong?

The diet débâcle is actually a small package tour of the whole shift. In a short space of time, our whole perspective on an issue changes. The center of the weight loss universe changes from calories to metabolism and from simplistic prescriptions to balance and health.

Secondly, this switch has everything to do with complex webs. What science has learned (or rather, *re*learned) is that the body is massively intertwined and the intertwining counts. One thing affects another which affects a third which turns around and affects the first. Understanding how threads blend and feed each other is central to understanding how the system works. Virtually nothing in this system has a simple constant effect — like more calories equals more fat. Indeed, outcomes are often counterintuitive.

Finally, the diet débâcle has everything to do with how scientific findings were coloured by tools and assumptions. Thus, though early researchers dealing with complex systems started simply and logically, many unwittingly engaged in a type of tunnel vision. They tended to look at one thing at a time in an artificially simplified situation assuming that this would not be a problem. This led to conclusions that were rigorous, repeatable, and incredibly simplistic. They were correct only in *very limited* controlled circumstances. Isolating and controlling create misleading pictures precisely because investigators eliminated complex ties and underestimated what this would mean.

So, nowadays, instead of seeing the body as a simple machine, we see it as an intricate, dynamic web. A billion years of evolution has produced a metabolic web that alters its operation in response to varying conditions — for example, starvation. The balance of that metabolic ecology determines whether any particular calorie gets converted to fat or not and the ins and outs of this ecology are not at all straightforward. Yet the final message is straightforward. If you want to lose weight, don't think about calories, think about the metabolic system as a whole and the imbalances in yours.

Interestingly, the result of the diet débâcle is a return to folkwisdom advice: eat a balanced healthy diet and exercise. The main insanity being stopped is the insanity of the last half century in which *the* scientific method was thought to be *the only* avenue to truth and folkwisdom based on generations of accumulated 'uncontrolled' observation was dismissed as mere superstition. As a recent medical talk show put it: 'between the 1960s and the 1990s a huge body of accumulated medical knowledge was discarded as being "unsubstantiated." We are now in the process of reclaiming some of the loss.'

The Simple Source of Insanity

By education most have been misled;
So they believe, because they so were bred.
The priest continues what the nurse began,
And thus the child imposes on the man.
                    John Dryden, *The Hind and the Panther*

The diet débâcle is part of a much larger switch. The traditional scientific view is based on the image of *single isolated* causes. Thus, if you isolate, control and break things apart, you are likely to get an image of causality that looks something like *one* thing causing another in a simple, unidirectional, sequential way because that is all that's left when one isolates and controls.

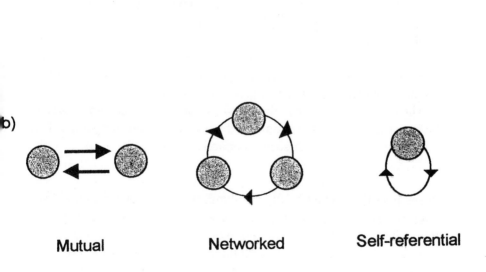

Figure 3. a) Simple causality versus b) complex causality.

Analytic approaches (ones that break-down, control and isolate) thus, beg us to believe in simple, even *single* causes no matter how complex the actual process. Examples of single-cause views of complex processes include: (1) calories cause fat, (2) cholesterol causes heart attacks, (3) natural selection causes evolution, (4) childhood trauma causes mental illness, (5) poverty causes crime, (6) competition creates quality, (7) work causes wealth.

Such ideas have been taught at various times in this century despite the fact that they are all but crude approximations of the real situation. Applying crude beliefs to complex problems, however, eventually creates a backlash. The diet débâcle is one example. There are many more. Take a question like how to reduce violence in cities? Issues such as poverty, poor education, child abuse, drugs, guns, restricted opportunity due to racism, sexism and classism, plus cynicism due to on-going injustice — these and other factors loop over and tie into each other. Political pundits, trading on the power of simple causes, sell the idea that a complex system like 'violence' has a single cause (their favorite one). But, in fact, all these variables affect each other such that no one has a constant effect or meaning. Unfortunately, simplistic approaches to complex problems create dysfunctional answers and these dysfunctional answers are coming home to roost in societies the world over. This is creating pressure to find something better.

Hence, nowadays, it is increasingly obvious that most causality looks like Figure 3. In complex systems such as the body — not to mention economies, societies, and the weather — causes blend and loop back on themselves. In such systems following single threads does not lead to *the* cause but, at best, a loop of causality and, at worst, a hopeless confusion.

The diet débâcle is thus the tip of the proverbial iceberg. Many of the issues that are treated simplistically are much more dangerous. This is particularly true in the socio-economic arena.

*   *   *

Please note that, scientifically speaking, there is no reason for blame. Scientists have known that the world was interwoven for a very long time. The problem is that the interwoven nature of the world can be overwhelming. It is overwhelming for scientific tools, social resources, and our merely mortal minds. The tools scientists use shape how they see the world. We all know the refrain: 'if all you have is a hammer, then the whole world looks like a nail.' Yet, researchers can only use the tools available. Hence, scientists had to start small and simplistically. We are where we are because they did.

Unfortunately, today we are stuck in perspectives that have passed their time. People's awareness of complex causality (webs) has been growing for years. A whole host of groups in every field imaginable have attempted to get other scientists and the public at large to realize that you can't understand much until you realize that everything really is a web — and that webs don't work like machines. Ecologists have been the most successful at this which is why people the world over are beginning to recycle and green movements are a force to be reckoned with.

Still, machine science with its deep habits of isolation and control has largely rolled on unperturbed. Assumptions of separability and simple causality are still the order of the day. Clearly, the tide has not yet turned. This brings me to the radical example.

About 30 years ago, a group of scientists discovered a phenomenon that they thought would turn the tide. This phenomenon was radical on two fronts. First, it revealed a beautiful type of motion that defied a host of traditional beliefs and yet was extremely commonplace (found from brains to planets). Secondly, its discovery helped reveal exactly why analytic methods *do not work* on most problems. The marvel they hoped would turn the tide is called Chaos. It too is a result of web dynamics.

Chaos!

Originally, the Greek word Chaos meant the infinite empty space which existed before all things. ... in present usage, chaos means disorder ... The technical Chaos I am going to speak about is nothing like total disorder ... Chaos is not disorder. Chaos is not randomness. Chaos is simple ... It represents a kind of global simplicity.

Michel Baranger, *A Chaos Primer*

Physics plays a unique role in science. God created Newton and all was light! Copernicus, Galileo, Kepler and Newton, physicist-mathematicians seem to have started it all and to this day physics sets our images of what science should be. Virtually every discipline from biology to sociology has used classical physics as its model of science. Tools, concepts, assumptions — threads of all types were taken up from physics and woven into each new scientific endeavour.

This is not surprising. Classical physics has been so successful that work on the material world often seems to be all but done. Physicists talk with confidence about finishing the TOTE (Total Theory of Everything) and many see an end for theoretical physics itself. If physics at subatomic levels will be over soon, how much could be left to know about straight forward systems like planets and pendulums? The everyday world seems all but sewn up.

Yet, this sweet picture of finality is crumbling. Many of the fields that tried to emulate physics now chafe under its constraints. It is a truism in psychology, for example, that the model of science handed down from nineteenth century physics is completely inappropriate for studying human beings. Nor is psychology alone. Radnitzky and Bartley sum up the biologist's perspective:

> Science ... has until recently been dominated both by physics
> and by a particular interpretation of physics ... Mayr notes that
> the philosophical accounts of physics do not apply to, are
> irrelevant to, are not true of, and have no equivalent in bio-
> logy. [In fact] biological theory and fact *conflict with* ... [the]
> interpretations of science stemming from physics ... (1987, p.7)

In short, clockwork physics still dominates, but it is not well-loved. Science in general is ripe for a Reformation but spawning a reformation requires discovering the fatal misperception in the traditional view. It also requires a demonstrably better model. This is where Chaos comes in.

The story of Chaos' discovery and exploration is one of the most perplexing stories in modern science. The meaning of Chaos is still a matter of active debate, and popularizers regularly misportray it. Yet, its importance seems to be without doubt. The reasons for this odd situation will become clear as we proceed but we can also side-step the debate. For our purposes, the easiest way to understand Chaos is as a type of web dynamics that changes our perception even in sewn up systems like planets and pendulums. Chaos shows that even physics' nearly perfect maps have room for Copernican change.

One More Body Brings a Very Big Change

The first bizarre thing about Chaos is that its story starts out in the solar system, the same system that Newton used to demonstrate the perfectly predictable clockwork universe. This time, however, the solar system provides an example of why absolute prediction is a myth and why physics is not almost finished.

As befits my story, the clockwork mistake was one of simple causality given too much credence. Thus, Newton worked his wonders using what is known as a *two-body* model. His equations describe how the sun's influence makes a planet move. Note that this is a perfect example of simple causality, one thing (alone) causing something else. Planets actually float in a web of gravitational effects but, because the sun is so huge compared to planets, one can ignore this web and still have a great deal of accuracy. Thus, the two-body model works well despite its simplistic nature. Indeed, it is still in use today.

Starting simply was necessary and useful, but even in Newton's day scientists knew that the two-body model was just an approximation. Furthermore, since scientists always try to improve things, the generation of scientists after Newton dutifully attempted to improve on his model by adding the effects of one more body, say a moon or another planet. This logical next step was called the three-body problem.

The three-body problem is one of the most celebrated problems in the history of science. For over one hundred years all the best minds in mathematics attempted to solve it. It defied them all. Apparently adding one more body (a little more *inter*dependence) made the problem a lot more complicated, as Figure 4 shows.

In 1892 the French mathematician, Henri Poincaré, made the first dent in the three-body problem. This is where the story gets bizarre. Poincaré did not actually solve the three-body problem, rather he showed that it *could not be solved using traditional techniques*. These last, of course, were analytical.[1]

Poincaré's work had a shocking implication. Adding *one more body* created a type of problem that couldn't be solved by breaking it down. This was not some imaginary addition. Everyone knew the body was there and had an effect. Yet, this addition changed the nature of the problem.[2]

The ultimate implication was that the math most physicists were using only works on *a very small percentage of the world's problems*.

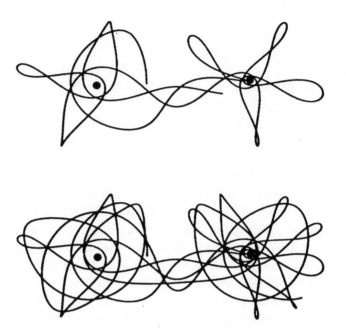

Figure 4. The Three-body Problem (From Peitgen and Richter, 1986, p.2).

With few exceptions, the interactions of three-or-more bodies create a type of behavior which cannot be understood by breaking it down. It is not just the solar system. When chemists study a hydrogen molecule, for example, they have a two-body problem: a huge nucleus affecting a small electron. A helium molecule, on the other hand, is a three-body problem. A nucleus and two electrons all affect each other. The history of chemistry thus followed the history of the solar system. Equations for the hydrogen molecule were solved early on and attempts to do the same for helium met the three-body barrier. Apparently a little more interdependence radically changes the problem regardless of whether that problem is chemical or planetary.

It would take the birth of new abilities for scientists to admit that the tools they had, were not all that was needed. But that would take a while. In 1892, few people had any idea that Poincaré's insight had much import. A grateful scientific establishment accepted Poincaré's work as a penetrating finding of little relevance to actual work on the solar system. Poincaré, however, devoted the rest of his life to developing new mathematical methods, ones that would work without breaking motion apart.

Chaos as Poise — A Ridge of Delicate Balance

Today people say that Poincaré discovered Chaos. Chaos challenges a host of classical assumptions, as we shall see below. But before getting to the strange side of Chaos, let me take a moment to build a solid sense of what it is.

Chaos is best thought of as a ridge of delicate dance which occurs when competing pulls create a place of balanced tension. Figure 5 shows how this works in the solar system. Hence, all celestial bodies (planets, moon, the sun, etc.) have gravity which pulls matter toward them. This means that the solar system is rather like a pond with multiple whirlpools, each pulling matter into it. These basins of influence butt up against each other creating little ridges where they

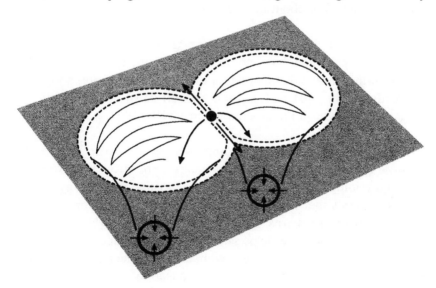

Figure 5. Boundaries of Poise between Gravitational Basins (Redrawn from Discover, Sept. 1994). From the perspective of celestial mechanics, a planet's gravity creates a deep well or basin of attraction. Anything that falls inside that basin is pulled toward the planet. Multiple bodies create multiple depressions with little ridges between them. These ridges are where Chaos and delicate poise hold.

meet. These ridges are where Chaos reigns. On them, forces are so balanced that it takes very little energy to move in any direction. The smallest nudge would send a rocket, for instance, into one well of influence or another. The right nudge would make it slide effortlessly along the ridge.

Places of chaos (poise) have always been there. Better models help us see it and seeing it may be useful, as NASA mathematician Ed Belbruno explains. Currently scientists sending rockets to the moon, still use the two-body model which gives a rather one-dimensional picture of the forces described above. One can see where the earth's pull ends and where the moon's begins. Hence, the current approach to going to the moon is to blast out from the earth's surface and ease into a parking orbit above the earth. At the right moment, the rocket then blasts out of this earth orbit and eases into a parking orbit around the moon. Current methods work but they require a lot of brute force blasting which uses a lot of fuel and costs a lot of money. Belbruno contends that one can use Chaos' delicate balance to do more of the work. As an article about his work says:

> One can use the instability of the ridge to your advantage ... If you use just enough energy to make it to the top of the ridge from the Earth side then, like a roller coaster cresting a hill, with just the right nudge you could roll down the other side and be caught in the moon's gravity well. (1994, p.78).

Still, Chaos is only mildly important in the solar system. My favorite example of its importance actually comes from brain research. Neurophysiologists Walter Freeman and Christine Skarda suggest in no uncertain terms that Chaos is part of what allows your brain to shift between different patterns, including patterns of thought and patterns of smell. Delicate poise helps your brain tilt into unexpected realms and new ways to proceed. Hence, without Chaos one might lie endlessly in the basin of some thought, unable to leap to something new. This idea is a bit more literal than one might imagine. Apparently nature builds Chaos into many systems as a way of enhancing creativity and learning.

Chaos is also important because it is common. It has been found in buckling columns, turbulent fluids, laser printers, the human brain and weather systems, not to mention the orbits of Pluto and the moons of

Mars. Entire volumes on Chaos — ranging from *Quantum Chaos* to *Chaos in Capital Markets* — have been written in recent years. Chaos has even been found in the Harvard Business School's standard inventory stocking problem. Apparently competing forces create a delicately balanced system in many places.

Finding the Order in Chaos

Chaos has become famous largely because of popularizations such as James Gleick's 1985 book, *Chaos: Making a New Science*. But, in all likelihood, it would never have become famous were it not for two very important inventions — twentieth century electronics and the computer. This takes us to one of my central themes. A new science is emerging because scientists finally have tools which allow them to deal with interdependence. These tools open new vistas which in turn are creating a very different picture of how the world works. This brings us back to Poincaré.

After Poincaré had shown that analytic techniques were limited, he and others began work on new approaches which did not rely on breaking apart. These approaches focused on patterns, shapes and forms. Topology and dynamical systems theory are both examples of these so-called 'geometric' approaches. In the beginning most physicists regarded these approaches as bizarre figments of mathematical imagination. Still by the mid 1900s they were pretty well developed.

Computers made the final difference. Scientists have known about interdependence for centuries but, when you have to do all calculations by hand, you do everything you can to avoid including more bodies. A real life example will bring home the point. Johannes Kepler set the scientific world on fire in 1617 by showing that Mars had an elliptical orbit. It took him nine hundred pages of handwritten calculation to do this — and that was a relatively simple path! In 1892, Poincaré almost went crazy trying to chart the three-body dance.

Today, however, things have changed. By the late 1970s computers could do more computations in a single second than were done by all the scientists who lived in the sixteenth century. Small wonder the scientific world began to shift. Computer speed and accuracy allowed scientists to include all sorts of factors they hadn't included before. Strange mathematical tools that had been developing quietly for years suddenly became practical. For the first time in history, scientist were able to explore web dynamics because they were armed with appropriate tools.

The birth of computer graphics made the idea of new vistas quite literal. Like the microscope in the last century, computers' ability to make patterns *visible* has made a tremendous difference. Poincaré had attempted to graph the dance of his three-bodies, but found it impossible to follow. Today computer graphics show us what he could not see.

This brings me back to order. Figure 6 (a) and (b) show the same set of data charted in two different ways. The first shows the traditional one-dimensional view of a variable as it goes up and down, apparently knocked about by unseen forces. The second shows a three-dimensional view made possible by computer-graphics. Here you see the shock of Chaos. Data which looks completely erratic from one perspective, is now shown to trace out a beautiful geometric pattern. Hence the catch phrase, there is *order* in what used to look like chaos.

The scientists who first encountered this order were dazzled indeed — in part, because of its implications. Scientists had long assumed that complex pulls meant messiness. Now the world appeared vastly more ordered than previously realized. A network of forces actually created a hidden design. Even simple webs could create subtle, beautiful, dancing order! The main theme of the new science was beginning. *Webs create pattern, structure and organization* — and now we can see it!

So, we have come to a unique historical juncture. For centuries, adding another body was the last thing a scientist wanted to do. Interdependence made mathematics miserable! But now, thanks to computers, times are changing. Furthermore, because there is order there is new hope for understanding.

So Chaos is common, it is orderly and it is often quite useful. Still, unless I miss my guess, you are still wondering why Chaos has created a lot of stir, which it assuredly has. This brings me to the strange side of Chaos and its famous enigma: while Chaos is exquisitely ordered, it is even more exquisitely *unpredictable*. How could this be?

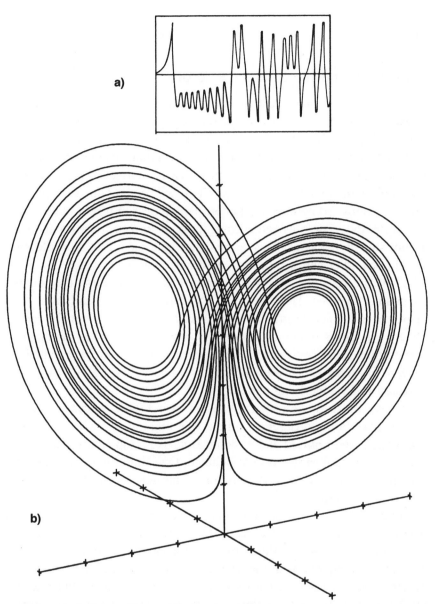

a)

b)

Figure 6. Order in Chaos: The Lorenz Attractor.
Figure 6 shows pictures of the same data seen (a) through the lens of traditional tools and (b) from a web perspective. Figure 6a is a classic time series graph, it shows the ups and downs of a variable as it moves along its sequential journey buffeted about by unseen effects. Figure 6b, on the other hand, shows the same data in graph called phase space. Phase space is made by giving an axis to each variable which means that each point in the plot represents changes in all three variables simultaneously. Eureka! Pattern is visible in the co-evolution of the three variables — in the picture of how they change together — but not in their separate sequential journeys!

Sensitivity and the Strange Side of Chaos

Chaos is a type of motion. Apparently, three bodies have the capacity to mutually affect themselves into an exquisitely structured dynamic dance. Three-pendulum swings sold in novelty shops give one a sense of how this works. Each pendulum has a repelling magnet at its base. As one pendulum swings down, it pushes a second out of the way and the third swings back in its wake. There will be smooth swings and sudden bumps. Sometimes the pattern will appear to repeat but just as you think the system as settled into its final form it makes a sudden abrupt shift in behavior. This is the dance of Chaos. It is an endlessly novel oscillating dance caused by interwoven effects.

There are several important features of this dance. First, the bodies are bound together. Thus, whether it is a pin holding pendulums together or a balance of gravitational forces, the bodies never fly completely off. Being bound by a web of forces is what makes the bodies curve around and come back. The pattern in Figure 6 (b) is called a *strange attractor* because bound bodies do curve back as if strangely attracted to an underlying pattern.

As we've seen, however, Chaos is also highly *sensitive*. Little nudges make a big difference. Like a spinning top, the whir of forces keeps the system poised and moving. But, like a top entering a rough area, balance makes the system delicate. One little bump can send it careening off in a wild new direction.[3] This sensitivity is what leads to Chaos' unpredictability.

Here is where things get strange, however, because when mathematicians say Chaos is unpredictable they are not making some loose claim that it is hard to follow. Rather, they are saying that, no matter how good the equations or the data, one will never be able to pinpoint exactly where a body in Chaos will be at some point in the future. Furthermore, they say these things for very concrete, rigorous reasons. Figure 7 explains.

So Chaos shows that the world is much more ordered than previously thought. But, this order is not the kind we are used to. Because there is order, we can understand and do much to steer our world. But because of Chaos' sensitivity, we will never be able to fully predict or control the system. If a dynamic system has Chaos, then any bump at all can make it change direction. Hence, the poetic

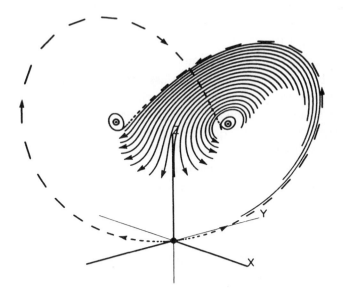

Figure 7. Diverging Trajectories (From Thompson and Stewart, 1986).
This figure shows bodies tracing out the pattern of a strange attractor. The lines that make up the attractor (called trajectories) can be thought of as the path a particular body might follow as it moves. As the figure shows, some trajectories that start very close, soon move in opposite directions. Now here is the trick to sensitivity. If a body were bumped in a place where the trajectories were very close, it would shift from one trajectory to another. The body would then move off in a radically new direction following its new trajectory. Thus, when the trajectories are very close, it takes only a very small nudge to send the body off in a wild new direction. This is Chaos' sensitivity.

In Chaos, the phrase 'very close' has a very precise meaning because the attractor is a fractal. In a fractal the same pattern repeats at ever smaller levels. Thus, though the figure doesn't show all the lines, the attractor is, in fact, honeycombed with trajectories at ever finer levels of resolution. Hence, if you zoomed in, you would find that between any two trajectories there would be another trajectory. No matter how many times you zoomed you would keep on finding new trajectories between the previous ones. The implication is that, no matter how small a nudge you can imagine, there would be always be a trajectory at that spot ready to sweep the body off in some new direction. Hence, mathematicians can show that during Chaos, the nudge needed is literally infinitesimal. Any microscopic nudge is enough to send the body off on a new trajectory.

name for Chaos is, the Butterfly Effect. The idea is that a butterfly flapping its wings in California could influence whether there are monsoons in China.

But Chaos is not just an interesting metaphor. Its unpredictability is real. For example, most of us assume that, if we plug the same numbers into two computers running the same equation, then the end results will always — always, always — be the same. Surely, this must be a fact! Yet, if an equation exhibits Chaos, running it on two different computers will produce radically different end points!

The reasons for this are mathematical, not mystical. Computers use finite-length numbers. Hence, they round off or truncate numbers during division and multiplication. As a result, different brands of computer generally have microscopic differences in their calculations. We don't usually worry about this because we *assume* that very small differences don't make much difference. Unfortunately, this is not true in Chaos. During Chaos, microscopic differences — twenty places past the decimal point and smaller — produce very big differences in the end number. Hence, if there is Chaos, computers running the same equations produce different end points.

Thus, the traditional belief that people can predict everything if they have the right equations is *wrong*. On the other hand, while the idea of absolute prediction dies, other possibilities arise. Hence, though Chaos is incredibly sensitive, it is also still incredibly ordered. Our two computers produce their radically different end points while nevertheless tracing out the same overall pattern. The equation always creates the same pattern. The overall geometry of chaotic behavior is quite regular and repeatable. It is the *path* of a body within the design which is unpredictable. This means Chaos is stable and regular but never repeats exactly the same way twice. It is a snowflake phenomenon.

The paradoxical nature of Chaos is actually an argument for Poincaré's strategy. Patterns hold! Use patterns and geometry, not analysis and point-by-point prediction. Nor is this a minor point. Governments which spend millions of dollars on simple causal models to predict the weather face diminishing returns. But those who study how *patterns* ebb and flow may get farther. The best weather predictions come from studying how patterns shift and turn.

So, Chaos curbs some of our more arrogant beliefs about prediction and control. Still, none of this explains why people thought it might turn the tide of clockwork thinking. Rather, as with all Big Change, the reason people think Chaos is important has to do with its human implications (not with science *per se).* People care about Chaos because it challenges a hateful image — that humankind can do anything because mathematics allows us to predict and control everything! This idea too is woven throughout our world.

The Fundamental Myth and the Dark Side of Science

> *In some sense, unlimited predictability is the fundamental*
> *myth of classical science.*   Ilya Prigogine

The idea that *everything* in the world can (at least in principle) be predicted and controlled has been called the foundational myth, and sometimes the fundamental myth, of classical science. Pierre Laplace, an eighteenth-century physicist and one of the great advocates of this idea, put it this way:

> Given for one instant an intelligence which could comprehend
> all the forces by which nature is animated ... [an] intelligence
> vast enough to submit these data to analysis, it would embrace
> in the same formula both the movements of the largest bodies
> in the universe and those of the lightest atom; to it nothing
> would be uncertain, and the future as the past would be present
> to its eyes.

Ah, the great hope! Given the right equations and precise initial conditions, everything — the weather, the evolution of the cosmos and a butterfly's sneeze — can be precisely predicted. Isn't this a fact? Physics seems to have demonstrated the truth of this principle in systems from cannonballs to quanta. Perfect prediction is sometimes cited as the aim of all science and even as the only real test of science. It is epitomized by Newton's Laws and the workings of the solar system!

Chaos, however, shows that absolute prediction is indeed a myth. Even if Laplace's vast intelligence knew everything, it couldn't predict the exact position of three pendulums, much less the evolution of the cosmos, unless it could use infinite numbers. God may know the exact end of the universe, but we never will.

But why should ending absolute prediction be a big deal? This brings me to the dark side of science. Modern science started as a dream that reason would overcome corrupt authority. Unfortunately, somewhere along the way science became swelled up with an arrogance of its own. This is not altogether surprising. If you teach people that they can predict and control the world, if you say that that is their job — well then, it is not so surprising that arrogance and running rough-shod might follow.

This point also applies to lay people affected by scientific beliefs. Machine science has made bending things to one's will seem like Man's manifest destiny. It is one of the main reasons we spit in nature's face with such great regularity, assuming we will always be able to predict and control our way out. It is also one of the main reasons we deify ourselves, seeing humankind as separate and above.

These kinds of ideas are now insidiously woven into every nook and cranny of our world. For example, in a controllable clockwork world, people assume that economies can be planned, controlled and predicted. Soviet five-year plans epitomize such thinking: if I add forty workers and five machines, in five years I will have X level of production. Hyper-planned economies seem ludicrous in light of the Soviet demise but variations on this theme still seem absolutely reasonable. A more subtle example is the belief in techniques — precise interventions that produce predictable, *controllable* results. This kind of thinking says: if I apply this technique to my children they will grow up happy or, if I present this propaganda to my employees, or the voters or ... (fill in the blank) ... it will raise their morale, make them more efficient — in short, make them do what I want. The belief that technique X will controllably produce result Y is very clockwork. And, no matter how often the children, employees, voters, etc. don't turn out like expected, people still believe that it is quite literal.

The fundamental myth also tends to bolster the idea that in people power can and *should* manipulate and control. Soviet five-year plans now seem ludicrous, but other ideas remain happily enshrined. Experts advise politicians and whole industries on how to manipulate people through clever public relations techniques and population analyses. The point here is simple. If you believe you can manipulate and control — if that is the point of numbers — it is hard to avoid the impression that you *should* manipulate and control. It's realistic. It's practical. It's efficient ... It's our job!

Dissect, manipulate, control! Innocent scientific beliefs have become pillars of less innocent activities. Chaos' assault on the fundamental myth has thus become a beacon of hope against the dark side of modern science. People are looking for it high and low, in the stock market, in epidemics and in arrhythmias of the human heart. And somehow just discovering it seems to be enough.

Popular accounts of Chaos have also resonated strongly with the lay audience, suggesting a deep common chord is being struck. The strength and breadth of this excitement has little to do with technical issues. Rather it arises from the deep and widely felt abhorrence of the dissection and control ethos and the arrogance it produces in science and society.

Let me now state the obvious. Many scientists hate this ethos as much or more as lay-people do. The problem has never been with science or scientists *per se*, the problem has been the unspoken attitudes which have been woven around innocent techniques. Those who abhor these attitudes in science and society now have hope. Chaos provides a rigorous way to deny the hated ethic and the barely glimmering hope of a profoundly different view.

Inklings of a New Science

The discovery of Chaos also proved to be but the tip of another iceberg. The computer and those vista-expanding tools were creating a revolution in science — though at a distressingly slow pace. At first the scientists who were developing the new ideas worked in isolation, with no awareness that they were dealing with common issues and reaching similar conclusions. Gleick's book outlines how these early workers found each other in the 1970s and how their disparate activities began to take shape as a 'new science.' He called it Chaos but there was much more than this. Fractals, attractors, bifurcations, turbulence, self-organization, emergence — a whole host of new findings were being born and they were all related. A new lexicon grew up and a theme was born. Webs don't work like machines — and new tools help you see why!

Gleick's book turned Chaos into a pop label for an entire field, sometimes called nonlinear dynamics[4] but meant generally as a new science. Web science was coming of age and with it a new view. Furthermore, the view that was emerging was more powerful and felt better than the one being left behind. Civilization was not going to lose science, rather it was going to get an expanded science that had a much bigger soul.

But Chaos did not turn the tide. Apparently the term Chaos did not work well. The new science with its broad goals was often confused with the one phenomenon, dynamic Chaos. Worse, both Chaos and the new science were confused with the vernacular meaning of chaos, 'wholly without organization.' Finally, too many insights that were important philosophically, were not seen as relevant in the everyday world. In the end, few people could see how Chaos related to anything they cared about.

The flurry of excitement that surrounded Chaos has largely subsided. Chaos now floats as but another uncombined bit in our already jumbled world. Apparently, knowing one's myth is a myth, doesn't necessarily make one give it up. It takes something more. I believe that the main reason the new science failed to take root is that it remained arcane. Jargon got in the way and so too did the urge to create hype instead of clarity. Hence, to my mind, the only way the new science is going to take root is if it is: firstly, clear; secondly, relevant to everyday life; and thirdly, linked to a deeply felt, motivating vision (spiritual).

This brings me to the awe-inspiring example and our first foray into the idea of a larger design. If we are ever to get our head, heart and soul back in sync, we had better begin to broach the delicate topic of spirituality and the great mystery that is the world. How do we get from concrete science to soaring soul? For both scientists and sages the connecting link is awareness of the design which permeates the world.

Unveiling the Invisible Hand

... but for harmony, beautiful to contemplate, science would not be worth following.   Henri Poincaré

When Big Change swells up, its effects are pervasive. The growing attraction to alternative perspectives on medicine, health, exercise and diet, for example, is also part of the crumbling of the clockwork view. Holistic perspectives are a natural return swing reaction to four hundred years of dissection. The process is obvious when you think about it. In every arena of society people are searching for alternatives to a system which seems to have gone distressingly astray by following analytic science.

Searching is also taking place in the area of spirituality and the need for meaning. Large numbers of people are returning to spiritual paths whether traditional Christian, alternative eastern or others more radically new. Highly educated people now openly acknowledge that they rely on intuition rather than rational analysis, many report synchronistic or paranormal experiences and many continue to believe in angels. Large areas of spontaneous popular culture have already made up their own minds about the story told by the clockwork view.

Regardless of whether one accepts these beliefs or not, it is clear that they all stem from a common instinct. There is a widespread and growing discomfort with the prevailing story of the world. Its inadequacy is becoming painful and there is a spiritual hunger for some more coherent account. All of this presses for some kind of new age.

Now, let me be clear, the new science does not support everything that has been said in the name of the New Age. It can, however, do a lot for providing a more coherent account of why secular and spiritual sages were speaking of the same world. Indeed, its true value lies in its ability to reconcile scientific rigour, spiritual perception and practical and humane concerns (our head, heart and soul). This section begins to explore how these might fit together in a physical world which we now realize is awesomely ordered.

The Great Ordering Oneness

Plotinus the Platonist proves by means of the blossoms and leaves that from the Supreme God, whose beauty is invisible and ineffable, Providence reaches down to the things of earth here below. He points out that these frail and mortal objects could not be endowed with a beauty so immaculate and so exquisitely wrought, did they not issue from the Divinity which endlessly pervades all things with its invisible and unchanging beauty.

St Augustine, *The City of God*

There is a thread running throughout the whole of scientific and spiritual thought — east and west, ancient and modern — that is rarely acknowledged today. It is that the exquisite order woven throughout the world is evidence of that ineffable process or reality which brought us to consciousness and which is still at work in the world today. This thread is being restored. This restoration is a core part of how the new science helps reconcile science and spirituality.

So let us remember the past. In the beginning science and spirituality were part of the same world. Plotinus the Platonist argued that the exquisitely wrought beauty reveals the Divinity which endlessly pervades all things. Medieval Scholastics and Enlightenment Deists also found ample evidence of God's invisible hand in the amazing intricacy of the everyday world. Divinity, the ineffable entirety which human beings call God, and *'that which orders all things and whose order permeates all'* are both part of the same thought and have been so for a very long time.

Secular thinkers too have been motivated by order woven as if by an invisible hand. Adam Smith set the foundations of modern economic theory in the eighteenth century and he talked often of an invisible hand of economic order that would make millions of little entrepreneurial actions benefit all. Henri Poincaré, the mathematician who discovered Chaos, spoke the thought which many scientists hold dear — 'but for the harmony, beautiful to contemplate, science would not be worth following.' Einstein said the same.

Some twenty-five hundred years ago the Greeks too realized that the world was ordered as if by an invisible hand and that harmony was its hallmark. Furthermore, being the great scientists they were, the Greeks also showed that the invisible hand was mathematically and geometrically very precise. This turns out to be important.

Figure 8. Golden Ratio relationships in Nature and Mathematics (redrawn from Frost and Prechter, 1990). The Golden Spiral shown opposite, is a type of logarithmic spiral. The ratio of one radius to the next is always 1.168, or 0.1618, if you take the smaller to the larger. The Golden Spiral is found in pine cones, sea horses, snail shells, animal horns, galaxies, hurricanes, DNA, sea waves, the tails of comets, and atomic particles in a bubble chamber. The curve it produces fits the accelerating rate of bacterial growth, the pattern by which meteorites rupture the earth's surface, and the death curl of a dying poinsettia. The Greeks and Egyptians both used the Golden Ratio to construct aesthetically pleasing buildings, and Renaissance artists such as Leonardo da Vinci used it to construct paintings and sculptures.

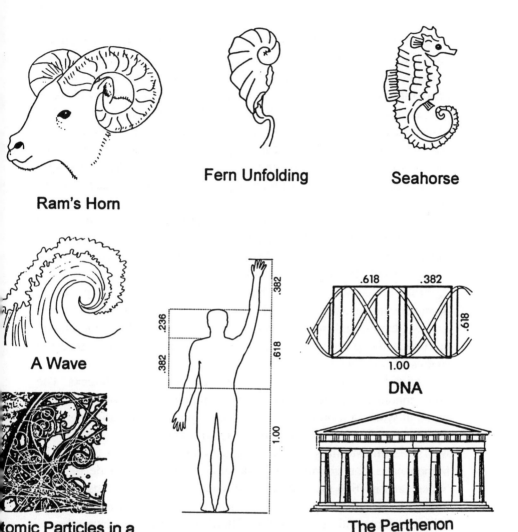

Ram's Horn

Fern Unfolding

Seahorse

A Wave

Atomic Particles in a Bubble Chamber

DNA

The Parthenon

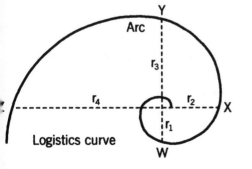

Logistics curve

Golden ratios

$$\frac{r_2}{r_1} = \frac{r_3}{r_2} = \frac{r_4}{r_3} = \frac{r_n}{r_{n-1}} = 1.618$$

$$\frac{r_1}{r_2} = \frac{r_2}{r_3} = \frac{r_3}{r_4} = \frac{r_{n+1}}{r_n} = 0.618$$

Even wonder why the spiral of a ram's horn looks so much like the spiral of certain sea shells? Or, why does a jellyfish with its tentacles hanging down look so much like a raindrop hitting a puddle and propelling a splash back up. And then there are flowers. They blossom into striking designs that take our breath away and every petal is placed just so, in common swirls and spacing patterns found through-out the plant world. The Greeks explored such questions and found that the invisible hand wove regular, precise relationships into shapes and patterns found in places high and low. They called these relation-ships 'sacred geometry.' Figure 8 shows the most famous precise number, the magic number *phi*, (.618), and how it plays out in an equally famous shape, the spiral found in hurricanes, galaxies, DNA, rams' horns, dying poinsettia leaves, pine cones, sea shells and atom trails in a bubble chamber (to name but a few).

From Pythagoras to Plato, the Greeks pursued the study of sacred geometry in all aspects of the world. They found recurrent ratios, angles, shapes, and number sequences in everything from the human body and the placement of leaves on a stem to the most pleasing shapes of buildings and vases.

Nor did the study of sacred geometries end with the Greeks. The great medieval mathematician Leonardo Fibonacci found the same ratios at work in a number series which represented a natural growth progression. Furthermore, Fibonacci's numbers (see Table 1) are found with the same startling regularity seen in the other sacred forms. The human hand, for example, is made of 5 fingers each made of three bones each in .618 ratio of length to each other. Your limbs are also made of three major parts (upper arm, lower arm and hand; femur, calf, and foot) with golden ratios. There are many more examples.[5]

What does it mean that the world is so intricately ordered? Greek, Egyptian and early Christian and Jewish philosophers believed that the sacred geometries were palpable signs of the Divine, the *mysterium tremendum* and 'that which is more than us.' The Egyptians saw *phi* as a symbol of the creative force in the universe, a force that evolved in endlessly unfolding series. Greek, Jewish and early Christian thinkers such as St John saw it as a sign of *Logos*, defined variously as the rational order of the universe, a life-giving force hidden within all things, and a universal reason governing and permeating the world. The Greeks used words such as 'Divine symmetry,' 'Harmonies,' 'Rhythms' and 'the One who orders by Art.' Plato described the 'Great

---

Fibonacci numbers:
    1, 1, 2, 3, 5, 8, 13, 21, 34, 55, 89, 144, 233, 377....
Ratios of adjacent Fibonacci pairs move toward Golden Ratios:
    ... 5/8 = 8/13 = 13/21 = 21/34 = 34/55 = 55/89 ... = 0.618
    ... 8/5 = 13/8 = 21/13 = 34/21 = 55/34 = 89/55 ... = 1.618

Table 1. Fibonacci Numbers and their Relationship to Phi.
Leonardo Fibonacci described his series as representing a natural growth
progression. For example, if one had a pair of rabbits which took one month
to mature and which produced another pair of rabbits each month thereafter,
(and all offspring followed the same pattern), then Fibonacci's series would
represent the total number of rabbit pairs each month: 1, 1, 2, 3, 5, 8, 13, 21,
34 ... There is nothing actually magic about these numbers except that they
do play out with remarkable frequency — most likely because they do tie into
some natural growth progression. They are also related to the sacred Greek
ratios. The Fibonacci series shown in Table 1 has the interesting property
that the ratio of any number to the next higher number is phi (.618) and of
a higher to a lower number is 1.618.

Ordering Oneness' as arranging the Cosmos harmoniously according to eternal archetypes or ideas. These insights were at the core of virtually all the great religious thrusts.

Most modern people, however, cast off the idea of sacred geometries and magic numbers as mysticism, awe without foundation. They do so for a number of reasons. One is that modern science has little understanding of why such shapes, ratios, angles and magic numbers come into existence, especially across such an incredible range of systems — from music to the patterns by which meteors strike the moon. Then too, having distanced themselves from religion after the Enlightenment, clockwork scientists want to avoid spiritual entanglements. To avoid the sense of religiosity that comes with awe, clockwork scientists tend to attribute the mystery of intricate order to nothing but chance (that is, accidents which coalesce without the aid of any deeper driving force). This last has become a key clockwork position.

The new science, however, makes it clear that there is more than chance at work in ordering the world. The Great Ordering Oneness weaves most of its design using energy and web dynamics. Still, it is going to take a lot of scientific pieces to explain why there is a Great Ordering Oneness. The next three Chapters all add to the plot. Here I look at evidence that all those sacred shapes, ratios etc. do stem from web dynamics.

The Greeks, of course, did not know exactly how sacred geometries came about. Until recently, modern scientists didn't know either. Now two French scientists, Stephan Douady and Yves Couder have created an experiment which helps us see that these ubiquitous shapes, ratios, etc. are a natural result of web dynamics. It even gives us a sense of what web dynamics look like. (Figure 9 shows their experiment.) The pulls and pushes of very real bodies create the patterns that pervade the world. These patterns are everywhere because the web we live in is comprehensively linked. It is a Oneness. Patterns are alike in precise ways because web rules and patterns are the same at all levels. This is not how we usually think about things, but it appears to be quite true.

Together such insights imply that science and spirituality need not be at odds. Science too begins to see that a deeper design permeates everything and that Oneness undergirds all. Scientifically speaking, there is a Great Ordering Oneness, which did create the order which permeates the world. The words are a bit too poetic for scientific tastes, but the dynamics which support the image are becoming ever more clear — as we shall see throughout this book.

The 'nothing but chance' idea created a nice barrier between scientific beliefs and the core spiritual awareness and imperative which has motivated thinkers for twenty-five hundred years. This barrier probably developed because the Scientific Revolution rose in reaction to religious oppression. Early scientists found it necessary to avoid any similarity in language or thought. But battles started back then have grown into an antagonism which is no longer appropriate. Science no longer needs protection. It need not press the idea that there is no Design.

The fact that web science matches the Design and Oneness aspect of traditional spiritual visions is among the most delicate insights in today's Big Change. Still, I believe pressure for reconciliation of head, heart and soul will come most strongly from a different direction — practical concerns in the everyday world.

Practical Implications Too

Everything is embedded in a web of forces whose rules and patterns play out in very real ways. To bring this last point home, I should also mention that Fibonacci numbers, *phi*, and other sacred ratios are also

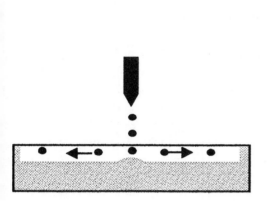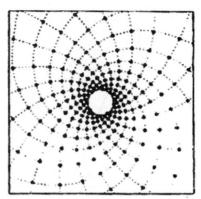

Figure 9. Douady and Couder's Experiment (Redrawn from Goodwin 1994). In this experiment, little drops of magnetized fluid are dropped onto a disk with a thin film on its surface. Magnets are placed around the disk such that drops falling in the center are pushed out toward the edges. The magnetized drops also repel each other. As a result successive drops arrange themselves into a pattern reflecting pushes from other drops and the field. The pattern one gets depends upon how fast the drops fall. For example, if you add drops slowly, each new drop is affected only by the drop that fell immediately before it. The other drops are already too far away to exert much influence. As a result, an alternating 180° pattern emerges as each new drop pushes itself other as far away as possible from the last. The faster you add drops, the more strongly earlier drops will affect each new one. At a critical rate, a strong interaction develops between drops and a stable pattern emerges. This pattern is known as the Golden Fibonacci Spiral. It is rife with all the ratios, angles and curves that the Greeks so admired. It is the result of a strong web of mutual effects pushing bodies into a particular arrangement.

found in the stock market. There is even a Fibonacci Traders Association which pursues these patterns in detail.

For example, in the late 1930s an American economist, Ralph Elliott noted that the number of Dow Jones Industrial Average (DJIA) points in the 1921 to 1926 bull market rise was exactly 61.8% of the final wave of that market which occurred between 1926 and 1928. A coincidence? The same relationship also held in the 1932 to 1937 and the 1949 to 1956 bull markets. In fact, *phi* and Fibonacci relationships are rampant in stock market turning points. Thus, in October 1977, Elliot's firm predicted that the DJIA would bottom out at about 740 because this point marked is exactly .618 times the length of the entire bull market rise from 1974 to 1976. Five months later on March 1,

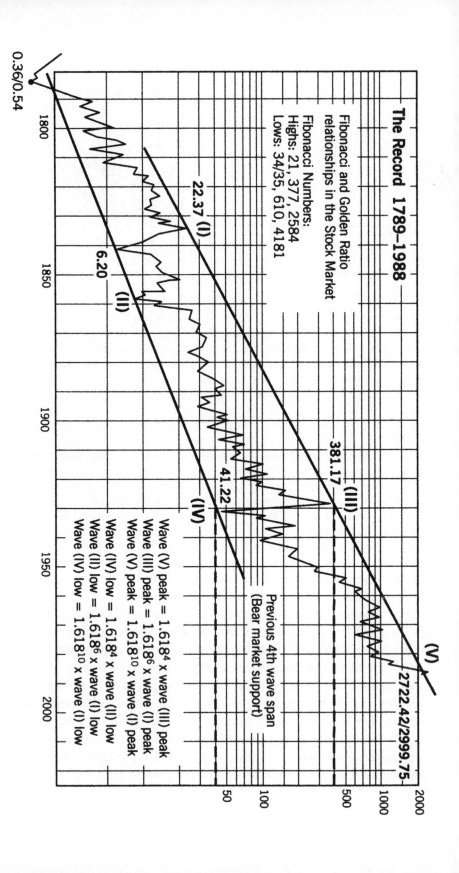

The Record 1789–1988

Fibonacci and Golden Ratio
relationships in the Stock Market

Fibonacci Numbers:
Highs: 21, 377, 2584
Lows: 34/35, 610, 4181

22.37 (I)

6.20
(II)

381.17

41.22
(IV)

(III)

(V)

2722.42/2999.75

0.36/0.54

Previous 4th wave span
(Bear market support)

Wave (V) peak = 1.618^4 x wave (III) peak
Wave (III) peak = 1.618^6 x wave (I) peak
Wave (V) peak = 1.618^{10} x wave (I) peak

Wave (IV) low = 1.618^4 x wave (II) low
Wave (II) low = 1.618^6 x wave (I) low
Wave (IV) low = 1.618^{10} x wave (I) low

1978, the DJIA bottomed out at 740.30. Figure 10 shows golden ratios in the stock market.

Why does the stock market exhibit sacred geometries? Because the stock market rises and falls in response to the pushes and pulls of a human web. Bernard Baruch said it well: 'What actually registers in the stock market's fluctuations is not the events themselves, but ... how millions of individual men and women feel these happenings may affect their future.' This web is made of people, yet it too follows the geometries.

Does this mean we can predict the stock market? Unfortunately, right now web geometries in the stock market are still only suggestive. Like Douady and Couder's drops, patterns shift depending on the strength of interaction between bodies. The investor web shifts with each new stock market turning point and we do not know enough to predict which way the next cast will go. The order is there (after the fact), but we can't tell which ratio will fall out at the next cast. We are left only with results that have an eerie order to them, the same kind of order that permeates the rest of the world.

The stock market example, however, helps people see why web dynamics are important. It isn't just spirituality or obscure science. Web dynamics play out in economics. It behoves us to figure out how.

Fractals — the Modern Version of Ubiquitous Order

So, web dynamics helps us see why order permeates the world and it also makes this order seem much more concrete and useful. Today's tools also allow scientists to see forms of order which the Greeks couldn't see. Fractals are the most intriguing of these new insights.

The world is vastly more intricate than dreamt of in analytic philosophy! Fractals bring this point home. Fractals are beautiful, useful and ubiquitous. They rise from processes we assume could create only disorder. But there it is, order! ... as the following story explains.

'The Chaos Game,' developed by mathematician Michael Barnsley, provides a startling demonstration of how exquisite fractal structure emerges out of what we assume should be a random mess. The rules of the game are simple. Draw three points of a triangle on a piece of paper and number the points (1,2), (3,4) and (5,6) respectively. Now

Figure 10. Phi and other ratios in the stock market (Frost & Prechter, 1990).

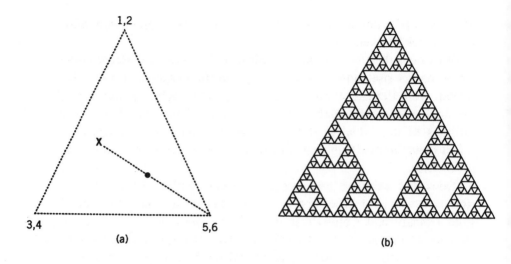

Figure 11 (a & b). The Chaos Game and a 24-hour run of it.

put a point anywhere on the paper. Roll a die. If the die comes up '5,' place a ruler between your starting point and the point labeled (5,6). Then make a mark halfway between two points. This mark is now your new starting point. Roll the die again. Place the ruler from the new start to the point that matches the die and make a mark halfway between. Repeat this process rapidly for about 24 hours — or run it on your home computer for a few minutes. Figure 11 shows the result. Delicate order emerges from a game that uses dice at every turn and begins with a random start!

Now there is nothing mystical about the Chaos Game. Though it's hard for our clockwork-trained brains to grasp, the rules of the game place each new point in a spot which continues a delicate string of relationships among all previous points. This means that all the points are invisibly connected. Even though each roll of the die causes the system to cast out in a random new direction, the rule keeps each new thrust connected with the past. Hence, each new point is shaped by all that has gone before. Ups and downs, zigs and zags, the process is rough and tumble, but subtle connectivity keeps weaving intricate order throughout the whole. The result is a fractal, another of new science's bizarre discoveries.

Fractals are also interesting because they help explain another ancient insight — the microcosm reflects the macrocosm, at every level.

The scientific term for this is self-similarity. It means that finer and finer versions of the same pattern repeat at every level.[6] (Figure 12 shows this in a fern.) We now understand why it arises. Self-similarity is produced by a process which keeps repeating itself, each time casting out from a current point. The process is a type of web because each cast keeps a tendril of connection to all that came before. In fractals, a subtle thread of relatedness runs throughout the whole.

Because fractal designs are fascinating and beautiful, they have had a burst of popularity. Art shows display them, as do tee-shirt salesmen. Fractals are important scientifically, however, because they are everywhere. Anything that is rough — with zigs, zags, scatter, bumps, or wobble — is likely to be a fractal and when you look closely, virtually everything is rough. Thus, more and more members of the new science are standing up saying that fractals *are* nature's geometry. Fractals are found in lightning bolts, coastlines, amoeba trails, snow flakes, electrical noise, music, the structure of quanta, and even cotton-prices on the stock market.

Figure 12. Self-similarity in a Fern (From Barnsley, 1989).

The Benefits of Orderly Scatter

So fractals are something of a sacred geometry for modern times. Furthermore, like other sacred geometries, they have practical implications. Nature uses subtly connected zigs and zags to create *important* structure. What structure? Let's use a story of how ants find food to give a sense of why fractal roughness is important in real life.

How do ants find food? Scout ants are sent out to search for food and when they find it, they return to the nest leaving a pheromone trail for their others to follow. Unfortunately, some 15% of the ants that sally forth on this pheromone trail get lost. These lost ants wander off leaving false pheromone trails of their own. Other ants follow these

Figure 13.
Fractal Ant Trails.

false paths. Some 15% of them get lost and even more false paths emerge (see Figure 13). Machine logic would say the pheromone process is flawed! It allowed individuals to deviate from the *true path* which the first scout left. The result is a tangled confusing mass of false trails. Isn't this obvious?

Actually, it is obvious only if you underestimate interdependence. Thus, Deneubourg and his colleagues have discovered an unexpected subtlety to the process. The confusion of ants falling off trails produces an intricate search pattern that is optimally efficient for finding food. Thus, food sources usually come in clusters which means undiscovered caches are likely to lie near the site already discovered. The scatter of ant trails creates a fractal pattern which intricately covers the high-probability area. Thus, fractal paths are an optimally efficient way to find food in a logically scattered world.

Apparently ants have been using Barnsley's Chaos Game. After millions of years of testing, nature honed in on an optimal behavior — one with a hefty inbred tendency to cast about, but which also has intricate structure because each cast is connected to that which came before. Ants go out one by one, but the pheromone-following rule gives order to their chaos. Every time an ant gets lost, it leaves a new path that subtly affects everything that comes after. At each cycle the landscape changes in a way that is intricately connected to previous cycles. The result is subtle indeed. We assume that getting lost and leaving a false path would produce *a random scattering* (with no order). But the ants actually produce a fractal patterning and this is a very different matter — there *is* a very subtle thread of relationship between every zig and zag.

Fractal structure helps other projects too. For example, lungs and ferns have a fractal structure because fractals increase surface area and more surface area means better energy exchange. This means that fractal order is there for a reason. It is a functional part of the design.

We come back to a recurrent theme. Being able to understand the world's pervasive order has a lot of practical implications. Fractals make this last point most strongly in fields like psychology, sociology, epidemiology and economics where traditional methods work poorly. Here the ability to measure fractal structure turns out to be very useful for exploring phenomena which were too complex for traditional tools.

Finger Prints for Patterns

Almost everything in the world is rough, but now we know that most roughness is fractal and fractals have order woven throughout the whole. Nowadays, researchers can *measure* fractal patterns in very precise ways. This allows them to chart delicate changes in the system that generated the pattern. It also revolutionizes measurement in the so-called soft sciences.

Where is the revolution? Let us take a simple before and after contrast. Researchers collecting data on, say a psychology experiment, are usually confronted by what looks like a messy scattering of points. Their goal is to find the order in that scatter. Most, however, have been taught to look for very simple order, usually a line. They assume that most scatter reflects error or some unrelated bump. In a web world, however, scatter is presumed to be part of the scheme of things (see Figure 14). It reflects the pulls and pushes of various interwoven forces. Furthermore, it probably has a fractal structure which means subtle relationships are riddled throughout the whole. Nowadays scientists can use new measures to study the processes which create this intricate order.

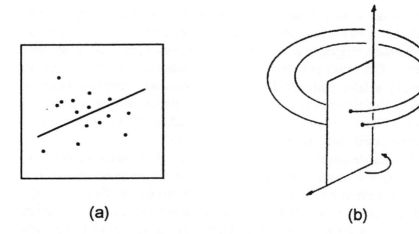

(a)   **(b)**

Figure 14. What Do You See in a Scatter? — Two Visions.
Figure 14 (a) shows a typical scatter of data points and the straight line that
most scientists are taught is probably the true path which these points were
meant to hit. Figure 14 (b) shows the new science image of the same data.
Some coherent process is creating the scatter. Each time around it hits
slightly differently — but this is part of the design. The scatter has a very
subtle fractal structure.

Precise measures of subtle fractal relationships let researchers create
a kind of fingerprint for patterns. Having a pattern's fingerprint allows
researchers to follow the processes that generated the pattern. For
example, EEGs monitor the electrical ups and downs from the brain
and EKGs follow the electrical pulses from the heart. The ups and
downs in both reflect pulls and pushes in a very interwoven system
(your body). Fractal dimensions in EEGs have been used to monitor
sleep stages, to follow mental tasks such as adding, and to predict
epileptic seizures and other pathological conditions. Fractal dimensions
of EKGs have been used to study the onset of heart arrhythmia.

The ability to measure very subtle changes turns out to be particularly useful in the soft sciences like psychology where the complex,
and the seemingly subjective have long stymied empirical efforts.
Redington and Reidbord, for instance, found that the fractal patterns
in heartbeats of patients during psychotherapy are closely related to
that patient's progress. Sabelli and his colleagues have also used
patients' heartbeats to find fractal patterns that correspond to specific
mental states such as anxiety, depression, and schizophrenia. The
results are precise and reproducible across many individuals.

There are also more uncanny examples. For instance, fractals help measure people's sense of seeing something versus seeing nothing.[7] How does one measure this? Well, think of watching clouds move by and looking for shapes in them. Researchers gave people a scatter of dots and asked them if they saw any shapes in these clouds. Their discovery? The fractal dimension of the scatter is an amazing indicator of a viewer's sense of seeing a 'namable object' versus 'nothing.' In fact, fractals turn out to be a good measure of many seemingly subjective things. For instance, fractals can be used to identify music from one culture versus another or sounds which are described as music versus noise. People identify computer-generated landscapes as being 'from earth' if they have a fractal dimension near the typical earth dimension of 2.3, and 'from the moon' if they are close to the typical lunar dimension of 1.5.

Apparently, nature has tuned us too. Human beings are sensitive to extremely subtle relationships among parts, but until the advent of fractals, scientists had no way to measure these subtleties. As a result, clockwork thinkers tended to doubt the validity of subtle perceptions, describing them as 'merely in the eye of the beholder.' Now, however, we find that subjective perception may be acute. Individuals are sensing extremely small, yet precise changes between parts of a whole. The astounding possibility in all this is that the ability to quantify subtle relationships may let the soft sciences become harder. Apparently a great deal of softness came from using the wrong tools (and assumptions).

*   *   *

This ends my brief tour of the new science's insights into the world's wondrous weave. If you notice, fractals are beautiful, ubiquitous and useful.

On the other hand, neither fractals nor the discovery of sacred order has been enough to turn the tide. Like Chaos, the ideas were too hard to understand. Almost no one mentions the link between sacred geometries and web dynamics and few people understood that fractals were useful as well as intriguing. So the popularists moved on. They soon found another label for the new science lurking in the wings.

Complexity!

*A revolution has been brewing ... mavericks from academe
... are gathering novel ideas about interconnectedness, co-
evolution, Chaos, structure and order — and they are
forging them into an entirely new, unified way of thinking
about nature, human social behavior, life and the universe
itself.*   Mitchell Waldrop

Complexity is a better label for the new science than Chaos in
many ways. After all, this new science is about how *webs create
intricate structure* and Webster's Dictionary defines 'complexity' as
'the state of being intricate.' Whichever label you choose, the point
is that both aim at the same vaguely visible new science on the horizon. In all cases, the key is the apprehension of order in complex
webs.

There does appear to be a slight difference between the Chaos and
the Complexity crowds, however. People attracted to the term Chaos
are more likely to gather data and generate equations and graphs much
like traditional physicists (indeed, many of them are traditional
physicists). They are also more likely to use the geometric techniques
from Poincaré and others. They will be attracted to the label, 'nonlinear dynamics.' Finally, Chaos folks are also more likely to be
working with relatively few interacting bodies.

The Complexity crowd, on the other hand, seems to be most
interested in how global patterns emerge from large numbers of bodies.
They tend to pursue this interest by doing *computer simulations*. They
set up computers as if they *were* webs. They then let these little
computer webs generate patterns. Figure 15 gives you some idea of
what this means.

Like life, a neural network is a dynamic, interactive web. Unlike
life, it is a perfectly malleable laboratory in which to study how
organization arises from a frenzy of mutual effect. The web above is
called a *neural net* because it was originally designed to simulate the
way neurons combine into that tremendously interwoven web we call
the brain. There are many types of such computer webs, however.
Cellular automata, genetic algorithms and artificial life are all forms of
computer-simulated webs. They all have similar benefits. Researchers

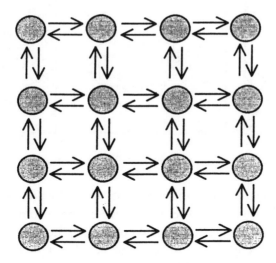

*Figure 15. Neural Network — An Interdependent Web of Little Computers.
Each little circle in Figure 15 represents a processor (a little computer) with
input and output wires connecting it to other processors around it. Each
processor accepts data from its input line, changes that data according to
some set of rules, and then puts out a response to one or more of its fellows.
The result simulates life. Each little computer receives signals out from its
fellows and sends signals back out. Effects ripple outward from a single point
and wash back in vastly changed form.*

can observe how the system evolves as they change operating rules
and other conditions.

Researchers can also use these simulations to study any problem.
Computer simulated webs are being used to model social systems,
economic systems, urban systems, eco-systems, brains, etc. The goal
in all cases is to study how back-and-forth local interactions produce
the patterns we see in real life.

Order from Frenzy

Awareness that global order could arise from individuals acting locally
with a limited set of rules began long ago. For example, in the 1950s
a Cambridge mathematician John Conway developed a program called
'The Game of Life' which showed how simulated cells acting locally
produced patterns which strangely resembled life. The rules of Conway's 'Life' are simple. Start with a computer screen divided into a

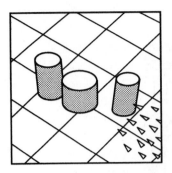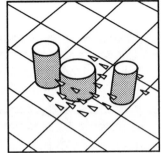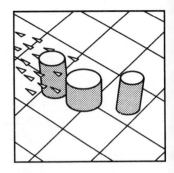

Figure 16. Boids Confront a Cluster of Pillars (Redrawn from Levy, 1992).

grid. Each square in the grid represents a 'cell' which is either living (black) or dead (white). These cells live or die according to a simple set of rules. If a living cell has two or three living neighbours, then it is happy and stays alive. If a living cell has less than two living neighbours, then it dies of loneliness. If it has more than three living neighbours, it dies of overcrowding. If a dead cell has exactly three living neighbours, they reproduce and fill the vacant cell. These are the rules of the game. Start with a random scattering of living cells, turn the computer on and see what evolves.

The results are fascinating. Glider patterns move across the plane, forming and reforming themselves over and over. Some patterns run through a series of stages that repeat over and over with regularity rivaling a traffic light. As mathematician Rudy Rucker put it, 'The screen fills with frenzied activity. Dots race around and clump into things like worms. The worms crawl around the screen, colliding and eating each other, casting off bits of stable debris.'

Some runs lead to the extinction of 'life' and some to stable oscillating patterns. Some patterns even spontaneously reproduce themselves. In the 1950s replication was regarded as a semi-mystical property of living systems, one of the essential differences between living things and dead things. But there it was. Replication emerged spontaneously from the frenzy of mutual effect operating under simple rules.

Simple as it seems, this and other simulations began to produce an important new sense of how webs work. Here, order emerged from *parallel activity*. The simulations above do not operate on an assembly line principle, with one processor doing one step and passing its results to the next processor which does the next step. No, each processor looks around and reacts to its own local situation. They do this simultaneously. At each moment they all stand up at once, look around, and react. They then do the whole thing over again using the changes that came from the last round. Patterns thus arise from back and forth action and reaction done in parallel. This is a lot like life, but it is not like our usual sequential images of how organization comes about.

Somehow separate cells reacting only to their immediate environment, produce a very fluid global-level organization. Organization emerges without orchestration from above and without any prexisting, step-by-step plan. The best example of how this works comes from Craig Reynolds' simulation of a flock of 'boids.' Reynolds had been fascinated by how a squawking field of blackbirds near his home would rise in a beautifully organized spiraling group and then move off in an amoeba-like mass. No head bird called out directions. The flock's undulating cohesion came from individual birds acting on local information according to some simple set of rules. Reynolds wanted to find those rules. To do so he invented his own variation on the Game of Life. Each cell — which Reynolds called a 'boid' — would notice what its neighbours were doing and adjust its own behavior accordingly. There were three basic rules. If its neighbours get too close, the boid moves away from them. If they get too far away, it moves toward them. Boids also try to match their neighbours' speed so that the group stays together.

Reynolds turned on his computer and after months of fine-tuning his rules, the behavior of his boids began to look a lot like a flock of real birds — even in very complex situations. For example, when confronted with a cluster of pillars, Reynolds' boids would temporarily split into two flocks which would flow back together at the end of the pillars, just as real flocks do (see Figure 16). Some of Reynolds' hapless boids would even slam into pillars while trying to avoid their neighbours, stop stunned for a moment and then move off to follow the flock. The behavior was so life-like that ornithologists started calling Reynolds to find out what his rules were.

So there it was. Coherent group behavior emerged from separate individuals operating on simple rules. The plan was not pre-ordained or handed down from above. It evolved from parallel activity. Many systems work this way. Scientists have used neural nets to explore much more than replication and flocking behavior. Some neural nets spontaneously exhibit sleep cycles. They go dormant after a period of frenzied activity. Neural nets can be used to find, copy and recognize patterns for which no equation yet exists. Genetic algorithms that simulate natural selection are being used to find rules of behavior for businesses, eco-systems etc. that produce optimal results over evolutionary cycles of varying lengths. The list of how computer webs can be used goes on and many of the results are very non-classical.

Does this mean that Complexity will succeed where Chaos failed? Right now it seems unlikely for reasons not unlike those which plagued Chaos. The term Complexity suffers from the connotation of being 'complicated' which puts people off and is often not the case. Just as there is order in Chaos, there is often simplicity in complexity. Then too Complexity has also suffered from the problems of popularization and what I call Hollywood science. Attempts to make Complexity seem exciting have left it seeming mostly like hype and a new techno-fad.

Finally, Complexity (as it is currently popularized) also has no sense of history and its own role in a much older push to understand the order which lies all around us. For instance, as one popular book says: 'This is a book about the science of *complexity* — a subject that's still so new and so wide-ranging that nobody knows quite how to define it ...'[8] Yet, complexity was defined long ago. Wrapped up in recent developments, most popularizers have simply missed its history. Let me rectify this situation and, in the process, give you a compact view of the whole story.

Intricacy and the Unexplored Realm

Puzzles that once appeared unanalysable become more susceptible to attack. What is more, the very nature of some puzzles are no longer what they seemed to be.

Jane Jacobs

We've seen that there is an amazing amount of order woven in our world. It is hidden high and low. Furthermore, most traditional tools can not see it. Let me now add that this is not a new idea. It is coming to public awareness because many threads are now converging to create an ever clearer picture. History makes the picture clearer still.

The term Complexity has the benefit of a long history whose story is rarely told but whose insights bear directly on the change of science and all that we have said so far. So, let me introduce Dr Warren Weaver, whose report to the Rockefeller Foundation in 1958 outlines a history of science that I think should become standard. As Weaver says:

> Speaking roughly, one may say that the seventeenth, eighteenth and nineteenth centuries formed the period in which physical science learned how to analyze two-variable problems ... Simplicity was a necessary condition for progress at that stage of science. (1958, p.432)

Weaver is describing Newton's very important two-body model. He is also pointing out that simple causality (plus analysis) has guided scientific images ever since. But, Weaver continues.

> ... It was not until after 1900 that a second method of analyzing problems was developed by the physical sciences. Rather than studying problems which involved two variables or at most three or four, some imaginative minds went to the other extreme, and said 'Let us develop methods which can deal with two billion variables.' That is to say, the physical sciences ... developed powerful techniques of statistical mechanics which can deal with what we may call problems of *disorganized complexity*.

Weaver is introducing one of science's other great developments, statistics. He says it works on problems of *disorganized complexity*. He explains using a billiard ball illustration. For three hundred years scientists focused on predicting the path of a single ivory ball as it glided across a billiard table. Eventually they could handle two or three such balls, but by the time they got to ten or fifteen balls, the problem became totally unmanageable. The imaginative minds mentioned above, then took a huge leap. They discovered that if one has a billiard table with millions of balls flying about, then (wonder of wonders!) the billiard ball system as a whole has certain reliable average properties. One can thus answer questions like: 'On average how many balls hit a stretch of rail every second?' One can also apply the same insights to other arenas and answer questions that help life insurance companies, for example, figure out the costs they are likely to have.

Statistical insights too have been important. But statistical properties arise from the helter-skelter of *non*-related behavior. Yet, most of the world's behavior *is* related. Weaver's story, therefore, continues. By the 1930s it became clear that there were many problems which did not fit the assumptions of either simplicity or disorganized complexity. Such problems were particularly rife in the human and life sciences. One cannot, for example, explain what makes an evening primrose open when it does using either simple causality or theories of non-related behavior. These approaches don't work on social evolution either. Rather a third set of problems exists which is inherently different from either of the earlier two. As Weaver writes:

> One is tempted to oversimplify and say that scientific
> methodology went from one extreme to the other ... and left
> untouched a great middle region. The importance of this
> middle region, moreover, does not depend primarily on the ...
> number of variables involved ... Much more important ... is the
> fact that these variables are all interrelated ... As contrasted
> with the disorganized situations with which statistics can cope,
> these problems also show the essential feature of organization.
> We therefore refer to this group of problems as those of
> *organized complexity*.

Weaver gives us the proper name for the kind of problem seen in human bodies, eco-systems, the weather, and fractals. The name is 'organized complexity' or alternatively 'ordered-complexity.' Jane Jacobs, the author of the opening quote, also suggests that the concept of order-complexity applies in places most people don't imagine. In 1961 she wrote:

> Cities happen to be problems in organized complexity, like the
> life sciences. They present situations in which a half-dozen or
> even several dozen quantities are all varying simultaneously
> and in subtly interconnected ways ... variables are not helter-
> skelter; they are interrelated into an organic whole. (1961,
> p.433)

Weaver's history helps clarify our current situation in a number of ways. First it says that science has been dominated by two types of problems: simplicity and disorganized complexity. Because these were first, we tended to assume everything was *either* simple (and analyzable) *or* so disconnected and disordered that only statistics could help. Retrospectively, we have been trying to cram everything into images which apply only to two extreme conditions.

We are just now beginning to open the middle ground and already the picture has changed. Forays into fractals, sacred geometries and the like make a very important point — most of the world falls in the middle ground. What is unique about this middle ground is that it is *ordered because it is interwoven*. These are not separate properties. Order in the world has a lot to do with web dynamics and profound connectivity.

Intricacy!

Weaver's story also gives us the proper names for all three types of problems and in doing so he helps reveal one source of confusion. Complexity is a bad name for the new science because it doesn't distinguish between ordered complexity and disordered complexity. Yet, the two are completely different. The key to the mid-ground is order *and* interweaving, not complex causality in itself.

Names have a wondrous ability to enlighten or confuse and right now we seem to be leaning toward the confusion side. To help avoid the confusion which already surrounds the term Complexity I have tended to replace the term ordered-complexity with the equally descriptive and as yet unencumbered phrase '*intricacy.*' Intricacy refers to the order which arises from interweaving.

Your body is, thus, intricate — not simple and not disordered. So, too ecologies are intricate and not merely complex. They are arranged such that one thing connects to another to a third, fourth and back again in an intricately ordered whole. Similarly, social fabrics can be either intricately-woven or frayed. The former is more likely to hold together than the latter.

The Missing Middle

Intricacy (order in interweaving) is found everywhere. It evolved for physical reasons. Hence, our budding ability to understand the patterns which go with orderly webs, is going to have a big impact on understanding a great deal of the world, in fact, *most* of the world. This leads to our first Copernican shift.

For a very long time we have been doing the best we can and assuming that it was all that was needed. Scientists tried simplicity. They broke things apart, hoping to find a simple cause. They then leapt to statistics and used assumptions about non-dependence. As a result most of us grew up assuming that these two approaches we had covered everything. Something was *either* amenable to statistics *or* to equations. There seemed to be nothing in-between, nor any need for any other techniques.

Now we find that the space between is actually filled with intricacy — the patterns, structure and organization produced by interdependence. Furthermore, intricacy is neither simple nor statistical. The two camps are thus changing into a continuum with a whole lot of unexplored territory in the middle. Thus, sometime in the future the scientific world is going to look like Figure 17. The mid-range is the ground of the new science.

This switch has two simple, but profound implications. First, both of our standard images — classical mechanics and statistics — are extreme cases. Simplicity only works when one variable is so overpowering (like the huge sun) that one can get away with ignoring other effects. Thus, classical mechanics was not wrong, its images are just restricted to a very few cases. Similarly, disorganized complexity happens when mutual effects so weak and so balanced that many-bodied behavior *is* effectively non-related. Normal curves do work some times. But statistical assumptions *are* assumptions. They are used at the cost of ignoring effects. In the end, there are always connections.

The second implication is a bit more jarring. It is now clear that traditional tools put scientists in the methodological equivalent of doing brain surgery with stone chisels and knives. We've been doing the best we can, but our best has been totally inappropriate for most of the world's problems. Intricacy defies the expectations of both earlier cases. Webs do not work like machines nor like billiard balls.

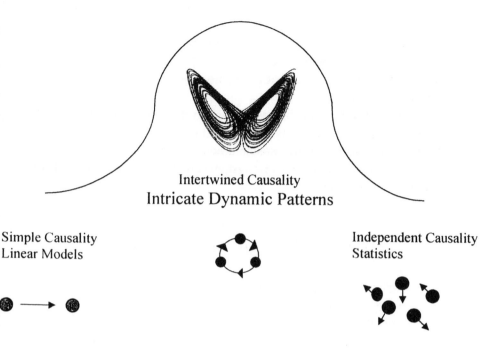

Intertwined Causality
Intricate Dynamic Patterns

Simple Causality
Linear Models

Independent Causality
Statistics

Figure 17. Science from the Broadened View of Interdependence.
Mathematically speaking, we've been using the extreme cases as the norm.
The new continuum is now being bridged mathematically. It turns out, for
example, that the mathematics of fractals butts up right against the mathemat-
ics of classical statistics. The equation that generates the normal curve, for
instance, is part of a broader equation, most of whose outputs are fractals.
On the other side of the world, Chaos theory butts right up against classical
mechanics. Take away one body and you have Newton's equations. As web
dynamics comes of age, we should be able to tell what techniques apply to
what kinds of problem.

Science is entering a whole new world — which happens to be the one
we most live in.

We can now phrase Poincaré's insight more clearly. Most of the
world is intricate. Most traditional methods are *inappropriate* for
intricacy. If you try to break intricacy down, you miss the point — its
organization. If you use statistics you glimpse order fleetingly but have
no idea what caused it or how it works.

All of this leads to one final shock. Now that alternatives are
emerging, it is becoming safe to say that we must change our tools if
we want to understand how the world works. This leads to the ultimate
implication of the new science. Twenty-first century science is still
embryonic, but it is already clear that its development will have

profound implications, particularly pragmatically. A huge amount of social, economic, and political power will go to those who succeed in developing a set of tools that are appropriate for intricacy and the as-yet unexplored realm.

Believe it or not, this brings us back to the start of the chapter. The traditional picture of nearly complete science armed with reasonably adequate methods is turned upside down. We know very little. Science is not nearly done and very few systems are adequately addressed. We are like our ancestors.

Crumbling, but still Emerging

When a great question is first started, there are very few even of the greatest minds, which suddenly and intuitively comprehend it in all of its consequences.

John Adams, 1776

Weaver's history helps us see that the new science is not altogether new. It has been developing for most of this century. What we are witnessing, therefore, is not a single discovery that revolutionizes our thinking, but a convergence of tools and abilities which make long-simmering ideas both useful and unavoidable. This is actually a lot like what happened with Copernicus. It does not, however, fit the usual lone genius story of how scientific revolutions arise. The hive mind has been chewing on this for a very long time.

Popular labels for the new science will eventually disappear as web-thinking becomes the norm. Why? Because this is not a new specialty, it is a transformation of science as a whole taking place for completely understandable reasons. Science as a whole is beginning to discover that you really can't understand much of anything unless you look at how webs create order, high and low. Science as a whole is also beginning to realize that the secret to understanding the world lies not in *un*tangling its weave, but in keeping the tangle and looking at the patterns it produces. When scientists start to do this seriously, their picture of the world changes.

How much could change? We have covered the long and the short of it. The diet example shows how web-thinking can radically change people's perspectives on everyday issues. Chaos and fractals show just how different web dynamics can be. Sewn-up areas have room for change, the fundamental myth finds a rigorous challenge, and underneath we find a world that the ancients knew. Apparently, adding a little bit more of what we already knew was there (intertwined effects) is about to shake up scientific images all over the place.

The new science also brings new reasons for a Reformation that are rarely mentioned. Weaver, Poincaré and now many others help us see why fields like psychology and biology have reason to chafe. The approaches handed down from clockwork physics are *not appropriate* for the phenomena in these fields.

Today, for example, financial analysts forecast market trends using linear, analytic equations (non-web kinds). Their forecasts are often wrong. We all know this. Most of us even know that what market analysts do is make best guesses given the tools they have. On the other hand, we tend to assume that the experts are on the right track and probably almost there. It rarely occurs to people (other than geniuses like Poincaré) that this wonderful machine science of ours *does not have adequate tools*. Something different *has* to be done because the tools in common use do not show a very realistic picture at all. That, however, is the hidden implication of the web revolution. No wonder the soft sciences chaffed!

The tide has still not turned. Yet, perhaps you are beginning to see why many people feel that a turning is inevitable. There is nothing here that is very disputable. People are simply beginning to include more of what they already know is there. Science is expanding. The surprise is merely the degree of change.

We've barely begun but already the shift in image is profound and also more appealing. This web world of ours weaves delicate and deftly-placed order all over the place. It finds no fault with the ancient sages and in the process it gives us new reasons for awe. This is not a clockwork world that can be easily predicted and controlled if we have the right equations. Yet, perhaps it is an understandable world, one we can live with, socially, emotionally, and pragmatically.

The threads that lead to the new science have been multiplying for some time. They are beginning to come together. What else could change? Let us look over the hill.

CHAPTER 3

ENERGY AND BASIC PRINCIPLES
OF CHANGE

We shall find that the flow of energy is a self-organizing
principle at both the macroscopic and the molecular level.

Harold Morowitz

If you look closely, you will notice that energy seems to play an important role in Eastern thought. Eastern medicinal approaches such as acupuncture base their theory of healing on restoring proper energy flow. Exercise and health disciplines such as Tai Chi and Chi Gong are also all about energy, with 'chi' being the Chinese word for it. New Age consultants have taken this thinking into business where they talk about energy flow in meetings and in a company as a whole. It is therefore apropos that energy should also play an important role in science's rethinking of the world. It does.

I've been talking a lot about math and computer simulations. But people doing computer simulations often leave out a key ingredient. To understand why organization arises in the real world we have to add energy. So where does the Great Ordering Oneness come from? What single principle could account for all the different kinds of organization — whirlpools, eco-systems and life? The answer has been known for a long time. Energy is the driving force behind a self-organizing universe.

If we are going to understand our world, therefore, we are going to have to understand at least the basics of energy flow. I start with an utterly simple example. The official name for this example is the Bénard cell experiment. Most people, however, call it the boiling soup model.

What happens when there's Heat?

Start with a pot of water at room temperature. Everything looks quiet, but inside, water molecules are colliding, bouncing furiously back and forth. If you put a fire under the pot, heat makes these collisions go faster. Indeed, they go faster and faster until they cannot go any faster — at least not through random collisions. Crisis! The current organization is going as fast as it can, but heat is pressing the system to go faster. The system becomes unstable and ripe for change.

Then, lo and behold, the system finds a way out. Little pockets of relatively hot molecules have been accidentally coming together and moving apart all along. Hot collections are lighter and more buoyant than their cooler surrounds. The unstable context now puts this characteristic to use. Little hot collections begin to float upward as a whole. Eventually some collection rises all the way to the top, loses its heat and sinks back down pulling other molecules along with it. The entire region suddenly erupts into a coherent circular motion. The system organizes itself into a pattern that moves energy faster!

But the saga of boiling soup is not over. If the heat is still on, molecules will move faster in the new circular motion until they can go no faster there either. The whole process repeats. Some naturally-occurring diversity will seed a new cycle. The system will *reorganize* itself into a faster, more intricate pattern — something like the figure '8' shown in Figure 18 (d).

So, what happens when there is heat? The three main points are:
- *Energy concentrations create a pressure to flow faster.* An energy build-up (like concentrated heat) creates a force which presses the system to move faster.
- *Organization arises to help energy move faster.* You can think of this as a bucket-brigade activity. Passing energy in an orderly fashion makes it move faster. This leads to a new perspective on organization itself.

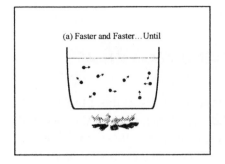

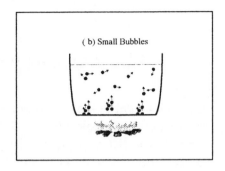

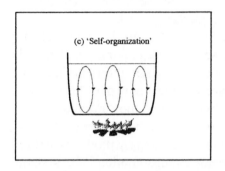

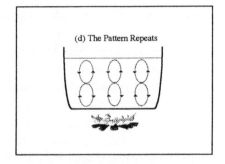

Figure 18 (a-d). From Random Collisions to Self-organization.
Molecules start by moving faster in their current pattern (random collisions).
When they can go no faster in that pattern, the system organizes itself into a
circular motion. If the pressure continues, the system will reach another
impasse and re-organize into a yet more intricate patterns — like figure '8's.
Each new stage moves energy faster.

■ *All organizations are flow structures.* They exist to make energy
flow. Energy is the glue which holds an organization together and
the fuel which makes it move. When there is no energy flowing
through, the organization falls apart. When energy flows poorly, the
system becomes fragile. What we see as 'organization' is actually
nothing but energy flow.

Boiling water (or the Bénard cell) provides a nice physical example
of how organization emerges from energy pressures. We can also use
it to see some of standard energy rules and patterns. For example, the
self-organization just described also follows a standard development
cycle shown in Figure 19.

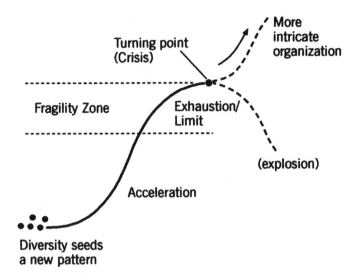

Figure 19. The S-Curve.
If the horizontal axis is time and the vertical is speed of energy flow, then you can also think of the Bénard cell as following a standard cycle of development. The elements of this cycle are: (1) Diversity seeds a new pattern of organization by tapping an energy build-up; (2) The organization grows by accelerating energy flow; (3) Size begins to reduce efficiency; (4) The system becomes exhausted and instability sets in (the fragility zone). It eventually reaches its limits; (5) Poised on the razor's edge the system can go either of two ways — more intricate or destroyed.

Rule 1: The S-curve

In the beginning, diversity seeds a new organization. A small tornado of organization rises by tapping a pool of pent up energy. This organization grows because it accelerates energy flow. All seems well. Unfortunately, as the organization grows, size begins to make it sluggish. Ironically, getting bigger — its very success — brings on its own exhaustion. Eventually, it will be able to go no faster in its current pattern of organization. Limit! Crisis! Instability sets in. The context becomes ripe for change. I call this period of instability, the fragility zone. The system eventually reaches a turning point.

Poised on the razor's edge, the system can go one of two ways. It can either give birth to a more intricate form of organization — or

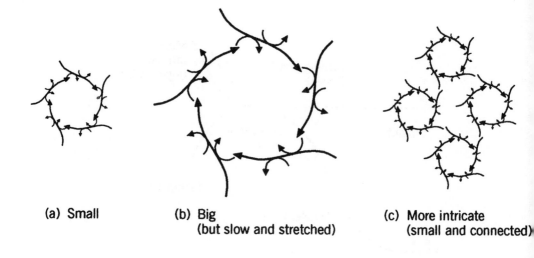

(a) Small **(b) Big** **(c) More intricate**
(but slow and stretched) (small and connected)

Figure 20. The Life Cycle of a Flow Structure.
An organization starts small and tight. If it cycles energy well, it grows
bigger. Size then stretches the bonds holding the system together. It becomes
less efficient and more fragile until it reaches a breakpoint. With luck and a
little diversity, the system may reorganize and improve flow by breaking into
smaller, inter-linked circles which pass energy more robustly throughout The
key characteristics of intricacy are first, small, and second, well-linked.

else. Super-purified fluids demonstrate the alternative. If you remove
all the impurities from a fluid and then heat it, it will still reach a
turning point. Unfortunately, when you remove impurities you also
remove the diversity which might seed a better organization. The
system explodes instead.

Rule 2: The Complexity Catch

This cycle also reveals a hidden rule. Size is the enemy of speed. The
bigger you get, the more sluggish you get. Furthermore, as a system
gets bigger the bonds holding it together get stretched thinner. They
eventually reach a break point.

Nature thus holds a hidden rule which I call 'the complexity catch.'
Getting bigger is tricky. You can't do it in one big circle because huge
circles fall apart. Nature prefers small circles because these are tighter
and faster. On the other hand, energy is also pushing to go faster. To
do this, small cycles have to link together, like a bucket brigade. Thus,
the trick to getting bigger is to stay small *and* well-linked.

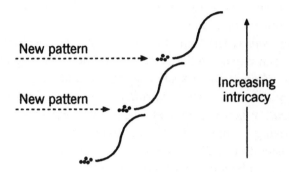

New pattern

New pattern

Increasing
intricacy

Figure 21. Increasing Intricacy and the Punctuated Pattern of Progress. Continual pressure produces a punctuated pattern of increasing intricacy. S-curves pile up with bursts in between. Over and over again, new-acceleration-limit-transformation. With luck, each new phase is more intricately organized than the last.

The result is increasing intricacy. When a big circle reaches its breakpoint, it breaks into smaller circles which link together (Figure 20). Intricacy, like a lace tablecloth, involves lots of small, interlinked circles. Energy actually pushes increasing speed *and* intricacy at the same time.

Rule 3: Punctuation!

The complexity catch also explains why the pattern repeats. Each pattern of organization comes into being, accelerates and reach its limits. Nature lights upon some new naturally-occurring characteristic and the system *re*organizes — more intricately than before. S-curves pile up, with little bursts of crisis and reorganization in between them. The result is a punctuated pattern of increasing intricacy (Figure 21).

I can now complete the boiling soup model. Turn up the heat full-blast. First, small bubbles form, then a string of bubbles up the side of the pan, and then gradually larger bubbles and undulations until a full rolling boil erupts. A series of patterns emerge and move through ever more intricate levels of organization — all to move energy faster.

Miscellaneous More

There are actually a lot of lessons to be learned from energy (and boiling soup). For example:

—*Timing counts.* The same fluctuation that vanishes without trace one moment, can transform the system at another. The fragility zone marks the place where a small spark may ignite a large change.

—*Change often emerges in parallel because of similar pressures felt throughout.* When the context is unstable, one sees lots of little hot parcels rising — much as one sees many little experiments with new society rising today. Thus, percolating change and parallel development are not just phenomena of boiling water. When a human system reaches its limits, searchers rise up from everywhere. In human systems, people call this Zeitgeist.

—*Change never happens exactly the same way twice, though the overall pattern is similar.* Water always boils. But the rolls never start in the same place or go in the same direction twice. Similarly, every seed crystal will have some necessary and some extraneous characteristics. Many crystals may seed the change, the one that does will add its idiosyncrasies to the outcome. The result is a blend of chance and necessity, lawfulness and idiosyncrasy.

—*Evolution is a property of the whole* and not just of specks inside it. Self-organizations do not arise solely from their own efforts or special qualities. They are always tied to a larger field which is pressing for a new way. Without the right context, great sparks simply fade.

One sees this last in life, but energy flow makes the reasons clear. Physicists tell us that all the matter and energy in a field are intertwined such that, if you pull on one corner, the tug is felt on the other. The field is a whole cloth. Similarly, all swirls of organization are connected because they all drink from the same energy trough. Ashes to ashes, dust to dust, little swirls of self-organization emerge and recede into the all embracing energy-flow field. So it is with energy.

All this leads to the reason for mentioning energy at all.

Energy-driven Organization in the Real World

The rules of energy flow play out in places other than boiling water. Chemical systems, for instance, follow the same rules because energy is at work there too. One big reason the world (and life) is more complex than water is that chemical systems can produce a tremendous variety of stable complexes which in turn opens up realms of behavior not possible in simple swirls like whirlpools. Carbon, the core element in living systems, is the most versatile of all, producing more varieties of compounds than any other element.

Since chemical systems can link into more complex forms, the results are more interesting. The outcome of self-organization in chemistry are the cycles and networks that riddle the world — and also our bodies. Your body, for instance, gets its energy because of a wonderful network of chemical cycles which we call metabolism. What is less often mentioned is that our internal chemical cycles came from and are still tightly linked to external ones like the famous carbon cycle. Plants take in carbon dioxide and give out oxygen. We take in oxygen, use it to metabolize our food, and give off carbon dioxide.

The whole interlinked system arose by the same rules seen in boiling soup. The carbon cycle, for instance, is actually part of a larger cycle which goes all the way to the sun — still following the same energy rules of forming cycles and creating speed. As Manfred Eigen says:

> The Bethe-Weizsacker [carbon] cycle ... contributes essentially to the high rate of energy production in massive stars. It, so to speak, keeps the sun shining and, hence, is one of the most important external prerequisites of life on earth. (1979, p.3)

Hence, despite all the differences between chemistry and fluid systems, most energy flow parallels remain: the S-curve, the complexity catch, increasing intricacy, self-organization and, of course, the close link between intricacy and energy-cycling speed. Thus, after years of study, self-organization czar Ilya Prigogine made the following comment:

Structure	F (ergs s^{-1} gm$^{-1)}$
Milky Way	1
Sun	2
Earth's climasphere	80
Earth's biosphere (plants)	500
Human body	17,000
Human brain	150,000

Table 2. Organizational Intricacy and Energy Flow Speed (after Chaisson, 1987).
If order is driven into being as a product of energy-flow, then what counts is how fast energy cycles per unit volume and mass. Physicist Eric Chaisson puts it this way: 'What is important is the rate at which free energy enters a system of some given size ... the operative quantity used to specify the order and organization in any system is the flux of free energy density, denoted here by the symbol F.' (F is energy flux per unit time and per unit mass). This table shows energy cycling speeds through various systems. Note that living systems require substantially larger values of F to maintain their organization. Conversely, intricate organizations like the human brain are the fastest energy cycling systems on the planet.

> We have systematically investigated the behavior of ...
> chemical networks of biological interest ... The surprising
> result was that, in fact, they share most of the properties of
> hydrodynamic instabilities. (1972, p.24.)

Does this commonality seem shocking? From an energy point of view, it shouldn't be. Energy can take many forms: electrical, chemical, thermal, etc. Energy moves back and forth between these types all the time. Furthermore, all forms of energy are interwoven. Thus, if the pressure is on, nature doesn't care whether energy flows via fluid rolls, electrical currents or chemical networks. The pressure is simply to move energy through whatever means available. As a result, patterns similar to those found in simple fluid systems are found in all sorts of systems, including chemical ones — and even life.

I should, therefore, add another piece. One reason scientists believe

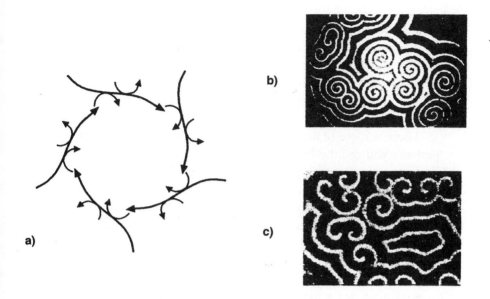

Figure 22. Chemical Cycles and Networks — (a) Symbolic, (b) Non-living, (c) Living.

The energy pressures that created organization in the Bénard cell, push similar changes in chemical systems. Here too diversity seeds new patterns and growth follows the S-curve. In chemical systems, however, increasing intricacy takes the form of networks of chemical reactions which spread cycles throughout the biosphere. Graph (a) shows the situation symbolically. (b) shows a nonliving self-feeding chemical cycle, the Beloussov-Zhabotinsky (BZ) reaction.[1] The BZ reaction strongly resembles (c) which is a living system, slime mold. The implication is that living systems, like slime mold, emerged out of non-living ones.

energy is behind organization and evolution is that the link between increasing intricacy and increasing speed holds from the largest systems to the most delicate ones, like the human brain.

Nobel-prize winning chemist, Ilya Prigogine, took the logical leap from these kinds of observations. He made the concept of self-organization famous in the 1960s through his studies of self-organizing chemical and hydrodynamic systems. He suggested that life arose from these.

The idea that life arose from chemical self-organizations makes sense because life is made up of exactly such cycles. Prigogine, however, also showed that both the living and non-living organizations exhibit similar patterns. They often even look the same. Thus, Figure 22 (b) shows the Belousov-Zhabotinsky reaction, a non-living chemical system which generates beautiful concentric rings that slowly travel outward from centers which arise spontaneously throughout the dish. This non-living reaction bears a striking resemblance to 22 (c), a living system, slime-mold.

There is more to the story of life than explained here, of course, yet perhaps you see the budding idea. Life too is an energy-flow system that emerged from non-living ones which came together in a radical new way. Furthermore, if this is true, then life also fits in a bigger picture. The chemical cycles that fill our bodies, are tied to ones which fill the atmosphere, oceans and land as well. Living systems emerged out of these and are still fundamentally intertwined with the larger self-organizing world.

Hence, the reason for introducing the Bénard cell is to lay the ground work for a grand idea: energy pressing to flow is behind all organization. It flows through our veins and those of the biosphere and the universe at large. Life, individually and collectively, is the product of energy flow and web dynamics. These two forces have been at work for billions of years. They are still with us today.

Dynamic Evolution — Interwoven and Driven by Energy

Energy is a pivotal part of a self-organizing universe. A lot of scientists already know this. Any biologist will tell you that energy is what makes eco-systems work the way they do. It is the tie that binds and the life's blood which sustains. It is the reason all is One.

Energy's ties to self-organization, however, also take us farther than mere connectivity. It helps us see the process of creation in a totally different way. If energy is the culprit, then evolution is radically rethought. Instead of being a result of sheer accident, evolution is process of increasing intricacy which started with pre-living systems, like whirlpools and chemical cycles. It proceeded through increasingly complex forms of life (Figure 23). What we call 'accidents' are part of this process because diversity is. But energy is the more central player. Furthermore, because energy embraces and connects all things, everything in the biosphere — the atmosphere, oceans, land and all life — evolves in a back and forth dance. The evolution of individual species is, thus, part of a larger picture and a more broadly co-evolving

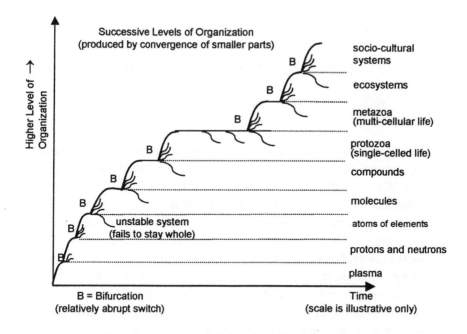

Figure 23. Increasing Complexity in Evolution (Redrawn from Laszlo, 1987).

whole. This is why, for instance, taking care of the environment is such a crucial issue. We and 'it' are inextricably entwined.

In a web world, evolution happens as a result of back-and-forth energy flow among all things. It happens fractally, at all levels up and down the ladder of life and the non-living world. Furthermore, though energy's role becomes more complex as one gets into life, underneath patterns similar to the ones listed above, still play out. This is actually a well-supported idea. Chapters 4 and 5 explain it more fully. I call the result Dynamic Evolution. It differs significantly from the usual Darwinian view.

Principles of Organization and Change

Self-entanglement produces beauty.   James Gleick

The energy view of evolution has been simmering in heretical circles for a very long time. It is becoming more solid today because it is meeting up with insights from the other big change, namely web dynamics (or, if you prefer, Chaos/Complexity) Together, the two create a remarkably consistent picture of how the world works, not as a simple machine, but as a dynamic, swirling energy web which weaves order high and low. Since web dynamics are so important, I'm going to integrate some of its principles into the now larger frame.

As we saw in the last chapter, web thinking (under many different names) is being applied in more and more disciplines. Engineers are beginning to use nonlinear models to understand why adding a road sometimes increases traffic congestion. Geologists are developing new ways to predict earthquakes using pattern recognition techniques on data taken from a web of sites around a target location. Medical researchers explore the origins and spread of epidemics using new types of patterns produced by complex interdependence. And finally, anthropologists are investigating the collapse of complex civilizations as interwoven events which follow common patterns. Scientists everywhere are beginning to discover that you really can't understand much of anything unless you look at how variables feed each other, inside and out.

Despite the diversity of problems, a few key concepts keep appearing over and over again. These concepts bind the new science together, creating an increasingly consistent image of how webs work. We've seen chaos, fractals and self-organization. This section summarizes a few other core concepts, starting with the most basic, the idea of common patterns.

Common Patterns and Universal Geometries

Why do sacred geometries hold from music to meteorites? Why are Fibonacci relationships found in the stock market and why are fractals found everywhere? The answer is that web dynamics produce similar patterns regardless of whether the bodies involved are cells, planets or human beings. This is a bit eerie, but it is not new.

The realization that there are common patterns which hold across fields is actually very old. Systems Theory, founded by Ludwig Von Bertalanffy in the 1960s, for example, derives largely from this observation. The use of similar mathematical equations on very different systems also assumes the existence of common patterns. Even the use of metaphors and analogies is based on awareness that similar patterns play out in very different arenas.

Today's technology, however, lets researchers make this point a bit more rigorously. Work in Universality Theory is a good example. Mathematicians studying all possible equations find that these produce only a limited number of possible patterns. This means that all systems, no matter how complex, fall into one of a few classes. All members of a class share certain common patterns of behavior. As a result, one can approximate any system using the simplest member of its class. As Cvitanovic says:

> The wonderful thing about this universality is that it does not
> matter much how close our equations are to the ones chosen
> by nature; as long as the model is in the same universality
> class ... as the real system ... This means we can get the right
> physics out of very crude models. (1984, p.11)

Universality provides a mathematical explanation for why common patterns of behavior exist. It also helps explain why the new dynamics works on systems as diverse as weather, population dynamics, pendulums, heart beats, and prices on the stock exchange. It also makes web dynamics much less overwhelming.

Coupling

There are a number of ways that a web world goes about organizing itself. *Coupling* is one of these.

Coupling is a process by which multiple bodies become bonded, essentially by nudging each other into synchronization. Cuckoo clocks give a nice example of it. If you hang a number of cuckoo clocks on a wall with their pendulums swinging in different directions, the pendulums will eventually start swinging in the same direction at the same

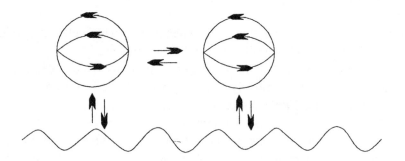

Figure 24. Symbolizing Coupling (Redrawn from Maturana & Varela, 1987). Some biologists argue that the primary path of evolution is through the coupling of previously independent forms into coordinated collectives (more in Chapter 4). The figure above, from two Chilean biologists, shows the graphic sense of this.

time. The reason for this is that each clock sends little perturbations through the wall and receives similar perturbations from its fellows. These small back and forth nudges push the clocks toward a common mutually-maximizing rhythm. Spontaneous synchronization! The many independent cuckoo-clocks couple into a larger, coordinated whole.

It isn't just clocks, of course. Coupling is common. Fireflies flash and tree toads croak in coupled synchrony. When you strike a tuning fork, your ear drum vibrates in coupled harmony. A more interesting example is the coupling of women's menstrual cycles. Women who live or work together closely over prolonged periods begin to menstruate at the same time. Women's menstrual cycles also tend to become coupled to the moon's phases, occurring most often at or near the full of the moon. This is why folk wisdom refers to a woman's 'moon cycle.'

Clockwork scientists tended to dismiss coupling, often because they couldn't find its cause — which brings me to the next point.

Subtle Causes and Hidden Connections

Clockwork science tended to discount small, subtle causes. Not so the new science. Chaos theory shows that extremely small nudges can make a very large difference. Coupling too is produced by extremely subtle prompts — small mechanical, electrical, chemical, vibrational or gravitational perturbations and back-and-forth effects. Clockwork thinkers overlooked all this in their usual rush to find large, clanging

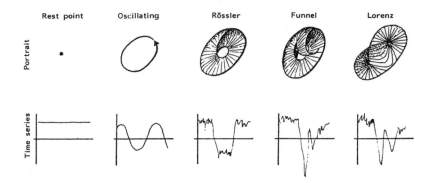

Figure 25. Strange Attractors (from Abraham and Shaw, 1987).
The upper figures show data seen the traditional way through time series charts. The lower figures show the attractors hidden in this same data.

causes. In the process they missed the river of fine bumps that are probably the largest cause of holistic order (see Figure 24).

New scientists thus believe that subtle causality plays a major role in connecting life. For example, engineers have long assumed that 'noise,' a kind of low-level electrical babble found in living systems as well as electronic ones, was worthless. It now appears that such noise may serve as a communication channel. Small fluctuations carried within the babble passes subtle information between biological organisms. Thus, electrical noise may serve the same function as the wall does in the cuckoo clock example. Electrical gibberish can carry subtle effects that help couple independent living bodies.

Attraction and Attractors

Another important way the world goes about organizing itself is *attraction*. In attraction, a web of forces pulls bodies into a pattern. The result is a dance whose momentum keeps everyone locked in line.

A whirlpool is a good example here. A whirlpool is nothing but a bunch of molecules chasing each other around, like a dog chasing its tail. But all those molecules somehow stay aligned in the shape of a funnel. A web of forces pulls molecules in and cycles them down, around and out the other side.

Physicists call this *attraction* because bodies are 'pulled' towards the pattern. (This web has tendrils.) They call the result an *attractor*. A whirlpool creates a funnel-shaped attractor. In a Bénard cell a circular attractor takes hold. In both cases, a web of forces has created a shape (or a pattern) which pulls bodies into its sway.

What is visibly true in whirlpools, however, is often mathematically true in other systems. This is more interesting. Attractors can grab all sorts of things and lock them in line. Figure 25 shows some of the resulting patterns.

Stability, Instability and Dynamic Dances

Note that the organizations above have a very non-materialist flavor to them. A whirlpool, for example, is not a fixed lump of molecules like a chair. It is a *dynamic dance*, a whir of motion held together largely by the momentum of its own spin. The matter involved in this dance doesn't even stay constant. Molecules come in at the top and circle out through the bottom in an endless stream.

Scientists call these kinds of organization 'dynamic structures' — because dynamics are crucial. Stop the momentum or break apart the forces, and the organization disappears as if it had never existed. On the other hand, this gossamer invention is also durable. Once the dance is going, its momentum tends to resist deviation. Thus, if you stick your finger in a whirlpool, it will keep its form and rebuild when you remove your finger. In the lingo of the field, the system has *structural stability*. The system is resistant to change because its dynamics are self-reinforcing.

We experience 'structural stability' in social systems every day. Copernicus, for example, became famous because he challenged the belief system of his day — and a tightly-woven, self-reinforcing system it was. John of Jandun could confidently say that no one would believe Copernicus' model was physical because the awesome inertia in a huge politically, financially, and socially entrenched web of humanity mitigated against it. The military-industrial complex, the health care system, the education system, the welfare system — words like 'stable,' 'self-reinforcing' and 'resistant to perturbation' are made for such as these.

But the flip side of the picture holds too. While dynamic systems often seem stable to the point of immutability, they also frequently fall apart. The medieval world, the Soviet Union, the Roman Empire, the Greek city-states, the Ottoman Empire, the Mayas, eco-systems and whirlpools — self-reinforcing systems collapse with great regularity.

What makes them fall apart? The hows and whys of structural *instability* are a pivotal area of research.

Reorganization and Sudden Shifts

We are now getting back to the lessons of energy flow. For instance, dynamic systems can come together, fall apart or *reorganize* into a new pattern. The official name for a sudden reorganization is a *bifurcation*. The classic example is a horse's gaits: walking, trotting, and galloping. Each gait represents a coordinated system of leg motion, a stable self-reinforcing pattern of nerves, muscles and moving limbs. Shifting between gaits occurs as a rather abrupt change of pattern, a sudden reorganization of leg movement.

There is nothing unusual about bifurcations, but their abruptness seems odd. Clockwork thinking tends to emphasize smooth continual change and portrays abruptness as the result of an outside force. Here, however, abrupt change is often the result of the system's own internal dynamics. This leads to another topic we've already discussed.

Pressure and Punctuated Change

What makes a system switch? In general, a system switches when the web of forces gets stretched to its limits, making the old way unstable. This is a very generic process. A horse, for example, goes faster and faster within one gait until it can not go any faster *in that gait*. It then shifts to a new pattern of leg motion that allows a faster speed — walk to trot, trot to gallop. The pressure to run faster, drives a horse to more intricate gaits.

This is just like what we saw in the Bénard cell, but adding generality helps. It isn't just horses, of course. Businesses go through a fairly well-known progression of organizational patterns as a company's size grows from ten to fifty to one-hundred fifty to one-thousand to ten-thousand employees. Companies switch patterns as size increases. Why? Because current organizational patterns are stretched to their limits. Flow is falling apart.

A system going through this kind of progression will experience a standard pattern of change — periods of stable sameness broken by sudden, reorganization. The official name for this pattern is *punctuated equilibrium*. It is extremely common. Virtually any developmental process you can think of follows this pattern — child development, cognitive development, stages of life, and so on. The eco-system version is called succession. Grasslands give way to pine forests and then oak forests, with each period ending in sudden, rapid change. Punctuated change is even being discovered in developmental processes that we once assumed were gradual. For example, growth in children, the evolution of scientific knowledge, and the evolution of life are all now seen as punctuated processes, not gradual ones.

Increasing Intricacy

This, of course, leads me back to the concept of increasing intricacy. More and more scientists are beginning to describe progressions like the ones listed above as types of increasing complexity (or increasing intricacy, as I call it). The concepts of developmental stages and more intricate organization dovetail quite nicely. Think of businesses, scientific knowledge, cognitive development ... or a horse's gaits. Whenever a system is pressed to its limits, it must reinvent itself in a new more intricate way.

Are these merely analogies? Maybe. But, then again, maybe not. I explore the role of energy and web dynamics in life in more detail later. One eventually gets to the place where analogy is all one can claim, but this point is much farther up than most people imagine. Even then, data from real systems seem to suggest that the same patterns are at work. Since this is the case, I'm going to explain the last three principles using analogies from higher up. After all, the most enticing implication of the new science is that energy rules and web patterns apply to human systems like businesses and civilizations. We might as well begin to see why they might.

Figure 26. Attractors and Bifurcation Points in Turbulent Fluid (from Abraham & Shaw, 1989).
This figure shows the progression of attractors that fluid moves through as stirring speed is increased. Each little box represents a bifurcation and the birth of a new attractor. The result is an overall pattern of punctuation.

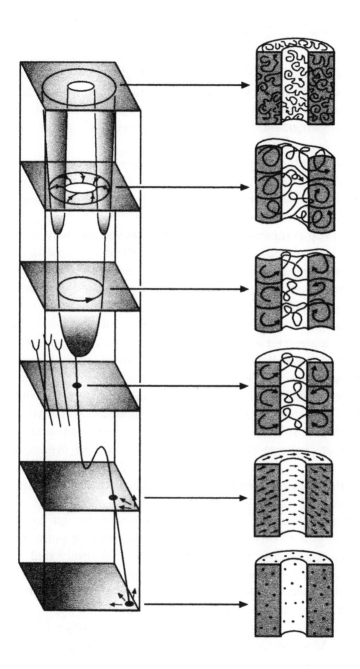

The Life Cycle of an Organization:
(or The Return of the S-curve)

We saw the S-shaped curve in the Bénard cell. We also saw it in the cycle of Big Change in Chapter 1. A similar pattern has been described in business, only here the three rough stages are: (1) delicate start-up, (2) well-integrated maturity, (3) dinosaurial decline (see Figure 27).

■ *Stage One — Start-ups.* Entrepreneurs with hot ideas create the diversity from which new economic organizations arise. If one of their little seed crystals taps an energy pool, a new organization swirls up (often like a tornado).

Start-up companies are unstable, however, and hard to get off the ground. Grass-roots entrepreneurs need capital to fund infrastructure. We should support them for therein lies the seeds of innovation and a next round of being. But many fail to gain stability. Those that do enter a new phase.

■ *Stage Two — Ascendancy.* Small to medium companies with decent infrastructure and a little economic cushion enter an optimal phase which ecologist Robert Ulanowicz calls *ascendancy*.[2] There is enough infra-structure and on-going flow that the company can weather economic ups and downs reasonably well. This is the solid adult phase.

On the other hand, ascendant companies are still small enough to be tight and still flexible enough to learn. Ascendancy, thus, involves a delicate balance between size and tightness of organization. You might say it requires intricacy. Optimal efficiency is a blend of small, well-integrated circles with energy and information flowing robustly throughout.

Organizations in their ascendancy are more apt to serve their society with quality and integrity. Community pressure only has an impact if a firm is still human in scale and firmly tied to a place. Integrated organizations serve themselves *and* the society because they are still closely coupled. The more such organizations an economy has, the healthier that economy is likely to be.

■ *Stage Three — Dinosaur.* Success, however, often brings size and inertia. Momentum and sheer distance over which information must flow lessens flexibility and ability to learn. Large companies tend to become bulky, bureaucratic and inefficient. Subgroups within the

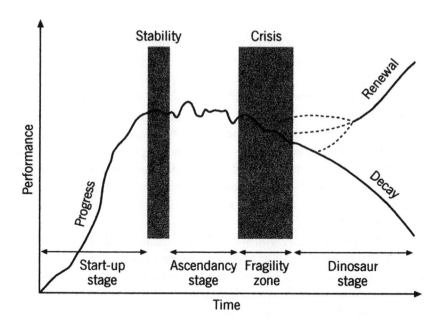

*Figure 27. The S-Curve of Organizational Life (Redrawn from Lawton &
Connors, 1996).*

organization become disconnected and insular. Divisiveness grows. The
organization itself loses touch with its environment and becomes
disconnected from the society it serves. Size, thus brings the downside
of stability, namely entrenchment and inability to change.

■ *The Fragility Zone* — The dinosaur stage also brings the fragility
zone. The system has gone as far as it can go and it is becoming
unstable. No amount of bulk or momentum will save it. Indeed, these
are part of the problem. Unless some spark of diversity seeds a new,
more intricate pattern, then the system is likely to collapse (or at least
cease to grow.)

The Complexity Catch, Part II

Visions of instability brought on by size and sluggishness brings me
back to the complexity catch. Have you ever wondered why big things
are built of smaller things which are built of smaller things still? Why
isn't your body made of one gigantic cell, for instance, and why can't
a business run with a thousand ungrouped people? The answer is that

intricacy is crucial to stability as well as efficiency. Small, intertwined circles mean solid infrastructure. Getting bigger tends to rip intricate fabric apart.

This is the complexity catch. Big groups must be composed of smaller ones because smaller ones are tighter and more efficient. But smaller ones must be well connected or the system falls apart. Found in fluids and throughout biology, this truism is particularly appropriate in social organizations which is why armies are organized into divisions built of brigades built of regiments built of platoons. In societies, intricacy looks like a close-knit social fabric. It is even behind the way an embryo develops.[3]

If you look closely, you'll see that intricacy and the complexity catch gives us a new way of conceptualizing a number of events taking place today. Corporate downsizing, for instance, reflects a failure to develop a more intricate type of organization, one with tighter ties and better flow. Downsizing does not solve the problem of how to stay efficient. It merely avoids it by shrinking. Though few people realize it, this is the complexity catch playing out in human systems.

The complexity catch helps us understand why getting bigger is tricky. It is not enough to grow in size. One must stay small *and* well-connected. Energy must flow robustly throughout. Failure to do so leads to instability which can bring the whole system down.

Figure 28. Organizational Intricacy versus Population Size (see oopposite). Carneiro studied how population and structural complexity grows in small villages. The plot shows the relationship between population size and structural complexity for 46 villages plotted on logarithmic coordinate paper. He estimated structure by counting the number of strong kinship bonds (uncle, mother, sibling etc.) and official bonds (council memberships etc). The graph suggests that there are relatively precise rules as to when a society breaks if it fails to increase its structural complexity. Furthermore, the slope of the line approximates the surface-volume law seen in biology. Population (P) equates with volume and internal structure (N = number of organizational traits) approximates complex surface. Fitted by eye, the ratio of these two is 0.6594, the breakpoint occurs at a two-thirds ratio, that is, 0.6666.

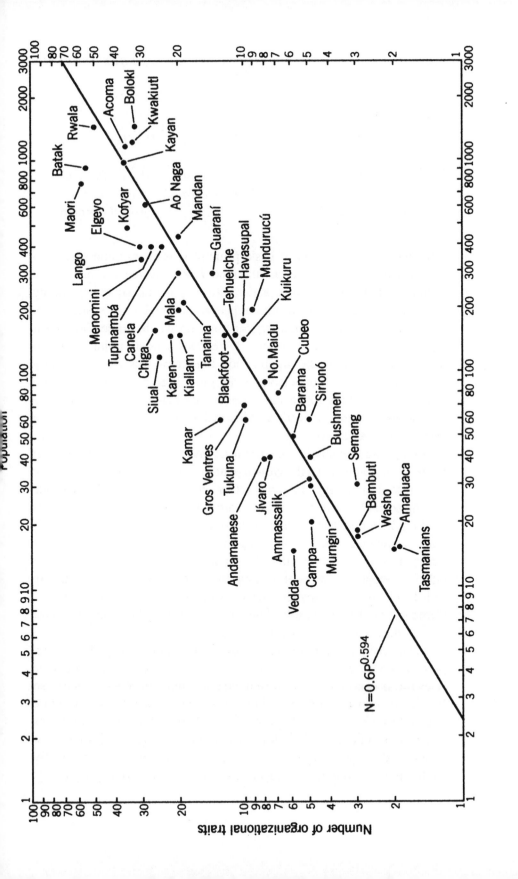

Rules for Rising and Falling

*If a society increases significantly in size, and if at the same
time it is to remain unified and integrated, it must improve
its organization.*   Robert Carneiro

This ends my discussion of basic principles of energy and organization. I leave you with one last thought. Just as sacred geometries are
found throughout the living and non-living world, so many energy
patterns and organizational rules appear to hold in human systems too.

For instance, as a human organization grows the forces holding it
together get stretched. It eventually reaches a crisis point with two
main possibilities. If the organization finds new ways to stay tightly
linked and mutually supportive, it can grow bigger and become more
powerful. If it fails to do this, subsystems begin to pull apart. The
organization begins to work at odds inside. We say it is fragmenting
and on the road to collapse.

While studying aboriginal societies, American anthropologist Robert
Carneiro discovered that the growth pattern of small villages fits the same
pattern seen in biology and fluids rather precisely. Apparently ideas like
fraying social fabric and crisis points are real. As villages grow the bonds
holding them together get stretched. At a certain point, the social bonds
reach a breaking point. In the case of primitive villages, the upshot is
straightforward. When a village's population reaches a certain size, it
either develops new ways of relating that keep the population integrated,
or it breaks into two smaller villages which get by on existing patterns.
Carneiro's studies suggest that human social break points occur at almost
exactly the same point found in biology (1967, 1987).

I shall have much more to say about these topics later. Meanwhile,
perhaps you are getting a sense of why this new science might be
relevant. If ideas like 'resistance to change' apply to social systems, so
too do the concepts of instability and the need for intricate structure
and robust flow. It is a bit eerie to think that human organizations
follow the same patterns, but it may be much more literal than most
people realize. Societies too are intricate dynamic systems. Apparently
we too must figure out how to stay small, well-connected and flowing.

CHAPTER 4

THE CREATIVE COSMOS

... we are not just an accidental anomaly, the microscopic caprice of a tiny particle whirling in the endless depths of the universe. Instead, we are mysteriously connected to the universe, we are mirrored in it, just as the entire evolution of the universe is mirrored in us.　　　　Vaclav Havel

Many ancients would agree with the opening thought. Plato described the Great Ordering Oneness. The Egyptians tried to decipher the rules of the Creative Force. Jewish and Christian thinkers explored *Logos,* defined variously as a life-giving force and a universal reason governing and permeating the world. In 500 BC, Heraclitus, put it this way: 'It is wise to listen, not to me, but to the Word, and to confess that all things are One.' Nowadays, science is beginning to see these things too.

Creation is a web whose design is intricate beyond comprehension. Today we are beginning to understand a bit more about why this is so. In this chapter I look at web dynamics role inside life and outside as well. I look more closely at energy's role in organization and evolution. Mainly, however, I look at how ideas discussed so far link up with a rethinking in biology which has been underway for a long time already. Biologists use different words but the ideas are the same.

The biologists' version of the Great Ordering Oneness is a theory called Gaia. Named after the Greek word for 'Mother Earth,' Gaia shows that each grain of life is fundamentally entwined with the land, oceans and atmosphere. Supported by evidence from many fields, Gaia also validates the idea that land, oceans, atmosphere and living organisms co-evolve in a back-and-forth dance. For example, not only did the atmosphere get its present balance of oxygen because of living organisms, but plate tectonics are also driven (at least in part) by organic growth. The image of bacteria growth affecting how fast we drift continentally is enough to give one pause. The 'biosphere,' as the great Russian biologist Vladimir Vernadsky called it, really is One.

Energy moves Gaia one step farther. It helps us understand why organizations emerge and why the biosphere is so fundamentally entwined. It also helps explain the oldest riddle of evolution: why the world moves toward increasing complexity. Sometimes organizations go up and sometimes they come down, but for the last four billion years the earth as a whole has evolved toward ever increasing levels of ordered-complexity. The cosmos as a whole has been doing the same for even longer than that.

Thus, the idea that we are the product of a creative cosmos — a Logos, a Great Ordering Oneness — is about to be rediscovered, in a way which is no longer vague nor merely poetic. It is, in fact, quite physical and increasingly well-explained. This means that Havel is correct. We are part of something much larger than ourselves. Havel also made his comment as part of a stronger point which I must make too. People in general and politicians in particular are searching for a key that will help our increasingly global civilization survive our times. Many people are hoping that the new view of evolution will provide that key. Havel's thought continues:

> The moment it begins to appear that we are deeply connected
> to the entire universe, science returns ... in a roundabout way,
> to man and offers him his lost integrity. It does so by
> anchoring him once more in the cosmos.

An Integral view of evolution does provide new reasons for hope and new reasons to care. It, much more than math, begins to change our view of ourselves and the world in powerful and productive ways.

There is, however, a problem. This majestic vision of how life evolved as part of a larger web faces a thorny battle for birth. The reasons for this have to do, first, with history and secondly with the way social systems have been built around the existing view of evolution. The clockwork opposition, in this case, is Darwinian theory.[1]

As with all long-standing traditions, there is an element of truth to Darwinism. It is only when one puts many pieces together, that one sees how Darwinians have mistaken a small part of the puzzle for the whole thing. It is much like what happened five hundred years ago, with Aristotle and Copernicus. A venerable older logic is seen to create a distorted picture because it is using the wrong center. There is no fault. Expanded vision, however, changes the picture significantly.

We want to believe that today's scientists will have no problem seeing the need for this change. Scientists, we are told, care only about logic and observation. They realize that views can change even in seemingly sewn up fields. Unfortunately, few people are dispassionate about this seemingly obscure subject. Rather, history and social realities are about to bite us again. Because of historical battles with religion, for instance, Darwinism has come to define itself as Scientific Truth which battles superstition. This position makes rethinking very difficult. Anyone who disagrees is labeled a crank no matter how much science they use. As a result, attacks on non-conforming scientists are less logical and more viciously personal than anywhere else in the new science.

Cultural weaving creates an even greater problem. A lot of social fabric has been woven around Darwinism — witness the incredible emphasis we give to competition and to images of behavior fixed in our genes. Social and economic theories have been particularly affected. As a result, Darwinism is more like the Crystal Spheres than one cares to imagine. A whole social world hangs in the balance. This includes traditional images of how economies run, how human beings work and how societies thrive. Small wonder a shift in evolutionary views is an incendiary topic.

Still, the pressure to move beyond Darwinism is strong and its source is not just science. Darwinian theory has been used to encourage all that is worst in human nature. It is now a mainstay of the social problem. So, let us review.

Another Dark Side of Science

The dominant Darwinian philosophy holds that evolution — *all* evolution — can be explained in terms of random mutations and survival of the fittest. Random mutations create the diversity upon which natural selection works and living organisms evolve through the gradual accumulation of such small hereditary differences. Better genes multiply because they win in the struggle to survive. The discovery of DNA in the 1950s made the theory seem indisputable. Scientists had found the physical control center of heritable difference!

Genes, sheer accident and survival of the fittest are *the* cause of evolution. Isn't this indisputable? Richard Dawkins, one of the most influential proponents of neo-Darwinism, thinks so, as he states in the opening of his book, *The Blind Watchmaker:*

> This book is written with the conviction that our own existence once presented the greatest of all mysteries, but that it is a mystery no longer because it is solved. Darwin and Wallace solved it. (1994, p. ix)

We all know this story. We know it because it is everywhere. The discovery of the gene turned this theory into a pillar of fact. Cultural weaving made it spread. As biologist Brian Goodwin says:

> It has become the basis for explaining all aspects of life on earth, or elsewhere. No aspect of human life is untouched by Darwin's theory of evolution, modified in various ways to apply to economics and politics, to the ... significance of art, and even to the history of ideas themselves. (1994, p.vii)

On the other hand, people in and outside of science have been decrying this view for as long as it has been around. We tend to imagine that it is only fundamentalists who object, but many scientists and humanists do too. Thus, the 'ism' which rose from Darwin has a very dark side. Darwinian evolution centers, not only on the idea that life is an accident, but also on selfish genes, weeding out the weak, adaptation to a status quo, genetically-determined superiority, and competition seen as war for domination in a win-lose game. It reads like an alpha-male manifesto and has been used to justify endless forms of oppression including subjugation, sterilization, and genocide of inferior peoples. Both Hitler and Stalin used Darwinian theory as a rationale for their work and Social Darwinism is one great rationale for why those in power are a meritocracy who must righteously use their power to preserve themselves as the best hope for the human race.

Evolution built in this baleful image has put a more destructive cast on the world than anything physics has to offer. Furthermore, this image has everything to do with the old Enlightenment devils, élitism and domination. Nor are these connotations accidental. For example, upon seeing the natives of Tierra del Fuego distribute goods equally among all, Darwin himself made the following comment:

The perfect equality of all the inhabitants will for many years prevent their civilization. Until some chief arises who by his power can heap up possessions for himself, there must be an end to all hope of bettering their condition. (cited in Goodwin, 1994, p.32)

One shudders to hear such talk even from a well-to-do white male from one of the great imperialistic powers of the time. One shudders because such thinking is alive and well today, now cloaked in the mantle of science. Thus, one's instinctive revulsion is blocked by a seemingly impervious web of logic! Selfish genes and survival! Evolution is well-explained!

Darwinian theory mistook a small part of the puzzle for the whole thing and, in the process, created a picture in which life was about struggle, selfishness and war. Many of the most destructive everyday practices in business, economics, politics and interpersonal relationships are rationalized by Darwinian theory, held up as Truth (with a capital T). Debunking the dark side of Darwinism is, thus, much more important than debunking physics' fundamental myth.

Evolution makes more sense as an interwoven process. This view opens the door to new insights and to a more positive round of cultural weaving. But, rethinking evolution requires details, not romantic dreams. So let us look at the birth of a new creation myth — an ever-more solid story of how life and humanity fit in a larger design. I begin with a look at how web dynamics work in life.

Web Dynamics and the Shape of Life

It is odd how science evolves. The idea that the shape of living organisms grew out of the same kinds of dynamics that create other physical shapes (like a whirlpool's funnel) has been around for a very long time. The curve of a ram's horn is identical to the curve of a hurricane. A raindrop splash and a jellyfish's shape also follow similar patterns (see Figure 29).

It is not surprising, therefore, that the first great school of evolutionary thought (called rational morphology) studied how living shapes come into being as a result of natural dynamics. William Bateson's

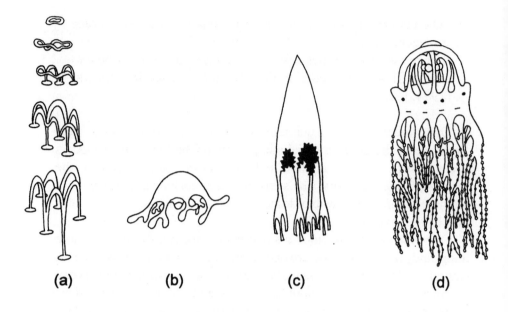

Figure 29 (a-d). Ink Drop, Paraffin, and Jellyfish (Redrawn from D'Arcy Thompson, 1917). The above figures show the similarities between biological and dynamical forms. Figure (a) is an ink drop diffusing in water; (b) is a species of Jellyfish; (c) is fuse oil diffusing in paraffin; and (d) is another species of Jellyfish.

book, *Materials for the Study of Variation* (1894), and D'Arcy Thompson's book *On Growth and Form* (1917), both explored these kinds of connections. The idea goes back farther than this. In 1790 Goethe observed that all organs found in flowers (sepals, petals, carpels, stamen) are variations on leaf patterns. The eighteenth-century French zoologist, Étienne Geoffroy Saint-Hilaire, argued that all tetrapod limbs were transformations of a single basic ground plan.

Rational morphology, however, has not been a dominant tradition in biology for over one hundred years. The reason is that Darwinism has a completely different way of explaining how life (including its shapes) arose. Darwinians see genes at the center of evolution. Genes hold the famous 'blueprint' for how an organism is built. The blueprint changes by random mutation — sheer accident. Since accidents drive change, any shape is possible. Selection then decides what stays. Since Darwinian theory won the nineteenth-century debates and since it claims to explain all evolution, rational morphology has become something of a quiet backwater pursued by eccentric specialists.

Yet, underneath a quiet exterior, this peaceful picture of evolution is changing — in part because the new science makes the connection between dynamics and shape more obvious by the day. Thus, Benoit Mandelbrot's book, *The Fractal Geometry of Nature* and Stewart and Golubitsky's book, *Fearful Symmetry: Is God a Geometer?* are amazing compilations of how interdependent dynamics create shapes from jelly-fish and flowers to DNA and galaxies. This means that the shapes found in living organisms began before there were genes and involves energy and web dynamics (not just accident).

But, this is the physicist in me talking. Biologists are apt to use different words. So, let me build a contrast between old and new ideas using a new scientist who hails from biology itself. Brian Goodwin's book, *How the Leopard Changed Its Spots: The Evolution of Complexity*, provides an excellent summary of the new science's progress in the biological sphere. He is, of course, not alone, but I will use his admirable work as bridge between the physics and the biology.

Webs at Work in Living Things

What physicists call self-organizing cycles, Goodwin calls a dynamic dance. I like his term. A back-and-forth flow of interactions among living and non-living elements create the development we see in life. In the case of a single-celled plant called Acetabularia, the dance involves mostly free calcium and the network of proteins which give the cell its form. As this network softens, stretches, bulges and twists, Acetabularia's shape follows suit.

Webs at work! Acetabularia grows an exquisite whorled cap atop a long stalk as the result of back-and-forth internal reactions. The protein network, called a cytoskeleton, reacts to the chemical environment. Growth, in turn, changes the chemical environment at various locales, thereby setting the pattern for the next round of the dance.

So, chemical webs create pattern, structure, organization — and shape. Working with a physicist, Lynn Trainor and a biologist/computer scientist, Christian Brière, Goodwin has been able to show how the whorl shape found in the caps of plants arise from a self-organized dance between internal chemistry and the network of

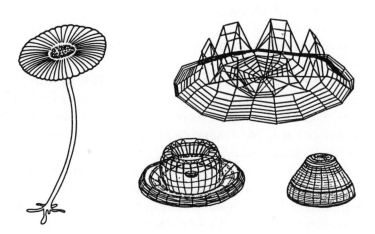

Figure 30. Acetabularia — Actual and Simulated Growth (Redrawn after Goodwin, 1994). The cytoskeleton shifts in response to free calcium in the environment. Conversely, cytoskeleton movement makes free calcium concentrations ebb and flow. It is an incredibly interdependent affair. Goodwin shows how this interwoven dance guides the evolution of the plant's shape over time.

teins which fills the cell. Figure 30 shows how their simulations mirror Acetabularia's growth.

It is not just this one plant either. Acetabularia belongs to a whole order of giant unicellular green algae, the Dasycladales. With a few tweaks, Goodwin's equations bring forth whorls like those found in all members of this order. This means that the same dynamic is behind all these variations. Goethe is made precise! Many different shapes are variations of one basic ground plan. This thought also holds for animal shapes including Saint-Hilaire's tetrapod limbs.

The Role of Neighbours

Limb development starts with a limb bud, an undifferentiated mass of cells which forms on the side of a developing embryo. A cytoskeleton dance similar to that found in Acetabularia is going on inside these cells and, in the early stages, this dance dominates the limb-growing process. But, limbs grow in *multi-celled* animals, so development also involves a dance *between* different cells. Here Goodwin's self-organizing dynamics sound a lot like Craig Reynolds boids:

cells are constantly exploring their environments by means of little cytoplasmic feelers — filopodia (filamentous feet) — that extend out from the cell ... Cell surfaces are sticky, so when filopodia of different cells encounter one another, they tend to shake hands (feet) and hold on. Then when the filopodia contract, cells are drawn together and stick even more strongly. (1994, p.149)

Intricate order comes from acting and reacting to one another! What controls the process? Is there some particular chemical signal or a lead cell? Like flocking boids, the limb bud's shape emerges from local exchanges between cells. In particular, as cells communicate with one another (mechanically and chemically), they develop a sense of where they are located in the whole. Cells change their behavior depending on the position in which they find themselves. To use a human analogy, one might say that bread-making cells emerge because they are next to flour-making cells which emerge next to farmer cells which produce wheat. In this case, muscle cells grows next to bone.

The image of cells who choose their occupation by communicating among themselves seems odd. Yet, it helps explain a perplexing fact of development which does not fit well with the usual story of genes. An embryo starts as a single cell with a single set of DNA. Yet, this single cell differentiates into many specialized cells: lungs, bones, heart, etc., which look and act very differently. How does any given cell know whether to become a lung or a heart if all have the same DNA and if DNA alone determines destiny? The answer, known for quite some time, is that each cell decides what to become based in large part on what its neighbours are doing. Thus, at early stages of development researchers can pick up a cell that is beginning to become a lung cell and turn it into a heart cell, simply by changing its location.

Though it is shocking to traditionally-trained minds, an individual cell's destiny is determined largely by what its neighbours are doing. Cells become bone or brain, depending on their place in the whole. Furthermore, this is very much a 'hive mind' effect. A seething web of communication determines what an individual cell becomes.

The implication here is that genes do not determine everything we are. This idea is very important because it helps liberate us from a view of genes which has become exaggerated to say the least.

Environment, interaction and experience all play a much greater role than we are usually taught. Genes are but one part of a very complex process.

Brain development makes the point even better. Hence, the same genetic material never grows the same *brain* twice because the way neurons grow is heavily determined by the activity they experience in early stages. Small differences can make a large difference, which is why identical twins never have the same personality. But environmental effects are stronger still. For example, in the 1960s neurophysiologists Hubel and Wiesel showed that what an organism *experiences* shapes what it can *see*. Hence, kittens raised in environments designed to exclude all vertical lines, could not perceive vertical lines. If vertical lines were excluded long enough, the kittens were never able to perceive them. In short, 'perception' and, even more so, 'intelligence,' is utterly wound up with environmental stimulation. This is not what we are usually taught, but evidence for this fact has been growing for forty years.

Neighbours, communication, environment and experience play a huge role in what we become! Dynamic evolution also has other shocks in store.

The Role of Stability and Simple Dynamics

In a Darwinian world, any shape is possible. Selection alone determines what improbable twists will remain. But in a web world only a few shapes are possible because many shapes are unstable. Biologists are beginning to understand this too. Self-organizing dynamics create stable shapes. Selection selects from these.

Oster, Murray and Maini, for instance, show that limbs of all kinds emerges from only three major types of activity. Cells concentrate, or group. They migrate along stress lines and either split into Y's (bifurcate) or bud off into a new group (separate). Group, bifurcate, separate! These three simple dynamics produce the familiar patterns of foot development (see Figure 31). Why these three? Because stability is crucial. Thus, small groups are stable and so are Y's. Three-way splits, on the other hand, tend to fall apart. Hence, the three main forms of behavior are ubiquitous because they are sturdy (literally).

These three humble motions have produced a lot of different variations, however. It is not just tetrapods either. Fish fins appear to

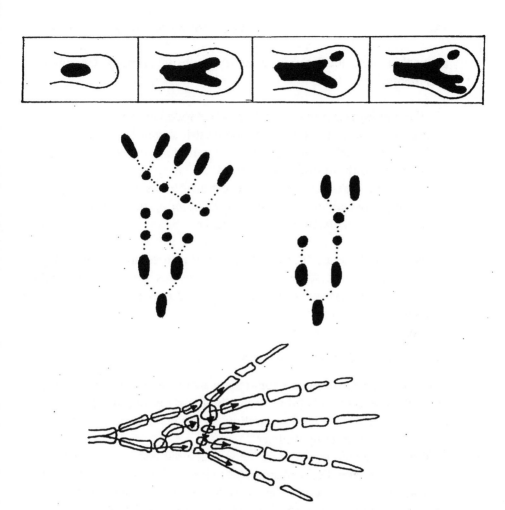

Figure 31. From Limb Bud to Foot (Redrawn from Goodwin, 1994).

develop via a similar dynamic process though without the bifurcation aspect. Indeed, a few simple, but stable self-organizing dances, seem to be behind a great deal of life's wonderful diversity. These dances are widespread because they are stable and because they arise spontaneously from naturally-occurring constituents. The same dynamic dances are found in many different kinds of living organism.

We are now entering touchy territory for biologists. We are saying that shape — which is the basis of all taxonomy — is a result of self-organizing dynamics. These dynamic dances exist without the aid of genes. Thus, similar living shapes reflect similar dynamics but not necessarily common ancestors or common genes. I will talk more about this later, but for now let us try to absorb some of Goodwin's comments:

> [Dynamic] principles provide a better foundation for understanding structure than historical lineages ...
>   ... Tetrapod limbs could have arisen many times independently in different lineages ...
>   ... The idea of a common ancestral form as a special structure occupying a unique branch point on the tree of life ceases to have taxonomic significance.

Ideas like these are biological heresy. But there are strong reasons why Goodwin and others are heading in this direction. To help understand why, Goodwin provides a more powerful example — the invention of the eye.

Eyes, Accidents and a Creeping Heresy

A great deal of traditional evolutionary theory hinges on the concept of accident and improbability. Rebel biologists have argued for years that sheer accident is hard to swallow as the main force in evolution. Their case is becoming stronger.

Eyes, for example, are intricately structured and many aspects of that structure must be in place before sight — or even sensitivity to light — begins to emerge. Yet, until some kind of function emerges, natural selection has nothing upon which to operate. Thus, a whole set of accidental, yet incredibly functional, connections would have all had to occur at once for movement toward sight to even begin. Yet, eyes crop up all over the evolutionary map. It is hard enough to imagine how random accidents could have produced such an astounding system once, but imagining it happening recurrently is even more fantastic. Darwin himself said the whole idea gave him a shudder.

In the days before web dynamics, biologists accepted sheer-accident arguments largely because physicists told them that matter didn't self-organize. But work in the new dynamics is beginning to cast doubt on the very existence of randomness (see Appendix A) and self-organization is seen as rampant. Hence, biologists armed with the new dynamics are reaching an important shift. As Goodwin says:

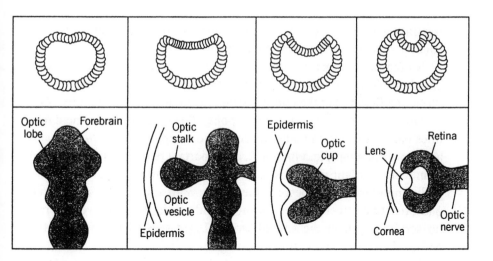

Figure 32. Developmental Changes Leading to an Eye (Redrawn from Goodwin, 1994). As the neural tube develops, it elongates (stretches). Two bulges then appear, as if in the process of separating. These bulges will eventually become the optic lobes. The bulges do not separate, but rather grow sideways until they reach the embryo's surface, the epidermis. Upon contact with the epidermis, they fold inward much like gastrulation. The optic cup is born. The epidermal cells react to contact with their own thickening and bulging. One bulge of cells does separate off. This group eventually become the lens of the newly forming eye. The optic cup now begins to differentiate into the retina with axons that cover the inside of the eye and then move down an optic stalk that will become the optic nerve.

What I suggest is that eyes are not improbable at all. The basic process of animal morphogenesis leads in a perfectly natural way to the fundamental structure of the eye.

According to Goodwin an eye's structure is produced by dynamics similar to those seen in Acetabularia and tetrapod limbs. Hence, if you look at a developing embryo, you are likely to notice two major events: gastrulation and neurolation. Embryos start as a sphere of cells which fold inward to create an inner multilayered hollow called the gastrula. The gastrula then stretches and folds again into a tube from which the nervous system will develop, hence the name, neurolation. These folding and stretching movements are the result of whole sheets of cells bulging and pushing each other into different positions. Yet, we've seen them before. They arise from exactly the same internal dynamics which produce shape in Acetabularia. The branching and separating seen in feet are also present, now accompanied by the equally robust operations of folding and stretching.

So the same dynamics are found throughout both plant and animal kingdoms. They contribute to many different ends. Here the result is not a foot or a flower, but the internal structure of an eye (see Figure 32).

Goodwin also makes a stronger point. The idea that the same dynamics can contribute to many different ends, applies to *function* as well as shape. For example, vitamin A, an important photoreactive chemical found in the plant world, is carried in many animal cells as well — including those which become the retina. With a few tweaks, the same photoreactive effect that serves photosynthesis in the plant world, ends up serving sight in the animal world. Light sensitivity, thus, started before there were eyes. It started in plants!

Such reasoning helps explain why eyes and sight might reasonably have developed independently all over the evolutionary map. The dynamic dances which form the basic structures and functions in living organisms, arise naturally. Stable ones, link and blend creating a tremendous amount of diversity. Because they emerge from pressures in the environment, they are likely to be found in many living systems. Once inside a living system, small tweaks will lead to variations which may be useful in many different ways. The same dance blossoms into amazing diversity and phenomenal new behaviors.

Self-organizing dynamics also aid the search for better ways by building in diversity. Systems which work well, emerge from fortuitous combinations, but such combinations are *not* the same as sheer accident. Like the Chaos Game, events we call accidents actually represent casts in an invisibly-structured game. Web patterns are similar but never exactly the same, (like snowflakes). They are designed to be endlessly unique because diversity helps discover helps explore the range of possibilities. Researchers thus say the Great Ordering Oneness uses diversity to cast about searching for new paths. That this bumbling search comes up with similar inventions many times is no more surprising than that water always boils, but never does so the same way twice.

Such ideas apply to more than just eyes, of course. Dynamics like the ones just described also produce hearts, brains, guts, limbs, leaves, flowers, roots, branches and much more. All of these are products of robust, interwoven dynamic processes — which exist independently of genes and are not sheer accident.

The Dynamics of Life and the Greater Whole

The view is spreading that the evolution of life is a
necessity, and the physical and chemical processes leading
to its emergence can be experimentally reproduced.

Vilmos Csanyi

So self-organizing dances like the ones inside whirlpools, play an important role in living organisms too. Still, this begs the question of how these dynamics got into living organisms in the first place. Explaining this, requires we look not only at the origins of life, but how life itself fits in a larger self-organizing process. This will bring me back to energy and also chemistry.

In the last chapter, I described energy's role in driving organization into being. The implication was that energy drives all evolution, living and non-living. This might be a Copernican thought, except there is already so much evidence to support it.

For example, researchers have known for a long time that the searing conditions on early earth gave rise to a profusion of chemical networks These follow the same energy rules described in Chapter 3. Increasingly intricate cycles form and the faster ones tend to proliferate. Chemical networks are relatively stable and capable of many variations. Chemical cycles on early earth, thus, began to spread over greater regions of space and longer periods of time. They emerged at microscopic and cosmic scales. The entire biosphere — earth, ocean, atmosphere and all living organisms — is riddled with them. I've already mentioned a few. Metabolism, the chemical dances by which your body converts food into the energy it needs, is built of just such chemical networks. These, in turn, are connected to cycles swirling around us, like the carbon cycle in which animals and plants exchange oxygen and carbon dioxide.

Self-organizing chemical networks set the context for life. Add the fact that early earth was a fiery place and the image of life as a flow structure becomes easy to imagine. Evidence that the right chemistry and the right hell-like surroundings produce conditions ripe for life has been growing for forty years. Thus, in 1953, Stanley Miller demonstrated that the basic building blocks of life, amino acids, form naturally given the conditions that were present on early earth. Hungarian biologist Vilmos Csanyi has shown that some chemical networks replicate themselves. As networks grow they spawn separate little copy-cat cycles out of left-over compounds and energy yearning to cycle faster. Self-organizing dynamics are the basis of reproduction too.

So, we begin to see that life's threads were forming long before the event. To fully understand why living organisms emerged from energy webs, however, we need to understand how energy fits some of life's more novel characteristics — such as finding food and following information. Let us, therefore, take the next step.

The Origin of Life-forms as an Interwoven Event

What makes life different from non-life? Focused on separate bits, clockwork thinking has tended to reduce living organisms to a small part of their mechanical nature. Thus, when physicist Erwin Schrödinger asked, *What is Life?* (in a 1944 book of the same title) his primary concern was: 'What is the biochemistry of replication?' His question spurred a generation of molecular biologists to seek answers and as a result we now have a much better understanding of the basic chemistry of DNA. But it leaves us wondering if that is all there is.

Schrödinger's book therefore reflects a past and continued bias — life equals replication. This comes from Darwinism's focus on heritable differences locked in genes, of course. Darwinists naturally see replication as the center of evolution. Thus, as physicist Freeman Dyson says 'in popular accounts of molecular biology as it is now taught to school-children, life and replication have become practically synonymous.' Yet, Csyani and others have shown that non-living chemical networks reproduce themselves. If chemical cycles replicate, how can replication be *the* defining characteristic of life? Besides, as Dyson points out, equating life with replication takes metabolism for granted. Yet, metabolism is the energy-cycling system which holds living organisms together and lets them move.

But it isn't just metabolism which is taken for granted. For example, compartments, those little membranes that contain metabolic processes, are also taken for granted, yet these too are necessary to life. There are many vital processes involved in life and researchers have been accumulating evidence that most of them began before life itself. In 1957 Alexander Oparin showed how a cell framework might have originated when oily liquids mixed with water to form stable coacervate droplets that provided a housing for metabolic cycles. In the 1980s, Sidney Fox showed that another form of housing, proteinoid microspheres, arises naturally under the conditions of early Earth. I've already mentioned that chemical networks replicate. In 1982, A. Cairns-Smith even described how irregularly distributed metal ions in clay microcrystals could have operated like genetic material in early cells. In short, all kinds of crucial processes began long before life and the evidence for this fact has been accumulating for at least forty years.

What then is special about life? My next comment should come as no surprise. If you focus on separate pieces, you miss the fact that the most important thing about life is that its various pieces work together in a highly functional way. Hence, life is not miraculous because of any *one* of its processes. It is miraculous because *all* these processes form a mutually-reinforcing web with some truly remarkable properties. Life is distinct from all that came before because long-existing threads came together in a totally new way.

So living organisms are amazing, first, because their parts work together. But is that it? Are living organisms compartmentalized, metabolisms that replicate? No. There is a bit more that is taken for granted. Some of life's most remarkable characteristics have to do with information, including the ability to follow information trails to food and also to choose different paths. These too must be part of the weave.

Pursuit of Wellbeing

The clockwork tendency to view everything through the lens of inanimate matter has made the animation of living organisms a delicate topic. But there it is. Living organisms actively pursue their own needs. They choose their own paths. They have self-directedness, intentionality, purpose and a host of related concepts that are much harder to find before life. How can these be integrated into the picture? Energy again provides a path.

Let us start at the bottom. Evolutionary theorist Rod Swenson points out that one really big difference between life and non-life is that non-living organizations are slaves to their immediate energy source, but living organisms are not. Hence, when you take heat away from boiling water, its organization dissolves. However, when you take energy away from a cell (light, for example), it will try to follow that energy source. Failing this, it will try to find a new one. Thus, living systems move freely between energy concentrations that help them survive. They even hold themselves together while they do this.

How do living organisms achieve this relative freedom? The first part is easy. Those crazy chemical cycles called metabolism generate enough energy flow inside to keep living organisms together while they move from place to place. The catch is that a living organization must find more energy (now called food) to keep itself going. Living organisms, therefore, spend their life pursuing the energy they need to survive. Active pursuit of food is harder to explain.

How did living organisms learn to find food? Though active pursuit seems unbelievable, it too probably started quite naturally. Swenson, for example, points out that 'seeking' might have started from a chance interaction with energized molecules. Photosynthetic bacteria, for instance, 'find' light by responding to a few photons, always moving toward higher concentrations. Interactions with photons might have caused movement. Gulping down a photon would be like taking an energy-pill. It could easily have started an internal cycle which propelled the system forward. Bacteria which exhibited such behavior would survive better and selection would take its course. Bacteria which moved toward light, however, would also be following a trail of energy to the food it needs to survive. It would be taking the first lucky steps in learning how to pursue food.

No one knows precisely how all this happened, but in an energy world one doesn't have to look far for possibilities. The right lucky reaction and life became a web which actively pursued energy for its own survival.

How Energy Created Codes

Life, however, is magic in another way too. Living organisms interact with their environment and pursue their own wellbeing. Then, somehow, valuable information about successful efforts are preserved in genes. Nature, thus, creates organizations from whirlpools to chemical networks, but only living organisms have means of preserving information about their own fruitful activity. Life passes learning on. Whirlpools do not.

So, life includes the notion of preserving learning. At last! Geneticists and system theorists agree! Information is coded in our genes! But let us go softly for we are reaching a change of image which is important to grasp. Geneticists tend to assume that genes 'cause' the system. Dynamicists are more apt to say that the system 'caused' genes. Let me explain.

Cyberneticist Howard Pattee points out that the phrase, 'information is coded in our genes,' also takes a lot for granted. For example, have you ever thought about what makes something a 'code' versus a meaningless pattern? Part of the answer had better be that the code is readable by someone or something. It must also be carrying some kind of information which produces a meaningful effect. Hence, the concepts of 'code,' 'reader' and 'meaningful effect' are inextricably linked. You cannot have one without the others.

Furthermore, these three have to work together in a tight fit which produces a functional results. Pattee calls this a *code-reader-effect* loop. You see it in living systems. In living organisms, the code (DNA) is read by RNA. The DNA helix unfolds a leg and interacts with surrounding chemicals to produce an RNA in that leg's image. The affected RNA then carries the effect out into the rest of the cell. It builds proteins which interact with enzymes to produce a meaningful result (a specific metabolic change with certain effects on survival). Clockwork thinking tends to focus on the code and take the rest for granted. But it is actually the way the code-reader-effect loop works *together* that is the miracle. Forming a loop that works requires exquisite matching. This only comes from eons of coevolution before there was a code there at all.

There is also strong evidence that the code came *last*, after a relatively functional loop was already in place. So DNA probably did not create the system by accident, the system probably created an information storage site by accident after the main organization was already in place. Physicist Freeman Dyson has even developed a theory which explains how information storage might have emerged. The bombshell is that, in this theory, the code appears to have come from *an energy flow crisis*.

Dyson's explanation starts with life's main energy-carrying molecule, ATP. This turns out to be almost identical to another molecule, AMP which is the main ingredient in RNA (the code 'reader'). Dyson imagines the scenario as follows. Early cells were compartmentalized chemical factories. They would have been full of ATP because these molecules are tied to energy cycling. They would have replicated like chemical networks do, with no genetic apparatus. According to Dyson, what happened next was probably a combination of crisis and lucky accident. If cells cycle a lot of energy, they have a lot of ATP around. A lot of ATP, however, creates an energy build-up and, as Dyson puts it, 'a dangerously *explosive* situation.' In this case, however, an explosion might have converted ATP to AMP which in turn would have created RNA which would begin to replicate itself. Researchers have already shown that this does happen.[2] Here is the interesting part. This home-grown RNA would already be matched to the existing metabolic web because it was built from AMPs which came from ATPs which were one of the core constituents of that web. If that RNA left remnants, these might have became RNA's more stable counter part, DNA.

If all of this is the case, then living organisms' ability to preserve learning was probably pushed into being by energy crisis. The matching between code, reader and metabolism would have already been in place, a result of self-organizing processes which came before. Having found a way to save beneficial tweaks to the system, however, living organisms began to accumulate learning as nothing had done before. Distinct from all that had gone before, life was finally born.

*   *   *

To summarize, in a web view, the wonder we call life is a multi-threaded, energy event. It was and *is* an integrated miracle which manages to follow information, metabolize food and preserve lessons. It is amazing and filled with fortuitous links, but it was probably also likely given the conditions. Hence, it may well have emerged multiple times, not just once.

While all this was going on, however, life was never alone. Because it is an energy event, life is also part of a much larger process involving a much larger whole.

Utterly Entwined and Co-evolving

We are led to a vision of the fundamental unity of all
processes.   Robert Ulanowicz

When the ancients said the force that created the world is, 'in us and more than us, at the same time,' they were quite accurate. In the final analysis, we are not a lump of chemicals, we are an delicately balanced swirl of cycles that is woven into all the other similarly balanced cycles swirling high and low. This image holds a more radical implication. Living organisms are not separate, they co-evolve with the larger whole.

The idea that each little tuft of life is intertwined with a much large whole with which it co-evolves, is truly Copernican in its perspective. Yet, it is also the logical extension of the scene that set the stage for life's origin. Energy is the fluid in which we float. It permeates everything. It shapes everything. It drives everything. What we call evolution is really an energy process involving the whole biosphere.

To ground these ideas, I'm going to explore how early life forms co-evolved with the atmosphere to produce the air we now breathe. This example, from Boston University biologist Lynn Margulis shows how back-and-forth pressures play out in the evolution of living organisms and eco-systems.[3] It also shows the S-curve at work in real life. The cycle of new-acceleration-limit has been at work for billions of years.

The Co-evolution of Life and the Air we Breathe

Early earth was not like today's earth. Not only was it extremely hot, but the atmosphere also had very little oxygen. How is it that we got from those days to these days? The simple answer is that living organisms changed the world. In turn, the world then shaped the way living organisms evolved. It was a back and forth affair.

When living organisms first emerged, they were little more than chemical cycles encased in a membrane. These little proto-cells fit well in early earth because they didn't need oxygen. This worked because they didn't need much metabolism. Human metabolism uses oxygen to break food down into energy-carrying molecules such as ATP.

Proto-life didn't have to work this hard because naturally-occurring ATP was floating all around.

Round One of life! Proto-cells lived by sucking up freely available ATP. They spread rapidly because the energy they needed was readily available. Still, this kind of life had its limits. As proto-cells multiplied, they began depleting free-floating ATP faster than it was being created. Free food became harder and harder to find. The pressure to find a new way grew.

Luckily, nature provided a host of possible solutions. Early earth was a cauldron of chemical cycles, all of which amounted to little proto-metabolic operations. Round Two probably began when some cells incorporated metabolic processes which produced ATP by breaking down more complex compounds.

The new metabolism was most likely a form of fermentation (which doesn't require oxygen). Anaerobes (bacteria which don't need oxygen) were probably life's second great twist. With little or no oxygen in the atmosphere, little anaerobic fermenters would have been perfect for their times. Able to break down compounds, they became less dependent on the increasingly depleted free ATP. Since they had tapped into a new energy source, they flourished. Fermentation is still the most common form of metabolism. Today's fermenting bacteria give us wine, cheese and sauerkraut. They decompose organic matter in sewers and our intestines, as in the case with *Lactobacillus*.

Fermenters also left by-products which still contained energy. This opened the door for other forms of life. A host of new symbiotic bacteria sprang up to use wastes of the old. Thus, as Margulis says:

> As time passed, microbes evolved that could make use of the different energetic waste products of the early fermenters. The fermentation end products of one species became the starting compounds — or food — for another. (1986, p.36)

Chains of life began. This was important because fermenters were rapidly creating a new crisis. Hence, when fermenters decompose organic matter, they release nitrogen into the atmosphere. Without a countervailing cycle, the fermenters would have released all the nitrogen into the air and living organisms would have died of nitrogen deficiency. Luckily one of the new symbiots developed a way to extract nitrogen from the atmosphere and convert it to organic form.

Today we call this process 'nitrogen fixation.' It is still vital to a healthy world. Symbiots thus created connecting cycles which helped keep life alive.

One might have thought anaerobes and their symbiots would go on fermenting, dominating the earth forever! But, as with all good things, success made the pendulum swing. Another limit rose on the horizon. Anaerobes and their symbiots were dependent on compounds being made by the sun. As they multiplied, they began depleting these compounds as fast as the sun could generate them. Depletion! Crisis!

Photosynthetic cells answered the developing need. Photosynthetic anaerobes capture light from the Sun and use it to convert carbon dioxide to organic compounds such as glucose. The birth of photosynthesis meant living organisms no longer needed preformed food. Success! Proliferation! ... Followed by limitation. Photosynthesis requires hydrogen, but anaerobes release hydrogen as a gas and it was constantly escaping into the atmosphere. Lack of hydrogen became the next crisis. Cyanobacteria became the new solution. Cyanobacteria get their hydrogen by splitting water molecules, a virtually limitless source. Splitting water, however, brought a new crisis — and with it a turning point of great importance to us. When cyanobacteria split water to get hydrogen, they release *oxygen* into the atmosphere as waste. Our atmosphere, the one with oxygen, was being born.

In the beginning, however, oxygen in the atmosphere was not such a good thing. Oxygen is poisonous to many anaerobes, even to some of the cyanobacteria that produced it. As it accumulated, many organisms were driven into small airless niches in mudflats and other nooks where they still exist today. Worse, high concentrations of oxygen are extremely flammable. Even today, rain forests and damp grasslands spontaneously burst into flames when their bacteria produce excessive levels of oxygen. Once release began, however, oxygen accumulated rapidly in the atmosphere — creating a threat to all life!

Luckily, a new brand of microbes began using atmospheric oxygen in photosynthesis. They took in oxygen and released carbon dioxide. The famous carbon cycle was born. Oxygen levels came down.

Nowadays people point out that anaerobes were the first form of life to so pollute the atmosphere that they drove themselves underground. Their stupidity was our gain, however, because their pollution made our type of life possible. Oxygen opens the door to a very efficient type of metabolism, one which moves energy at a much faster rate. In turn, faster energy flow is what allowed living organisms to get more complex. As Margulis says:

> [oxygen] provided cells with enough energy to grow larger and become structurally more elaborate ... It was the prerequisite to the origin of the eukaryotic cells that became the building blocks of larger organisms. (1986, pp.54–56)

We have returned to energy. Oxygen laid the foundation for more complex forms of life because it created faster metabolisms which meant faster energy cycling and greater structural complexity. Complexity in living organisms is also a product of increasing energy flow. The ultimate result was the human brain — the most intricate, the fastest-cycling and the most oxygen-dependent system on the planet.

Energy, Eco-systems and Intricacy

Margulis' example helps ground the idea that living organisms, atmosphere, oceans and land are all part of a single energy ecology. It also helps us see the dance. Complex interwoven eco-systems were born from back-and-forth pressures. Living organisms affected the atmosphere which then set the stage for the next round of evolution. Energy was always the invisible link.

Increasingly complex forms of life also arose alongside faster energy cycling. Figure 33 also shows this co-evolution in terms of the infamous S-shaped curve. Here, more oxygen, faster energy cycling and increasing complexity all go together. Furthermore, though you can't see it, this big curve is actually composed of many smaller ones which correspond to each new biological innovation. The top of each curve represents a type of maturity, a maximum for that particular pattern. It also represents a jumping off place for another evolutionary thrust. Hence, tops also represent a fragility zone with a potential for catastrophe. Some of these are easy to see. For example, had some clever microbe not completed the carbon cycle, high oxygen levels would have ignited the atmosphere and life would have become a memory. Apparently, the trick to evolution, is to find a new way before the limits of the current round create a disaster.

Finally, this process shows the yes/and part of evolution. Particular forms of life have their personal evolutionary stories *and* they are also part of a larger story. Individuals and whole are never really separate.

We are all part of one embracing energy-flow process. This brings me to the biologists' version of the Great Ordering Oneness.

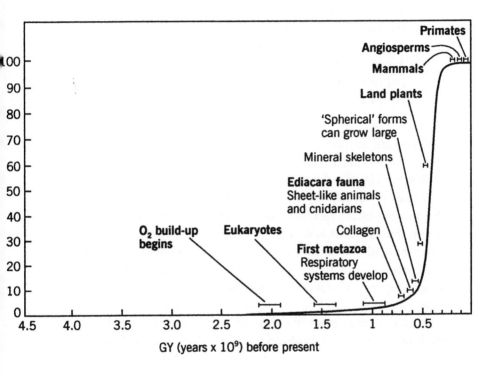

Figure 33. Acceleration of Metabolic Rates (From Swenson, 1989b).
The figure shows how living organisms' increasing complexity and faster energy cycling have co-evolved with atmospheric oxygen. The horizontal axis is given in billions of years before the present (GY=years x 10⁹). The vertical axis (%PAL O₂) shows percent of Present Atmospheric Levels of Oxygen. Note too, that metabolic rate is a good measure of energy-cycling in living organisms and oxygen is a major factor in metabolic speed. Thus, rising oxygen levels imply faster energy cycling. Finally, since energy allows living organisms to get more complex, the rise in oxygen and metabolism both imply more complex forms of life. This is seen in the progressively more sophisticated (intricate) forms of life in the chart.

Gaia and the New Biology

[The Gaia Hypothesis] brings together proof that the dense network of mutual interactions between the organic and inorganic portions of the Earth form a single system, a kind of mega-organism, a living planet ... According to this hypothesis, we are parts of a greater whole. Our destiny is not dependent merely on what we do for ourselves but also on what we do for Gaia as a whole.   Vaclav Havel

If you want to find the soul of the new science, you need look no farther. They call it Gaia.

Vaclav Havel's description of Gaia is quite correct. First proposed by James Lovelock, the Gaia Hypothesis has provided ample evidence that the biosphere functions as an intricately ordered, self-maintaining whole. Energy flow and material cycles go up through the atmosphere, down through the oceans, in through plant and animal life both simple and complex. This flow is integrated in a massive self-reinforcing, self-sustaining way. Co-evolution and the invisible hand of order? It is all there.

It is also more extensive than we have yet discussed. Even tectonic plate movement is recognized as part of the process. For example, as Richard Monastersky says, in an article entitled 'The Whole-Earth Syndrome':

> ... it is now clear that the separate regions (crust, mantle and core) are engaged in a multichannelled conversation. Across major boundaries and thousands of kilometers, these sections exert profound effects on one another. (1988, p.379)

How far does it go? As Sahtouris puts it, 'the whole Earth, from innermost core to the magnetic fields surrounding it, is one systematic entity.' Slowly but surely everything affects everything. The world is a very intricate web indeed.

Then too, it isn't just Earth. The stars are involved too. Meteorites brought chemical compounds that were essential to the birth of life and some people believe that the first fusions were made deep in space. As Csanyi says: 'There are exciting theories that assume a very important role for star dust not only in the origin of life but in the birth of present day stars.' Apparently the Great Ordering Oneness involves a whole creative cosmos, not just the earth.

Gaia theorists bring new breadth and specificity to the image of the Great Ordering Oneness. I refer readers to any of their many wonderful books. Yet Gaia is also but one part of a whole new biology which fits hand in glove with the new dynamics. Physicists and biologists are now beginning to realize that, under their differing words, lies a common picture of the world.

The New Biology

If one hangs around with people doing computer-simulations, one gets the impression that they were the first to see the new world. This is not true. Biologists, particularly a band of heretical biologists who make up what is called the 'New Biology,' have been working on the interwoven world for a very long time. And — big surprise! — many of their theories connect nicely to the ones coming from physics and math. Furthermore, I think the way biologists tell the story has distinct advantages. For example, biologists see increasing complexity in terms of cooperation, symbiosis and committed collaboration among living beings. The image of cooperation has a very different feel than complexity. It helps one see the human implications more clearly.

Committed Collaboration

The Portuguese Man-of-War looks like a single jellyfish, but it is actually a collection of individual organisms which act like a whole. Wolves hunt in packs with highly-evolved cooperative behavior. Packs survive better in harsh climes this way. Your body too is a collective of cells which take up different occupations (depending on what their neighbours are doing) to form an incredibly functional whole. Though Darwinians don't mention it much, cooperation is an extremely beneficial arrangement.

The new biology contains a tremendous heresy. The main way life has become more complex is through cooperation! Organisms band together for mutual benefit. Cooperative groups survive better than individuals. Over time some cooperatives become so tightly coupled that

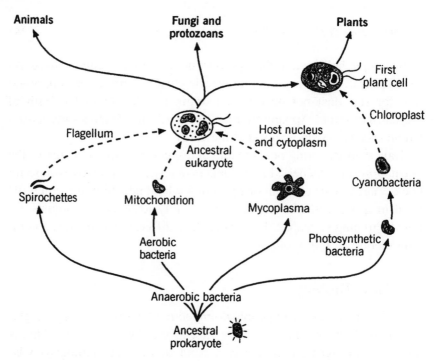

Figure 34. Increasing Complexity Through Serial Symbiosis (Redrawn from Margulis, 1971). The simplest known cells are non-nucleated bacterial cells called prokaryotes. The early forms of life were probably much like prokaryotes today. More complex nucleated cells, called eukaryotes, emerged after the oxygen revolution and are what most of us think of when we use the term 'cell.' Many of the organs in a eukaryotic cells are remnants of what used to be independent prokaryotic cells. Similar integrations take place all the way up the ladder of life.

they become an inseparable whole, a new 'unity' as biologists call it. This incredible integration turns out to be the main basis of the step-ladder of life (see Figure 34).

After the oxygen revolution, for example, cells became sophisticated, adding internal organelles such as mitochondria, flagella, and nuclei. These organelles, however, actually represent previously independent life forms which became so chemically coupled that they became a single unity. One reason for believing this is that they have separate genetic material. Hence, as Margulis says:

> Other biologists, including myself, believe that independent,
> free-living microbes joined together, first casually, then in
> more stable associations. As time passed, and as evolutionary
> pressures favored such symbiotic unions, the partner microbes

became permanently joined in a new cell composed of
interdependent components ... Three classes of organelles —
mitochondria, plastids, and undulipodia — once lived as
independent prokaryotes, an idea that would account for their
separate genetic material. (1982, p.78)

It isn't just cell organs either. Margulis also argues, for instance,
that land plants emerged through symbiotic coupling, this time between
lichens and photosynthetic algae. Lichens had learned to live on land
and were resistant to extremes of hot and cold, wet and dry. Algae, on
the other hand, had the advantage of being able to produce their own
food through photosynthesis. Algae and lichens living in close
proximity at the edge of ponds began to form stable, mutually beneficial cooperatives. The cooperatives got the benefits of each partner
and eventually the whole melded into one organism. Land plants,
hardy and able to photosynthesize, began to move over wider and
wider ranges of terrain.

To Darwinian-trained minds the idea that cooperation is the main
avenue of evolutionary improvement seems fantastic. Yet it makes a
lot of sense. Collaboration is more apt to give rise to creatively new
wholes which, like land plants, can pioneer new realms. The parts
which make up these wholes have already been tested by selection and
are known to work. When organisms which are good different things
band together, they form a whole which can do more than either. Biologists call this synergy (so do theologians).

Evolutionary pressures favor such pacts. Growth pressures also tend
to push them into being. For example, as early cells multiplied, those
in particularly fertile regions would have started to cluster and grow
on top of one another. This turns out to be a problem. In an overlap
situation, cells on the top have access to the sun, but they can't get to
water and nutrients. Those on the bottom have access to water and
nutrients, but they don't have access to the sun. Thus, as life multiplied, those on top *and* bottom both faced death. Crisis! Famine! Many
died (see Figure 35 overleaf).

Some cells, no doubt, learned to destroy their neighbours in order
to survive. But apparently another innovation also arose. Through some
quirk of diversity, a lower-level cell passed water up to an upper level

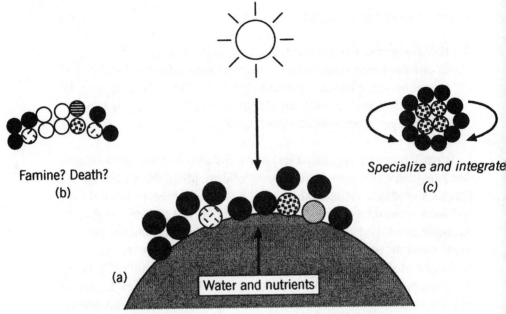

Famine? Death?
(b)

Specialize and integrate
(c)

(a)

Water and nutrients

Figure 35 (a-c). Pressures toward Committed Collaboration.
Figure 35 shows how crises fall out of the natural dynamics of growth.
(a) shows cells beginning to pile up and some (the white ones) beginning to
die; (b) shows one option — many die; (c) shows the other option, specialize
and integrate, form a new more complex cooperative. Both options occurred.
Committed collaboration was selected because individuals survived better.

cell which, in turn, passed some of its food molecules back down. This
simple act allowed both cells to survive. It also allowed each to
specialize in a task which meant they became particularly good at it.
Specialists working together have an evolutionary edge over an organism which tries to do life all alone. The way to create strength, therefore, was to follow a new theme — specialize and integrate!

Collaborations probably started out of necessity, not altruism, but
the results were phenomenal. For billions of years cells learned to invent new occupations. Each new profession off-loaded work from others and opened new possibilities. Gut cells, lung cells and nerve cells
are all specialists whose efforts produce very complex, and incredibly
functional wholes. In the process, the whole became more powerful.

Members also became more mutually dependent. Eventually, cells
became so specialized that they could no longer live without their
fellows. They depended on one another to survive, individually *and*
collectively. I call this situation 'committed collaboration.' It means
everyone's life is on the line.

Survival of the Fittest Group

I mention this story for a reason. It helps explain why our body is built of specialist cells which cooperate for the good of one and all. (Selfishness is dangerous in an interwoven world). It also helps explain why the human body is a collective of specialists which, nevertheless, emerged from a single cell with a single copy of DNA.

Margulis points out that early cells reproduced by division, leaving two identical clone copies of the parent. Clones would have multiplied, clustered and grown on top of one another — creating exactly the situation described above. Specialization probably proceeded from there. Previously identical cells begin to differentiate while also developing symbiotic relationships with each other. Clone clusters eventually learned how to circulate oxygen and nutrients throughout the whole. This is what breathing and digestion are about.

The magic of multicellular life is that cells which took on specialized tasks managed to preserve life's lessons in a common genetic set. This is why an embryo with a single set of DNA produces cells which decide whether to be lung, brain, or bone, depending on what their neighbours are doing. Hence, eventually, the clone cluster also began reproducing as a whole. Clone cells started with the same genetic set, but somehow this began to preserve lessons learned from *communal living*. How could this have happened? The basic argument is that natural selection started working on the group. As Margulis says: 'Natural selection acts to preserve the members of the clone [cluster] as a functioning unit ...' (1982, pp. 130f)

The idea that selection works on a group is Darwinian heresy, but the idea is not new and it is gaining credence.[4] Collaborative groups are obviously more powerful than separate individuals. What we know of embryo development also fits the theory of group selection. Finally, there is growing suspicion that environmental pressures also push back on DNA. I discuss this idea later but notice we've already touched on the logic. An energy accident probably created genes. The links between genes and pressures in the rest of the cell are still tight.

However it happened, it is clear that the common genetic set came to reflect learned cooperation. This is not how we are taught to imagine life, but it appears to be closer to the case. Environmental pressures and a lot of trial-and-error produced wholes which exhibit amazing behaviors because millions of specialists are bound in committed collaboration.

* * *

We have learned that collaboration is the best way to survive and thrive, especially in difficult times. Living organisms also get more complex through collaboration. Meanwhile, they are still embedded in that larger co-evolving dance. Biologists are now finding that this dance follows another famous web-world pattern — punctuation. This too challenges a traditional view.

Life's Big Bang

Darwinian theory argued that evolution was gradual, a slow accumulation of random variation. New biologists, however, say evolution is punctuated, it is pock-marked with sudden developmental bursts.[5] As Levinton says:

> [Life's] increase in complexity seems to have been anything but steady. Most of evolution's dramatic leaps occurred rather abruptly ... (1995, p.84.)

Now there is no one theory which explains all punctuation. Indeed, some punctuations appear to be the result of meteor strikes. Yet, at least some also appears to be a result of energy co-evolution. The best example of this is the Big Bang of Animal Evolution. Bursting forth about 543 million years ago at the start of the Cambrian period, this bang brought truly complex life, the kind with brains and back-bones. It too appears to be the result of entwinment and invisible pressures at work in the world. This is how it happened.

Single-celled life ruled earth longer than any other form. Earth formed four to six billion years ago and the first fossil evidence of blue-green algae emerges about 3.6 to 3.4 billion years ago. The first nucleus started about two billion and the first multicelled algae about 1.75 billion years ago. All in all, the world was an ocean of complexifying blue-green algae for about three billion years.

Then, apparently, things changed with a jolt. In perhaps as little as ten million years living organisms went from a few crude multicelled algae to roundworms, mollusks, jellyfish, sea cucumbers

Figure 36. A Brief History of Biological Evolution.

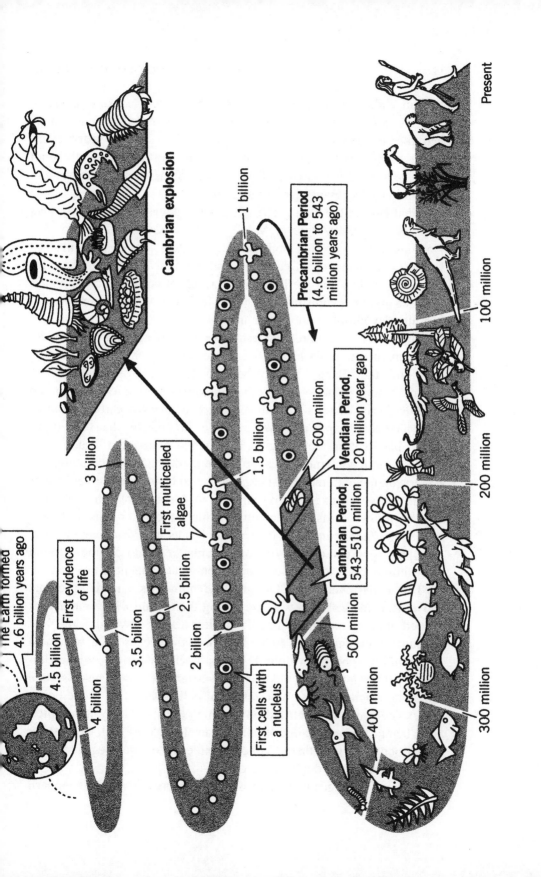

Cambrian explosion

The Earth formed
4.6 billion years ago

First evidence
of life

First multicelled
algae

First cells with
a nucleus

Precambrian Period
(4.6 billion to 543
million years ago)

Vendian Period,
20 million year gap

Cambrian Period,
543–510 million

4.5 billion
4 billion
3.5 billion
3 billion
2.5 billion
2 billion
1.5 billion
1 billion
600 million
500 million
400 million
300 million
200 million
100 million
Present

and an endless parade of arthropods, the ancient cousins of crabs, lobsters, spiders and flies. Even swimmers with rod-like spines emerged, the precursors of our own Chordata phylum. In fact, nearly every major branch of the biological tree emerged in a fantastically brief time, geologically speaking. This sudden jolt is what biologists call 'Evolution's Big Bang' (see Figure 36).

What caused the bang? The story being developed by researchers such as John Grotzinger at M.I.T., Andrew Knoll at Harvard, and Douglas Erwin at the Smithsonian Institute, is very similar to Margulis' explanation of early life and the air we breathe. These researchers believe that the Bang was a result of co-evolution going on between living organisms and the environment. Oxygen and energy cycling played out in another round.

Knoll, for example, suggests that the bang was driven by environmental turmoil that helped infuse the seas with oxygen. By the time of the Bang, the carbon cycle was well established. Photosynthetic algae took in carbon dioxide and released oxygen and organic decay bacteria took in oxygen and released carbon dioxide. The photosynthesizers, however, were limited to the thin light-accessible layer on top and soon, a tremendous mound of dead matter began forming underneath. This blocked them from their carbon-cycle cohorts on the bottom. Living organisms had boxed themselves in. For life to grow and expand, oxygen had to cycle more fully (because oxygen allows a faster metabolism which allows organisms to get bigger and more complex). But, as Knoll puts it: 'For oxygen to rise, the planet's burden of decaying organic matter had to decline. Around 600 million years ago that appears to be what happened.'

The actual event probably involved numerous threads. Tectonic movement, for instance, was rife during this period. Huge mountains surged up and equally huge landslides came down driving vast amounts of organic debris to the bottom of the oceans. Guts were also beginning to appear, and John Hayes, a biochemist from Indiana University, speculates that this made a difference too. Those simple conduits which put waste out, left fecal pellets dropping to the ocean floor. The bacteria which fed on organic debris suddenly found their food being 'express mailed' to the ocean floor. They followed taking the carbon cycle with them. Carbon dioxide and oxygen began to cycle more thoroughly throughout the oceans.

With more oxygen to aerate tissues, living organisms of the modern variety could now emerge. Organisms started getting much larger with even early ones reaching lengths of three feet or more. Expanded opportunity also made a difference. Oxygen in the oceans opened up new places to live. According to open spaces hypothesis Cambrian organisms were like homesteaders in the American West. An aerated sea suddenly opened a huge tract of space and a swarm of new life forms emerged to take advantage of it.

Novelty built by shifts in existing dynamics also played a role. By the time of the Bang, living organisms had been testing their internal dynamics for billions of years the genes inside life were already linked by the hundreds in vast complex webs. This meant that a lot of variations could be cobbled together from twists of existing blends. Hence, as Jarmila Kukalová-Peck of Canada's Carleton University says: 'Arthropods are all legs, including legs that evolved into jaws, claws and even sex organs.'

Many threads came together and the foundations of life as we know it began. With the possible exception of *Bryozoa* which shows up just after the Cambrian, there is no record of a new biological phylum emerging after this explosion. All the ancestors of today's life were here.

Why haven't more bangs occurred? Some researchers invoke the open-space theory. They argue that after the initial rush, it became harder and harder for newcomers to establish footholds. Other researchers argue that once the big genetic networks had been established, they became more and more difficult to change. There was enough tinkering room for crude precursors to develop modern marvels like wings and the human brain, but the heyday was over. Complex genetic webs had complex ripple effects. It became difficult to do more than tweak them without killing the host.

Another Set of Copernicans

Today biology is still in its pre-Copernican period.
Ludwig van Bertalanffy

We have now come to the beginning of complex life, with a growing sense that biologists and physicists see the same interwoven world. Life was not an accident, it was an interwoven energy event.

Furthermore, webs do produce similar patterns at all levels, including increasing complexity, S-curves, punctuation and self-organized dances.

Yet, many of these ideas challenge establishment views. For instance, we find that genes do not control everything. Here evolution is punctuated, not gradual. Living organisms do not merely adapt to a status quo world, they actively change the world. Land, oceans and atmosphere co-evolve in a back-and-forth dance. Cooperation is the main path of improvement and commitment to the common good plays a bigger role in survival than self-centered individualism. All these ideas are revolutionary — and they are getting easier and easier to see.

A powerful synthesis is brewing between the new dynamics and the new biology. Threads from many different directions are making the new evolutionary synthesis more substantial by the day. Biology is rife with Copernicans. What new world do they see? It is time to put some pieces together. This section explores how the Dynamic view of evolution differs from the Darwinian view.

Beyond Darwinism

The revolution in evolution is particularly important because it has the potential to reverse a belief system which is both grim and exceptionally supportive of the worst parts of human nature. Darwinian theory centers on images of antagonism, zero-sum games and self *regardless* of anyone or anything else. It tends to validate ruthlessness and people who dominate other people. It tends to deny people's ability to change. Hence, as Goodwin puts it, our children are now taught that living things are 'complex molecular machines controlled by the genes carried within them.' Furthermore, the most notable aspect of our genetic controllers is that they are selfish — as Richard Dawkin's 1976 book, *The Selfish Gene,* attests. Selfish, manipulative genes created us and define us today. Dawkins puts it more powerfully:

> [genes] swarm in huge colonies, safe inside gigantic lumbering robots, sealed off from the outside world, communicating with it by tortuous indirect routes, manipulating it by remote control. They are in you and in me; they created us, body and mind; and their preservation is the ultimate rationale for our existence. They have come a long way, those replicators. Now

they go by the name of genes, and we are their survival
machines. (1976, p.219)

Dawkins' view of selfish genes and machine bodies is chilling. Yet,
we teach it in schools. Darwinists tell us this view is part of the high
cost of looking objectively at the world. It is actually part of the
high cost of having not understood interweaving.

Darwinism, however, is crumbling. As Stephen Jay Gould, the
eminent Harvard paleontologist says: 'The synthetic theory ... as a general proposition, is effectively dead, despite its persistence as textbook
orthodoxy.' As it unravels, so does a huge rat's nest of beliefs which
have become a haven for ideology in its ugliest forms. Let us start
exploring how much could change by revisiting an old friend — genes.

A New View of Genes

Darwinism says nothing about self-organization or energy or entwinment in the biosphere. It does say a lot about genes, however, and
genes do play an important role. Genes are part of the new view, they
just don't look the same. For example, the new dynamics makes it
clear that genes do not define, control and start everything. Web dynamics produce most shape and function. Neighbours, experience and
environment also play big roles.

How do genes fit in? Genes came late and completed a circle. They
were a final link in feedback system between metabolic processes,
cellular actions and natural selection. They preserve lessons, much like
a notebook.

Goodwin describes genes as 'control parameters.' They affect
patterns and the timing of events, but they work only within a range
of possibilities defined by self-organizing dynamics. It is rather like a
nozzle on the end of a garden hose. The nozzle has a range of potential patterns and twists of the nozzle determine which of these patterns
one gets. Genes define the amount of twist. For example, researchers
are beginning to show that all plant organs — sepals, petals, carpels
and stamen — represent variations on a leaf. (Goethe was right.) A
few small chemical tweaks determine whether a leaf becomes a petal
or a stamen. Hence, when genes which hold the tweak for a petals or
stamen are *removed,* the plant merely produces leaves instead. Genes
merely serve as parameters to a system which has a life of its own.

Genes also work in webs. Genes interact, activate each other, limit each other's ranges, and turn on and off depending on what others are doing. Goodwin, for example, describes how patterns of five overlapping Hox D genes determine where a particular kind of digit appears on the hind limb of a chick. These same genes also determine the position of digits in cats, but a cat's digits look different. Thus, some genes affect what a digit looks like, others affect where it appears and others determine the number. None of them contains a whole blueprint. Timing and even position play a role in the result.

Genes as Part of the Web of Processes

The view of genes is also changing in a more radical way. Genes are traditionally viewed as inviolate. In true clockwork form, the sacred genetic blueprint is essentially *separate*, 'sealed off from the outside world' as Dawkins puts it. Cosmic rays create random mutations, but traditional theory discounts virtually all other sources of genetic change. Furthermore, isolation is crucial to the Darwinian view. Isolation was necessary to preserve the purity of the species and individually-won lines of better genes.

But random mutations are not the only way that genes change. In fact, genetic material is exchanged all the time in a wide variety of ways including gene transfer from micro-organisms and exchange during sexual encounters. And, contrary to traditional images, this mongrelization is important. Genes are worked on by life at large. As Goodwin says:

> viruses and plasmids ... travel from host to host, picking up
> and delivering genes randomly on the way. This mixing of
> the gene pool results in an effective search through the
> potential space of ... possible forms suitable for the habitat.
> (1994, p.177)

The idea that genes are mixed and tested by the vast web of life is shocking. But there is another heresy lurking in the wings. Genes are also affected by what happens in the environment. Working with Indian corn in the early 1970s, geneticist Barbara McClintock discovered that genes on chromosomes rearrange themselves and even change in reaction to environmental stress. By the late 1970s other researchers confirmed McClintock's so-called 'jumping genes' in other species. By the late 1980s John Cairns and his colleagues at the

Harvard School of Public Health were beginning to show how environmental pressure changed genes. For example, when lactose-intolerant bacteria are grown in a lactose medium, some of the bacteria undergo mutations which make them tolerant. How did this happen? Researchers have known for a long time that genes affect RNA which affects proteins which affects enzymes which affect the body in many ways. In this case, information flowed the other way. Enzymes coded to a particular gene pushed back to change the gene itself.

What does all of this mean? It means that genes are part of the great web-process too. Effects go two ways. Environment and the great hive mind of life push back and forth. As Briggs and Peat put it:

> On many levels, the DNA code seems less a blueprint than an exquisite feedback relay center ... DNA feedback is coupled with other feedback inside and outside the individual organism — an instance of the cooperative, coevolutionary process that sustains and transforms the life on the planet. (1989, p.161)

The End of Genetic Determinism

Genes are important, but they work somewhat differently than usually portrayed. What difference does the new view make? The biggest concept to fall is the exaggerated image of genetic determinism.

Clockwork philosophers tell us that science runs on reason and objective data alone. This is what differentiates our world from the medieval one. Unfortunately, it is not true. Metaphors are mistaken for fact and enshrined as unchangeable truth all the time. When this happens we become just as medieval as our ancestors. The idea that genes are immutable and 'control all' is an example of the triumph of story over reason. Down's Syndrome, a gene-based problem that leads to severe developmental effects, provides a good example.

What experts 'know' affects real people. Since Down's is gene-based, most doctors also 'know' the results are inevitable — this is what orthodox genetic determinism teaches. Hence, in the world of genetic determinism, the only approach to Down's is to fix the gene.

In a web view, however, genes are only one part of a complex cycle. Hence, the genes associated with Down's actually affect the production of certain enzymes. The absence of these enzymes leads to certain chemical deficiencies which in turn affect development.[6] Most geneticists simply see this as the way genes determine. Yet, the complete story holds another possibility. Intervention can be made at many places in the cycle. For instance, medical researchers such as Henry Turkel have used diet and nutrient supplements to reduce the chemical deficiencies and thereby mollify Down's effects. These attempts have met with apparent success and have been widely used in Japan.

Apparent success is not enough, of course. To fit the sensibilities of science, controlled studies must be done. So, Turkel and various colleagues documented their results with copious volumes of objective evidence. Japanese physicians, for example, have treated thousands of Down's children since 1964 using Dr Turkel's treatments. They report that virtually all children improve in general health. About two-thirds improve in physical function and about one third in mental functioning.

These results led Turkel and his colleagues to apply for approval for their treatment from the American Food and Drug Administration (FDA). Unfortunately, administrators at the FDA were trained in genetic determinism. The FDA sent Dr Turkel many dismissive letters and finally wrote him that, since Down's is a genetic disease, it is incurable. There was no point wasting energy looking at data because the results are inevitable unless you fix the gene! (see Turkel, 1985)

The FDA's dismissal of data is an example of how people disregard ideas which do not fit current beliefs. It also shows why belief systems are insidious. Why is it that everywhere you look experts agree? Because studies which might counter their beliefs go unfunded, unexamined and unpublished — and scientists who suggest them go un-positioned. We are much like our ancestors.

Genetic determinism highlights our own medievalism. We are not completely open to facts. We cling first to our stories. But the story gets worse. Add the idea that natural selection always puts the best people on top and one gets the stuff of which ideological nightmares are made. The Meritocracy of Selfish Genes!

The Fallacy of Inherited Superiority

In classical physics if you had the right equations, the future was determined. In classical biology, once your genes were set, your future was equally determined. The sacrosanct blueprint contains all and controls all. There is nothing you can do. Furthermore, selection means the best individuals always rise. Thus, those who hold power have the right to lord over others because they have better genes. Élites hold their position because of congenital superiority. The rest of us should consider sterilization lest we pollute the gene pool.

The combination of genetic determinism and survival of the fittest (individual) has been used in exceptionally vile ways. It is a mainstay for ideologues who believe that a breed of innately superior individuals should rule inferiors. This too affects real life, even today. For example, in 1994 two American sociologists, Charles Murray and Richard Herrnstein, wrote an infamous little book called *The Bell Curve* which reiterated the age-old claim that intelligence differences between races are genetically determined. They also claimed that, since intelligence was pre-determined, government attempts to aid disadvantaged youths in programs such as Head Start, were ill-advised because there was no reason to believe such programs could change things. Herrnstein had already written an earlier article suggesting that economic status depends on IQ which, he held, was utterly determined by genes. He therefore concluded that as America developed into a true meritocracy, it would develop a hereditary upper class. *The Bell Curve* elaborates this idea into an emerging 'cognitive élite' whose rule will be inevitable because their superiority will be genetic and therefore unchangeably pre-determined.

Meritocracy and a hereditary upper class! Don't bother trying to help the disadvantaged! But perhaps this is just a hard fact of life. Murray and Herrnstein deny any ideological intent and point to statistics. They are simply grounding the idea of innate superiority scientifically. Of course, in doing so they are reinventing the idea of a hereditary aristocracy and that most famous twentieth century ideology, fascism. You will perhaps recognize the basic idea — some people are innately superior and these better people should rule, unhindered by dissenting inferior peoples who should probably be exterminated as a way of eliminating inferior genes.

Now, in a world where environmental events determine whether one can perceive vertical lines, the idea that intelligence is pre-determined at birth is utterly ludicrous. Rather, what human societies mainly have is a self-sustaining cycle of privilege. Those with money get better food, better education, better contacts and better jobs — which allows them to pass these things on to their children. It is this cycle of social effects that accounts for most social differences.

Many researchers have, thus, attacked Murray and Herrnstein for ignoring a tower of countering data. Unfortunately, 'reason and fact' are not the only things which run society. Hence Murray and Herrnstein benefited from what everyone 'knew.' Their work was hailed by pundits because it was consistent with the dominant story — selfish genes, survival and genetic determinism! It was also hailed because certain segments of the population already believe that their innate superiority justifies their privileged position in society. Sometimes this is done innocently. But it is often done for traditional reasons. Those who hold coercive power always say their role is an inevitable part of the natural order.

Genetic determinism and selfish-gene thinking are a blight on modern thought. They riddle our world with toxic and dangerous ideas that affect real people in real ways. But as long as we're exploring the dark side, let's look at another dangerous Darwinian pillar, the importance of antagonism and war.

War or Cooperation?

> *All nature is at war, one organism with another, or with*
> *external nature. Seeing the contented face of nature, this*
> *may at first well be doubted; but reflection will inevitably*
> *prove it to be true.*   Charles Darwin

Knowing leads to doing! and the kind of world we have hangs in the balance. What do we 'know'? Look around you, the world is a cruel, uncaring place replete with war, genocide, and horrific crimes. Nature is 'red in tooth and claw.'[7] What besides cunning ability in life's ruthless struggle could help individuals survive? Nature is ruthless and so are we! Darwinian theory tells us so.

Take the case of World War I, a fine example of the horror of war. Pressed to kill, pressed to survive, foot soldiers on the Western front faced each other from trenches often for months at a time and often across distances of only a few hundred yards. In this gruesome setting a powerful grassroots philosophy emerged. It cropped up everywhere. Despite numerous efforts, the high commands on both sides were unable to stamp it out.

What horror did it advocate? It was known simply as 'live and let live.' Embraced by foot soldiers on both sides, 'live and let live' produced an etiquette of unofficial truces, of firing to wound not kill, of not shelling roads used by supply trucks, and even of extensive fraternization made possible by the extended periods and short distances over which soldiers faced each other. The recollections of a British officer illustrate these unsanctioned ethics:

> I was having tea with A Company when we heard a lot of shouting and went out to investigate. We found our men and the Germans standing on their respective parapets. Suddenly a salvo arrived but did no damage. Naturally both sides got down and our men started swearing at the Germans, when all at once a brave German got on to his parapet and shouted out 'We are very sorry about that; we hope no one was hurt. It is not our fault, it is that damned Prussian artillery.' (Rutter, 1934, p.29)

There are many such stories from life and the last lines of this quote have a distinct ring of authenticity. Yet, this story of ethics and humanity emerging in the midst of war makes no sense to a Darwinian trained mind. Why? Because the second soul of Neo-Darwinism is competition — and not just competition as trying to do better, but war between competing selfish genes for domination of the species and from thence the world! As Thomas Huxley, Darwin's friend and defender put it: 'The animal world is on about the same level as a gladiator's show. The strongest, the swiftest and the cunningest live to fight another day ... no quarter is given.'

War and selfish genes form an inseparable core at the center of Neo-Darwinian evolution. Yet, something strange is happening. The odd part about the new view of evolution is that working together' — cooperation, symbiosis, collaboration — emerges as the primary player. Nucleated cells are built of previously independent life forms. Land plants come from lichens and algae. Even chemical cycles live longer by feeding each other. When you think about it, almost all increasing complexity, from molecules to civilization, comes from smaller parts working together in collaborative wholes.

Cooperation is also not just found inside living organisms. It abounds in places both large and small where it rounds out the connective tissue of life. Examples are legion. Bees cross-pollinate and many types of plants cannot live without them. Microbes live in the digestive systems of most higher animals and help break down food. *Lactobacillus* is an example in human digestion. Protozoans living in a termite's digestive tract are what allow it to digest wood. As Augros and Stanicu say 'A termite without protozoans in its gut will starve to death despite ingesting normal quantities of wood fiber.'

Large forms of life cooperate too. For example, baboons and gazelles frequently congregate as a way of increasing safety of both. Baboons have superior vision, gazelles have superior smell and aggregate is safer because both species respond to each other's warnings. Then there is cleaning. The tickbird cleans the rhinoceros, egrets clean various cattle, and dust mites eat dander from humans, cats and dogs that would otherwise fill up your house! The Egyptian plover enters a crocodile's mouth to feed on leeches and emerges unharmed. The list of cooperative behaviors goes on and on.

So cooperative behaviors connect the web of life. Where is the competition? Well, actually once one stops seeing the world through Darwinian glasses, it becomes harder and harder to find. For the most part life seems to avoid antagonistic competition like the plague. For example, similar species in the same eco-systems avoid competition by seeking out different niches. Take the two species of cormorant which occupy the same shorelines in Britain. Darwinian thinking would predict that these animal would be locked in a ruthless struggle, but in fact, one species eats sprats and sand eels while the other eats a mixed diet — notably absent in sprats and sand eels. Eating different food keeps species from competing for resources. Everyone does better.

Augros and Stanicu cite many more examples of how living organisms avoid competitive games. I'll cite a few:

> Coexisting species appear to use resources more or less opportunistically. We find little evidence that they are currently much concerned about competition with one another or that competition in the past has led to an orderly community structure. [John Weins and John Rotenberry after a three-year study of breeding bird communities]

> ... when competition is observed, it often appears inconsequential. Perhaps a fiddler crab scurries into a hole on a beach only to come running out again, expelled by the current inhabitant.

But the crab simply moves off to find another hole. [Ecologist, Daniel Simberloff]

In the desert, where want and hunger for water are the normal burden of all plants, we find no fierce competition for existence, with the strong crowding out the weak. On the contrary, the available possessions — space, light, water and food — are shared and shared alike by all ... This factual picture is very different from the time-honoured notion that nature's way is cut-throat competition among individuals. [Plant physiologist, Frits Went]

Ruthless struggle between species can be induced artificially in the laboratory, but it is difficult to point out clear examples of mutual harm between natural species undisturbed by man. Many ecologists and others experienced in field studies of animals candidly admit that the theoretical expectations are not borne out by the observed fact. Actual competition is difficult to see in nature. [Entomologist, P.S. Messenger] (1988, pp.90–93)

The point here is simple. Competition is not the omni-present governor of life we have been led to believe. As biologist Lewis Thomas puts it:

One major question needing to be examined is the general attitude of nature. A century ago there was a consensus about this; nature was 'red in tooth and claw,' evolution was a record of open warfare among competing species, the fittest were the strongest aggressors, and so forth. Now it begins to look different ... The urge to form partnerships, to link up in collaborative arrangements, is perhaps the oldest, strongest and most fundamental force in nature. (Cited in Augros and Stanicu, 1988, p.117)

Fitness Through War?

Another of Darwin's core ideas was that the living organisms got better because struggle allowed the fittest to rise. This idea did well in part because it resonated with the Enlightenment idea that free men should be allowed to rise to whatever heights their talents would allow. This view of competition as freedom for diverse talents was and is one of the great icons of Enlightenment civilization. Small wonder Darwin used it as a centerpiece of his theory.

Unfortunately, Darwin saw competition as war, not freedom. Survival meant guarding one's plate at all times and beating up others to get the contents of their plates whenever possible. This is not what Adam Smith meant when he said traders should be free and it is not how enterprising serfs became free men in the birth of capitalism. But, Darwin's story won. The image of competition as war now dominates Western thinking.

As a result, thoughts about what helps one survive are also viewed through the lens of war. This is why images of conquest, killing and selfishness are rife. Indeed, today, proficiency at war — aggression, self-serving cleverness, ruthlessness etc. — so define fitness that everything else seems unnatural. Entomologist E.O. Wilson, one of the great proponents of Neo-Darwinism, states that one of the great tasks of his sociobiology is to explain why paradoxical behaviors like love, nurturing, altruism, peacefulness, self-sacrifice, etc. come into being. As he says: 'How can altruism, which by definition reduces personal fitness, possibly evolve by natural selection?' (1980, p.3)

Wilson and other Neo-Darwinists explain nurturance, altruism and caring by invoking complicated epicycles of selfish genes. It *is* possible to do so, of course. But selfish genes cannot explain the origins of life or shape. They cannot explain why the biosphere evolves as a whole because, as Swenson says, 'There are no competing earth systems.' Hence, epicycle arguments fit the category of well-meaning attempts to bolster a view whose center is fundamentally misplaced.

Fitness in an Interwoven World

> *Fitness acquires a new meaning ... the ability of a species to play a coherent role in the web of ecological processes.*
>
> Robert Ulanowicz

Nowadays people are beginning to notice that the war model of fitness does not work very well. It encourages destructive behaviors in individuals, businesses and societies. Indeed, Wilson's question is better asked in reverse — how can a society which encourages antagonism, ruthlessness and selfish personal ends possibly hope to survive and prosper?

The new view is important because it helps reverse this vision. We've seen some of the differences already:

- *Cooperation* is a survival principle because groups are more powerful than individuals.
- *Commitment* to the common good is important because societies are a form of committed collaboration.
- *Diversity* is important because it provides seed crystals for new ways.
- On-going *learning* is important because we never have a perfect view. (I discuss learning in Chapter 5).
- Competition as *freedom* is important because this is part of diversity.
- Competition as war is a destructive habit.

In a web world, one must also remember that individual fitness is never separate from the larger whole. We all drink from the same energy trough. We are all built into an intricate web. Everything we do comes back around (eventually). Physicist-ecologist Robert Ulanowicz outlines the meaning of fitness in such a world, succinctly. In an interwoven world, fitness means 'the ability to play a coherent role in the web of processes.' Synergy is our most important business.

This is an important idea. It is also a very old one. It amounts to a rediscovery of something the ancients knew but that we have forgotten — harmony. Why do primitive people live in such rapport with nature? The answer is that they know that people live in a web of creation and that any group that tries to live at the cost of that web soon destroys its own vehicle for life. Therefore, groups and individuals which do not maintain a coherent role in the web of processes, eventually die out. This is the meaning of fitness in a web world. It realizes that personal survival is tied to group survival and the web of life up and down the line. The reason this vision of fitness is so different from Darwin's is that it stems from a deeper awareness. In the long run, *we are not separate, but bound together*.

Hence, this version of fitness, so well-articulated by Robert Ulanowicz, has also been articulated by virtually every great spiritual and moral tradition. The Buddhists call it 'right living.' The American Indians called it living with the great circle. Modern thinkers call it developing synergy. I discuss its role in economics in Chapter 8. The goal of the game is not to win but to improve flow. This is best done by joining hands and circles. Harmonious flow makes individuals *and* wholes more powerful.

Guarding and Growing

This harmonious view, however, should not be confused with the belief that love will automatically solve all problems. The latter is naïve. Interwoven fitness thus has a complication which I should mention.

Hence, the caveat. Darwin took the cherished notion of competition and linked it to war. Yet, Darwinian fitness also made sense to people because they could see that sometimes life does involve a zero-sum game. Someone lives and someone dies. Any concept of fitness, thus, has to contend with the need for defense and with one form of life eating another.

I should mention that both defense and consumption have an energy basis. Consumption is easy. The food chain (in which one form of life eats another) is part of the energy chain. Self-defense is actually more interesting. The birth of self-organizing networks, for instance, also meant the birth of self-defense. Your body's immune system, for instance, started as a chemical self-defense system. Outside intrusions can destroy a chemical network and networks which survive must have cycles which help thwart these. Your immune system grew out of processes which helped dampen intrusions which threatened the home chemical system.

So, even non-living systems find a need to protect themselves. The notion of self-defense leads, in turn, to an important refinement of what might otherwise be a simplistic view. Thus, fitness involves both maintaining oneself *and* working well with the outside. Finding a balance between these two is the main reason that fitness is so very complex.

Still, this two-edged type of fitness is also familiar. It harkens to another ancient image: some protect and some sow that all may live. This is the medieval organic whole. Someone has to grow food, build houses and take care of connections. This is harmony. Still, the need to protect oneself means that guarding and defending are important too. Someone has to watch out for enemies. Affinity for one side or the other leads to two powerful cultures found widely in the animal kingdom and in human societies. I call the two cultures Guardians and Synergists. One side protects and destroys enemies while the other builds synergy that all may live.

But as long as I'm pointing out parallels, let me mention one more.

The calamitous fourteenth-century helps us see these two cultures in a new light. Both are valid, but both can run amuck. Synergists run amuck mostly through naïvety. They ignore the need for defense and become ripe picking for an outside system. When Guardians run amuck they move from defense to war for personal gain. Medieval knights became agents of chaos when they started using their habit of violence for personal gain instead of for social defense. Guardians who promote themselves at the cost of the home web are a common cause of social destruction. Hence another ancient truth: war for personal gain (the Darwinian ideal) is a main source of social demise.

The trick to differing roles is that both sides are valid but both must remain committed to the greater good. Parity between the two is also crucial. This helps keep either side from running amuck.

Fitness is a complex topic about which too little is known. How can one tell whether to cooperate or defend, to be open or distrustful? Computer simulations are suggesting one rule of thumb. Explorations of a game known as the Prisoner's Dilemma[8] show that, in a self versus other game, the most productive long-term strategy is 'tit-for-tat.' One extends the hand of cooperation to one's fellow and if they accept honestly the bond is made. If they deceive, however, one treats them in kind. I believe the adage is: 'Fool me once, shame on you. Fool me twice, shame on me.' In tit-for-tat, however, the home system must be willing to forgive the other if it changes its behavior. Computer simulations that follow these rules survive and prosper better than others. Presumably, so does life.

*   *   *

To summarize this section simply, stories make a difference. Most people do not know the facts of evolution and they do not understand the numbers. They rely instead on the story they have been told. The result is cultural weaving. Even people who would like to believe otherwise feel compelled to accept poisonous ideas. The *story* seems tight and experts agree. Thus, thanks to cultural weaving, genetic determinism, inherited superiority, fitness through war and all of their dangerous and destructive implications are broadly accepted and even more broadly applied. A whole string of experts will tell you that human beings are fundamentally self-serving and that human nature — from why women are passive to why men are killers — is unchangeably set in selfish genes.

We need to see the world differently for many reasons: scientific ones, social ones, spiritual ones. Most of all, we need to see in a way which reconciles instead of incites. We are on the edge of just such a frame.

The Web of Life and Energy

The oneness of all life means that the same streams of life energy runs through all the veins of the universe. It is this stream which binds all life together making them One ... A realization of this Oneness should do much to eliminate discrimination, especially against colour, race and caste.
From *Essentials and Symbols of the Buddhist Faith*

The idea that energy is behind the world's order is not new. Buddhists and Taoists have said it for centuries. Even western scientists have been describing energy's role in evolution at least since the turn of this century.[9] Biologist and mathematician Alfred Lotka, for instance, had this to say in 1922:

Boltzmann pointed out that the fundamental object of contention in the life-struggle and the evolution of the organic world, is available energy. In the struggle for existence, the advantage must go to those organisms whose energy-capturing devices are most efficient

Lotka also points out (rather dryly) that energy pushes the system to go faster and get more intricate at the same time. Energy prefers small tight circles which are well linked because this helps it cycle rapidly and robustly throughout. This is why your body is fine-grained and highly interwoven. It is also why the biosphere is filled with cycles great and small. Thus, Lotka continues:

... In every instance considered, natural selection ... operates [so] as to increase the total mass of the organic system, to increase the rate of circulation of matter through the system, and to increase the total energy flux through the system.

Nowadays a host of biologists will tell you the same thing. Eco-systems, for example, move through a succession of dominant forms, from grasslands to pine forests to oak forests. And each new system cycles more energy per unit time and density than its predecessor. Energy and intricacy go together.

Newer views of energy also help explain another familiar experience, namely, the increasing pace of change. Energy actually pushes three things in tandem: (1) increasing energy flow, (2) increasing intricacy, and (3) increasing pace of change. Hence, your sense that evolutionary epochs have been getting shorter, is not just in your mind. As Petters-son says:

> Many people feel that things are changing faster, nowadays, than during the time of their parents or grandparents ... Hither-to, this acceleration of change has seemed a purely human phenomenon, confined to our own lineage ... However, there is evidence, from long before man, of a general long-term accel-eration during the greater part of biological and social evolution. (1978, p.201)

So, maybe we should take this energy idea seriously. It would help reconcile east and west, ancient and up-to-date. The idea is not fuzzy or ill-founded. All things considered, the evidence for energy playing a pivotal role in evolution has been growing for a very long time. Why then hasn't it caught on? The answer to this question can be put in a single word: entropy.

The Second Law

In physics, the study of energy is called thermodynamics. The second law of thermodynamics says that entropy always increases. According to common interpretation, this means that the natural flow of the universe is toward disorder. Since physicists describe the second law as virtually in-disputable, biologists studying evolution have been put on the spot. If the universe is running downhill toward disorder, then life — indeed, all ordering — must be an accident that runs uphill against the flow.

This view of the second law has had a profound impact on the western view of life, evolution and nature itself. It is the main reason that spontaneous organization still seems unscientific. It is the main reason Darwinists felt obliged to say that life is a sheer accident and evolution an accumulation of such accidents. Everyone knows that order is unnatural!

Thermodynamics, however, is undergoing a Copernican shift for the same reasons explained throughout this book. Expanded understanding changes vision. In this case, traditional energy stories are built on well-studied systems at or near equilibrium. Most of the world, however, is nowhere near true equilibrium. Scientists are beginning to expand into the realm of non-equilibrium and far-from-equilibrium systems. In lay terms, this means they are beginning to broach the broader-case world.

This shift is important because it shows that the idea that 'order is unnatural' comes from studying very limited-case systems. Entropy cannot even be measured in the far-from-equilibrium case (which is most of the world). It is not even well-defined there. Hence, the image of a cosmos that is running *only* toward disorder reflects a limited case, not necessarily the world at large.

Expansion is also bringing a new interpretation. This view sees order as *part of an expanded view of the second law.* The elegant insight is that the second law can cover both order and disorder, depending on the force available. Energy concentrations create a force which pushes the system to move faster. This is when the system self-organizes and moves toward increasing intricacy. When there is no concentration, the system runs downhill as expected. Both conditions increase entropy. (Figure 37 explains the logic.)

These simple insights produce an elegant idea, we can reconcile order and the second law by adding a *rate factor.* As Swenson puts it, the second law should read, 'entropy increases *at the fastest rate possible.*' Here the word 'possible' refers to whether there is a pressure pushing energy to flow faster. Nature produces entropy very rapidly, while it's producing order. It produces entropy slowly, when it is winding down. Hence, the focus on entropy has been misleading. Using energy helps us see that pressure is the key concept. Order is a by-product of pressure to flow. Entropy is also a by-product of flow. Swenson (1988) suggests this idea specifically in his Principle of Maximum Entropy Production (MEP) and Brooks and Wiley suggest it broadly in their book entitled, *Evolution as Entropy.*[10]

*   *   *

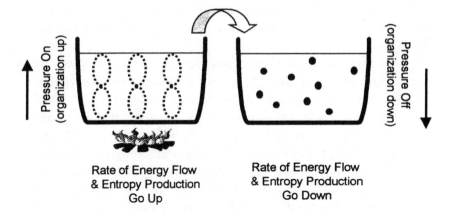

Rate of Energy Flow
& Entropy Production
Go Up

Rate of Energy Flow
& Entropy Production
Go Down

Figure 37. Why Order and the Second Law need not be at odds.
Since entropy can't be measured in the far-from-equilibrium case, one approach is to use energy flow to approximate entropy production. Energy flow is what produces entropy. Thus, the rate at which energy flows should be roughly equivalent to the rate at which entropy is produced. This is a helpful idea because people can measure energy flow in far-from-equilibrium systems (where they can't measure entropy).

Energy also helps us see that nature produces order or disorder depending on the context. When concentration creates pressure, energy flows faster and intricacy (order) is likely to increase. Entropy production also increases because energy flow does. When pressure falls off, the world winds down. Order decreases, energy flows more slowly and entropy is produced more and more slowly.

This brings me to the reason for mentioning entropy. Reconciling order and the second law would be very important. It would build a final link between biologists and physicists struggling to understand the same interwoven world. Life and evolution would be seen as natural products of a profoundly entwined, energy-driven web.

Dynamic Evolution

> *In the eyes of science ... man's creator becomes the vast*
> *interwoven fabric of all evolving nature ...*   Roger Sperry

The quest for a Dynamic theory of evolution has been simmering in heretical circles, at least since the time of the great evolutionary debates in the mid-1800s. A long line of thinkers have contributed to the idea including Spencer, Lotka, Vernadsky, Velikovski, Von Bertalanffy, Prigogine, Laszlo and a host of others too numerous to list. You can see the idea back as far as Goethe and even the ancient Greeks. Sperry summarizes the idea today. The web of the world and, grander still, the creative cosmos at large authors the order we see about us.

If Dynamic Evolution were to become the norm, then we would be reconciled, east and west, ancient and up-to-date. The Buddhists, for instance, are right. The streams of energy run through all the veins of the universe, binding all life together. Our separateness an illusion. Energy created life and the cycles that swirl up through oceans, atmosphere and land. We are built of and tied into all that is.

The new science helps us see even more. Evolution is filled with re-current patterns because energy and web dynamics are built this way. The Greeks saw sacred geometries. Now we see fractals, intricacy, S-curves, the poise of chaos and much, much more.

The web world is a subtle seamstress who weaves order high and low. Its patterns exist at the finest and most subtle depths of reality and yet it is also at work in our everyday lives. A life-giving force and a universal reason permeating the world? In us, of us, and more than us, at the same time? Scientists and prophets are beginning to say many of the same things.

What Difference does Web Thinking make?

> *A human being is a part of the whole called by us,*
> *'universe', a part limited in time and space. He experiences*
> *himself, his thoughts and feelings, as something separated*
> *from the rest ... This illusion is a kind of prison for us,*
> *restricting us to our personal desires and to affection for a*
> *few persons nearest to us. Our task must be to free*
> *ourselves from this prison by widening our circle of*
> *compassion to embrace all living creatures and the whole of*
> *nature in its beauty.*   Albert Einstein

Our world is beginning to look different indeed. This is not a violent, empty universe. It is a creative cosmos which gives birth to new order at the flick of a butterfly's wing. We live in an order-producing universe whose design we are but barely beginning to see. Awe returns. A sense of belonging returns. Yet science is still with us. The world is being re-enchanted and demystified at the same time.

I started this book pondering how much could really change. The tide has not turned, but hopefully the shape and extent of this great metamorphosis is a bit more visible. So let me review.

We are asked to embrace ideas such as 'nature is at war' and 'life is an elaborate way to for DNA to replicate itself' as part of the high cost of looking objectively at the world. But Neo-Darwinism is unraveling. Gould says it is already effectively dead. Margulis puts it more delicately:

> We consider naïve the early Darwinian view of 'nature red in tooth and claw.' Now we see ourselves as products of cellular cooperation — of cells built up from other cells. Partnerships between cells once foreign and even enemies to each other are at the very roots of our being. They are the basis of the continually outward expansion of life on Earth. (1982, p.138)

The new story of evolution is more relevant to most of us than the new dynamics. Darwinism coloured our view of ourselves and life seen through its lens was grim. Individuals were out for themselves and the superiority rose through selfishness and war. No wonder many religious traditions balked at this view. The subtitle of Dawkins' book, *The Blind Watchmaker*, says it all: *Why the Evidence of Evolution Reveals a Universe without Design.*

Happily this cultural web is unraveling and as it does it begins to seem like a self-reinforcing rat's nest that no sophisticated person would believe. We even begin to see what retrospective absurdity might look like. Bodies are not mere housings for selfish genes. We are not an accident and we are not pre-programmed automatons.

Happily too, the cultural web which is about to replace the old is both more coherent and more appealing. Appealing? We have been trained to believe that science teaches mainly harsh truths, so the concept of 'appeal' seems unscientific. But the appeal is obvious and well grounded. Cooperation is the central avenue of evolution. Competition *as war* is a very restricted aspect. Yet the Enlightenment icon remains, now returned to its original meaning. Competition *as freedom* plays an important role because the universe is in the business of casting about to learn. The socially beneficial side of freedom is its role in creating diversity.

Energy does tie us together in a set of cycles that are intricate beyond comprehension. Stars, rocks, plants, animals and human beings great and small are bound together in an invisible design. Alive and harmonious? You can almost hear the next century's historians:

> ... Once upon a time Westerners imagined themselves alive but going nowhere in a universe without design. Most things were assumed to be either dead, unconscious or unfeeling. Science was associated with control, manipulation, dissection and often with the end of the world. Competition drove evolution and anomalies like altruism were explained as complicated epicycles of selfish genes. The world was neither enchanted nor loving. But that view unraveled and a new one emerged ...

Many people hope that understanding the *physical reality* of the Great Ordering Oneness will provide the key for a more sane civilization. Alive, appealing, collaborative, embracing, meaningful, humbling, inspirational, profound — words like these are important today for very practical reasons. The clockwork view did not speak to the basic questions of human being. It tended to discount those questions as being irrelevent or illusion. This drove people away from the modern view because it seemed sterile and meaningless despite its great feats. This need no longer be the case. Science is rediscovering ancient wisdoms. Our head, heart and soul may yet come back together.

CHAPTER 5

THE MIND OF GOD, MANY AND ONE

The Universe is built on a plan, the profound symmetry of which is somehow present in the inner structure of our intellect.   Paul Valéry

Evolution did not stop with life *per se*. At the very least it built brains from which sprang minds from which sprang consciousness, the greatest of the world's many mysteries. This chapter takes up the question of brains, minds and consciousness. The not-so-surprising implication here is that these greatest of creation's wonders are also part of the story. No longer in long, slow cycles of blind self-organization, somehow the Great Ordering Oneness found a way to build a system which consciously shapes the world and itself as if by plan. More self-aware and more potentially powerful than anything that has ever existed, thinking beings are a world-transforming force in their own right.

There is, of course, a reason I haven't mentioned much about mind. Mind is even more incomprehensible to clockwork thinkers than life. Early clockwork thinkers thought that we were merely separated, mind from body. Later ones described mind as an epiphenomenon, an illusion of a few lifeless chemicals. After all, when you break brains down, there is no mind to be found. Traditional evolutionary theory has essentially ignored mind, preferring genes instead. All of this is likely to end in the relatively foreseeable future.

Currents of change can already be seen. Once a taboo topic, consciousness is becoming an increasingly common subject in the popular press. Books such as *The Celestine Prophecy,* for instance, paint a picture of humanity reaching a new level of consciousness. People trapped in the cloying maze of modern reality, suddenly discover an invisible web of awareness growing within themselves and others. Individually and collectively, human beings are struggling precariously toward a new, more integral perception. The potential is high. So is the need. The birth of a new level of consciousness seems to be part and parcel of the project to save the world.

I am not going to tell a romantic tale of New Age seers in the Andes. It is important to stay more grounded than this, lest the realists in the audience run for the hills. Yet I also believe there is a valid intuition behind such works. Books like *The Celestine Prophecy* are part of the same instinctive reaction to clockwork omissions seen elsewhere. Clockwork bleakness strikes again. Millions of highly educated people the world over now read such books and harbor secret hopes that they are true.

Understanding the science behind this intuition, gives human hope a better foundation. Thus, brain researchers too are hoping that new understandings of consciousness will help bring about a global civilization which is less apt to destroy itself and the world. Their hope seems particularly reasonable since mind and consciousness are so central to the human condition. Indeed, I would make a stronger statement — one *cannot* understand our condition or our times without understanding the phenomenon of mind, including ways of looking at the world and patterns of collective knowing.

Today, powerful new views are building which will have a profound effect on our sense of ourselves. They quite literally redefine what the human project is about. Not a lumbering automaton or a ruthless beast, here human beings (one and many) become the ultimate learning system, the finest and foremost spark of a learning world. That is the story that will unfold here, it will simply be much more integrated into the larger story of evolution than most people imagine.

The theory of mind presented here is new in its fine points — largely because I include the energy connection and other rarely-popularized points. Yet, the core image is again remarkably old. Mind is a natural, interwoven outcome of a much larger flow. What is interesting is its implications for our times.

The Enigma of Mind

I doubt whether there is a more decisive moment for a
thinking being than when the scales fall from his eyes and
he discovers that he is not an isolated unit lost in the
cosmic solitudes, and realizes that a universal will to live
converges and is hominized in him. Sir Julian Huxley

Any pursuit of mind and consciousness should start with a necessary admission: there is no universal agreement as to what these are, much less how they came to be, or how they work. Most people try to understand mind by focusing on brains. Still, no matter how much we know about brains, there remains an explanatory gap between brain operation and the enigma of mind. This explanatory gap is what led reductionists to describe mind as an illusion of brain chemistry. As emergence becomes more scientifically acceptable, however, so does mind.

The new brain science, thus, brings with it a new interest in the age-old mystery of mind. In most new views 'mind' is more than the sum of brain parts, but it is nevertheless a phenomenon of this real world. The more daring even wonder how consciousness came into being.

How does the new science approach the enigma of mind? Our three old friends — energy, organization and the Great Ordering Oneness — provide some new paths by which to tread deftly through the minefield. Hence, here 'mind' is mostly a matter of *dynamic organization*, the ways bits of matter work together to produce the mind-like behaviors (described below). Minds arose from older self-organizing drives which came together in radically new ways. To properly understand mind, therefore, we must begin long before there were brains.

Mind, From the Bottom Up

... if we expect to get anywhere with the mind-body problem
at the brain level, then our concepts must at least be
adequate ... to explain the symbol-matter relation in single
cells where it all started. Howard Pattee

How can we understand mind as a type of organization? A dictionary provides the first clues. One of its definitions of mind is a 'system which exhibits purpose, intention, or will.' What Pattee suggests in the opening quote (1982), is that the best way to build an understanding of mind, is to look for the earliest possible stirrings of these three. When you do this, you find that mind-like behaviors started long before brains. If you start at the first stirrings, you can then follow mind-like behaviors throughout evolution. Here, human consciousness appears as the cutting edge of a long-standing drive. What follows is an energy story of mind from the bottom-up.

Actually, we've already started the journey. In the last chapter, I described how early cells began to search for food. This is a very mind-like thing to do. What few people mention is that finding food involves a new kind of energy activity, one in which small amounts of energy provide information about something else. Thus, whether there is a chemical trail or a pattern of light bouncing off food, cells must find food by following energy trails which lead to a bigger energy concentration in the vicinity. These small bits of energy are information in its physical form. Life had to learn to follow energy information in order to eat.

Pattee points out, therefore, that early life represents the first type of mind. Cells don't think and they aren't self-aware, but they do begin responding to information in a functional way.

Note too that the entire cellular system is tied up with this pursuit of information. For life to reach food, little energy blips from outside must trigger some form of locomotion that moves the cell toward its food. In turn, locomotion (whether by flagellum or pseudopod) requires energy from the cell's metabolic cycles. Hence, metabolism has to speed up in order to answer the demand. In short, an entire, interlocked system must kick into action in response to little energy nudges from the outside. Furthermore, the system must respond differently to different kinds of nudges!

If you look closely, you'll see that this means 'mind' activities (such as following information) and 'bodily' activities (metabolism and locomotion) are inseparable. Getting food requires that the ability *to perceive* information and *to act* appropriately be linked in one connected loop. Survival depends on this. If any part of the loop doesn't work, the cell does not get food and dies. This means that a whole lot of systems inside the cell had to co-evolve in tight conjunction from very early on. Furthermore, internal cycles had to be intertwined in a *functional way* from the start.

If you put these kinds of ideas together, a fascinating picture begins to emerge. First, mind-like behaviors started long before brains. These mind-like behaviors appear to be based in energy, now in the guise of information. Secondly, mind elements and body elements are One. Break the chain anywhere and the system doesn't work and the cell doesn't survive. Life, therefore, had to be a kind of well-wired, little proto-mind from the beginning. Finally, if you look at mind from the bottom-up, you find that what is most special about life is exactly its mind nature. Life is an integrated perceiving-acting system. It also manages to preserve information in its genes. It is much more than self-organizing. Biologists Humberto Maturana and Francisco Varela sum up the image nicely: 'To live is to cognize.'

Increasing Intelligence

Obviously, nature did not stop with the mind of a cell. Hence, looking at mind from the bottom up, also opens the door to an aspect of evolution I haven't mentioned yet. Not only does nature make things more physically complicated, she also makes them smarter. As living forms evolved, they learned to handle more and more information in more and more complex ways. Handling more information in more complex ways also led to more intelligent action. Thus, the path from cell minds to human minds is notable for *increasing intelligence*, as well as increasing intricacy.

Increasing intelligence is still tied to energy, but in a very different way. Hence, what we call information starts out as small energy blips. The energy in these blips is minuscule compared to the big build-ups which push shapes (like whirlpools) into being. In life, however, small nudges actually move more material than the big build-ups. For instance, it takes less energy to get you to move your finger away from a hot stove, than it does to make a whirlpool rise.

Rod Swenson at the University of Connecticut, thus, points out that life involves two distinct types of energy interactions. First, there are what he calls 'mass-driving gradients.' These big energy flows are the kind that maintain a whirlpool's shape. Inside living organisms, these flows form metabolism, the energy cycles which allow life to move and hold itself together. Thus, mass-driving gradients are behind an organism's overall structure and motion.

An organism's activity, however, is also governed by microscopic energy blips (information). Hence, bacteria find desirable resources by perceiving and acting on a trail of observables — that is, a fine-grained energy trail *related* to molecules they consume. Information is based in energy, it is just very fine-grained energy with a level of indirection. Hence, Swenson says living systems respond to 'patterns' in energy flow.

Living organisms, therefore, are made of energy flow *and* they follow energy patterns. Both sides are essential. Furthermore, life's two energy interactions are integrated — which is why mind is never separate from body.

This integration also creates a great irony. In living organisms, subtle patterns are more powerful than big build-ups. Hence, as organisms began to respond to information in more complex ways, larger and larger amounts of matter moved in response to smaller and smaller bits of energy. As a result, increasing intelligence is accompanied by increasing *responsiveness* to ever more rarefied patterns. By the time one gets to reading words on a page, entire populations move in response to incredibly microscopic bits of energy. This is strange way to put it, but it is true.

Now, we certainly don't know how all this came to pass, but it is not so hard to imagine why it might. Natural selection favors every addition which helps life follow information *better* because following information is the main way life survives. The connection to physical energy became fainter and fainter as life (especially with brains) began to respond to very complex patterns. Yet, underneath, the phenomenon of information is still based in energy.

A Brief History of Better and Better Minds

Why did evolution move from the cellular mind to the wonder which is our brain? Oddly enough, the need to maintain collaboration played a major role. We know that mind and body are integrated and that life is a committed collaboration. In such a world, growing apart is deadly because responses *dis*-integrate. Let us see, therefore, how the pressure to stay collaboratively connected has contributed to increasing intelligence from nerves to brains.

The Birth of Nerves

Life brought the miracle of responding to information to find food. Still, though early cells represented a great leap in information processing, from our perspective they are crude. Their responses are knee-jerk and their horizons are limited. How did life get from there to here? The path is actually quite understandable.

As evolution proceeded, single cells gave rise to multi-cellular organisms. As we saw in Chapter 4, many-celled organisms are actually collectives of specialist cells bound in committed collaboration. Once upon a time specialist cells were capable of independent lives, but millions of years of evolution forged them into a whole whose members need each other to survive. Herein lies a rub of great importance to the evolution of mind. A living organism *has to stay integrated to survive.* Cells coordinate their activities by circulating chemical and electrical signals. Information must circulate thoroughly so that each cell can do its job intelligently. Lung cells, for instance, have to know what is happening with the legs because moving a leg requires more energy which requires faster metabolism which requires more oxygen. (This is why we breath faster when we run.)

Failure to communicate well inside, therefore, leads to death just as fast as failure to perceive information from outside. Limbs, eyes, guts, and so on, can only do their job if signals are timely and correct. If your lung cells don't get signals from your legs, for instance, they won't increase oxygen which means your legs won't get enough energy to catch the rabbit.

This brings me to the point of mentioning all this. As organisms got bigger, internal communication became harder. Information exchange happens easily when cells are in close proximity. But signals dissipate over distance. As bodies got bigger, member cells began to lose touch with each other (literally). The whole began to fall out of sync. Unfortunately, when cells depend on one another for basics such as oxygen (lungs) and nutrients (gut), growing apart can be deadly.

Because losing sync is deadly, the evolutionary pressure to find a way to stay connected grew. No doubt many organisms died as their internal collaboration began to fail. Others stopped growing and settled into a safe niche. Yet eventually, through some quirk of diversity, some organisms developed a new means of staying cooperatively connected. A new type of specialist cell emerged whose job was to carry signals between distant groups. We call them nerves (see Figure 38).

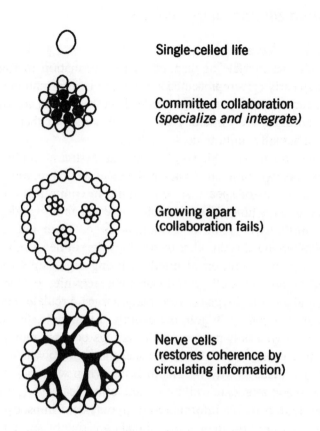

Single-celled life

Committed collaboration
(specialize and integrate)

Growing apart
(collaboration fails)

Nerve cells
(restores coherence by
circulating information)

Figure 38. Growth Crises: from Clone Clusters to Nerve Cells.

Nerves are particularly important because they allowed the organism's mind-nature to grow more sophisticated. The quality of an organism's response to the outside world depends almost entirely on internal collaboration which in turn depends heavily on information flow. Mind-body integration is crucial! Nerves improved intelligence by increasing information flow which in turn improved collaboration. More cellular specialties could develop and life became vastly more complex and sophisticated too.

Brains — The Pattern Repeats

Evolution was not through, however. In simple forms of life, such as the giant sea slug today, a single nerve cell often serves a whole organism. But as life became more complex, the same pattern of growth and crisis played out again. As bodies grew bigger, collaboration began to fail again. Pressure to stay connected grew.

At first, nerve cells multiplied forming multi-lane information highways as it were. Nerve highways brought signals from all over and spread information throughout. Where nerves overlapped, signals from many directions intermingled. At dense cross-roads, a new kind of cell began to emerge. We call this one a brain cell.

Brain cells had a unique view. Positioned atop a cross-roads with information pouring in from all over, the information they got was rich and multi-dimensional. As a result, brain cells began to respond to extremely subtle patterns in complex streams of energy (information). The horizons this opened up were truly vast.

Brain cells responding to rarefied patterns in massive amounts of information were actually beginning to respond to conglomerate pictures. Complex pictures helped organisms see contexts and make choices. The brain's owner began to see how any bit of information fit in a larger whole. For example, an organism with a brain is able to see that food *and* a predator means something different than food alone. Unlike a planaria which responds to information in a knee-jerk way, life with a brain began to learn to decipher and choose. As brains learned to synthesize ever more complex pictures, questions of how bits fit got complex indeed.

Brains also allowed life to develop complex responses based on subtle nuances in the outside world. Sitting astride mixing centers allowed brains to coordinate incredibly complex response patterns involving all parts of the body. Like a keystone on top, brains solidified life's ability to perceive and act as a truly coordinated whole. Thus, brains are what brought life out of the ooze and allowed multi-cellular organisms to locomote with legs and fins.

The irony of brains is that 'staying connected' produced a whole new stage of evolution. Brains and other mixing centers (like ganglia) helped an increasingly-vast collective act like a truly coordinate whole. Mind-like behaviors also began to take the forms we associate with minds today — choices, contexts, significance, meaning. We are still deciphering like mad. Underneath, however, the same evolutionary principles applied. United they stood! Multicellular organisms became a multi-level society of mind because selection favored cells that (1) worked together for the common wellbeing and (2) stayed linked.

The Fractal Nature of Mind and Body

Note, however, that the brain did not become the sole arbiter of intelligence nor the controller of everything underneath. This is a machine image. Local cells don't just send information to the brain and wait to be told what to do. Instead, most bodily responses are handled locally and a lot of processing is done at various stages from bottom to top. Processing information at lower levels increases the speed and often the appropriateness of the response. It is also one of the reasons one's body can operate on auto-pilot while one's thoughts spin off into space.

Nature thus built new levels of intelligence while keeping the old. Furthermore, everywhere you look, cells work in groups. A brain is a mind system which is still integrated into a larger mind system called the body which is organized into smaller working groups, like lungs and liver. The whole thing appears to work on a subsidiary principle reminiscent of one used by the medieval Catholic Church — decisions should be made at the lowest level possible.

This, of course, does not fit our usual picture of how a hierarchy works. It means instead that intelligence is *distributed* — fractally, down to lower levels. This kind of organization is crucial. Without it, life would be too slow and stupid to live.

Social Learning in Higher Organisms

Nature also did not stop with brains. Organisms with brains became great sorters of information who chose paths based on subtle patterns. Freed from knee-jerk responses, animals with brains began to explore the world and to learn lots of new lessons. Most of these lessons were stored in the brain of the beholder, in circuits etched by experience. (They were not stored in genes.) Storing lessons in the brain allowed organisms to learn faster and to learn without having to die.

Still, there was a problem. Lessons stored in a brain were lost when the individual who owned the brain died. The next great evolutionary development was the ability to preserve lessons by passing them between different individuals and across generations. The two big agents here were modeling and signaling. They too started for understandable reasons.

Since cooperation enhances survival, animals began to congregate in families or herds. Communication between animals in a herd has the same benefit as communication between cells in your body. Whether a honey-bee dancing directions to a cache of nectar or a deer signaling the approach of a predator, communication between members is an old and honoured way for individuals to survive better by working together.

Animal communication, no doubt, began in the usual haphazard way, with twitches that eventually became associated with a meaning. These eventually developed into clear signals. Active signaling also brought modeling. Young and old alike learned common signals and worthwhile patterns of behavior. These began to trickle down the generations. The herd was now working on patterns of perceiving and acting. Learning accumulated from many members was preserved over increasing periods of time. All of it enhanced survival.

The Social Nature of Mind and Learning

> Brains consist of neurons, which in turn are composed of
> organelles, molecules and atoms. They are designed by
> biological evolution to work in pairs, families, tribes and, by
> cultural evolution, to work in cities, nations and empires ...
> biologists have largely neglected those biological properties
> by which brains join together in social cooperation.
>
> Walter Freeman, Neurophysiologist

Notice the parallels in the patterns discussed so far. In the web view, cooperation is the central path of evolution. Cooperative groups depend on communication between members to survive. Growth, however, pulls groups apart and makes collaboration break down. Hence, developmental leaps often come from an invention which helps keep the group integrated.

Perhaps the most unusual observation in the new science, therefore, is that each mind is a many-bodied *society of mind*. New levels of intelligent action always arise from the cooperative, intricately-ordered activity of smaller parts. The farther up the line one goes, the more clearly those smaller parts are seen to be individuals which once lived independent lives. A complex eucaryotic cell, for instance, is a society built out of previously-independent life forms. Its mind-like behaviors depend on collaboration among individuals. The idea holds all the way up to brains. As Margulis says:

> Our nerve cells are the outcome of an ancient, nearly immortal
> marriage of two arch enemies who have managed to coexist:
> the former spirochetes and former archaebacteria that now
> comprise our brains ... These former free-living bacteria are
> inextricably united. They probably have been united for more
> than one thousand million years. (Cited in Combs, 1995, p.40)

The idea that all minds are built of lower societies and into higher
ones, fits nicely in a self-organizing world which builds macrocosms
out of microcosms. It helps us come to grips with the fact that intelligence is distributed throughout our body and is not just limited to our
brain. It is startling because it puts community at the center of mind
as well as body. It is also important because it helps us rethink human
societies.

The Cutting Edge of Collaborative Learning

In human beings, signaling evolved into language which made passing
information extremely precise. Speaking allowed highly-structured information tapestries to be shot from one brain to another. When
writing emerged, these tapestries could be stored outside human bodies
and compared and contrasted over huge periods of time. People living
today, for instance, can benefit from learning accrued by people who
lived five thousand years ago.

Language and writing add tremendous survival value because they
allow lessons from many individuals to be synthesized into extremely
precise patterns of knowing and doing. Eventually, these highly synthesized systems of knowing and doing became what human beings call
culture. Myths, paradigms, worldviews and scientific theories are all
made of these.

In human beings, cooperative learning became unbelievably refined.
Language allowed learning to accumulate at tremendous rates. Information tapestries became knowledge webs which grew over the ages.
Where nature had once searched the realm of possibility by casting
about blindly, human beings now search the realm of possibility with
brains which process huge amounts of information from personal,
group and historical experience in order to maximize the foresight,
planning and prediction. These big brains eventually gave rise to self-
awareness, which we call consciousness.

Evolution's second side, increasing intelligence, was leading to more and more mass being moved by ever more subtle blips. As Swenson says:

> In this way, the explosion in mass communication and globalization going on at present is but a new phase of ... the same evolutionary order-building behaviour started some four billion years ago.

The Learning Universe

That which created us, designed us to create back.   J.S. May

Mind too evolved as part of the larger process. It went from crude information-following behaviors to truly astounding activities like language, writing and culture. It appears to be involved with energy, especially of the information variety. It is a very social process.

Energy's role in this process became invisible with the advent of brains. No one can follow how physical energy gets transformed from blips to meaning through the bio-chemistry of brains. We are responding to patterns in masses of information, to *flows about flows about flows*. Nevertheless, energy parallels still play out. Increasing intelligence is accompanied by greater intricacy and energy flow. The human brain is the most intricate and fastest energy cycling (per unity density) system on the planet. Furthermore, brains also help increase energy flow in the world at large. This is particularly true of big-brained humans who began restructuring the outside world as part of their drive to survive. As a result, human organizations such as cities also increase energy flow.

But seeing mind just as increasing energy flow is not very satisfying. So, let us look at a more appealing explanation which also fits the facts. In this story, human beings try to understand the world because the universe itself is trying to learn. We are the leading edge of a learning universe, the product of an evolutionary push that endlessly strives to find new ways. This story, from evolutionary theorist Rod Swenson, is easy to understand. Yet, in it, our view of ourselves and the world is utterly transformed.

The Stages of the Learning Universe

Swenson starts by pointing out that evolution is a learning process, the primordial one. Learning is induced by problems. In energy terms, the universe is faced with the problem of how to distribute energy as fast as possible given the inertia and the disorder that abound. It learns in that it configures and reconfigures itself toward greater and greater intricacy and efficiency. Learning is not intentional. Like a baby growing, the goal is not in mind. But it is directed toward future states which are more intricate, and more 'developed.'

Furthermore, the pressure to flow faster also involves a pressure to learn better ways. Each stage is a current-best solution that works until the things it cannot do, the efficiency it cannot achieve, creates a shortfall and a crisis which begs for something more. At each stage the field uses diversity to cast about in search of new ways to flow. The field also searches by cobbling existing pieces into new forms which produce astounding new behaviors. (Physicists call this coupling.)

With each cycle, the universe also learns how to perform some activity better. Table 3 shows first four stages of the Learning Universe.

We are the epitome of the fourth stage. With humankind, the Great Ordering Oneness has produced an organism which can restructure the world more powerfully than anything that has ever existed. Yet, since our brains were created by the Oneness (as well as earned by us), chauvinism is not appropriate. We too are servants of a higher process. Our project is to endlessly strive to learn more.

This brings me to the final and most intriguing assertion of the Learning Universe story: a fifth stage is now waiting in the wings. Conscious beings should eventually evolve to the place where they begin to actively shape the world, not for selfish personal ends, but wisely, responsibly, and for the good of the whole. Books like *The Celestine Prophecy* are not so far off. Fully conscious beings become stewards of the world because they 'know' that they are part of something larger. They serve themselves, their fellows, the biosphere and the larger process because everything is intertwined. Fully conscious beings become the ultimate agents of the evolutionary process because four billion years of learning has taught them to see how pieces fit. The fifth great stage is Integral Consciousness and global learning aimed at the greater good of the planet.

- **Shaping change.** In the beginning the universe found ways to organize shapes and networks which made energy flow faster.

- **Life-forms pursuing information.** In the second stage, the universe learned how to build systems that began to learn on their own. Life-forms followed information and moved about in hitherto unknown ways. The universe learned faster because living organisms learned faster and preserved more.

- **Brains organizing information into tapestries.** In the third stage, brains accelerated learning even more, and even more amazing behaviors emerged. Individual learning was now preserved in brain circuits etched by experience. Modeling allowed individual learning to be passed to others and preserved in habit patterns passed from generation to generation. The universe began to learn as never before because brains began to learn more intentionally and to preserve exquisite details of experience.

- **Communal learning via culture.** The fourth great stage of learning came with the human brain and society. In fourth-order organizations, such as science and human culture, learning moves beyond the individual's lifetime and is turned back on the environment. What is learned is how to restructure the environment itself, now with tools. The ability to learn intentionally and cooperatively makes learning rates explode.

Table 3. Four Stages of the Learning Universe.

* * *

We are the leading edge of a learning universe. We have the capacity and the need to help the world as ourselves. Still, apparently we aren't there yet. Rather, at the moment, we seem to be more of a threat to the world, than a caretaker. Hence, right now, the Learning Universe view seems a bit hard to swallow. The pragmatist looks around at the current violent, dysfunctional state of the world and doubts that a vision this gentle could have much basis in fact.

Chapter 7 deals specifically with the paradox of brilliant human beings who seem to thrive on destruction. But to understand why we are such a strange blend of killer and angel requires we understand the specifics of our brain and its evolution. That is the story next.

The Evolution of Humanity's Society of Mind

The concept of societies of mind is extremely important because it allows us to rethink human societies as a collective struggling to act as an intelligent whole. There is already ample reason to believe the analogy holds. Hence, as Gaia's James Lovelock says:

> What is remarkable about man is not the size of his brain, no greater than that of a dolphin, nor his loose incomplete development as a social animal, nor even the faculty of speech or his ability to use tools. Man is remarkable because by the combination of all these things he has created an entirely new entity. When socially organized and equipped with a technology even as rudimentary as that of a Stone Age tribal group, man has the novel capacity to collect, store, and process information, and then use it to manipulate the environment in a purposeful and anticipatory fashion. (1979, p.132)

Lovelock's point is simple. What is unique about humankind is that, *as a collective*, we gather, digest and apply information to help us survive and prosper like no other species. This is our evolutionary strategy. We are not swift of feet, strong of body, sharp of tooth or clever in niche finding. We can change our behavior dramatically and we are very, *very*, good at discerning patterns.

We bet our survival on behavioral flexibility and the pursuit of better ways of knowing. In the process, we gained dominance of the earth. And the one most overlooked fact is that now, as in the primordial beginning, creating better ways of knowing is a profoundly social event.

We've also seen this image before. I started this book with the image of a hive mind, a great web of humanity reaching a turning point in an on-going evolution of ideas. We are part of an invisible dynamic network that is struggling to learn, in ways often unknown to itself. The glimmering possibility is that this is the normal state of affairs. We belong to a vast human society of mind which digests billions of bits of information coming from billions of individual minds. Every once in a while, our hive mind begins to come to new conclusions. That is what is happening today.

There are concrete reasons for believing that human civilization is a powerful (if struggling) society of mind. This idea also provides an image of humankind which is both strikingly different and strikingly reasonable. It is not selfishness and killing which define us. We are an information pooling, picture-making cooperative which is centered on a quest to understand the world.

So, the idea that civilization is a struggling society of mind is not lightly based. The goal of this section is to lay out why it makes sense in concrete terms. I start with why the human brain has several personalities because of how punctuation has played out.

Our Three Brains

> ... the brain has followed a now familiar formula. It has been a cooperative effort between separate and relatively autonomous subsystems ... In this respect the brain follows the basic pattern for the entire human body, itself a cooperative venture between the living cells that make up its various organs ...   Allan Combs

Human beings have not one, but three brains, each of which appears to have been the result of separate bursts of evolutionary activity. This fact is very important to the story of humanity's society of mind because each of these brains comes with a personality. Hence, we are not the result of a unified brain, but of a society of three brains each with their own personality.

In the 1930s Swiss psychologist C.G. Jung noted that people have a committee of personalities inside their head, a cast of differing voices which often pull in different directions. Brain research now suggests there is a physical basis for at least some of these voices. Thus, each of our three brains has a great deal of self-sufficiency. Each appears to have its own type of intelligence, its own motor, memory and other functions and even its own peculiar sense of subjective experience.

Each new brain emerged on top of an earlier one, but underneath its predecessors still functioned and affected the whole.

Our three brain-personalities are particularly important because they affect our social relationships. Hence brains brought more than the ability to move legs and fins. They also brought complex interaction patterns between individuals, including nurturing, modeling, mating, self-defense and much more.

Our three brains are most important, however, because they represent three distinct survival strategies. Thus, each brain arose from pressures in particular evolutionary juncture and each personality reflects the strategy that successfully answered those pressures. We carry all three with us to this day.

Since these three brains and their personalities profoundly influence human society, one must understand them to understand it. So let us look more closely. The most famous description of our three brains comes from Paul MacLean's 1969 book *The Triune Brain*. He calls the three, the reptilian brain, the paleomammalian brain and the neomammalian brain.[1] Their personalities are as follows:

Crude ...

The *reptilian*, or the 'lizard brain' as it is sometimes called, is the core brain for all vertebrates from early reptiles on up to mammals. This brain is famous for routine, repetitive and instinctual behaviors. Stylized mating rituals, migratory behavior, imprinting, threat displays, fleeing and patterns of home-building are its forte. It is heavily involved with the autonomic nervous system including systems that regulate heart and respiratory rates, digestive functions, and bodily cycles such as sleep and sex.

What we should envision with this brain is a scurrying lizard, with flicking tongue, blinking eyes, and fixed patterns of behavior with little flexibility and no thought. Still, we should also realize that this brain is largely responsible for early vertebrates learning to live complex lives in complex environments, particularly dry land.

Warm ...

The *paleomammalian*, affectionately known as the 'furry mammal brain,' comes next. It was literally plopped on top of the lizard brain during a later burst of evolutionary activity.

The difference here is mainly emotion and behavioral flexibility. The lizard brain has a crude type of emotional system shared by fish and salamanders, but with the paleomammalian brain, emotion becomes much richer. This richness has two great benefits: faster learning and richer social relations. As neuropsychologist Allan Combs puts it:

> the unique quality of the mammal is its ability to experience emotion, and through it to benefit from personal experiences, retained as emotional reactions to predators, friendly members of the same species, and so on. It also allows close emotional bonding between mating partners, parents and infants, members of families and larger extended groups. (1995, p.41)

Thus, where the lizard brain tends to react rigidly and acquire new behaviors slowly, the furry mammal brain learns faster and reacts with more diverse and flexible behaviors. The icing on the cake is that new forms of emotional bonding support a richer, more coherent social life — and with it better social learning. Mammals nurture their young and cubs play together as youths. Both activities enhance learning.

Thoughtful ...
The third brain, the *neomammalian* or 'thinking brain,' is the most recent of all. It is found only in higher primates — most notably ourselves. It is famed for vastly improved pattern recognition and problem solving (including tool making). It is also notable for increasing flexibility. Thinking beings can invent their own behavioral patterns to a remarkable degree. In humans, this brain is the seat of complex cognitive skills such as language, reading, writing, arithmetic and beyond.

Since the thinking brain is so crucial to humankind's society of mind, let us take a closer look at how it came to be.

The Big-Brain Project

Our first brain, the lizard one, represented a phenomenal advance in coordination which allowed life to become more complex. Unfortunately, it was inflexible. Our next brain, the furry mammal one, was a great leap because richer emotion improved individual and social learning. Yet, at some point it too was not enough.

Why did we develop big — hyper-sensitive, pattern-recognizing — brains? Like many questions in science these days, this one is a topic of hot debate fueled by a flood of recent findings. I present here, not a final answer, but a budding theory of how our own big brains emerged in conjunction with legs, language, tools and environmental upheavals. The astonishing outcome was a society of mind such as the world has never known.

But, let us begin at the beginning. Four to six million years ago the apes that would become humankind came down from the trees and started walking on two legs.[2] Eventually they also began making tools and engaging in sophisticated information exchange (talking). This earned them the name hominid. Then, as the story goes, millennia of walking, talking, and tool-making accelerated brain growth, producing the well-known bulge of our big brains. Why did all this happen? One thing most researchers agree upon is that two-legged walking came first and led to the rest. But explaining walking is tough. As Stephen J. Gould once wrote:

> Upright posture is the surprise, the difficult event, [it involves] the rapid and fundamental reconstruction of our anatomy. The subsequent enlargement of our brain is ... secondary ... an easy transformation. (1980)

So why two legs? Early researchers believed that the first tool-making hominids evolved in South Africa about two million years ago and that they lived in open grasslands. Hence, the traditional Savannah theory holds that our ancestors descended from the trees as their habitat changed from forest to grassland. Adaptations to stable grasslands then produced bipedalism which allowed free use of the hands for tool making. The Savannah theory, however, is undergoing severe attacks as new evidence suggests that environmental shifts may have been more frequent and jarring than previously realized. Changes went not only from forest to grassland but from forests to lakes and back again, perhaps numerous times. For example, research at Olorgesailie in southern Kenya has uncovered evidence of dramatic environmental changes from 1.2 million to 500,000 years ago. The most noticeable changes are found in the structure of large lakes. Most early hominid skeletons have been found around such lakes.

What do lakes and frequent jarring shifts have to do with walking? Well, first the watery element fits with the Aquatic Ape theory of human origins first posed by Oxford University zoologist Sir Alister

Hardy in 1960.[3] This theory holds that early hominids lived in partially aquatic environments and that such environments produced walking as well as numerous other distinctive human features such as hairlessness, subcutaneous fat, refined finger control, ventro/ventral sex, and the ability to consciously control breathing (this last being a prerequisite to complex speech).

The aquatic explanation of walking is easy to understand. It is also supported by the only other example of upright walking. Hence, many animals stand up on two legs briefly, to reach food or look about, but only one other primate, the Proboscis monkey of Borneo, *walks* on two feet — and it learned to walk on two legs while crossing stretches of water between the mangrove trees in the swamp in which it lives. As the monkey travels through the swamp, its head has to be elevated while its back legs push. Water helps support weight during walking and eventually an upright posture evolves. Presumably, early hominids experienced similar aids and pressures.

Other human traits also fit a watery background. Thus, fat babies float; smooth hairless skin moves easily in water; and fine motor control is common in shallow feeders (for example, raccoons). Conscious breath control is necessary for swimming under water. Even the long Omega-3 fatty acids needed to make large brains are best derived from marine food chains which humankind shares with other big-brained mammals such as dolphins (who apparently went back to water completely).

So a watery background helps explain walking, better finger control, and precursors to talking. Frequent jarring changes then hearken to an even more important cause of our nature — the need to be *flexible*. Repeated climate change makes flexibility a crucial survival strategy with clear advantages over fixed or slowly changing responses. Discerning subtle patterns makes complete sense in this situation. We change our behavior by changing our mind. Collaborative learning also makes sense. The richer the perspectives, the richer (and more accurate) the resulting tapestry. The best way to survive frequent change is to pool information, synthesize it by communication and then change one's behavior based on a new view. This idea is becoming reasonable. As Richard Potts, an archeologist at the Smithsonian Institution in Washington, D.C. writes:

> The ratio of brain size to body size in early hominids had
> remained similar to the ratios for other primates. As a result of

repeated climate and habitat shifts, however, hominid brains
began to bulge ... This discovery dovetails with preliminary
evidence that stone-age groups responded to recurring crisis
situations by pooling information and making effective
collective decisions. (*Science News,* 1995 p.359)

Rethinking Human Nature

We can now reconstruct the origins of human nature from an interwoven perspective. Many threads came together to make us a talking,
tool-making, pattern-recognizing, information-sharing animal such as
the world had never seen.

Two of our brains, mammalian and thinking, spurred the transformation. The furry mammal brain produced the social bonding needed
for sharing and group learning. The neocortex began with our ape ancestors, but continual crises plus aquatic additions now paved the way
for a new burst of development. The picture-building process seen in
brains, thus, accelerates in human tribes. Where brains create rich
tapestries by gathering information from many cells, human societies
create tapestries by pooling information from many individuals.
Collecting information and developing pictures became a way of life
that defined human groups.

Not only did individual brains become astute at pattern-finding, but
pressure to collaborate pushed talking which, in turn, increased brain
development. Thus, pooling information improved talking and talking
led to better pooling. It was a circular, mutual-effect affair! It also led
to more complex social relationships and group abilities which grew
more sophisticated by the age.

Then too, that wonderful finger dexterity, born of shallow feeding,
began to be applied to tools. Where our lowest brain coordinates our
bodies, the thinking brain extends our bodies and our ability to act on the
world by inventing tools. Humankind began its epic journey as 'shaper of
the outside world' that would culminate in today's 'master of the universe'
mentality. What is often overlooked is that we have a two-way relationship
with our tools too. We build tools, but tools also shape human societies.
They extend what we can do, but they also tend to shape what we believe
— leading to the 'if all you have is a hammer' adage. Human societies
actually *co-evolve* with their tools.

Yet, of all the characteristics we possess, flexibility is the most important. Thus, our thinking brain has a paradoxical personality whose main characteristic is *ability to change itself based on the patterns it perceives*. This brain allow us to redefine our relationships with others and the world depending on the patterns it perceives. As a result, we build our societies out of what we think we know. We have come back to James Burke's thought — 'Knowing leads to doing!

Our new view of human nature is now complete. Human societies represent a major advance in learning, one that blended individual contribution and community commitment into a totally new form. Individuality brings richness through diversity of perspective. Emotional bonding brings sharing, caring and modeling. The combination makes human societies looser than insect societies such as ants, but closer than many mammals societies such as cows. (We are neither rigid automatons nor disinterested by-standers.)

Our great strategy lies in our ability to learn and to change ourselves via culture. We survived upheavals by changing ourselves rapidly. There is already evidence that Cro-Magnon Man, the direct ancestor of modern human beings, survived where Neanderthals did not because Cro-Magnon showed greater ability to change behavior in face of changing environment. It was the ability to change appropriately that counted, not brain size *per se* (this last is a materialist assumption).

* * *

A complex blend of upheavals and other conditions, thus, made us the leading edge of the learning universe. Talking, walking, finger dexterity, big-brains and close bonding eventually created a society of mind more subtle and powerful than any before or since. We became a pattern-recognizing, information-sharing animal such as the world had never seen — one that preserved lessons in highly-structured little vibrations called words. These vibrations became the most powerful mover of mass in the history of the world.

Nature was still not through, however. The next stage brought pressure for individual minds to develop some distance from the collective in which they lived. Such separation might seem at odds with community-building, but it actually makes sense. Rich tapestries come from diverse views. The unexpected implication here is that individuation is good for the community. It increases accuracy by increasing the richness of input.

The next great evolutionary thrust was the evolution of consciousness. It involved the long, slow birth of 'selves' which see themselves as separate and distinct from the whole. The up-side of this evolution is that individuals with distinct egos make richer contributions. The downside is that big egos have now become so self-absorbed that they do great harm to larger wholes at all levels from family to planet.

The Evolution of Human Consciousness

I do not propose to solve the enigma of the relationship of
consciousness to the brain ... My own view ... however,
places consciousness in a considerably larger context while
at the same time not denying its involvement at the level of
the brain.   Allan Combs

Hominids bring us to the beginning of complex minds and also to the glimmer of historical times. Cro-Magnon emerged 70,000 to 40,000 years ago and the great cave paintings about 20,000 years ago. Mesopotamian civilization and recorded history began about 6000 years ago (4000 BC). The gap between then and now is getting small. It is, therefore, time to leave the biological story and begin the journey to historical times and the kind of mind that experiences the world consciously. Consciousness researchers ask the delicate question: what *kind* of minds live inside big brains?

How did consciousness — defined in Webster's as, 'an inward sensibility of something' — come into being? Once multicellulars grew brains and sense organs like eyes, they could see their own bodies and the first crude awareness of self could have emerged. From this point of view even lizards have at least some form of consciousness. Still, most people skim past lizard-level consciousness in search of the more alluring question: what about our own?

The story of human consciousness too involves punctuation and cycles of co-evolution. Researchers base their theories of early stages on studies of cave paintings, burial practices, etc. and of later stages on writings, sculpture, philosophy. They also cross-check their theories by studying primitive peoples today who follow behavior patterns similar to ones seen long ago. For example, some remote tribes still have rituals similar to ones practiced by Cro-Magnon. Many insights into how consciousness changes come from studying peoples who act similarly today. The point is that, while the theories described here are clearly speculative, the sense that consciousness has evolved through stages is grounded in a lot of observation and evidence. It is not just New Age fantasy.

Gebser's Stages of Consciousness

What are the stages of consciousness? There are many theories. I use Swiss philosopher, Jean Gebser's theory of consciousness as described by complexity researcher Allan Combs in his book *The Radiance of Being*. The punctuated pattern should be familiar.

Gebser believed that consciousness evolved through stages. New forms emerged on top while underneath earlier forms still played a role. Each stage of consciousness has a distinctive perspective, personality and subjective experiences of the world. Each brings a different perception of time, space and of how individuals fit in the larger world. Finally, each stage also brings distinctive patterns of how people relate to each other. Hence, each implies a different kind of culture with a unique experience of the world.

Gebser described five major types of consciousness — *archaic, magic, mythical, mental,* and *integral* (see Table 4). Their history is as follows:

1. Archaic Consciousness. Archaic consciousness belongs to the time when our hominid ancestors were still at one with the natural world. Gebser often likened it to a state of deep, dreamless sleep. The self experiences itself as completely embedded in the world and is not aware of itself as separate. Humankind is said to live in perfect harmony with Nature and probably in complete identity with it.

Who had this type of consciousness? Perhaps all three-brained primates have this type of consciousness, certainly the very early hominids are candidates. Hence, the archaic state is meant for protohumans who did *not* exhibit a recognizably human culture (that is, with tools and language). *Australopithecus*, a vegetarian ape that foraged in Africa from five to one million years ago, for example, and Homo habilis who dates from about 4 to 1.5 million years ago probably had archaic consciousness. *Homo erectus*, 'the Peking Man' who lived from 1.5 million to 75,000 years ago, may have represented a

1. **Archaic**	Embedded in nature (little different from animals)
2. **Magical**	First symbols (greater separation from the world)
3. **Mythical**	First cities, first myths (also the Agrarian Revolution)
4. **Mental**	Individuation for richer contribution (also the Age of War)
5. **Integral**	Strong selves *and* strong bonds (not there yet ...)

Table 4. Gebser's Stages of Consciousness.

transitional case because hand axes found during their late period indicate that they were becoming adept tool makers.

2. Magical Consciousness. The next stage of consciousness, magical consciousness, brought language, adept tool use and also a new form of imagination seen in the beginnings of ceremony and symbolism.

Neanderthals, some 500,000 years ago, are thought to have had magic consciousness. They made a variety of tools and engaged in speech (albeit a crude speech, judging from throat development). More importantly Neanderthals were also the first to bury their dead ceremoniously as if to issue them into an afterlife. Bodies were often placed in sleeping postures, legs curled up and head cushioned on one arm, or in fetal postures, as if to suggest a sleep from which one might awaken or a hope of a rebirth. In some cases whole families have been found with a man and a woman placed heads together and children at the woman's feet. Some Neanderthal finds even show evidence of religion in the form of bear worship.

These kinds of ceremonial practices mark a change from earlier times. Many scholars believe they signal a budding awareness of self as separate from nature, a form of individuation. This awareness brought a new concern with what happened to individuals even in death — hence new care with burials.

The new awareness also brought a new concern about how to influence an increasingly separate world. Magic consciousness thus also brings humankind's first attempts to manipulate the world through symbols. Magical consciousness gets its name because the first symbols were used for magical substitution. For example, paintings of animals in the cave sanctuaries such as Lascaux and Les Trois Frères, have been repeatedly struck by stone projectiles, presumably spears used to kill the animal magically before the real event. In short, just as voodoo practitioners hope to kill people by sticking pins in symbolic substitutes (dolls), so early man apparently tried to influence the killing of real animals by jabbing painted ones.

Gebser believed that all magic started with symbolic substitution of one object for another. Yet, we must go slowly here. People in earlier stages of consciousness experienced the world very differently than most modern people do today. To understand magic consciousness one must realize that, in this stage, symbol and actual are experienced as *equally real*. Thus, when Pygmy tribes in the Congo kill pictorial animals and actual animals in exactly the same manner, they experience both hunts as being equally real. Whenever we insist on taking our beliefs and views as equal to reality, we too are harkening back to this time.

Gebser believed that magical consciousness reached its heights with Cro-Magnon and his cave paintings. Yet, this stage (and all the others) is still buried within us. This has both pros and cons. Magic consciousness is crude by current standards, but it also has a richness of community which is still buried within us today. As Combs says:

[Magical consciousness brings] a deep sense of community ...
of belonging to a family or any other group of people. Music,
with its ability to transport us out of the moment, is also a
product of magic consciousness. On the negative side, there's a
tendency for the magic structure to hold too tightly to other
persons, sometimes refusing to allow them space to breathe.
There's also a very dangerous tendency to follow the drumbeat
of collective ideological movements, religious or politically
totalitarian, as was experienced so widely before the Second
World War and all too much today. The only remedy to these
tendencies is to shift one's attention to the more recent
structures of consciousness. (1995, p.102)

Cro-Magnon, however, was probably also a transitional case and 20,000 BC probably marks the beginning of a slow transition to a new phase. This time witnessed an acceleration of tool making and social development which led to the kind of societies which mirror our own.

3. Mythical Consciousness. The next stage, mythical consciousness, was certainly in full sway by the time of the Neolithic farming revolution, which is usually given as around 14,000 to 8,000 BC.

Nomadic life was giving way to stationary communities. Sophisticated speech was now the norm and so too were sophisticated tools. Animals were domesticated, crops were planted and villages blossomed into cities. Staying in one place allowed new technologies to flourish. Crafts like pottery and weaving emerged alongside the wheel, boats, musical instruments, and painting. New social specialties from policeman to priest grew with them. Religious symbolism became sophisticated and focused on the idea of fertility and bolstering life. The concept of law was invented and also central political control. In short, human societies began to look much like our own.

By 6500 BC an entire Old European civilization based on agriculture was well established throughout Eastern Europe and the Near East. This society brought commerce, metallurgy, new forms of artistry and even early forms of script. It probably also marked the height of mythical consciousness.

Mythical consciousness gets its name because this was the time of myths. Language was now sophisticated and the telling of tales was beginning. These stories allowed information to be preserved and passed along through time. Myths also helped usher in a new sense of time that is at least somewhat linear. This was probably not the modern sense of time, but what Gebser calls *temporicity*, the feeling of being *in* a certain time, for example, during the reign of a certain king. Hence, mythic tales take place 'once upon a time' or 'long ago and far away' and have a sense of an enchanted time that has long since escaped the world of day-to-day affairs.

This sense of enchantment also fed another theme The imagination that began in magical consciousness ripened into a deeper reverence for nature and the life force. Spirituality took a theme appropriate to the new agricultural society. This theme was the bountiful Earth/ Mother Goddess.

The Goddess image was reflected everywhere. Thus, archeologists studying this era have uncovered large numbers of female figurines standing or seated, usually naked, often pregnant, and sometimes holding or nursing a child. But we must go slowly here lest we impose our own biases on these people too. Many experts argue that exaggerated breasts and pregnant abdomens symbolize fertility and were used to beg the Goddess for help with crops. No doubt this was partly the case. Yet, other researchers say that the people of mythical times felt a more present force. They were, after all, still immersed in nature and in tune with it in ways we no longer are. This meant their experience of spirituality was more direct. Hence, as American mythologist Joseph Campbell says, Goddess images point 'not to a new theory about how to make beans grow but to an actual experience in the depth of that *mysterium tremendum* that would break upon us even now if it were not so wonderfully masked.'

Hence, Goddess images probably represent recognition of and gratitude to the life force at work in the world. UCLA archaeologist Marija Bimutas calls it, 'the celebration of life energy.' We might call it the first articulated awareness of the Great Ordering Oneness.

Yet, this awareness was also blended with a new step toward individuation. No longer utterly embedded in Nature or lost in the tribe, humankind became a child of nature, at once awed by and grateful to the life force. Mythic consciousness thus brought humankind's first covenant with nature. This age was 'the time when humankind discovered its own soul and that of the world at large,' as Combs says. It expressed both in the worship of life.

Mythic culture thus brought the first high forms of technological, artistic and spiritual culture. It brought the main inventions of civilization from weaving and the wheel to cities. It climaxed in the great artistry and technology of ancient Greek civilizations, such as the Minoans on Crete (circa 3000 BC to 1500 BC). One might have imagined that this wondrously creative and soulful age would have simply continued to ever greater heights. But times change and with them humankind.

The deep mythic experience, formed during the neolithic period carried over into ancient civilizations such as Sumer, Egypt, and Homeric Greece. But, by then, signs of a new mode of consciousness were emerging, one with a greater sense of individuality and ego. Then too, there was a crisis of some sort. Somewhere between 4000 and

2000 BC, the Old Society civilization underwent a major transformation. Apparently consciousness changed with it.

4. Mental Consciousness. The next stage was mental consciousness, the time when thinking came into its own. Hence where stone tools signaled the change from archaic to magical consciousness, so cognitive tools highlighted the change from mythic to mental consciousness. Number systems began to appear in the Middle East about 3500 BC and by about 3100 BC writing was well developed. Time as the linear quantity we know today began, along with recorded history itself. The first calendars from the Middle East are found around 2800 BC. The first libraries are found in Egypt around 2500 BC.

Writing gives researchers a better glimpse into changing experiences. The Epic of Gilgamesh written about 2700 BC, for example, suggests self-reflection is becoming strong. Having failed in his quest for immortality Gilgamesh experiences an almost existential crisis, an exquisitely personal emergency not seen in recordings of more ancient myths.

The new stage, of course, also brought a new emphasis on thinking — especially as separate from feeling. Not surprisingly, this new type of consciousness places the sense of self somewhere in the head. This contrasts with earlier tradition seen in ancient Greeks and Native Americans who experience their essence as being in the heart.

Centering oneself in one's head brings, in turn, what Gebser called a *perspectival* element of consciousness. We perceive the world as if it comes in through our eyes and informs a 'self' which is located in the head right behind those eyes. This new perspective also reflects another major development, the birth of highly individuated egos. No longer embedded in Nature or the tribe, the separate, self-aware, and often self-serving ego emerges.

Evolving slowly since the time of Egypt, evidence of the new mental consciousness is strong by the classical Greek period (circa 600 to 400 BC) which brought us science, philosophy and drama. Socrates likened the soul with pure thought and by 480 BC Parmenides would say: 'For thinking and being is one and the same.'

Strongly associated with reason and critical thinking, mental consciousness had arrived. By the time of the Roman Empire some five hundred years later, the ego had become a highly individualistic, self-reflective center of inner life. Thus, where classical Greek statuary pursued universal perfection, busts of Roman citizens became studies in character and attempts to capture individual uniqueness. Autobiographical documents such as personal diaries also appear in Rome. Historian Morris Berman who traces the development notes that periods of strong self awareness are usually accompanied by sharp increases in the use of mirrors. As he says, 'Mirrors became so popular in Rome that they were even owned by servants; Seneca reported his disgust at one Hostius Quadra, who had himself constantly surrounded by mirrors.'

We are still in the age of Mental consciousness, but the next stage, Integral consciousness, is simmering. It is simmering because the current age is exhausted and a new way is needed. Let me take a moment, therefore, to expand on the problems that Mental consciousness is facing.

The Problem with Rational Thought

Mental consciousness begins the story of rational thinking — but, it is not the story one might expect. Gebser stressed that rational thought was not the pinnacle of mental consciousness. Indeed, he described it as an inferior form, a distortion of the true mental miracle.

Gebser said that each form of consciousness had an authentic and a distorted form (or as he said, an *efficient* and *deficient* form). The authentic form of mythic consciousness, for example, created myths which encapsulated deep insight in metaphoric form. We have a hard time grasping the deep meaning and hidden accuracy of such myth because we no longer understand the symbolism. The result is the distorted form of mythic consciousness — myths as tall tales. The stories of the Greek gods, for example, were eventually told as colourful yarns not intended to convey real meaning.

The authentic form of mental consciousness is *menos:* balanced thought which evolves through discussion. The object of balanced thought is to improve through dialogue and continual rethinking. Socrates' dialectics and Plato's *Dialogues* are examples. Rational thinking is a distorted form because it was characterized by *ratio,* or as Combs says, 'by divisive, immoderate, hair-splitting reason.' The entire object of rational thought becomes to pick things apart, often as a destructive act. The quest to refine understanding is lost to obsessive love of haranguing over microscopic bits. Small wonder Gebser saw it as inferior. Understanding its inferior nature is of importance to our times because this hair-splitting thought is often held up as the one true form of thinking. Gebser writes:

> *Ratio* must not be interpreted ... as 'understanding' or
> 'common sense,' *ratio* implies calculation and, in particular,
> division ... This dividing aspect inherent in *ratio* and
> Rationalism ... is consistently overlooked, although it is of
> decisive importance to an assessment of our epoch. (Cited in
> Combs, 1995, p.110.)

Rational thinking, therefore, is divisive and often destructive. If you add egos which can become big and self-absorbed you can see some of the threads which lead to a change. Self-centeredness and focus on division tends to thwart balanced, evolving thought *(menos)*. Instead, one gets rigidity and an inability to go beyond one's own perspective instead. Human learning shrivels.

These kinds of distortion help push a new stage of consciousness which Gebser believed was in the offing. On the other hand, a more pressing problem is simmering.

The Great Transition: — from Collaboration to Coercion

Mental consciousness came with a new society, of course. The catch is that the epoch which brought it is best described as the Age of War (or, if you prefer, the Age of Empire-building). Hence, Mythic culture was shunted underneath and a new more violent culture rose in its place.

The Neolithic culture of Old Europe and the Middle East flourished in peace and prosperity for thousands of years. Then, in a crisis that would mirror that of many civilizations yet to come, it ended in a relatively abrupt, mysterious and violent manner. No one really knows what happened. Theories abound. Natural disasters may have been part of the problem with tectonic movement creating new rounds of floods and earthquakes. The story of Atlantis, for instance, is thought to come from a volcano and tidal wave that destroyed an Old Society civilization on the island of Thera in the Aegean circa 1628 BC. The other major theory is that the pre-ancient world was rocked by waves of barbarian invasions from nomadic Indo-European (Kurgan) tribes from the steppes to the east.[4] Whatever the cause, disaster and disruption appear to have brought a period of cultural regression and stagnation.

Villages vanished as did painted pottery, frescoes, shrines, sculptures and script. The development of Old Society civilization came to a halt.

Whatever the cause, the most notable effect of the crisis period of 4,000 BC to 2000 BC was a large and distinctive shift in the direction of war. Metallurgy, for example, had been known for some time, but Old Society metal implements were religious, domestic and agricultural. Weapons of war were distinctly absent. The 3500–2500 BC time period, however, brought the Bronze Age and with it bronze weapons such as daggers, maceheads, and thin sharp axes. These appear first along what are believed to be the routes of barbarian attack — hence the theory that invaders brought change.

But, bronze weapons were just one symptom. The whole culture changed. Burial practices, for example, also changed. Large-boned male skeletons began being accompanied not only by weapons and riches but also by the skeletons of sacrificed women.

Mental consciousness was thus forged in the fires of what I call the Great Transition, a shift from a social system based on the life-force and mutual contribution to one based on war and domination. The contrast here is important. The original Neolithic culture was agricultural and egalitarian. Its people often lived in large townships where land and all principal means of production — for example, animals, plows and looms — were held in common. Social power was viewed as a responsibility, a trusteeship used for the benefit of all. Elder women or the heads of clans administered the distribution of the fruits of the Earth which were seen as belonging to all members of the group.

In short, the Old Society had a fundamentally cooperative social organization and absence of fortifications and weapons attests to the fact that they lived in peaceful coexistence. It was this peaceful society which brought many of the core inventions of civilization as we know it — from the wheel and metallurgy to farming, pottery, music and religion. The palaces, arts and technologies — including indoor plumbing — of Minoan civilization show the heights to which it led. I call it a *mutualist* society because it is based on mutual benefit between members.

This cooperative culture was replaced by a socially-stratified patriarchal society that exalted war. The contrast in ideology is striking. Where weapons were nonexistent in Old Society imagery, the New Society symbols were the dagger and battle-axe. Where Old Society religion focused on the cycle of birth, death, and regeneration, embodied in an Earth/Mother Goddess, the New Society worshipped virile, heroic warrior gods that forced their bloody will on the world. The biggest difference of all, however, was in social organization. Riane Eisler, perhaps the most famous researcher of the Great Transition, calls this a *dominator* society, characterized by:

- A hierarchical social structure dominated by strong-man élites
- Accumulation of wealth for status
- Coercive social power
- Private ownership of land and means of production
- Slavery and human sacrifice
- The reduction of women and children to the property of men
- A central focus on war and militarism.

Dominator beliefs soon made struggle and war the order of the day. The Tigris-Euphrates valley, an invasion crossroads in Eisler's terms, spawned a series of aspiring empires — Sumerian, Babylonian, Assyrian and Hittite — known for their bloody ways. Sumer is often credited with inventing organized warfare as we know it. Yet, each of these societies also had a base in life-centered times and a memory of mutualism in a time before. Sumer is a good example. Sumer's early legends refer to the Supreme Deity as 'Queen of Heaven' or 'the Mighty Lady, the Creatress.' Written about 2300 BC, the Urukagina Reforms of Sumeria even includes a requirement that food grown on Temple land be used, not just for priests, but for those in need '*as it had been in the times of old.*'

These kinds of contrasting before-and-after images have led some scholars to argue that the Garden of Eden is a myth about the Fertile Crescent. The harmony and abundance of early times was replaced with the baleful struggle for existence in a time of subjugation and endless war.

Mental consciousness, thus, grew up in a battle between radically different cultures. This struggle is particularly apparent in spirituality, one of the key aspects of consciousness. Hence the new culture brought Gods who exalted war. Religion also became part of the political control structure. As a matter of expedience, the king often served as head priest or even proclaimed himself a God. Religious hierarchies that pulled resources up and issued commands down became common. The new culture also remade older Gods in the new order's image. Struggles between the life-force Goddess of the old religion and new, violent, vengeful, male insurgents such as Horace, Marduk, Zeus, and Yahweh ensued. The recording of ancient traditions, thus, often includes a blending of old and new myths as priests rewrote ancient stories. This is clearly seen in the Bible with its conflicting images of a compassionate and a vengeful god.

More about these two cultures later. Meanwhile their struggles set the stage for mental consciousness and all the history to follow. We are still in this Age. For the last five thousand years human societies have been centered on war, empire-building and domination. The social structures listed above remain and so do many of the violent cultural ways. Human societies have not always been this way, but most are today.

5. Integral Consciousness. Mental consciousness is still dominant, but there are problems. Indeed, many of today's problems can be traced to deficient aspects of mental consciousness.

Thus, the down side of the strong ego is the grandiose ego with its need to be the center of attention. The down side of balanced evolving thought (*menos),* is divisive, hair-splitting rationalism. Add a society centered on dominator imperatives and one gets the two egos of modern times: the embattled, lonely ego, and the arrogant, self-centered ego which sees the world through the lens of conquest and domination. Naturally enough, individuals and communities both fail with alarming frequency. Gebser's description of failure, thus, echoes those of many observers of the Modern condition.

> Isolation is visible everywhere, isolation of individuals, of entire nations and continents ... in the political arena in the form of ideological monopolistic dictatorship, in everyday life in the form of immoderate, 'busy' activity devoid of any sense-direction or relationship to the world as a whole; isolation of thinking in the form of the deceptive dazzle of premature judgments or hypertrophied abstraction devoid of any connection with the world. And it is the same with mass phenomena: overproduction, inflation, the proliferation of political parties, rampant technology, atomization in all forms. (Cited in Combs, 1996)

Unfortunately, since mental consciousness still dominates, many academics view it as the highest and final form of consciousness. Gebser, however, saw things differently — in part because he had lived through the worst effects of the calamitous twentieth century.

Born to an aristocratic family in Poland in 1905 and studying in Berlin until encountering Nazi Brownshirts in 1933, Gebser had little hope for a world controlled by men's egos. In the winter of 1933, however, he was struck by a realization that would become the core of his life's work. This realization was that a new and radically different form of consciousness was beginning to emerge. He believed this form of consciousness, *Integral consciousness*, had the potential to transform the fabric of civilization from top to bottom just as mental consciousness had done in its time.

Gebser spent many years charting evidence that Integral consciousness was emerging. His book, *The Everpresent Origin,* details that evidence in a impressive array of cultural forms including physics, mathematics, biology, sociology, philosophy, jurisprudence, music, painting, and literature. For instance, Gebser believed Integral consciousness brought a growing ability to make multiple view points appear as integral wholes. He saw this new ability evident in the paintings of Pablo Picasso and Paul Klee, for example. It suggested a new freedom from possessive, ego-based consciousness. The new consciousness also brought a new sense of time as a tangible experience, and not the abstract quantity known since the age of Newton. Gebser pointed to the works of writers such as T. S. Eliot, Hölderlin, and Rilke as evidence of this new sense of time. Born of World War I's lost generation, these writers cherished the reality of each moment, thus generating a revolutionary new fullness of existence.

Paradoxically, while time became more tangible, the experience of reality also became more fluid, or as Gebser called it, *diaphanous.* Using the Buddhist term *Void,* Gebser described this new experience as 'a spiritual transparency by which we experience the whole almost as the whole lives through us.' He argued that this transparent quality came from a new spiritual awareness which was again grounded in felt experience of the creative force which permeates the world.

This new spiritual awareness was important. Mental consciousness had brought institutionalized religion heavily involved in social control. Such religions invariably moved toward increasingly rigid and often hair-splitting beliefs that smothered the spiritual awareness from which all true religions emerge. Integral consciousness brought a new spiritual depth, one which contained a solid clarity missing in earlier forms. This clarity was supported by a more integral reason and new scientific abilities to apprehend the design in which humankind is embedded. Thus, no longer an awed child or an arrogant adolescent, humankind returns to its spiritual roots, now with a more lucid awareness of the *mysterium tremendum.*

Gebser saw a danger, however. Powerful contact with spiritual roots often left soulful selves lost in the light. These souls follow blindly, without judging ideas critically or cross-checking their validity, these last traits being mental consciousness' great strength. Thus, Integral consciousness had a deficit form, *diaphainon*, a shining through of spiritual light which lacked substance.

Well-meaning New Age romantics, filled with the light, but unable to separate quality from quackery, are an example of *diaphainon.* Unfortunately, the lack of grounding makes this kind of spirituality a natural feeding ground for charlatans, megalomaniacs, and psychopaths in many guises. The rise of charismatic cults producing horrific ends in this century is a sign of *diaphainon's* inability to discern. Jim Jones, David Karesh, Aum Shinrikiyo — the list is long. Charismatic leaders' ability to play on blind passion, is one reason that it is important to keep the new vision well-grounded.

*   *   *

Gebser hoped that the twentieth century's great calamities were part of the birth struggle of a new way. He viewed the outcome as uncertain, however. Hence, though he believed humankind's only hope lay in the embryonic new consciousness, he found that most people were still mired in egoistic, rationalistic consciousness and that the power structures that supported these traits still seemed secure. As he said:

> ... the coming decades will decide whether a fundamental
> transformation will occur during the next two generations or
> not for the next two millennia.

The Evolution of Consciousness Revisited

Gebser's work helps us see that the evolution of consciousness is not a figment of New Age imagination. Whether you believe his theory in detail or not, this and other research makes it clear that changes have taken place *inside* our big beautiful brains. Consciousness changes are directly relevant to the kinds of cultures human beings produce.

The contrast between Integral and Mental consciousness also helps us see our crisis more clearly. Individuation enriches the community, but the pendulum has swung too far. Modern individuals often lose all sense that they are contributing to anything larger than themselves — a predicament enshrined in the image of selfish genes. Small wonder fragmentation now plagues the end-of-the-millennium world. As biologist David Sloan Wilson says, 'Western societies seem to spawn far more self-absorption than sacrifice for any greater good.'

Self-absorption among some, however, spawns the opposite among many. Frightened and alone selves often fall prey to blind, yearning need. They willingly submerge their identities to charismatic leaders and commit atrocities — usually in the name of community and soul.

Add the centrality of war and you get the modern world. The age of Mental consciousness has left us (1) brilliant but disconnected, (2) powerful but vicious, (3) antagonistic and often self-destructive.

This list helps us understand the direction of the return swing. Learning is enhanced by strong selves *and* strong bonds. The two must go together. Strong selves without strong bonds produce self-absorbed egos who ravage society and the world. Strong bonds without a strong self is the basis of pathological conformity. Integral consciousness must have both because either side without the other can lead to disaster — a society with very little group intelligence and a lot of destructive tendencies.

A New Look at the Learning Universe

The story of the stars, that of life, of human beings, and of thought, are one and the same story.   Yves Coppens

We are back to our own time, now with a new sense of how our minds fit in evolution and history. Thanks to the Enlightenment, rational thought spread across the world along with public education. Human societies of mind now reach phenomenal levels, best seen in that most rapidly-learning society of mind, science. On the other hand, big egos and the idea that war is central to the world also leave us ever-floundering on the edge of extinction. How can we achieve a more viable way? The next section explores some of the obstacles to human learning in detail. Meanwhile, let me close with a review.

Clockwork thinkers were apt to argue that life was an anomaly going nowhere. Consciousness was merely the latest pin-stripe on the lumbering automaton that selfish genes call home. An alternative view is emerging, however.

Just how differently might our descendants view the world? Perhaps they will believe that humankind's great strategy is a mind one. Our inquisitive, collaborative nature was forged in a caldron of crisis. From this came our one defining task — 'knowing and doing' in ever better forms.

Then too, perhaps our descendants will believe that the Great Ordering Oneness gave us consciousness that we might consciously aid in the project of creating an ever-more harmonious, well-flowing world. After all, when mind is seen as a project of the world (and not just a human quirk), then one has to wonder whether the ability to see so far has some aim beyond, say, making money.

And so the noble thought. We were born of a universe which is driven to learn and this urge is implanted deeply in us. Following this urge is what makes us who we are. Following this urge *together* has made us the most remarkable creatures on the face of the earth. It is time we started using those big beautiful brains to envision something wiser and more loving than parochial self-interest and quality through war.

Humankind is not a finished product. Our ultimate place in history remains to be seen. Our existential question looms large. Yet, there is reason for hope. We can remake ourselves rapidly. That is what culture is for. We have done so many times before. So while our straits are dire, our potential is still great. If anything emerges from the ideas in this chapter, I hope it is that humankind's strategy is *learning*, done in community and aimed at wellbeing — our own, our society's and that of the world with which we are so tightly bound.

PART III

THE HUMAN PREDICAMENT

The only devils in the world are those running around in our own hearts — and that is where all our battles ought to be fought.

Mahatma Gandhi

CHAPTER 6

THE NATURE OF HUMANITY
AND THE WORLD

*It is the customary fate of new truths to begin as heresies
and to end as superstitions.*   T.H. Huxley

Every once in a while, an old way of looking at the world begins to
fail. That which it cannot see starts to become a problem. That which
it says is enough, turns out not to be. At such times, accepted truths
return to their original status — fallible theories. Slowly a new set of
visionaries step in and make progress. People struggling with the
puzzle in front of them, find themselves contributing to a much larger
whole. This is how Big Change happened four hundred years ago. It
seems to be happening again.

When new insights finally start coming together, change seems
abrupt. As if out of the blue, one sees a new picture. As if out of the
blue, the old picture begins to seem absurd. In 1632, when the
medieval system was beginning to fail, Galileo Galilei wrote an
incendiary little book called *Dialogue Between the Two Chief Systems
of the World.* It outlined all the reasons why there was an old and a
new way of looking at the world — and why the new was obviously
superior.

It is time to have history repeat here too. We need to see that there
is an old and a new scientific view of the world — and that the new
one is superior. We need to see this for a very specific reason. Just as
at the crumbling of the medieval view, many of our current ways are
not working. We pollute the planet and seem unable to stop. Our economic systems are often great on paper, but dismal in real life, with
millions without proper food, shelter, education or opportunity. Our
communities and families lie in tatters and life is often frenetic and
empty. Many believe that if the current round of 'knowing' keeps up,

we will destroy ourselves — socially, politically, economically and spiritually — probably in the near future.

Failed webs and unraveling social fabrics give rise to a turning time. If we are lucky, a new type of knowing will arise and with it a new civilization. What will it be like?

Deep Ecology

Scientists see in the process of evolution a forward march,
not toward more destructive competition, but toward more
foresight, insight, wisdom, and love. These persons ...
believe that the trend from the material to the spiritual,
from the amoeba to man, will inevitably continue toward
superior heights of love and wisdom, however, threatening
present developments on earth may appear to us now.

Eric Chaisson, Physicist

In 1950 most educated people looked out on a clockwork world. Progress was being pushed by technology. The object of the game was to win! ... or, alternatively, to conquer, dominate and control. Men were economic beasts whose quality was marked by money. Life was going nowhere in a universe without design. Yet, the horror that Western civilization experienced in the first half of the century, eventually mellowed into a soft emptiness with a hole in the middle.

In 2050, most educated people will probably look out on a very different world. A Dynamic Web World will differ from the machine world in many specific ways. (Appendix B summarizes some of these.) Yet, what most people want to know is how the new world will feel.

In its simplest form, the new science is about seeing everything as an ecology. Your body is an ecology — an energy-driven web of chemicals and cells working together for balance, harmony and the common good. An economy is an ecology, which may work or not. The world is a fractal of ecologies, nested spheres of life, biosphere and societies of mind. Furthermore, the biggest of these ecologies gave us birth. Most of what we see is the result of an unfathomably intricate process which the ancients called the Great Ordering Oneness.

The ecological vision being born is thus vastly more profound than the environmental version which gave us the term. Philosophers call this type, deep ecology. It implies awareness that the Great Ordering Oneness created us and is with us now, as long ago.

This profound ecology renews images and vows that are as old as the hills. We again find ourselves embraced by a great mystery, more awesome than we can fathom and yet more creative than we have dreamed. Energy binds us to the biosphere and all things high and low. Learning to survive and prosper in this world has a lot to do with learning to live in sympathy with the web, up and down the line. Thoughts like these have been echoed by every great religion and culture for thousands of years.

Human nature is also rethought in an old, yet new way. Our ancestors realized long ago that mind is what makes us special. We are now beginning to understand why. If we follow energy delicately, we find that the same process that created life also created mind. The universe itself is embroiled in a search for better ways. Here humanity's great strategy is the pursuit of understanding — a project done best in community where tapestries are rich. Here our drive is clear. Learn *better* ways! No model is final. Learn with your fellows. Diversity makes us wise. Find a coherent role. Build a coherent world. The call echos from all sides.

In this view too, love is part of our brain. It is not only natural, it is crucial to the bonding to each other and the greater task that we need to survive. It is necessary to health, sanity and a better way of being. It is, as the sages say, the more advanced strategy. If we used it and our big brains more, we might just blossom into the majestic phenomenon we have the potential to be.

Today, therefore, we face a web view of the world which is radically new and remarkably old. What does it look like? Table 5 (see pp.268–9) sums up the scientific view now visible on the horizon.

The Lessons of Dynamic Evolution

If the cosmology listed here were to take root, the society which would arise would, no doubt, be much different from the one we have today. Yet, the view listed above is still too general to help us build a workable new society. Therefore, let me highlight the three key lessons of dynamic evolution:

A Creative Universe

There is a creative force at work in the cosmos. Scientists can now describe the physical paths of the invisible hand. The sun pours energy over us and the universe expanding from the Big Bang presses the cosmos as a whole. As long as such pressures exist, the universe in general and our world in particular will be creating order, little dynamic dances which seek out better ways to flow. We and all that we see are the result of this creative drive.

The One is Many and the Many are One

The ancients used this phrase to convey deep meaning, we can use it to convey physical meaning. All forms of being are part of one process. They are differentiated aspects that emerge from, contribute to and then recede back into an ongoing flow. Entity and field are inseparable and co-effecting. The two are inter-playing aspects of one thing.

Deep Ecology and the Rediscovery of Ancient Contemplations

The inseparability of all things takes ecology to a deeper level. It is not just that living things are curiously interconnected. Our connectivity and our existence, each and all, are part of an unfolding process which created us, directs us and to which we contribute. Ancient ideas return in new light. 'In us, of us, and more than us, all at the same time' – the words are mystical, the meaning is real.

Becoming Members instead of Masters

This vision also implies that, though we may be the leading edge of our own small pond, we are not the center, the power, the end-all of Being. We are members of a community of Being with rights, privileges, duties, and conditions of membership. We are part of a chain of Being that will not end with us. We have a role, as all members do. If we care to continue, the trick to continued existence is clearly in going with the process, not just ourselves. Thanks to Chaos, we also see that there are definite limits to our ability to know and control. The implication here is that humankind will always remain a member of the world, not its absolute master.

A Co-Evolving Universe

We are members of a creative unfolding, based in simple local actions but also of infinite interwoven complexity. Immeasurably small differences will keep evolution forever beyond our control. Yet, while we cannot be masters of this process, we are not slaves to it either. We co-create this unfolding. Each living moment arises out of a creative act played out in millions of places all over the globe. Furthermore, everyday activity, in all its microscopic uniqueness, is important in a way classical science never imagined. Subtle causality fills the world. Each of us registers in the great mystery of the world. Buddhists, thus, call our relationship to the world a 'dependent co-arising.'

A Cooperative Universe

In a web world, cooperation is the central path of evolution. The way you increase ability is to build new forms out of old by collaborating in ever more intricate ways. Specialize and integrate!

A Universe in which Integrity counts

Integrity is an interesting word. It comes from the same root as 'integral,' meaning *whole*. To have integrity, then, means to act in ways that sustain and nourish the whole. Once beings become bound in collaboration, the concept of integrity takes on new meaning. Members need each other to survive. To act in ways which harms the larger whole – whether society or planet – is to undermine one's own well-being. This is the deep meaning of committed collaboration. In an interwoven world, integrity and commitment to the common good are crucial.

A Learning Universe

In a web world, learning is a process going on all around us. Our own struggle to learn makes sense as part of this. We now stand on top of a long ladder of learning with a new form of Integral Consciousness possibly at hand. If we become aware of the profundity of our embedding and the benefits of living in sympathy with the web, we may yet become the wonder that the Great Ordering Oneness gave us the potential to be.

Table 5. Web World — A 21st Century Cosmology.

- *Learning* — The universe itself is in the business of finding better ways. Mind, from cell to human, is part of this project. Humankind is the penultimate learning system on the planet.
- *Collaboration* — Collaboration is the best way to survive and thrive in a web world. Learning itself is done best in groups.
- *Intricacy* — There are energy rules behind organization and change. These include the S-curve, the complexity catch and the need for periodic reorganization. The concept of intricacy helps us see that the way to stay sound is to nourish the fine-grained structure which lets a society flow. The challenge of intricacy is to keep smallness under an ever-growing umbrella of connective tissue.

All three of these lessons are intertwined. In the human condition, a more intricate social system supports a more collaborative learning system. Small entwined pods of intelligence work together for the common good. For this to work, information and resources must flow throughout.

Unfortunately, clockwork thinking has been blind to all of these lessons. As a result we learn poorly, we collaborate poorly and we regularly destroy our own best connections, the fine-grained ones. Failure in all three now leaves us hanging on the edge

This brings me back to the beginning of the book. Virtually all of today's downfalls come from our view of the world. We are like our ancestors. The cycle is complete. Societies fail when a pumped up sense of correctness keeps them from dealing with the misery and dysfunction which is building anew. Habit and entrenched power block productive change. Yet, if we do not invent a better way, our society will crumble.

Today's beautiful vision, thus, comes with some ominous overtones. If we are going to survive our times, we need to invent some new ways. Since issues play out everywhere — in politics, economics, and spirituality as well as science — we are going to be reinventing in parallel. Luckily, the hive mind has been at work. Rethinking is already in progress in fields like education, economics, politics, urban planning, sociology and the like. The next chapters explore some of these endeavors.

We are also going to have to take the lessons of dynamic evolution seriously. The rest of this chapter lays the groundwork for seriousness by exploring two key issues more thoroughly. The first is the changing view of human nature. The second is the role of intricacy and evolution simmering underneath. First, our nature.

Rethinking Human Nature

In the clockwork view, we were mostly a result of selfish genes. Nastiness was fixed centrally in our nature. In the web view, human beings are complex, as playful and loving as we are competitive and self-serving. Furthermore, mind is central to our nature. We are much more wide-ranging and innovative than anything stored in our genes.

This contrast of views, however, is not specific enough to help us deal with social realities. The web view is also a bit too sweet. If we are to survive our times, we must also understand the dark side of human nature which has plagued us these many years. Selfishness, cruelty, empire-building, enslavement and destructiveness: if we do not understand these, we cannot hope to avoid them.

Everyone can see this dark side. It is the crux of a great deal of history. Darwinian theory dealt with it by putting it at the center of evolution. It said that war and selfishness were at the center of nature's plan. The unusual levels of cruelty and organization which human beings bring to the project are merely the result of nature's fine tuning.

The web view deals with our dark side differently. In this view, war has been the centerpiece of western culture for about five thousand years, but it is not the only way we have been. Before this we had a partnership agrarian culture. It was dominator culture which brought us coercive hierarchies, privileged élites, exploited peasants, and empire-building as a way of life. It also brought inhumanity, cruelty which is invariably designed to maintain some form of exploitative control.

Because dominator culture has been central as long as we have had writing (and history), one can understand the Darwinian mistake. Nineteenth-century thinkers assumed that the whole world worked like their society did. Unfortunately, their theory tended to support the pattern by making it seem inevitable and even good. This is why Darwinism has been embraced by despotic systems from Fascism and Communism to Social Darwinism.

In a web view, selfishness and war are not at the center of human nature, except that we have made them so. Human beings are designed to change. Today there are powerful reasons that we must change. Unfortunately, the habits and incentives that maintain the old ways are deeply entrenched.

Countering the ugly three — war, selfishness and inhumanity — is going to require some sound thinking and some even sounder science. It is also going to require we build a socio-economic system which sustains a more collaborative way. The first step in this direction is to build a better understanding of why we have the cultures we have. This better understanding must of necessity start with how the human brain affects the types of societies we create. Brain research helps us see why human beings are complex in a specific three-tiered way — we are crude, warm and thoughtful. Each of these brains contributes to the kind of society we get.

Our Two Cultures ... and the Paradoxical Third

Our present minds are formed, and in turn helped to form, two antithetical types of social systems with markedly different functional thrusts ... An understanding of this duality is important for those who wish to see the world's peoples living in greater harmony with each other ...

Michael Chance

Thomas Sowell once wrote an interesting little book called, *A Conflict of Visions*. Its thesis was that social philosophers could be divided into two camps, those who saw humankind as basically good with society as the corrupting influence, and those who saw humankind as basically selfish and wicked with government and authority holding that wickedness in check. Cooperative or selfish? Mutualist or dominator? What is our *true* nature?

Let us now suggest that we are not one or the other of these, but *both* and that apparently these two cultures are related to our two lower brains, the lizard and furry mammal ones. Our thinking brain sits on top of these two. It creates belief systems which channel these two deep currents. The kind of society we get rises from the balance struck between the three (see Table 6).

Linking and Ranking

People who study animal behavior have observed two cultures throughout the animal kingdom (including human beings). Here I

Thinking brain
Talking and very active learning ... mental maps, continual rethinking ... paradoxical personality

∧

Lizard brain		Furry mammal brain
Out of the ooze ... rigid, stylized ... favors ranking	| | |	*Bonding and emotion* ... faster learning ... betters group learning ... favors linking

Table 6. Our two cultures and the paradoxical third.

describe the work of ethologist Michael Chance, a strong spokesman for this two-culture observation.[1]

The lizard brain brings a pattern which Chance calls the *agonic mode*. This style is characterized by individuals arranged in a series of social levels or ranks with high-ranking individuals exerting great influence over those below and lower-ranking individuals directing most of their attention to those above. The structure is a hierarchy built on status, intimidation and posturing. Among monkeys, for example, dominant individuals regularly threaten subordinates who retreat and return submissively thereby reassuring both sides that the system is powerful. Because threat is such a fundamental aspect of the structure, most individuals' attention is taken up with security. As Chance says:

> Individuals become concerned with rank, convention, and
> maintaining good order, as an expression of this inbred
> security [need] ... social timidity, obsequiousness, shyness,
> sycophancy, and other forms of culturally identified lack of
> social initiative can be seen as rooted in primitive submissive-
> ness and other traits, such as snobbishness, as being derived
> from an exaggerated awareness of social rank. (1992, p.6)

It all seems quite familiar and Chance and his colleagues have found this type of culture in birds and fishes as well as mammals. It undergirds what Eisler calls the *dominator culture* in human beings.

Researchers, however, also find what Chance calls the *hedonic mode* over the same wide range. This mode centers on linking and undergirds what I have called *mutualist culture*.

Mutualist culture is heavily tied to the furry mammal brain and its warm bonding emotions. As Chance says, 'here the assuaging qualities of appeasement are transformed into the reassuring gestures of individuals who are mutually dependent.' Among chimpanzees, for example, when groups split up to go foraging, less confident individuals seek and are offered reassurance from older, more confident leaders through contact and gestures. Individuals tend to form networks of personal relationships that offer mutual support. Leading is done through encouragement and the main social bonds are nurturance, mutual benefit, and, for want of a better word, love. Because attention is not tied up with self-defense and security, individuals tend to be more creative and the system more flexible.

Now, oddly enough, this mutualist mode also seems familiar. There is such a thing as working together toward a common goal and a common good. Sometimes people *do* feel like a cherished part of a family, a team or a community. Many of us have experienced the kind of bonded, egalitarian, 'in this together' working groups that come from this kind of mode and, wherever we go thereafter, we yearn to be in one again.

Bonding and love are profoundly important aspects of human nature. There is also more than sentimentality at work here. Nature bred bonding emotions into us as part of an extremely important strategy. Bonding encourages diverse individuals to work together in a way that is supportive, collaborative, creative and committed. The early Neolithic Old Society exemplifies its potential for peaceful coexistence. In fact, as we shall see in the next chapter, this powerful mammalian part of our nature is central to commitment and creativity in all human societies.

Pros and Cons

Contrary to the usual Darwinian descriptions, it is relatively easy to see both cultures at work in our daily lives. They are everywhere. Natural disasters, for example, often bring out people's mutualist side with heroic efforts being put forth not for selfish ends, but for a deeply-felt need to serve something higher than oneself. One's image of a good teacher, a warm family, community concern or of an old-time craftsman who honours quality and integrity as part of his craft — all these are mutualist images.

The mutualist mode tends to be championed by spiritual traditions as correct, by working-class people as honest, and by radicals as the direction of hope. Even street gangs find their strength from the deep need to belong. Abandoned by the larger society, the disenfranchised of the world form mutual-support families of their own.

Still, while mutualist bonding beckons us, it is domination which tends to frame our existence. Dominator culture tends to be espoused by those who seek power over others. It is seen best in big business, combative politics and materialist obsession. It is also seen in scientists who use debate, not as the forge by which learning is refined, but as an alpha-male opportunity for prowess and intimidation. The flip side of the dominator coin is seen in followers who keep élites in power through conformity, sycophancy, obedience and hero-worship. Thus, dominator culture requires controlling egos on one side and subservient ones on the other.

The dominator mind is closely associated with the lizard brain and has many of its pros and cons. For example, the lizard brain reacts to displays which means appearance (and not necessarily ability) is very important to rank. In a dominator social structure, intimidation keeps members focused on maintaining alignment with superiors, but it also leaves little energy left for inventiveness. Indeed, as anyone who has lived in one knows, such structures tend to suppress inventiveness and to create many reasons *not* to speak one's mind. Dominator culture, thus, tends toward rigidity and focus on the status quo. It is a great way to conserve habits, but a terrible way to learn. Since rank and intimidation are central, dominator culture also has a great affinity for war. War is after all a perfect way to establish rank through intimidation, appearance and force. Because dominator culture keeps people in line, it can also be extremely efficient, at least for short periods where little learning is required. Finally, dominator leaders also stir deep primitive yearnings. The hope that a strong-man will save us if only we obey, is extremely powerful.

The mutualist mind is the more advanced learning mode. Strong bonds and mutual support aide creativity and group learning. For instance, when people feel safe, they express their opinions in the name of getting a better result. Jane Jacobs calls this pattern, *dissent-in-the-name-of-the-task*. It is found all over the world, from ancient times to the present. The group learns by pooling insights, not by conforming. Bonding also encourages initiative which is freely given and filled with all the ability the individual has to offer. When such groups agree upon a common strategy, individuals take it upon themselves to further that strategy, without anyone forcing them to do so. The main reward is the respect of fellows and personal pride. It is this kind of emotional motivation which makes mutualist teams the most creative, rapidly-learning organizations on the face of the earth.

But mutualist structures can also be upset by insecurity — particularly, as Chance puts it, 'by prolonged and frustrated competition.' For example, Margaret Powers, one of Chance's colleagues, describes how a mutualist chimpanzee social structure broke down in the Gombe Stream Reserve in Tanzania after bananas were locked away for large parts of the day. Competition escalated and eventually the chimps' usual mutualist mode broke down and members of one group began hounding and killing members of the other. Thus, threat, struggle, or prolonged competition is likely to restore a dominator mode. Fascists, for example, came to power in the 1930s as the result of depression and weary people looking for a strong-man savior.

*   *   *

Now, most of these insights are familiar. This is a richer, more realistic picture of the world we all know. The only new idea is that *both* modes are real. Thus, Eisler's dominator culture is probably not just an invention of invading outlanders. On the other hand, neither is the mutualist mode a weak tendency that can be squashed forever through force or fear.

We are not mutualist or dominator, we are both. These modes are not a matter of gender, race, intelligence or class. Individuals generally specialize in one mode or the other, but this is usually a result of training, circumstance and personal preference. The fact that certain groups tend toward one mode or another is more a result of social pressures than hardwired inevitability. The classic example here is men and women. Women tend more toward mutualism because their traditional role is mothering. Yet, mothering too has to be learned and women are just as capable of being dominators as men — a fact certain business women and politicians have demonstrated aptly in recent years. Conversely, men are just as capable of being caring parents and supportive human beings as women. In short, most people are capable of both modes and no society yet has managed to change this no matter how much they force stereotypic roles.

The web view also helps us see that both cultures have their problems. Domination is prone to instability through rigidity and unfairness. (Force and obedience never work forever.) Mutualism is prone to instability through crisis and greed. Dominator tendencies are always there and crisis tends to throw us back into this lower state.

Awareness of both cultures, thus, gives a better sense of why the human condition is so fraught with paradox. Human beings — individually and collectively — are built of two very different minds intertwined in one social body. What then shall we do? This brings us to our third and most cherished brain. We are capable of being wonderfully caring and cooperative *and* of being remarkably crude and coercive. Over these two potentials arches a brain capable of tremendous variation. Michael Chance sees our third brain, the thinking one, as the best hope to integrate our two deep cultures in a sustainable way. I would concur.

Weaving Those Reality Webs

A society's fitness is determined by its social cognitive map.
Robert Artigiani

The thinking brain is an odd duck. It is a phenomenal pattern finder. It got big by talking, therefore, it is highly social. It was forged in a crucible of crisis, so its big reason for existence is to allow its owner to be more flexible and to learn faster. The net result is a mind more powerful than anything else on earth. The result is also a personality that can (and will) change itself depending on how it views the world.

The thinking brain's personality is paradoxical. It is capable of tremendous change — like that seen in Dr Jeykll and Mr Hyde. Yet, it is also capable of the Optical Illusion Effect — keeping people so locked in their current view that they literally do not see things that really exist. This paradox explains why views can be entrenched and, yet, why entrenched views are regularly swept away. Furthermore, the paradox applies both to individuals and groups. Entrenchment and changeability are two sides of the same coin.

The most important aspect of the thinking brain is its role in creating human realities. We've been here before. Humankind's great strategy is to build ever better pictures of how the world works by pooling information from many perspectives. Human beings then build social realities out of what they think they know. Little back and forth bumps of close-knit interaction slowly brings about a belief system (world view, mental map, etc.) that comes to unite and define a people. Knowing leads to doing! — and soon, a reality web, an embracing social reality, is born.

Since I discussed cultural weaving and reality webs earlier, I will not belabor the point. Table 7 lists a few of the characteristics of our thinking brain that clockwork thinking tended to overlook.

The Hinge Point of Our Condition

Our thinking brain is both the main cause and the best remedy for our predicament. It creates the belief systems which direct most human behavior. Its ultimate implication is that what people believe is the hinge-point of human progress. Societies, therefore, do engineer most of their members' behaviors — often unwittingly. Social engineering starts from the day a child is born and generally proceeds via habits and assumptions. Unfortunately, because we underestimate the flexibility and self-determination of our reality webs, we tend to assume that the way we 'are' is inescapable. We tell ourselves that nature (not our own beliefs) made us this way!

The great crime of the human condition is that what we regularly teach stultification despite our flexibility and potential for intelligence. Today, for instance, studies show how girls — told they can't do math, sports, etc. — slowly succumb to such instruction. Half of our society is trained *not* to live up to its potential. If you include racism and classism, the percentage is much higher still. This kind of suppression is socially destructive.

Why do societies stultify their own people? History answers here. Most stultification is a direct result of dominator systems. Stultification makes perfect sense in a dominator system because dominator systems are based on subjugation. The society trains certain people to keep their place so as to give others power and privilege. This is a cultural system. Privilege however requires rationalization. Hence, all

- Because mind is part of the physical world (and integrated with body), the human mind and its mental maps are *more physically powerful* than usually imagined. Studies of Multiple Personality Syndrome, for example, show that brains are capable of flipping between different patterns of organization (attractors) which is why different personalities can live in the same body. What is shocking is that bodily characteristics change along with personalities. One personality, for example, may have diabetes and another may not. One may have allergies or heart disease and another may not. All this occurs in same body. Body patterns change along with patterns of mind because mind and body are integrated.

- Because mind is integrated and emotion is part of it, mental maps are also every bit *as emotionally real as they are cognitively compelling.* This is why children from upwardly-mobile families can get suicidally depressed over average grades, while a few miles away inner city youths live in a gang world that sees violence, promiscuity and a variety of deadly pastimes as normal and necessary. Each group sees and feels little choice. They live – and die – accordingly.

- Because knowing leads to doing, *the idea that people's beliefs create human realities is much more literal than most people realize.* A good example comes from a study in which teachers were told that certain children in their class had tested in the brilliant range. The children had actually been selected at random and many had tested as slow. But teachers who believed they were brilliant, subtly helped them to become so. By the end of the year these children *were* testing as brilliant. The moral? Never underestimate the power of beliefs.

Table 7. Overlooked elements of mental maps and the thinking brain.

dominator societies have explanations for (1) why those who benefit from exploitation deserve to do so; (2) why people who are used and abused should keep their place; and (3) why God (or nature) made this so. Thus, in dominator systems 'the way things are' is always explained as a necessary natural order.

Dominator systems emerged at a particular time in history, but they still colour western civilization today. I discuss their reasons for being below. Meanwhile I leave you with a dark thought. Dominator beliefs contribute heavily to social collapse. Ossification, worldliness and greed? These characteristics rise as dominator élites solidify control and begin to see themselves as separate from their own society. Soon simple exploitation turns into more rampant pillage. Remember those fourteenth-century knights! It may take time and a huge amount of suffering (because we are remarkably pig-headed) but eventually the old will crumble under the weight of its own dysfunction.

Humanity's urge to rethink will eventually spring back. This leaves only two major questions involved in human evolution. The first is how much self-destruction is required before we change our view of the world. The second is whether we will be able to conceptualize a *better way* — one which does not center on domination.

Intricacy and our Two Deep Cultures

War is not an instinct but an invention. Jose Ortega y Gasset

Brain research teaches us three things. First, we are remarkably flexible. Secondly, we have two deep cultural currents running underneath. Finally, for historical reasons we seem to be stuck in domination and stultification.

The question now arises as to why human beings developed dominator culture given that mutualism is our more creative — and enjoyable — mode. The answer to this question is important because it may help us see what we need to do to next if we are to give birth to an Integral Age.

If dynamic evolution holds for the human condition, then the answer to 'why dominator culture arose' must have something to do with co-evolution, S-curves and the movement toward increasing intricacy. It should have something to do with the need to maintain coherence in order to maintain collaboration. It probably also has something to do with survival pressures coming from a changing environment. These are the kinds of things that drive change in the web view of the world.

There is evidence that all of these factors did indeed play a role in the change from mutualism to dominator society some five thousand years ago. Understanding how and why they did helps provide a very different perspective on cultural evolution and also on the shift which we hope is at hand. Let us review.

Our Two Cultures: Past and Present

Once upon a time, human beings lived in agricultural communities, close to nature and each other. This was the time of Mythic consciousness, when people worshipped the life force at work in the world. In this now misty time, societies were essentially mutualist. People worked together creatively and cooperatively without coercion, overseers or the incentive of getting more than the person next door. Quite the opposite. People were apparently bound by the realization that they needed each other. People played different roles, but, like any intelligent society of mind, the aim was to survive and prosper by working together. Hence, in this culture:

- Social power was viewed as a responsibility, a trusteeship used for the benefit of all;
- Social relationships were largely egalitarian. Roles differed but they were definitely more equal than exploitative.
- There was a solid sense of being in the world together. Since everyone worked, the fruits of the Earth were seen as belonging to all. Land and major means of production were held in common.
- People worshipped the life force at work in the world.

This was also a very creative society. Most of the mainstays of civilization came from this time including: the domestication of animals; the invention of specialist professions; the first true religions with symbols and temples; the beginnings of trade and trade networks; the invention of centralized political authority and the idea of law — not to mention technologies such as pottery, weaving, writing; metallurgy, boats, the wheel, musical instruments, sculptures, frescoes, and a thousand other amenities.

These early cultures were far from idyllic. On the other hand, they were not, as is often taught, merely a pre-cursor to true civilization which, according to Darwin, required some chief who could heap up possessions for himself. The Minoans, for example, developed vast multi-storied palaces, networks of paved roads, viaducts, farmsteads, harbors, reservoirs, water pipes, and inside sanitary systems — not to mention the exquisite paintings, statues, mosaics, and vases all done in a joyful artistic style. And, despite the sophistication of their culture, there were no military fortifications, depictions of battles, caches of weapons or tombs with chieftains covered in riches and surrounded by servants slaughtered to accompany him in death.

This mutualist mode of civilization also arose in many places in relatively similar time frames. It was not solely a product of the Old European and Near East societies that Eisler describes. China, for example, apparently also started in this mode (see Jiayin, 1995). So, too did the Indic civilization which originated along the Indus river valley in northern India as early as 14,000 BC. Covering 300,000 square miles at its height (where pharaonic Egypt covered less than 15,000) and boasting metallurgy, art, complex architecture, paved roads and cities, the Indic civilization also produced the great spiritual traditions which are being rediscovered today. And, wonder of wonders, this longest-continuing civilized tradition also appears to have started as mutualist society, not a coercive one. As Feuerstein writes:

> Remarkably, war technology is not well represented in the archeological artifacts, and there is no evidence of any extensive military conflict which is also true of Sumer for the period prior to around 2000 BC. The early Indic civilization appears to have been largely peace loving ... Rebellion and revolution were not part of traditional societies, as they are today. (1996, p.75)

In short, mutualist societies are not an anomaly. They appear to have arisen in at least several places in the world in roughly similar time frames. They appear to have been the natural starting stage for civilization for understandable reasons. People who live by growing things learn to work together peacefully because everyone benefits from cooperation. Such cooperative societies are more likely to value harmony among themselves and the larger world. They are also more likely to be creative because improvements benefit everyone. Since one still finds cooperative enclaves the world over, one can also say that mutualism never completely went away.

On the other hand, this appealing kind of culture is clearly no longer dominant. Somewhere between 4000 BC and 2000 BC it receded and a new culture began to rule. Societies like Sumer, which had once operated on partnership principles, turned to empire-building instead.

Domination and The Age of War

Oligarchy: a government resting on a valuation of property, in which the rich have power and the poor man is deprived of it. Plato, *The Republic,* 350 BC

The dominator view started somewhere around 3000 BC. Since it began around the same time as recorded history, it has long been viewed as the basis of civilization. Hence, according traditional theory, the first civilizations (as opposed to just cities) appeared in ancient Egypt and in the Tigris-Euphrates river valleys around 3000 BC. Today's society followed directly from such as these. Yet, what was being born, was not exactly something about which we can rejoice. As one textbook on Western civilization describes the innovation:

Each of the great valley states was ruled by a despot: a king who was also a priest, if not actually considered a God. He ruled through a privileged class of nobles and priests, who commanded a professional army. His subjects had no appeal from his decisions. They obeyed orders, worked hard and turned over much of their crops as taxes to support the bureaucracy. Bureaucrats included such experts as engineers, scientists, priests, clerks who kept tax records, lawyers to argue disputes, and judges to settle them in accordance with law ... After these very great innovations of urban civilization, these societies apparently changed very slowly. (Brinton, 1964, p.8)

In short, a new social system arose which was centered on bureaucracies and despots — a system I call *coercive hierarchy*. This system also came with a new economic focus. The élites who ruled dominator societies made their living through war. Thus, where collaborative agriculture was the hub of early mutualist societies, the new culture brought a very important new economic system — *conquest and subjugation.*

The distinction between going to war and making a living through war is very important. Human beings, no doubt, have always fought. Fighting for survival started long before man. But, it is only with so-called civilization that organized fighting becomes oriented toward three peculiarly human ends — accumulating land/possessions, enslaving other people, and endlessly trying to expand so as to do more of the same. Today we call it empire-building. It has many forms. What one must remember is that, once upon a time, this too was new.

The invention of war for conquest explains why the 3000 to 1000 BC time-frame found a series of aspiring imperial powers — Sumeria, Babylon, Hittite, Assyria, Chaldea — meeting up with the Egyptian Pharaohs who made their own periodic excursions for plunder and slaves. The élites who benefited from these excursions actually made their living by plundering abroad *and* exploiting at home. Hence, élites acquired land by conquest and owning land gave them rights to its fruits regardless of whether they actually labored or not. This system also brought tyranny — planned viciousness which is designed to maintain power over others.

It is easy to see why Eisler calls this *dominator* culture. Its distinctive elements include:

- A hierarchical social structure dominated by strong-man élites,
- Accumulation of wealth for status,
- Coercive social power,
- Private ownership of land and means of production,
- Slavery and human sacrifice,
- The reduction of women and children to the property of men,
- A central focus on war and militarism.

The dismal nature of this list, however, begs the question as to why this system took root so widely and why it still seems immutable today.

What Happened to the Garden?

Humanity stepped out of nature, entering into an artificial environment where an affluent minority coerced the impoverished majority to work for the collective good ... Why would these noble savages have ever left the Garden? Why were they foolish enough to create societies that were hierarchical, unequal, coercive, and militaristic?

Robert Artigiani

Why did humanity step out of the Garden and create coercive societies? Eisler believes the Old Societies were overrun by invaders who forced their social system on unwilling populations. This certainly appears to have been the case for many, including the Minoans of Crete. Yet there is also an intricacy explanation of why hierarchies came about. This explanation is important because it helps us come to grips with the benefits of the system. Coercive hierarchies remain because they are more effective in certain ways. They are, in fact, an example of increasing intricacy.

The Birth of Coercive Hierarchies

> *Civilized societies, the hierarchical militaristic ones, extract*
> *work by what Herbert Spencer called 'coercive*
> *cooperation.'*   Robert Artigiani

The idea that civilization is based on empire-building and using social power for selfish ends is depressing. It is depressing because this situation is still so rampant as to seem inevitable and most of us feel quite helpless to do anything about it. Most of us also understand why dominator culture continues. It appears to be more powerful than the mutualist culture which still lurks inside most societies.

Dynamic evolution provides both a confirmation and a caveat to this picture of dominator efficiency. This section looks at the downside — the confirmation. From a strictly academic point of view, the birth of coercive hierarchies did involve the birth of a more efficient type of social organization. American anthropologist Robert Carneiro even describes how this more intricate organization came into being through a punctuated pattern of evolution not unlike that seen in the Bénard cell.

Carneiro starts by pointing out that hierarchical civilizations tend to arise in bounded or constrained regions, of fertile land, including the Nile valley, the Tigris-Euphrates, the Huang Ho, the Indus and the coastal valleys of Peru. Evolution within these regions tends to proceed through a pattern as follows.

When land is plentiful, tribes in a desirable valley tend to be semi-nomadic and well dispersed. They may have deadly quarrels, but these quarrels usually involve prestige or revenge, but not land *per se*. If a conflict is particularly bloody, a tribe will simply pick up and move. Thus, when land is plentiful, tribal collisions serve to spread groups evenly around the region. In vast open areas such as the North American plains or rugged areas such as the South American central jungles and the Australian outback, this pattern may continue for centuries.

But *constrained* land changes things. When desirable land fills up, the region enters a new phase. Deadly quarrels begin to take a different form. Since it is no longer easy to flee, land becomes an issue. The focus of war changes from revenge and prestige to controlling space. The frequency and importance of war begins to increase.

At first, tribes try to annihilate their opponents. This eliminates threat and opens new land. Eventually, however, some chief hits upon the idea of subjugation. A defeated village is allowed to remain on its land, but it is forced to become a subunit of a larger political unit controlled by the victor. Separate tribes become coupled into a larger collective.

These new political organizations are not only bigger, they are also more coordinated. Individuals who were successful in war are assigned the task of administering the new areas. They maintain law and order and collect tribute (later called taxes). They also mobilize work groups to build roads, irrigation works and fortresses. These efforts are usually done in the name of war, but many also improved economic activity in general. Roads, for example, increase all sorts of exchange. Conquerors also demand tribute which must be paid by producing more. Hence, as Carneiro puts it, 'subjugation squeezed out an untapped margin of food productivity.' Administrative classes live off this increased productivity and create constant pressure on the lower classes to produce more.

All of this should seem familiar because its effects are still with us today. What is depressing is that, in this view, subjugation fits the increasing intricacy scenario. It produced a new, more efficient structure which was based on cooperation, if of the coercive variety. Its effectiveness is loathsome, but obvious. Élites use coercive hierarchies to pull resources from the grassroots. This allows them to create concentrations of wealth and power which they apply in focused ways — such as castles, armies, roads and armaments.

Concentrated power also opens the door to new rounds increasing complexity. As Carneiro puts it, 'Villages were succeeded by chiefdoms, chiefdoms by kingdoms, and kingdoms by empires.' A fractal of structures emerged, all of it made possible by coercive hierarchy's wondrous ability to concentrate power and apply it in focused ways.

Naturally, coercive hierarchies soon spread far beyond their original constrained region. Their existence also put pressure on other societies to develop bureaucracies and despots of their own. This pressure too can be seen in terms of intricacy and coherence. Villages, for instance, had existed in the mythic mutualist days, but once a village grows beyond about 350 people, traditional mutualist ways start to break down. Community members no longer know each other deeply enough to mobilize rapidly for defense or other common needs. Hence, some anthropologists believe that despots and bureaucracies were necessary for societies beyond a certain size. One man deciding for all and using an efficient system of enforcement, allowed fragmenting societies to act as a whole. Without them, the society couldn't take coherent action rapidly enough to survive. The situation is very similar to the one which led living organisms to develop nerves.

The Next Punctuation

So, dominator civilization is bad because it is based on subjugation and exploitation. It is not a sustainable form. Yet, coercive hierarchies and empire-building élites came to dominate the world because they are powerful. They can concentrate resources and coordinate efforts on much more massive scale than their more primitive predecessors. The Idyllic dies before the onslaught of terrible dominator efficiency. Carneiro's theory simply adds awareness that the invisible hand of web dynamics may be involved. A hierarchy is more intricate and more energetically efficient than simple mutualist circles.

Does this mean that exploitation, élitism and command/control are the royal road to efficiency and hence intrinsic to complex societies? Success and thousands of years of cultural weaving have certainly made this mode seem inevitable, the way things *must* be whether one likes it or not. Yet, our century — and many before it — can also be thought of as a debate on the alpha-male effectiveness question. For example, twentieth century Fascism, the epitome of an alpha-male dominator hierarchy, was defeated by democratic, mutualist rabble. The fall of the Soviet Union, the struggles in Easter Europe, there are many examples of the vicissitudes of coercive hierarchies and their owners.

Today, there is also a new way of explaining the likely outcome of this long-standing debate. This brings me to the upbeat side of the story, the caveat. Today, the same invisible hand of dynamic evolution

is being used to explain why a new type of socio-economic system —
and the Integral Age that goes with it — is now in the offing. Thus,
from a strictly academic point of view, coercive hierarchies are now
exhausted and a more intricate type of organization is needed.

Today we find that information-up/control down hierarchies are simply
too slow to handle the pace of change and level of complexity of the
modern world. They also tend to suppress innovation. This makes them
bad at learning. Finally, empire-building and exploitation builds wealth for
a few at the expense of many. This creates socio-economic tension and a
system which grows more fragile with every turn.

There are also new reasons to return to collaborative ways. The
mutualist current which runs deeply within us creates greater initiative
and intelligence at every point in the society. It increases creativity and
commitment to the greater good. It increases bonding and lessens
social tension. All of these characteristics are vital for a complex,
information-based civilization which can destroy itself more insidiously
and more completely than any society in the history of the world.
Quality counts in an information age and quality comes from committed, collaborative culture.

Mutualism, however, must become more intricately organized if it
is to take back the world. Mutualism works well in small circles, but
small circles are easily destroyed. The only way to resist dominator
pressures is for small circles to join hands in a collaborative network
that is broader and tighter than anything domination can provide.

Hence, from a web point of view, civilization needs a new pattern
because command-and-control hierarchies have major *effectiveness*
problems. War and subjugation is a bad way to do business in today's
complex world. A more intricate way would make us more powerful.
What system could be better? I believe, as many do, that the next
socio-economic form will have to be:

- more networked than hierarchical,
- more collaborative than coercive,
- more mutual than exploitative.

If done well, these characteristics would make societies more
creative, more cohesive and better at learning. The question is how do
we get there.

The Integral Challenge

We are now in a position to understand humanity's past and our hoped for future in a dramatically new way. To whit: we are discovering, not only that we are embraced in a web world, but also that the rules and patterns of this wondrous web hold in human systems. These patterns include co-evolution, S-curves and the motion toward increasing intricacy. Furthermore, the need for intricacy can be used to explain why we have come from a mutualist beginning, through a dominator era and now stand on the threshold of an Integral Age.

The web view does provide a very different context for understanding what is happening today. For example, it now becomes clear that the kind of Big Change I described at the end of the medieval world is actually but one small cycle in a much larger fractal whole. Small cycles are embedded in large ones which periodically include the emergence of a new level of consciousness. Consciousness, in turn, is entwined with social, political, economic and spiritual systems. Hence, each new stage of mind co-evolves with a new socio-economic system including: a dominant way of making a living; a main kind of social structure; and a specific kind of religion. In the Mythic Stage, for instance people lived by agriculture and had a mutual-benefit type of society. They worshipped the Life Force. The Mental Age brought big egos, coercive hierarchies, vengeful Gods and the concept of making a living through war. Table 8 sums up our sojourn so far.

Many people hope that the turning we face today represents the final days of the Age of War. If so, the rise of Integral Society would involve a major shift in social, political, economic, spiritual and scientific systems. It would also reflect the stirrings of a new stage of consciousness, one which is more aware of its embedding in the greater whole. Integral Society would emphasize learning, interdependence and stewardship. It would emerge for logical reasons. This entire century has been a lesson in the fallacy of big egos, self-centeredness and fitness through war.

Yet, there is more to understand than this. If the cycles of human history fit dynamic evolution, then the need to work together, to maintain coherence and social intelligence, play a major role in social change. Growth is a tricky business. It pulls organization apart. It makes

Stages of consciousness Main social structure *Main economic form*
Integral consciousness   ? Networked mutualism Synthesis of information *The Age of Wisdom* **Mental consciousness**   3000 BC Coercive hierarchies Living-by-taking (conquest, subjugation, pillage) *The Age of War* **Mythical consciousness**   15 000 BC Mutualist cooperatives Agriculture *First civilization, cities and specialization* **Magical consciousness**   500 000 BC Organized hunting bands Hunter/gatherer *First symbols* **Archaic consciousness**   2 million BC? Loose bands of individuals *Foraging*

Table 8. Stages of Consciousness and Socio-Economic Systems.
This table shows the first four stages of consciousness along with the major social structure and economic system that came with each. As with brains, new systems rise on top of older forms which still operate within. Older socio-economic ways do not go away, they just becomes less dominant. Mutualist modes, for instance, still continue underneath the war-centered system which came with mental consciousness. Note that I have not given the Industrial Revolution its usual major place because, while the economic method changed, the social and mental structures which dominated them did not.

communication difficult. It causes cooperation to fail and this makes an organization prone to regression or collapse. This is why new eras often have something to do with the need for gretaer intricacy.

The hidden message here is that the ways we devise to stay

connected and committed to the greater good, are crucial to any great turning. Vision and values alone are not enough. Inventing a system to maintain our dreams is perhaps the more crucial need. One might call this the Marxist dilemma. The idea of an equitable society is good, the question is how can it be made real now that we know that governments alone cannot create it.

One challenge of an Integral Age, therefore, is to figure out how to nurture intricacy and collaborative learning in an increasingly complex world. What makes some people stay committed to the greater good while others circumvent it? How can people stay connected when size, speed and distance pulls a society apart? What kind of social structure would answer the needs that coercive hierarchies do, while not succumbing to the destructive tendencies inherent in the dominator mode. These are the kinds of questions that go into a sustainable civilization. I explore them throughout the rest of this book.

We are going to have to build a more networked, more collaborative and more mutualist civilization. This must take place world-wide. Such a task would seem overwhelming were it not for the fact that it has been in progress for thousands of years already. Our mutualist tendency never left. It has been developing all this time. We may need only a few more straws for this already ladened back.

Many people hope that World Wide Web is a budding nervous system for a planetary mind. The Web is certainly an important step because it allows information to flow to all corners and not just up and down a tree. Unfortunately, the Web is not yet designed to aid wisdom, commitment or quality. Information accumulates like a giant vat of junk mail. The Web also doesn't reach everyone and this is crucial to maintaining coherence. Finally, many parts of the Web are still being run according to dominator principles. These parts accelerate the practices which are pulling us under. One need only think about how electronic communications help wild swings in the stock market to see that this wondrous new invention is not a panacea.

The World Wide Web is a crucial step, but it is not sufficient. In the end, culture determines the meaning of any given invention.

The Struggle to Reinherit the Earth

*The gradual development of social equality is at once the
past and the future of mankind. To attempt to check
democracy would be to attempt to check the will of God.*
                                                    Alexis DeTocqueville, 1835

The first step in realizing why a form of mutualism may return is to
realize that it has not lain dormant. For five thousand years civilization
has been centered on empire-building, but for much of that time
mutualism has fought back. At various times and in various places it
has surged back producing a fractal landscape of rises and retreats
embedded in one overall push. DeTocqueville saw that push. If we are
to get past our current dominator proclivities, we need to see it too.

The story is actually straightforward. Thousands of years of cultural
weaving now makes it hard to believe that dominator principles aren't
at the core of human nature. Yet, mutualist patterns never really went
away. Rather, invaders conquered early mutualist societies and yoked
them into service. The result is the kind of system we know today.
Dominator élites accumulate personal wealth as a mark of status and
amass community wealth for purposes of war (personal, corporate, religious or national). Dominators dominate the power structure which
straddles most societies and they create incentives to follow their
views. Yet, underneath, partnership patterns still exist.

Hence, most societies (and people) are still schizophrenic, with one
culture living inside the other. If you scratch most societies just a little
bit, you will find that the old culture is alive and well. When parents
sacrifice for their children, when a businessman cares about his community, and when preachers tell us to love one another — then
mutualism lives again.

It is this unsung mutualist core that performs the lion's share of
productive work. It is also this unsung core that makes human life
worth living for most people all over the world. Indeed, it is deep,
abiding mutualist values — freedom, equality, justice, compassion,
love, mutual support and equal effort — that also stir people's souls
enough to make them take a stand against what often seems like
irresistible forces and immutable status quos. These mutualist ideals are
so powerful that they have formed a common theme running throughout the history of the world. De Toqueville saw it. American civil-

rights legend, Martin Luther King saw it too. After studying history and the Bible he summed up the sentiment as follows: 'The arc of the universe is long, but it tends toward justice.'

We can also make the story stronger. As we shall see in the next chapter, true civilization flowers, precisely when mutualism advances. It declines and frays when dominator beliefs surge back. The result has been an S-shaped curve of rises and falls scattered throughout history. This pattern is actually obvious for anyone who cares to look. For example, there was a time when knights served God, chivalry and the organic feudal whole and there followed a time when knights began to serve themselves, destroying their world as they went. The Medieval organic whole was originally built on common commitment and the principle that worldliness and greed should be rejected because these had destroyed Rome. The Medieval world rose on this premise and declined exactly as its mutualist ethic declined. Knights always fought, but in the first case it was for common defense and in the second case it was to accumulate money. The first was of mutual benefit and the second one-sided benefit. Chaos ensued from the latter. Crisis then gave rise to another round of common-cause. The Enlightenment, for example, was a mutualist resurgence that rose in reaction to corrupt, self-serving authority — that is, a dominator ethos.

If we are going to change our world, it is important to realize that mutualist ideals are powerful. They are also common across time and cultures. Underneath a bewildering variety of cultural masks lies a common human urge to live together in freedom, compassion, justice, and love — and without war or exploitation. This urge is not so hard to understand. It implies a common heart beating all over the world. It is much more powerful that we usually imagine. Chapter 7 outlines the role mutualism has played in founding cherished ideals in science, government, religion and society at large. It then looks at how a renewed dominator ethos destroys great societies.

Life in the Learning Universe

If the world is dynamic and evolution is natural, why is
transformation so hard?   Barbara Lawton

This ends my outline of the changing view of human nature and the
human condition. Let me summarize.

The web view is sweet, but complex. It paints a breathtaking vision
of cosmic evolution and a world ecosystem struggling to be One. It
anticipates much that is happening today and gives it a new frame. The
World Wide Web, for example, is being described as a budding
nervous system for a planetary mind. If billions of minds all over the
world can learn to work together for a greater good, then we may
stand a chance for an Integral Age.

Yet, this transformation is not a certainty. It is important, therefore,
to understand the hidden pressures which undermine our best intentions. Here we find that learning, collaboration and intricacy are
crucial, but these are not easy to maintain. We are smart, but dominator patterns still encourage stultification. We are sophisticated, but
habit and insularity can keep us from learning as we should. We grow
apart, but we barely understand that this is a problem. Web science is
knocking at the door with a whole new way of looking at things. It is
more powerful and extremely relevant to our times. Yet most people
do not see it. So we wallow in old ways and cannot imagine an alternative. No one has time to put pieces together.

If dynamic evolution really does hold in human societies, then the
challenge of an Integral Age is to figure out how to nurture intricacy
in an increasingly complex world. If we don't figure this out, our
collaboration will fail and so will our civilization. There is also a more
immediate problem. We are the most flexible, self-determining species
on the face of the earth yet we are currently following old habits into
self-destruction. Why do we do this? Both our deep cultures are strong,
but domination still dominates. The next chapter takes a closer look at
the role of the dominator dream.

CHAPTER 7

THE CYCLES OF CIVILIZATION

When I despair, I remember that all through history the way
of truth and love has always won. There have been tyrants
and murders and for a time they can seem invincible, but
in the end they always fall. Think of it. Always.

Mahatma Gandhi

You cannot understand our times without understanding the epoch battle between our two deep cultural currents — mutualism and domination. It has been running continuously for five thousand years.

People have been aware of this battle for a very long time. We are on the cusp, therefore, of a radically new and yet remarkably old view of history. Popularized versions of this view talk of how the Patriarchy arose in a time long ago and still weaves its tendrils of oppression into much that we do. This story, however, tends to create a rift between men and women which is false and destructive. Women can be just as oppressive as men and men have often been the champions of the humane way. Therefore, I am going to tell the tale more along Gandhi's line.

New science ideas actually link up with a theory which is very old and which has nothing to do with gender in itself. Over a thousand years ago, St Augustine said there were two cultures struggling for the hearts of men. Their battle played out in the ups and downs of transient civilizations. One culture seeks to build a city on earth that reflects the great design. This culture espouses harmony, synergy and common wellbeing. The other culture is centered on war and worldly things, particularly power and wealth. Since this culture originally achieved power through conquest and subjugation, it often finds torture and killing necessary to maintain the exploitative edge. Everyday callousness and repression, therefore, is part of a larger, more reprehensible scheme now supported by an entire socio-economic system.

Contrary to our usual impression, both deep cultures are found in virtually all societies, past and present, primitive and sophisticated (and among male and female members). Hence, in most societies, the two cultures lie side by side. On the other hand, they don't lie still. A great deal of history is defined by the oscillations between them. For example, cherished values such as freedom, justice, equality, compassion, and serving a larger design (that is, spirituality regardless of creed) all represent a deep mutualist urge. Westerners call these Enlightenment ideals, but they actually represent a project that humanity has been working on for thousands of years. A deep mutualist dream has been pushing for the entire time that domination has ruled.

The two-culture view thus helps us see the cycles of history more clearly. The pendulum swings. There are periods when social justice and common-cause move forward and times when the return of rapaciousness undermines a great society. As a result, civilizations go through an S-shaped evolutionary curve, one that starts with a swelling mutualist soul and ends with malaise and renewed exploitation.

The goal of this chapter is to outline the role that mutualism plays in founding civilizations and establishing cherished ideals. I include it because today's turning requires we understand the strength of our humanity and the powerful role it has played throughout the last five thousand years of history. Ours is not the first round. The humane side of humanity has been struggling to live free of the self-serving for thousands of years.

To make web patterns and their connection to the mutualist dream more substantial I am going to describe how a world-wide series of mutualist surges, swelled up into one grand, historical boom roughly twenty-five hundred years ago. I call this boom the Big Bang of Civilization because we are quite literally still reeling from its effects. It set the stage for all that we hold dear in government, science and religion.

Civilization's Big Bang

For our fight is not against flesh and blood, but against the rulers, against the authorities, against the powers of this dark world ...   Ephesians 6:12

Animal evolution had a Big Bang which set the stage for all the major species today. Western civilization is much the same. Though it is rarely mentioned, the foundations of western civilization's most cherished traditions were almost all laid in a brief golden burst from 800 to 200 BC. Most were laid between 600 and 400 BC — a mere two hundred years. All of them represented a mutualist return.

First, classical Greece burst forth in this period, founding western traditions of science, democracy, philosophy, drama and the arts. Secondly, the Romans also forged their Republic during this time, founding traditions of law, civic duty and political self-reform. Finally, and least mentioned of all, the Axial Age of spirituality developed the concepts of wisdom, compassion, and humanitarian action and set them at the heart of the world's great religions. In all regions of the civilized world, prophets and sages began to create new and remarkably similar ideas about the nature of the sacred and how to live life that are crucial to this day. Taoism and Confucianism emerged in China and Hinduism and Buddhism in India. The Hebrew prophets evolved new versions of monotheism in Israel and the Greeks gave birth to the philosophical God which led to rationalism in Europe. Parallel ideas emerged even in regions with no commercial contact, such as China and Greece. Hence, though it is rarely mentioned, underneath the various dogmas, all the religions mentioned above share a common core perspective known as the *perennial philosophy*. This philosophy argues for love, compassion, justice, equality and harmony. It is, therefore, of a mutualist vintage.

Awareness of our two deep cultural currents, allows us to see the story of this time as the single most powerful upsurge of mutualist mores in recorded history. This alone makes the tale important. Yet, the new science's rediscovery of the Great Ordering Oneness also allows for an even more unusual view. Across the world, the prophets and sages of these times ended up developing very similar insights — which is why philosophers since ancient times have described a common *perennial philosophy* lying at the core of the world's great religions. The source of their inspiration was also similar. In essence, these seers quieted their ego, immersed themselves in the mystery and listened to the voice of the greater Reality which is woven into each of us. Today, scientists can understand both the perennial philosophy and the source of inspiration in terms of a now physically-discernible Oneness which did create us and is woven into all things. Appendix C summarizes the Perennial Philosophy and looks at how understanding the Great Ordering Oneness might affect the Integral view of spirituality and religion.

The Return of the Dominator Ethos

To whom can I speak today?
Gentleness has perished
and the violent man has come down on everyone.
                    Ptahhotpe, twenty-fourth century BC, Egypt

The foundations of Western civilization's most cherished beliefs were all set in a brief golden period which reached its pinnacle between 600 and 400 BC. Think of it: science, democracy, Republican virtue, citizen soldiers, civic duty, ethical conduct, social justice, and a transcendent, compassionate God who urges love and right living as the truest form of worship—all in a few hundred years. All of these thrusts were also bound up (one way or another) with reaction to dominator abuse. They involved the struggle to build a society founded on liberty, equality, justice, common wellbeing and a sense of order in the world. Furthermore, most efforts in science *and* religion were aimed at understanding the ordering force which undergirds the world and embraces humankind. It was a world wide phenomenon.

Unfortunately, progress toward a loving world and a mutualist society does not run smoothly. The various flowerings faded and most ended in disaster.

Decline of the Classical Age

'The idea of a lawful world that could be known by reason was so exciting,' as Artigiani says, 'that Greek thinkers explored an endless array of ideas in a 150 year intellectual explosion of almost unequaled creativity.' But then the dominator ethos of *arete* (glory-seeking and prowess, not ethics) surged back and wanton competition set in. Leisured intellectuals would gleefully compete, trying to advance their own theories and to publicly annihilate their fellows. The real victim, however, was collaborative learning. Never of much use to the common man, fine ideas spun off into space.

Athens' worldly success also brought a new dominator pride and rationalizations of power still found in theories today. Plato's *The Republic* shows the shift. Its chronicle debates between Socrates and

Glaucon. Socrates champions the idea that societies must continually pursue justice by refining their understanding of what it meant and exploring better ways of achieving it. Glaucon, on the other hand, champions the dominator view that 'might makes right.' He argues that for men of the ruling class, justice and law are merely matters of expedience. Justice, he says, is merely 'a compromise between what is best — doing wrong and getting away with it — and what is worst — being wronged and not being able to get revenge.'

Such philosophical debates, of course, reflected a deeper problem. Glaucon's idea that might is right and justice merely expedience, emerged from a deep dominator perspective that would soon play out its natural pattern — self-destruction. This brings us back to the habit of war for personal gain.

Athens had formed the Delian League in an effort to unite the Greek cities for mutual protection. Unfortunately, Athens' great general Pericles saw Greece united under Athenian rule and largely for Athenian benefit. Athen's relations to its fellow states became more and more self-serving. Eisler cites a message that says it all. Athens was preparing to annex a small Greek city called Melos when the Melosians sent an envoy begging for mercy and justice. In their reply the Athenians tell the Melosians bluntly that they are not interested in right or wrong, merely what is expedient. Their message put it like this, 'the question of justice arises only between parties equal in strength, while the strong do what they can and the weak suffer what they must.' Athens' ruling class operated on dominator principles and cooperation for the greater good was not part of their vision.

Unfortunately, pitiless self-service generates the same in response. Resentment grew in the other states, particularly in Sparta which had dominator aristocrats of its own. In the wars that followed, Athens and Sparta took turns devastating the entire peninsula — razing towns, cutting down olive trees, sowing salt and killing large numbers of people. It was a perfect fore-runner of the calamitous fourteenth century replete with plagues and famine caused by ruination of crops. Greek unity and culture disintegrated.

Aristotle (384–322 BC), Plato's most celebrated student, thus presided over the now fading Greek miracle. He extended science like almost no one else. As tutor of Alexander the Great, he is responsible for salting Greek thinking in a place that would keep at least the intellectual aspects of the miracle alive. But dominator thinking was now in force and he added to its rationalization. In his *Politics*, he argues that nature is built of elements that are meant to rule and elements that are meant to be ruled. Aristocrats are meant to rule slaves and men are meant to rule women. Anything else violated the observable and, hence, 'the natural order,' a phrase used by generations of dominators thereafter.

As Greek glory was ending, however, Rome's great rise was beginning. Justice and collaboration had been growing for three hundred years and power had grown along with it. After reducing Carthage, its main Mediterranean rival, to a vassal state, the war machine then began to roll. Conquest succeeded conquest.

Unfortunately, intoxicated with their sudden rise to power, the new generation of statesmen departed form the wise policies of their great predecessors. They fought mercilessly and ruined the countries they conquered. They then put those countries under governors who ruled like despots trying to amass enough money in their brief tenures to last for the rest of their lives. Conquered peoples paid for this greed in blood, slavery and back-breaking taxes. Still, governors were not the only greedy ones. Tax collectors, bureaucrats and contractors who sold goods to the army, all gouged their share. As wealth poured into Rome, the ancient simplicity of Roman life gave way to avarice and a love of pomp and luxury. The great Roman character began to dissolve as vice and corruption flourished.

Enough has been written about Rome's fall that I will not belabor the point. Instead I turn to its effects on Christianity, the pivotal western religion.

Dominator Effects in Religion

By the first century AD the Roman Empire was well on its way to decadence. The taste for opulence continued throughout the Imperial period. The rich amused themselves with splendid feasts and the poor with their free bread and circuses. Remote lands were ransacked to support them both. Yet, beneath the gaudiness, decay was taking its toll. A powerful yearning for meaning afflicted both rich and poor. Growing numbers of people sought a pillar of meaning in a crumbling world and many found their solace in the upstart religion called Christianity. It became the official religion of Rome with Constantine's conversion in 312 AD.

What is less often mentioned is that Rome's fall had a profound effect upon Christianity not all of which was good. Have you ever wondered how it is that Christianity, a religion of love, came to be used to justify torture, mass murder and suppression of thought? The answer has nothing to do with Christianity's core values, but with the politics of power as it began to play out in religion. Christian institutions were swept up into power issues, precisely because Rome was going down hill.

Becoming the official religion of Rome, therefore, was not altogether good because power politics tended to corrupt the heart and soul of Christianity. Constantine, for example, probably converted because he believed Christianity would make him victorious in battle. Since he boiled his wife alive and murdered his son soon after, we should not imagine that his conversion meant that he had actually adopted Jesus' teachings. Rather he appears to have been following expedience and superstition.

Similar problems of Christian meaning versus Christian religion became rampant. Soon Christian beliefs themselves were swept up in the politics of power. Doctrine, for instance, became a political football, with economic and political issues undergirding the religious ones. As a result, compassion, moral imperative and concern for deep meaning were gradually replaced with literalism and required obedience to élite-controlled teachings. This process was well underway by the time of Constantine.

Required infallible orthodoxy became a more central issue in Western Christianity than it ever was in Judaism, Buddhism, Islam or even Eastern Christianity. Required doctrine eventually became the rationale for torture, mass murder and suppression of thought in the Middle Ages and most of the victims were Christians. Spiritual concerns were used to justify such harm, but issues of money and élite control often lay underneath. Hence, in the greatest conversion of all time, the worship of the God of Love began to spawn cruelty, bigotry, coercion and closedmindedness. Christians were taught that 'faith' means unquestioning adherence to élite-defined doctrine. This conversion colours many people's sense of religion today.

The return of the dominator ethos in religion is witnessed by a grotesque conversion. The deep values that touch people's hearts are used to support the habits which they were originally meant to oppose. While I am at it, however, let me also point out that the problem of dominator corruption is not limited to religion. It affects all institutions in a similar way. For instance, when a scientist stands up to demolish his opponent using weapons from personal attacks to social status, then that scientist is acting out the principle that 'might makes right.' Whenever this happens, science ceases to be the pursuit of understanding and becomes merely another attempt to establish control. In this small act, the entire meaning of science is corrupted. The false God of winning is substituted for the real God which is understanding. False Gods appear in many spheres.

The Causes of Social Distress

Humankind holds two visions — one which enabled us to live well and in harmony with each other and the world and another which brings us to the brink of extinction ...

Daniel Quinn

Two distinct ideals of human society lie behind history. One is based on self *regardless* of other. It values rank. The other is based on self *and* other. It seeks a collaborative society based on mutual benefit. When the dominator ethos returns it tends to undermine a great society.

If knowing leads to doing, then it is dominator thinking that will kill us. Thus, if we are going to avoid the cycle, we must understand in detail why the dominator ideal does not work. This is the story I take up here. I explore two descriptions of the usual cycle of rise and fall, one from archaeology and the other from sociology. The first gives a sense of how the social body falls apart and the second how the social mind decays. The two are related, of course. Hence, I also explore how these cycles might fit a web view of failed collaboration, failed intricacy and failure to learn.

But first, we should note one thing. Dominators usually claim their ways are necessary because they work better. Here we see the other side of the coin. Élites often do well right up until the time the society collapses around them. So when someone tells you, for instance, that the pursuit of gluttonous gain is necessary and good, then you must ask the long-term question — good for who and how long? In the end, dominator dream usually leads to devastation at home and abroad. It is not a sustainable form.

The Standard Cycle

The collapse of urban cultures is an event much more
frequent than most observers realize ... Often, collapse is
well underway before societal élites and decision-makers
become aware of it, leading to scenes of leaders responding
retroactively and ineffectively as their society collapses
around them. Sander Vander Leeuw, Archaeologist

Archaeologists too are beginning to echo themes seen elsewhere in the new science. A new breed of researchers emphasizes interdependent entities, similarities in pattern, and stages of evolution. They describe evolution as: 'some kind of development ... in which cultural phenomena became increasingly complex, although in individual cases there is some kind of devolution.'

Enter the nasty word, 'devolution,' a topic of great concern in archaeology. Hence, though debates about causes are heated, most archaeologists agree that, when it comes to civilizations, what goes up, frequently comes down. Sander Van Der Leeuw, a Belgian anthropologist, puts the point succinctly in the opening quote. Collapse is quite common and it usually surprises élites.

Why do urban cultures, also known as 'complex civilizations,' collapse? Experts agree that each collapse is at least somewhat unique, yet there are also common patterns. Working with a complexity study group headed by the dean of British archaeology, Sir Colin Renfrew, dynamicist Harry Erwin outlines the typical cycle. Note that it is a blend of intricacy, growing apart and dominator beliefs.

Stage One — Small and Mutual
Social evolution usually begins with the population growing mostly in the countryside with small cities beginning to form. In this stage, the society is likely to be a relatively egalitarian agricultural or semi-nomadic society. For example, in the Age of Judges, the Hebrew tribes were mostly shepherds with strong egalitarian modes. Both men and women could be generals or Judges. Warriors were also mustered from their tribes which made them loyal to their people instead of an employer-king.

These kinds of mutual-benefit societies exist most often when people are close to the land and each other. As the population grows, this changes.

More specialist craftsmen emerge and trading expands. Merchants and craftsmen begin to concentrate in cities and this attracts more people.

Stage Two — Growth Spurt

Stage Two begins with a sudden leap in urban population. If social stratification didn't exist before, it soon begins. Invaders may subjugate, lured in by attractive city wealth. Alternatively, a local chieftain may rise to power, often by promising wealth through war. The Hebrews, for example, converted from thirteen shepherd tribes to a traditional kingdom when attractive Caananite wealth brought out their own imperialist urge. The leap is thus often accompanied by a shift. Some combination of size, greed and conflict with other groups begins a conversion from a relatively egalitarian mutual-benefit system to a dominator one. Stratification is the academic term for classes and ranking based on privilege and exploitation. These are supported by an economic system called a 'funnel' which is designed to move wealth toward the top. (I discuss it later in this chapter.) Both are usually accompanied with an increasing use of war as a way to acquire wealth.

Still, the urban leap usually means the society is prospering, so optimism is likely to be high. People of all classes embrace society's theory and see themselves as part of a noble whole. Late Stage Two is often a golden time such as the high medieval period or the rising Roman Republic. People believe their society will last forever. But it doesn't.

Stage Three — Evolution Shaped by Élite Power

In Stage Three, the cycle begins to go too far. City wealth and opportunity attracts more peasants. Urban population grows and so does social distance. Élites become more and more separate from the peasants.

Élites are also becoming more powerful. Horses, armaments and retainers have to be paid for by taxing the peasants. Taxes increase. More wealth moving up then tends to increase ostentation in the upper classes. This in turn, creates a desire for better things which creates yet new means of extracting wealth from workers. Raising rents, reducing wages, favorable debt and usury laws — there are many ways to extract more.

Money is used to build more power. It buys slaves and soldiers loyal only to the noble. Greater power then leads to increasing self-service. In the late days of the Republic, for example, generals with personal armies occupied Rome recurrently, slaughtering opponents and forcing the Senate to their bidding. In this way, powerful élites

begin to influence social evolution in a way that serves their own interests but not necessarily the common good.

By late Stage Three, élites begin to lose touch with their society —
especially at lower levels. Concentration of power and a shrinking
sense of community has led to an élite class which is effectively decoupled from its own people. Suffering from tax burdens and other
abuses, the quality of peasant life begins to go down hill.

As élites decouple from their own people, they become more tightly
wound up with their peers. They fortify personal or family power by
strategic alliances. They become absorbed with the moves of their
rivals. There are likely to be a number of power centers with élites
who cast longing eyes at nearby wealthy cities. Keeping rivals at bay
is likely to spawn an arms race as local élites become increasingly
concerned with defending and controlling their markets. The irony is
that élites become so embroiled in their rivalries, that they bleed their
home system until it crumbles. Enter Stage Four.

Stage Four — Decoupled Élites and Rapid Decline

Élites dwell on the moves of their rivals and are out of touch with
their people. To impress and defend, élites pour money into big
armies, impressive castles, and impressive adornments which symbolize their power. They also pour money into payoff schemes, like bread
and circuses, which help salve local discontent over a system which is
less and less mutual. Finally they also deviate more and more from
their traditional role, which, in most societies, is fiduciary (internal
justice and external defense). They brandish cherished icons, but these
are now corrupted. Rhetoric masks pursuits which have little to do
with the icon's original intent. False Gods slowly replace the originals.

Powerful and arrogant, élite wellbeing climbs, while lower-class
wellbeing drops precipitously. The calamitous fourteenth century is a
good example of Stage Four. Caught up with each other and how to
advance their own wealth, Europe's knights went about the countryside
pillaging, extorting ransoms and maiming peasants. Famine, plagues
and endless wars? Peasants do not do well in Stage Four.

Signs of Failing Times

Late Stage Three and early Stage Four, however, are often a high time
for élites, so it is not surprising that they may not see anything wrong.
Erwin lists the signs of failing times as follows:

- *Élite power and wellbeing increases and is manifested in displays of wealth* — castles and palaces in the times of kings, churches in the times of faith, commercial buildings and private homes in the times of business.
- *Élites become heavily focused on maintaining a monopoly on power inside the society.* Laws become more advantageous to élites. Privileges become more pronounced and penalties more violent.
- *The sense of belonging to a community diminishes.* Previously mutual benefit systems become increasingly dominated by patronage systems. The very wealthy support their pet causes, while large numbers of people are unable to find a role.
- *The middle class shrinks and there is an increasing gap between the haves and have-nots.* The quality of life in most of the society drops. Outbreaks of disease become more massive and virulent as malnutrition and over-crowding increase. Life span decreases. The misery index mushrooms — witnessed by homicide, suicide, drug/alcohol abuse, and increasingly senseless and horrific internal violence.
- *Ecological disasters increase as short-term focus pushes ravenous exploitation of resources.* Forests are razed and land is worked to exhaustion. Exhaustion of home resources pushes élites to conquer and exploit farther and farther afield.
- *The system becomes much harder to manage.* Long-standing social patterns end and chaotic dynamics emerge.
- *There is a resurgence of conservatism and fundamentalist religions.* The society's golden theory is brought back to help ward off disaster, but it is usually in a corrupted form that serves primarily to preserve status-quo power relationships.

We have come to the stuff of which class warfare is made. The golden age wanes. Theory conflicts with reality at ever increasing turns. Erwin notes that Stage Three and Four are usually rife with class conflict. The social theory that melded people into an organic whole — be it the Roman Republic or God's Design — is now more facade than substance.

By late Stage Four élites begin to understand that something is wrong, but their discovery usually happens too late and their efforts are too haphazard. Their remedies often contribute to descent instead of countering it.

Stage Four is not inevitable, just common, as are the other phases of the cycle. It has played out in classical Greece, Egypt, Mesopotamia, the Valley of Mexico, middle and late Roman Antiquity, early Anglo-Saxon Kingdoms and China, to mention a few. It may be playing out today.[1]

Domination and the Human Ecology

Lo! Man has proved a tyrant and a fool.   Koran (33:72)

What happens to dominator civilizations? Decoupling and fraying bonds? Competition and greed among the powerful? Destroyed social root system? Yes. The end of an advanced society is usually a complex affair in which everything seems to go wrong at once. Ecological disasters such as dustbowls and flooding meet social disasters such as epidemics, riots and malnutrition. T. Patrick Culbert put it this way in his description of the Mayan collapse:

> Discussions of what caused the collapse ... pointed fingers simultaneously at almost every aspect of environment and society ... Variables were so tightly interwoven and under such general stress that almost every juncture was vulnerable ... the most interesting cause of collapse may not be the specific factors that initiate the process, but the failing structure that allowed perturbations to amplify throughout the system.

So, the answer to 'what goes wrong' is: *everything*. Dynamically speaking, however, the cause is fragility. Underneath élite self-praise, the society's natural and human ecology are growing ever more brittle — socially, politically, economically and spiritually. The reasons for this are relatively clear. Caught up in their own concerns and habits that work for themselves, élites quite literally bleed their home ecology until it crumbles. Resources are funneled disproportionately to the top. When they reach the top, they are used to fund destruction, control and impressive displays, not a healthier society. Élites are doing so well and their rationales are so tight, however, that they rarely realize that this is a problem until it is too late. The root problem is that the dominator system is based on exploitation and uncurbed power and this problem tends to get worse with size and success.

Since we still use dominator assumptions, we too are prone to the 'tyrant and fool' cycle of civilization. Since we exhibit all of the signs of failing times, we may even be farther along in the cycle than one might imagine. How might we avoid a Stage Four? It might help to understand why societies which were once golden become fragile instead. Here we find that, while everything goes wrong, socially speaking, there are three main problems:

- Decoupling
- Draining
- Cognitive corruption (an originally vibrant belief system is turned to other ends).

Here I draw out the first two. The third will take a section of its own.

Decoupling — Broken Bonds and Failed Collaboration

Human ties are very important. They help keep people committed to the good of the social whole. Unfortunately, as an organization gets bigger, distance grows and bonds break. Decoupling is a result of the complexity catch. Subgroups grow apart. Social collaboration begins to fail.

Decoupling happens easily in dominator societies because coercive hierarchies encourage a sense of separation and alienation between top and bottom. An already thin commitment to the common good grows gaunt and breaks. Decoupling is also particularly dangerous among élites because they have more power. It happens at all levels, but élites press the system to follow their interests regardless of the effect on the larger whole.

Hence, one of the most noticeable aspects of failing times is that the society's élites cease to function as part of the organic whole. They become fixated on the moves of their rivals and lose all perspective on what their society needs for health. Wound up with themselves and others of their ilk, they pursue their self-interest to the death of their society. They often won't see a problem because they are insulated. Everyone around them agrees!

This same pattern plays out whether it is railroad magnates of the late 1800s, Roman generals of the first-century BC or modern politicians battling each other. It is why fourteenth century knights who once brought order, began to bring chaos instead. The implication for us is simple, if distressing. Beware a society where human ties no longer bind. Committed collaboration is about to fail. Failing bonds and collaboration create fragility and a system designed to fall apart.

As élites pursue their habit of pillage, however, a more insidious problem builds. Warring rivals need money to press their cause. This brings me to the second cause of fragility.

Draining — Dominator Economic Practices

Coercive hierarchies are bad because they create alienation between top and bottom. Dominator economic practices are bad because they funnel wealth from bottom to top. As élites become more wrapped up with their rivals, funneling accelerates. Exploitation grows along with armaments and impressive displays. Hence, though social collapse involves many threads, economic failure is usually the most prominent. The French Revolution, for instance, came on the heels of financial collapse. Similarly, the medieval world crumbled after nobles and clerics began indulging their taste for the finer things and bleeding the peasants to do so.

Economic failure also has a particular appearance: ostentation grows at one end while misery grows at the other. Since dominator economic practices grew out of subjugation, this outcome is not actually surprising. The end is merely a more extreme form of the beginning, one made worse by greater power and less sense of community.

If we want to find another way, the first step is to realize that funneling is not the only way. Indeed, we already know the alternative.

A Contrast in Economic Vision

> *When one is studying aggression in different cultures ... one of the things one looks for is the degree to which economic distribution is set up according to the siphon method or the funnel method. These two methods do not correlate with stages in human progress, but they are relevant to the kind of individual behaviour that occurs.* Ruth Benedict[2]

Most of us have wondered why some people are incredibly rich while a few feet down the road others sleep on the street and can't feed their children. Today, theorists usually attribute this situation to intrinsic abilities. Economists have been listening to Darwinists! They believe people at the top got there because they are good. Success accurately reflects value. Presumably people on the bottom stay there because they are bad, apparently in most ways. Gross inequities are merely the natural order of things. There is nothing we can do — or so we are told.

If we are ever going to do better with our world, we had best come up with a more realistic explanation of why starvation exists next to gluttonous wealth. The first step in countering this naive picture is to realize that not all societies have horribly distorted distributions of wealth. This means that gross inequities have much more to do with the society's belief system, than with any intrinsic economic laws or inevitable natural orders.

This brings me to Ruth Benedict, a solid, well-known American anthropologist who penned the opening quote and with it, the first solid insight into why current explanations of inequity are at best naive and, at worst, self-serving. She helps us see that what we have is not the only workable way. After looking at a lot of cultures, Benedict came to the conclusion that economic systems fall into two main types, which she labeled: *funnels* and *siphons*. These reflect exploitative systems and mutual-benefit ones respectively.

Funnels — Dominator Habits in Economics

> *This system depends upon certain men's claim to the labor*
> *of others, or upon ownership or rights given to favored*
> *persons ... It reaches its highest development where there is*
> *'interest' and where wealth can be used to obtain forced*
> *labor.*

Funnel economies are designed to move wealth toward the richest persons. As Benedict says: 'The collective wealth has only one prime destination, the person who already has valuable possessions.' We've seen it before. It is the pattern which came from subjugation. Funneling continues today with more civilized forms of leverage and more enlightened claims to disproportional gain. Benedict describes some of these in the opening quote. Unfortunately, regardless of how the funnel is implemented, its social implications remain the same. Funneling creates anxiety and social tension everywhere. As Benedict says:

... no man in the funneling system can reach a security from which he cannot be dislodged either by other rich men ganging up on him, or by failure of crops, or by death in his family ... His only security lies in having, not merely property, but more property than his neighbour. He is driven into rivalry with his peers and he must outdo them, or better yet, undo them if he can. He is driven into rivalry not because he is a bad man or because he is ungenerous, but impersonally, because the system works that way. Copying the rich man, the poor man competes too and tries to outdo other poor men.

Funnel systems foster anxiety, competitiveness, anger and aggression which afflicts all classes. Because personal security depends on outdoing one's neighbour, people are pushed into aggression and no one feels they can stop. One has to pursue economic war because everyone else is too. Life in a funnel is therefore very distressing. Dominator economics create a self-fulfilling prophesy of struggle and war.

Siphons — Committed Collaboration in Economics

Being constantly at war is not a good way to create a healthy, sustainable society. Therefore, it is important to realize that this is not the only way. Furthermore, the other way has always been with us. The alternative, siphon economies, are best thought of as common-cause economies. Assets and human energy are applied where they are needed and in a way that is mutually beneficial. Benedict calls them siphons because they tend to draw wealth away from stagnant concentrations and spread it throughout the community. Siphon societies do this by encouraging wealth to pass from hand to hand. Benedict writes:

Thus, if one has fields, one's neighbours gather at work bees and one feeds and entertains them at planting, hoeing and reaping seasons. The siphon system ensures great fluidity of wealth; if a man has meat or garden produce or horses or cattle, these give him no standing except as they pass through his hands to the tribe at large.

People in such societies often have differing roles and ranks, but here rank is not used as a means of leverage, privilege or exploitation. Rather, roles are fiduciary. They are oriented toward serving the com-

munity and involve responsibility, not advantage. The difference between fiduciary and exploitative roles is easy to see. In the highland
clans of Scotland and among the plains Indians of North America, for
example, the chief's job was to organize common-cause efforts and
make sure that all members were cared for. Chiefs did not get rich off
other people's labor. Hence, in a circulating system, the prize is honour, respect and the reciprocating commitment which comes with
service to the greater good.

Wrapped in funnel anxieties, many modern people find these
rewards too flimsy. We want to know how to safeguard our personal
security and we assume the only way to do this is by accumulating assets. Siphon societies, however, are actually reassuring places because
they are of necessity built on the premise of social solidarity — no one
suffers more than the rest. People are aware of their mutual dependence. Because of this, they focus on serving the society *and* themselves. The social side of siphons is, thus, very different than that of
a funnel. Benedict states:

> Since everyone is provided for ... poverty is not a word to fear,
> and anxiety, which develops so luxuriantly in funnel societies,
> is absent to a degree that seems incredible to us. These are
> preeminently the societies of good will, where murder and
> suicide are rare or actually unknown. If such societies have
> periods of great scarcity, all members of the community
> cooperate to get through these periods as best they can.

If we are to successfully navigate our times, it is also important to realize
that common-cause economics are still active the world over. Islam, for
instance, still asks its adherents to follow a set of economic practices
designed to ensure that the weak are cared for and that each person realizes
a role in the ever-growing circle of communities, from family and city, to
world and cosmos. Islamic economics is still a major force for everyday
Muslims in many countries. The heartland of America also still has habits
of common cause. Many people there are but a generation from small-
farmer or immigrant enclaves where the bonds of community meant
something. People in such communities help one another in ways large
and small. Our images of craftsmen and small-town businessmen who take
pride in personal integrity reflect this culture.

The commitment and integrity which flourishes in this culture creates a sense of assurance which softens some of the grimmer aspects of existence. The social benefits of siphons also explains something most of us know but rarely manage to articulate — namely that such systems serve as beacons in our dreams. Most of us don't want to live by anxiously scratching out for Number One, bravely denying the possibility that illness, divorce, accident, age or economic downturn will leave us at the mercy of an uncaring society. We yearn for some long-past 'good old days' in when belonging, sharing and caring seemed natural. We imagine that once upon a time work and love went hand in glove and both made life worth living.

Our imaginations are not actually so far off. Human beings can and do live in societies where solidarity is central. Such societies are more peaceful and satisfying. Hence, we actually know these kinds of common-cause economies. Sharing threshing machines at harvest, trading child-care services and helping out the aged or infirm — these kinds of unsung economic activities are natural parts of most societies. Such activities have nothing to do with accumulation *per se*. They have everything to do with surviving together by working for the common good as well as oneself.

Siphon and funnel systems have the same relationship as mutualist and dominator cultures, of course. Thus, most modern societies are schizophrenic with the siphons and mutualism living within a power-structure built on funnels and domination. If we are ever to navigate our times, it is important to grasp the key difference between them.

■ Funneling is based on self *regardless* of others. It promotes accumulation of personal wealth and emphasizes acquisition of power and privilege. It encourages struggle with one's fellows.

■ Siphons are based on self *and* other. They promote justice and common wellbeing. People play different roles and have different incomes, but they feel bound to the community. The society goes up and down together.

This brings me to the point. We often overlook common-cause economics because they don't seem to count. We forget them because they are increasingly hard to find. But mutual-benefit economics are important. Far from being Utopian, if a society becomes too much of a funnel and too little of a siphon, it will begin to look like Rome in the later days. Élites flourish, but they sit atop a slowly dying world.

Building an Economic Bubble

Successful imperialism wins wealth. Yet, historically,
successful empires such as Persia, Rome, Byzantium,
Turkey, Spain, Portugal, France, Britain, have not remained
rich. Indeed, it seems to be the fate of empires to become
too poor to sustain the very costs of empire. The longer an
empire holds together, the poorer and more economically
backward it tends to become.   Jane Jacobs[3]

Funneling may be done by individuals, businesses or governments. All
funneling does harm. The organized governmental variety, however,
is generally the most destructive (think of Louis XVI). Élites trying to
build or maintain an empire, funnel faster in order to pay for their
pursuits. The result is a bubble economy: the shimmering wealth of a
few obscures the increasing misery of many.

   This leads to the great paradox of dominator economics. Empire-
building tends to destroy the home world. Imperialists hope to out run
the problem by gobbling up prey. But the food does not circulate
throughout. The body of the beast starves, while its head grows fat.
Thus, though we assume empires are desirable, big empires actually
tend to create grinding poverty in the home populace. Other lands are
pillaged to make élites incredibly wealthy, but the home world withers
nevertheless. This paradox is a result of funneling and it is still at
work today.hy do grand empires tend to wither, not thrive? Let us look
at a more modern example. In 1984, years before its actual end,
economist Jane Jacobs forecast the demise of the Soviet Union for
economic reasons. The Soviet socio-economic body was going necrotic
largely because its élites were funneling resources into imperial
necessities such as the arms race. Jacobs' more interesting insight was
that the Soviet situation was not an unusual case. Socio-economic
necrosis is often a direct result of economic activities used to build and
maintain empires. Jacobs calls these activities 'transactions of decline.'
The reason for the name is simple — transactions which build empires
also sew the seeds of decline. The root problem is that empires are
held together by military power and bribes, not committed
collaboration. As a result their care-takers must use certain economic
techniques to hold the empire together. Jacobs' list of transactions of
decline, include:

- Maintenance of large militaries;
- Economic structuring that centralizes control and fosters dependence on the state;
- Economic placation of rebellious factions in the form of subsidies, pensions, welfare, etc.

These should all sound familiar because they are still common today. They help shore up political entities brought together by force and their basic forms are very old. Unfortunately, payoffs, central control and military spending channel economic energy into ends that do not give back in kind. Money goes into artificial controls and often into nothing but smoke.

Why channel so much energy into militarism, placation and control? Jacobs emphasizes that most nations do not pursue these transactions today for simple reasons of powerlust. Rather, most élites see themselves as performing the job their society hired them to do — hold the system together. As Jacobs writes:

> ... Germany supports French agricultural regions because if it didn't, the European Economic Community would break down, and France insists on the subsidies as a condition of its membership because otherwise France could not contain the anger of its farmers or the ever simmering threat of separatism in the country's south.
>
> Canada frankly calls its systems of national equalization payments to poor provinces the sinews that hold the country together. It combats separatist sentiments in Quebec in the same fashion that the English combat separatist feelings in Scotland: by reminding pensioners and other recipients of transfer payments ... where their money is coming from. (1984, p.213)

This self-destructive pattern is also found in societies which do not see themselves as empires *per se*. Indeed, social theories that sound wonderfully enlightened often end up more self-destructive than the more obvious imperialists. For example, from Jacob's point of view, the Soviet and Chinese communist economies were/are not significant new episodes in economic history, but rather traditional imperialistic economies cloaked in new theories. Both systems over-ran old empires on the brink of dissolution and succeeded in reconsolidating them by force of arms. Thereafter, both depended to an extreme degree on transactions of decline — military spending, payoffs, etc. — to hold their political units together. In the old Soviet Union, for example, whatever wealth Soviet cities created was promptly devoted to subsidies for other parts of the nation and purposes of the state. The only thing that changed significantly in China and the Soviet Union was the greater efficiency and ruthlessness which the communist regimes brought to the task of holding their sovereignties together.

Becoming policeman to the world, arms races such as the cold-war — one does not have to see oneself as building an empire to fall into the trap. Unfortunately, transactions of decline drain economic health regardless of motive.

This brings me to another of Jacobs' forecasts: American decline. What is her logic? Massive military spending, a huge centralized bureaucracy, payoffs to foreign governments, home corporations, and welfare recipients — the pattern is uncomfortably clear. Even Reagan-era trickle-down theory which rejected Big Government, nevertheless proudly promoted gluttonous military spending. Deficits skyrocketed as never before. President Bush proclaimed that this spending had won the cold war — and maybe it did — but it also damaged the robust side of the American economic web. Arms races are a standard imperialist necessity and they accelerate decline on both sides.

And so, Jacobs' point. Regardless of motive, when nations employ transactions of decline they enter the list of imperialistic economies likely to decline shortly after having reached their pinnacle of glory. Imperialist practices, even in their most well-intentioned forms, are destructive of the synergetic side of life and economies. So watch closely for the three main draining activities.

- Prolonged and unremitting military production,
- Prolonged and unremitting payoffs and subsidies to potential discontents and also allies,
- Heavy promotion of trade between advanced and backward economies.

We are back to the beginning. Draining eventually wreaks havoc. Imperial governments pull wealth from the grassroots and then use most of it to fund control, cronyism and impressive displays — not a healthier society. Élites at the top will not see anything wrong because they will be surrounded by a shimmering bubble of wealth (see Figure 39).

They don't see an increasingly fragile human and natural ecology because their world is filled with power and privilege, not misery and injustice. Élites drain their home societies often without realizing that this is a problem. They create dustbowls, moneyless mobs and malnutrition.

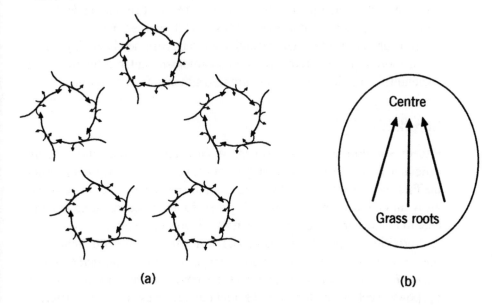

(a) (b)

Figure 39. An economic ecology versus an economic bubble built by a dominator funnel.
In a web view, an economy is an ecology. Like all ecologies, energy must flow robustly throughout to keep the system healthy. Intricacy means energy flows in fine-grained cycles throughout an incredibly entwined, maze-like whole. Funneling, however, tends to create a large bubble of wealth with very little infrastructure underneath. This bubble looks good from the outside and especially from the top, but it is actually very fragile. The internal eco-system is dying.

The Corruption of Head, Heart and Soul

> *Sorotkin does not say that Western Civilization is about to fall, although a collapse as devastating as that suffered by ancient Rome is always a possibility for an advanced sensate society such as ours.* William Bainbridge[4]

Dominators have a particularly insidious effect on belief systems. The more powerful élites become, the more they twist the society's cherished symbols to fit their sensibilities. As they become more powerful, their interests also tend to diverge more from common good. Ancient icons remain but they begin to serve different ends. False Gods have replace golden ideals. Deep need goes unmet.

Spiritual and intellectual corruption are thus common in ending times. Pitrim Sorotkin, the famous Russian sociologist, centered his theory of societal rise and fall on it. I now turn to his theory for a better view.

Sorotkin's Cycle

Pitirim Sorotkin had reason to care about cycles of civilization. As an official in the democratic Russian government overthrown by Lenin during the First World War, he had seen how an idealistic surge could be swept away and replaced by a tyrannical system based on coercive power and able to countenance seemingly boundless levels of cruelty.

Sorotkin escaped to the U.S. and founded the Harvard School of Sociology in the 1930s. His 3000-page master work, *Social and Cultural Dynamics,* documents analogous cycles of common-cause ideals replaced by power-seeking materialism throughout the ages. He uses different words to trace out cycles like those of Greece and Rome, but the essence is the same. What I call mutualism fits with what Sorotkin calls *ideational culture*. What I call dominator mode fits what Sorotkin calls *sensate culture*.

Sorotkin's words make more sense in many ways because many societies are militaristic throughout their cycle. The key in Sorotkin's cycle, then, is how a society with common-cause ideals turns into a society of scrapping, self-serving, materialists. What kills a society here is the shift from working together to serving oneself regardless of others.

Sorotkin's description is also helpful because it shows how two-culture tensions produce an S-shaped curve from common-cause to parochial interest. Let us start with the up-side.

The Spiritual Spur

> ... *at its birth, a civilization bases itself on a coherent set of*
> *spiritual beliefs which give it strength. To the extent that its*
> *[ideals are] successful, it grows and develops.*

According to Sorotkin, civilizations which have an impact on history, start as integrated wholes. People at all levels see themselves a part of a honourable society. Commitment is high and generally freely given. The most powerful cultures also have a view of reality which is essentially spiritual. People see themselves as engaged in a larger mission which requires they look beyond themselves and serve a greater good. It is this spiritual spur which gives wings to people's feet and energy to their efforts.

This spiritual vision need not be of a 'God' *per se*. The key is dedication to what Sorotkin called a *transcendent*, a design larger than individual men and even larger than the current state of the culture. This dedication to a larger design has practical benefits. For instance, it helps justify learning, that is, continual social change toward ever better approximations of the ideal. Roman plebes, for example, spent three hundred years establishing a habit of political self-reform and the end was a civic character in which all classes took pride.

Successful cultures work hard at moving everyday life toward their vision. Roman citizens worked at building a Republic out of civic virtue and political self-reform. Medieval men worked at building the City of God on earth. Enlightenment men worked to reinvent civilization to reflect liberty, equality, compassion, reason, and social justice. There are many examples.

Pursuit of ennobling ideals also gives a sense of meaning to life. There is a mission. Furthermore, because most people in the society feel drawn to the mission, it helps harness intelligence and initiative at all levels. Many hearts willingly pursue the same cherished end.

A society engaged in an ennobling mission is the most powerful organization on the face of the earth. Bonded individuals seeking an ideal also create a powerful society of mind. They are the ultimate example of 'think globally, act locally.' Sorotkin called these 'ideational cultures.' I would call them learning societies.

The Rise of Sensate Materialism

... As time passes, [a society] slowly loses its grip on its
spirituality, doubt sets in, and the culture becomes
progressively more sensate.

The catch is that societies must keep on learning. Societies that become successful, however, are likely to become complacent, believing theirs to be the one true way to do civilization. Money and power are also likely to attract the self-serving. This leads to the other side of the curve. Sorotkin believed a *sensate* mode also lay dormant within these societies. It begins to rise.

A sensate culture's aims are materialistic. Sensates emphasize acquisition, accumulation, pleasure and power. They usually try to realize their aims through exploitation of other people and the external world. They range from manipulative to malevolent. Concepts like common good and serving a larger design are not high on their list. Rather, sensates believe that reality is strictly what lays before one's eyes. There is no design, no deeper meaning and no direction except that made by individual will. Since there isn't any larger mission, there is also no reason to serve a cause higher than oneself. Might and cunning are the only right and reality is what the powerful create.

Glaucon in late Golden Greece spoke for this group and late clockwork science seems to have become a rationalization of it. Yet, Sorotkin actually saw three varieties of sensates.

▪ *Active sensates* use empire-building and technologies of war to bend the external world to their materialistic will.

▪ *Passive sensates* indulge themselves in pleasures of the flesh.

▪ *Cynical sensates* do not attempt to dominate the material world openly, but rather shift their face to suit in a calculated attempt to profit from the power of ideas. They often appear to be serving traditional ideals, but this is a ruse for their real aim which is personal profit, power or control.

Cynical sensates are the most dangerous kind because they intentionally manipulate fears and heart-felt hopes in a calculated attempt to profit from the power of values. Any icon is up for grabs. Right-wing pundits, for example, turn 'freedom' into 'laissez faire' defined as the right to be rapacious without caring whether one is serving the society or destroying it. Cynical sensates invariably claim to be driven by principle, but this is only a ploy. Unfortunately, after a while it becomes hard to tell what the truth is.

In this century Capitalist, Communist, and Fascist sensates, have all used idealistic ruses to mask power-grasping ends. Fascism and Communism, for example, were each billed as a common-cause rise, yet the élites of each group became more ruthless and oppressive than their more openly dominator predecessors. The Washington DC body politic is another example. American cynical sensates train followers to manipulate cultural icons (such as freedom). The hope and fear these icons generate is then channeled into self-serving ends and the veneer of integrity is shamelessly thin. Indeed, manipulation is done quite openly, explained by that ultimately pragmatic belief — 'winning is everything.' The cynical circle is complete. Deceit is valid because, after all, there is no design except that which is made through might.

Malaise and Incendiary Conditions

> ... At the extreme [the society] is so thoroughly sensate that it lacks a spiritual core and dissolves or is conquered by a stronger civilization that is still in an ideational or idealistic phase.

False Gods and clever ruses, however, obscure paths toward a better society. People swimming in a sea of lies, can no longer tell what is really going on. Floundering in a world which no longer makes sense but which they are told is golden, people become despondent. Soon power seems unchallengeable, corruption impenetrable and malaise immovable.

Undirected anger grows with disenchantment. Pockets of frustrated human energy begin to litter the landscape, looking for a home. Anger bursts forth sporadically in various places. Riots, senseless violence, substance abuse: the signs are understandable, if distressing.

Eventually, shrinking wellbeing and pent-up frustration in the great core of society, the middle class, brings the society to the brink. One sees this in America today. Surveys show that 80% of the American populace feels alienated from — and disenfranchised by — the two major political parties and the system as it stands. Americans no longer believe the system is serving America's mission or moving toward its ideals. They no longer believe their government is pursuing intelligent strategies for the common good. Rather, their government seems aimed at serving special interests regardless of how this affects the people as a whole. Ideals appear to be shams and concern for the common good a farce. Yet, Americans are not alone. Similar feelings are found in most developed countries.

The Fragility Zone

> The mad mob does not ask how it could be better, only that it
> be different. And when it then becomes worse, it must change
> again. Thus, they get bees for flies, and at last hornets for bees.
>
> Martin Luther, 1526

Free-floating human energy creates incendiary conditions which radicals with sparkling alternatives can ignite. A host of sparkling alternatives bubble around, popping up everywhere in response to growing disenchantment. New ideas become as thick as fleas.

Paradoxically, incendiary times also bring a fragility which makes learning easier. The system is now poised on the edge. It becomes more sensitive to nudges (no matter how massive its momentum). This is the time of Chaos, wild swings and great sensitivity. Poise, however, makes tipping to a new way easier. If the society manages to seize a positive alternative, it may find a way to reinvent itself without undergoing a catastrophe. Reinvention amounts to breaking out of entrenched habit

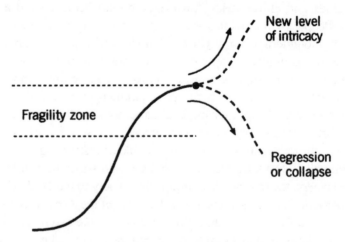

Figure 40. Fragility and a Turning Which Can Go Two Ways.

patterns which now thoroughly stifle learning and common-cause needs. Reinvention also includes renewed commitment to the mission, that is, to pursuing the dream of a society built on justice, compassion and soul.

Reinvention can happen without collapse. The Enlightenment, for example, was fed by radicals who popped up everywhere and it was eventually embraced by people of all classes, even absolutist monarchs such as Frederick of Prussia. Japan's Mejii Restoration in the late 1800s is perhaps a better example. With European powers knocking at their door, the Japanese had to drop their feudal system with its bickering warlords or they would become a colony of Europe. Their switch from feudalism to a modern nation-state was accomplished in about twenty years.

Unfortunately, a society in the fragility zone can turn either way. Clever manipulations brought by cynical sensates create lots of problems. People swimming in a sea of lies grasp at bright lights, but they have no way of knowing if there is quality behind them. Given the degree of pent-up energy, it is easy to see why things might get worse instead of better. The fog is thick, but people are desperate.

If the downside takes hold, then corrupted old-thinking will rise. This is why ending times are marked by a resurgence of conservatism and fundamentalist religions. Believing that what is good for them is good for everyone, conservatives press reform in exactly the wrong direction. They become more authoritarian, more doctrinaire and more coercive. Locked into maintaining their personal advantage, they block all but trivial improvements.

The downside of the curve leads to regression and possibly collapse. It can also lead to a take-over by a more ruthless set of dominators. The Russian Revolution, for example, brought Stalin, not the egalitarian society intended. (see Figure 40).

Gore Vidal tells an illustrative story. If you throw a frog in boiling water, it will jump and scream and try to get out. If you put a frog in cold water and then heat it to the boiling point, it will die without complaint. So it is with a slowly building cloud of confusion that is killing a golden tradition. The change happens so slowly that neither élites nor commoners sense much amiss until the damage is done.

None of this is inevitable, however. It is just likely given how coercive hierarchies work and how dominators build their dreams.

Cycles, ever Cycles

... the Golden Age, was said to be an age of paradise, a time
when humankind lived completely in the bounty of nature ... the
Age of Silver, was also much like a paradise, but human
distance from nature had increased ... the Age of Bronze,
brought with it aggression and distrust ... Finally, with the Iron
Age 'came trickery and slyness, plotting, swindling, violence
and the damned desire of having.'

The observation that civilizations go through cycles of rise and fall
— which have a lot to do with fraying bonds and self interest run amuck
— is thousands of years old. The archaeologists' standard cycle is not new,
nor is Sorotkin's story. The description in the opening quote, for example, was developed by the Roman poet Ovid some two thousand years ago.
Writing during the last days of Rome's Republic when civil war brought
the rise and subsequent assassination of Julius Caesar, one might assume
that Ovid was merely describing his time. But, then, the story of bountiful
paradise turned to endless in-fighting and greed is much like Sumeria's
story — only Sumeria was two thousand years before Ovid.[5]

History does repeat, even for us. Today, signs of failing times abound,
from malaise and the surge of fundamentalism to plagues like AIDS and
eco-disasters like global warming. There is even a nasty growing gap.
Shimmering wealth obscures growing misery. Such signs bespeak a social
structure which is unable to live sustainably, inside or out.

Great observers from time immemorial have also said that most of the
problem has to do with the return of the dominator ethos. What most great
observers don't point out is that the penchant for both cultures is found
everywhere — in men and women, top and bottom, all cultures and every
'ism' you can think of. This means, for instance, that one cannot identify
foes by labels alone. Most traditional splits, such as Christians against
Muslims or management versus workers or men versus women are
misleading. Within each of these groups are people who share the same
deep dream — justice, compassion, freedom, equality, and harmony with
the greater design. Within each also are people who are dominators.
Regardless of the theories they espouse, they are actually seeking power
and privilege regardless of the cost to others.

Dominator thinking is humanity's true enemy and it is still with us today. Hence, we teach our children that everyone is out for themselves, that nature has no design, that warring rapacious genes create quality, and that one should never try to reign-in ruthless competitors because they automatically produce the best of all possible worlds. We assume that our social system is an inevitable 'natural order' in which some people were meant to rule and others to fall through the cracks. Exploitation still runs rampant, now justified by economic necessity. *Arete* — glory seeking and displays of self-serving cleverness — are encouraged among élites. No one talks about curbing power for the common good.

What can we do to block the dominator ethos? I am hoping that Integral insights may help. For instance, the lessons of dynamic evolution are: learning, collaboration and intricacy. All of these can fail.

- *Draining (Failed Intricacy)* — A human society is like an ecology. It is made sturdy by strong bonds, fine-grained connections and robust flow (intricacy). Human ecologies are also made strong by spiritual spurs, mutual benefit and common-cause ideals. These create intelligence and commitment which is distributed throughout.

  Dominator habits run against all this. Dominator systems run best on a simple classist structure held together through leverage, privilege and intimidation. As funneling increases, so does anxiety and aggression. Grassroots shrivel and the system becomes unstable. The human ecology crumbles.

- *Decoupling (Failed Collaboration)* — Size and exploitative habits also pull a society apart. As élites become powerful and more distant, human bonds break. Absorbed with their rivals, élites undermine their own society. They won't see a problem because they are doing well.

- *Corruption (Failure to Learn)* — Coercive hierarchies breed entrenchment and corruption. Institutions which originally pursued the greater good, eventually become maintainers of absolute truths which are enforced regardless of how much they harm. The God of Love becomes a rationale for torture. Freedom becomes a rationale for pillage. Survival requires a new leap of learning, but those in the hierarchy often feel a vested interest in suppressing reform.

Our own times become a bit clearer. Our élites are often insular and absorbed only with their rivals. Empire-building continues under an economic guise, yet the same old signs arise. Look again at the signs of failing times and ask yourself: is the economic system in front of us aimed more at (a) justice and common wellbeing? or (b) accumulation of wealth and expansion of exploitative power among élites? Western civilization at large is currently pursuing the latter in hopes that it will automatically produce the former. It never has before.

If we want to avoid regression (or collapse), we are going to have rediscover ennobling ideals which give wings to people's feet and commitment to their souls. If we are going to reinvent ourselves intelligently, however, then we must look more closely at socio-economic problems and possibilities. The next chapter explores how web thinking plays out in economics.

CHAPTER 8

THE ECONOMIC DEBATE

Not understanding the nature of complex systems, we regularly
create our own catastrophes, all with the best of intentions.

Jeffrey Long

So, how are the world's economies doing anyway? The Soviet Union fell, so presumably communist economic principles are flawed. America, the epitome of Enlightenment Capitalism, self-interest and competition, stands triumphant! Or does it? Throughout the developed world something is not quite right. But what is wrong?

Apparently it is hard to say what is wrong. There is a malaise, but experts disagree as to whether there is good economic reason for gloom or whether it is just sour grapes. A story aired on America's National Public Radio (NPR) in January 1995 is a good example of the debate. The story was on middle-class anxiety about the economy — an anxiety which abounds right now. Unfortunately, the experts were divided as to whether this anxiety was a reaction to *real* problems or just alarmist tendencies. After all, the numbers were good! At the time of the airing, the American economy appeared to be growing so fast that the Federal Reserve had just raised interest rates to avoid inflation.

Some of the show's experts thus pointed to numbers which said incomes were up and the economy was great. According to this group, anxiety was really about other things: crime, welfare and too much government. As one said, 'I think people are disgusted with too many taxes.'

Other economists took a different stance, however. They said wages were declining, the gap between rich and poor growing, and that the economic implications of this were real. Most everyday Americans sided with this group, as a survey by researcher Ethel Kline suggested. Kline asked people a now standard question: 'If the economy is doing better, why are *you* feeling so insecure?' She quoted the survey results as follows:

A good 25% think that the statistics are lying. I'm not sure if they
think there is a conspiracy about cooking them but they certainly
think that somebody is getting it wrong. Another 25% said things
change faster on top than on the bottom and eventually the
improvement in the economy would trickle down into their lives.
But the rest, the majority, said ... that what is going on out there is
that the economy can no longer support the kind of growth that
many of us grew up expecting and wanting.

Thus, most people and a number of experts believe that middle-class
anxiety is a reaction to real changes in the economy. One of these experts
argued that the post-World War II boom was an aberration and virtually
everyone in American public life knew it. People differed only in who they
blamed for the boom's end. Conservatives blamed people like welfare
mothers for pulling the country down. Liberals blamed the labor force
saying it needed better training. Kline put the average person's sense of the
reality like this:

I think the fundamental source of middle class anxiety is that
people know, no matter what the economists tell them about the
numbers, that this economy is in a period of restructuring, that
there is no job security, that whatever job growth exists is erratic
and not necessarily in good jobs. The IBM workers who used to
think they had a job for life are now completely wiped out ... They
now see minimal security anywhere ... In their hearts, they believe
they are going to have to lower their expectations.

This economic restructuring is also creating a sense of betrayal. With
the advent of the global economy American corporations are no
longer seen as concerned with America or its workers. Economic growth is
seen as expanding élite wellbeing, but not middle-class wellbeing
and certainly not lower class wellbeing. This feeling is born
out by numbers. Wealth is going up at only one end of the spectrum.
Between 1980 and 1992, incomes in the top quarter went up 15% while
those in the bottom quarter went down 6.8%.[1] The top fifth now takes in
49.1% of the total income while the bottom fifth takes in 4.4%. The plight
of the poor is so bad that of the 35 million families in poverty over two-
thirds had a least one person working. Small wonder a sense of
betrayal is growing. Those at the top argue for an end to minimum

wage, while workers at the bottom have to work two jobs to feed their children.

But why is this happening? What if anything can be done about it? The experts had little advice. One thought technology was making jobs obsolete. Another blamed the advent of the global economy. As he said, 'How do Americans compete in a world of six billion people, most of them willing to work for less than we are?'

Similar feelings are expressed throughout the developed world. So people sit in a malaise, with only a vague sense of what is wrong and an even vaguer sense about what to do. Economists can be found on both sides and even the most optimistic theories seem to assume upper-echelon wealth is enough. There is, however, an ominous possiblity. Writing in 1984 well before the collapse of the Soviet Union, Jane Jacob said:

> Today the Soviet Union and the United States each predicts and anticipates the economic decline of the other. Neither will be disappointed.

Jacobs based her forecast on economic evidence. Anthropologists make the same point more simply. The pattern now being played out in America and elsewhere in the developed world has happened before with great regularity. It is the pattern which precedes every great social collapse. Historically, a shrinking middle class and a growing gap between rich and poor indicates a bubble economy. A shimmering facade of élite wellbeing obscures lower class misery and socio-economic fragility.

* * *

Economics is where all the threads of human complexity come together with a vengeance. Belief systems, social patterns, and whether we can feed our families, are all rolled into one. Today, economists face two particularly thorny dilemmas:

- They are trying to understand a highly-entwined system using clockwork tools and assumptions. These often misportray webs but are highly institutionalized.
- They work with a system which is heavily laced with dominator thinking. This thinking is well-rationalized thanks in large part to Darwinism.

We should have sympathy for economists because theirs is a leviathan task. We should cajole them because Jeffery Long is right: 'Not understanding the nature of complex systems, we regularly create our own catastrophes.' Warning signs already abound. Let us start with misleading math.

Economics and the Madness of Method

Could it be that the nation's economic experts live in a statistical Potemkin village that hides the economy Americans are actually seeing?
                    Clifford Cobb, Ted Halstead, and Jonathan Rowe

Economists were some of the first researchers to realize that their system was interwoven and that this was important. Unfortunately, they too have been limited by the tools available. Following the lead of seventeenth-century physics, most economics is still based on simple causality, linear models and underestimating intricacy. Not knowing that this is a problem, economists often exacerbate the crises they seek to avert. They do so unwittingly, often with the best of intentions. How much could economic theory change? Let us start with how adding one more connection, radically alters the traditional picture.

Big Change Hidden in a Small Addition

In 1990 Brian Arthur wrote an article on economics for *Scientific American,* one of America's premier scientific journals. What great advance did this article describe? The addition of positive feedback to economic models. Positive feedback is the technical name for a feedback loop which creates an increasing spiral of return. It is best understood via the cliché, 'the more you have, the more you get.' The classic example is the VCR market in the early 1980s.

In the early 1980s when VCRs were just beginning, two formats, VHS and Beta, were vying for supremacy. Both emerged at about the same time for about the same price and with roughly equal market shares. The market-share of each seesawed for a variety of reasons in the beginning, but as demand built up, a feedback cycle suddenly clicked in. Video stores originally stocked both formats but this required high inventories. As the number of available movies grew, the pressure to stock only one format grew too. Forced to choose, stores began to select one format over the other based on what format they thought their customers wanted most. This put pressure on the customers to choose and they began buying their VCRs based on their perception of what format would be most available in stores. Each side fed the other and a feedback cycle of 'the-format-that-has-more, gets-more' took root and accelerated. At some point the momentum of that cycle tilted in favor of the VHS format leading it to take over virtually the entire VCR market. The choice of format became locked in and VHS became what Arthur calls, a 'frozen accident.'

Arthur uses phrases like 'frozen accident' and 'locked-in' because there is strong evidence that Beta was a superior product available for an equal price. Thus, VHS cannot be said to be the best choice in any absolute terms. Rather, small bits of strategy, happenstance and luck produced an exaggerated and unpredictable result that dominated the course of the VCR market thereafter. Nor was the VHS lock-in a quirk. Arthur shows that positive feedback and frozen accidents are common. The rise of Microsoft's MS-DOS as the standard operating-system for U.S. personal computers is also an example. Software vendors writing for one system (or another) created a 'the-more-you-have, the-more-you-get' cycle which eventually locked most vendors into Microsoft's format though many others would have worked.

Positive feedback is common and easy to understand. So, why is it controversial? Mainly because it radically alters the theoretical picture of economies. Traditional models are based entirely on negative feedback.[2] These models paint a nice 'best of all possible worlds' picture of economic life which is deeply cherished. Negative feedback is the idea that every economic event will be countered by the very reactions it creates. High oil prices of the 1970s, for example, encouraged energy conservation and increased oil exploration and this created a predictable drop in prices by the early 1980s. Negative feedback tends to stabilize the economy because any major change will be offset by the very reactions it generates. Economies built of negative feedback move to a single equilibrium point which marks the most efficient use and allocation of resources under circumstances. Hence, if negative feedback is the *sole* stuff of which economies are made, then we can feel safe at night because what we have is what should be. A free economy automatically corrects itself and gives optimal solutions. Our models tell us so.

Unfortunately, as Arthur says, 'this agreeable picture often does

violence to reality.' Negative feedback does exist, but when you add the
equally valid phenomenon of positive feedback, all the neat images go
away. For example, positive feedback makes microscopic differences
balloon. One cannot predict which competitor will be chosen and one
cannot say that the winner represents some kind of optimal best choice.
Thus, positive feedback pushes a major perceptual shift similar to the ones
seen in other fields. Arthur writes:

> Conventional economics texts have tended to portray the economy
> as something akin to a large Newtonian system, with a unique
> equilibrium solution preordained by patterns of mineral resources,
> geography, population, consumer tastes and technological
> possibilities ... one should in theory be able to forecast accurately
> the path of the economy as a smoothly shifting solution to the
> analytical equations governing prices and quantities of good.

In short, what we have is an economic version of clockwork thinking.
Economics, for example, aspires to be an exact science in the image of
Newton. If one cannot predict, one is not scientific. This situation suggests
an intensely human reason why positive feedback was not incorporated
earlier — a large body of self-reinforcing clockwork theory and its well-
employed adherents find it distasteful because it threatens everything they
have been taught. As Arthur explains:

> 'Multiple equilibria,' wrote Schumpeter ... 'are not necessarily
> useless, but from the standpoint of *any exact science* the existence
> of a uniquely determined equilibrium is of the utmost importance
> ... [multiple equilibria] is a chaos that is not under analytical
> control.' ... increasing returns would destroy the familiar world of
> unique, predictable equilibria and the notion that the market's
> choice was always best ... When Hicks ... surveyed these
> possibilities he drew back in alarm. 'The threatened wreckage,' he
> wrote, 'is that of the greater part of economic theory.' (1990, p.93)

Since positive feedback helps us see economies a little more like a web,
Arthur's recommendations should also sound familiar. He argues that the
new dynamics and the new math helps us understand additions like
positive feedback while still being able to do science. Absolute prediction
and control may have to go, but the new math does not mean an end to

economic science, only a shift in focus. Pattern and the dynamics of change are the key.

Positive feedback, however, is but the tip of a very large iceberg. Other mathematical measures mislead even more. The GDP (Gross Domestic Product) is perhaps the biggest of these.

How Big is the Misperception?

> *... the GDP not only masks the breakdown of the social*
> *structure and the natural habitat upon which the economy —*
> *and life itself — ultimately depend; worse, it actually portrays*
> *such breakdown as economic gain.*
> Clifford Cobb, Ted Halstead, and Jonathan Rowe

In October of 1995, *Atlantic Monthly* had its own front page spread entitled, 'If the Economy is Up, Why is America Down?' This article, written by economists Clifford Cobb, Ted Halstead, and Jonathan Rowe, focused on another mathematical disaster. The subtitle was: 'The GDP is such a crazy mismeasure of the economy that it portrays disaster as gain. A new economic barometer might transform society.'

Why is the GDP a disaster? The GDP is a seemingly innocuous measure of economic activity. It measures activity by tracking how much money changes hands. It treats every money exchange like a gain. It never asks whether the exchange helps or hurts people or the economy. It also ignores everything that doesn't involve direct money exchange, including all barter, volunteer, and household work. Its adherents claim that the GDP indicates wellbeing and that everyone should strive to increase it at all times. They have convinced so many people that 'money activity' equals 'wellbeing' that upping the GDP has become a national pastime that defines American society.

What could be wrong with this? As currently handled, the GDP counts destructive activity as good and argues that a great deal of vital activity is irrelevant. It cannot tell the difference between a bubble economy and one with sound structure. Economists pumping up the GDP encourage destructive behaviors and destroy vital ones, all in the belief that they are doing good. Their incredible misconstruction is quite literally destroying the fabric of American society. Cobb and his colleagues make their point so well I shall simply quote them:

The more the nation depletes its natural resources, the more the GDP increases ... [GDP] portrays the depletion of capital as current income. As former World Bank economist Herman Daly puts it, 'the current national-accounting system treats the earth as a business in liquidation.' Add pollution to the balance sheet and we appear to be doing even better. Pollution shows up twice as a gain: once when the chemical factory, say, produces it as a by-product, and again when the nation spends billions of dollars to clean up the toxic Superfund site ... It shows up again as medical bills rising as a result of dirty air.

The GDP totally ignores the distribution of income ... so enormous gains at the top — as were made during the 1980s — appear as new bounty for all ...

It ignores much of the nation's most important work, from caring for children ... to volunteer work in its many forms. Such activity is the nation's social glue. Yet because no money changes hands ... it is invisible to conventional economics ... [This] means that the more our families and communities decline and a monetized service sector takes their place, the more the GDP goes up and the economic pundits cheer. Parenting becomes child care, visits on the porch become psychiatry ... both government and the private market grow by cannibalizing the family and community realms that ultimately nurture and sustain us ...

When kids are talking with their parents, they aren't adding to the GDP. In contrast, MTV helps turn them into ardent, GDP-enhancing consumers. Even those unwed teenage mothers are bringing new little consumers into the world ... So while social conservatives ... are rightly deploring the nation's social decline, their free-market counterparts are looking at the same phenomena through the lens of the GDP and breaking out the champagne.

By the curious standard of the GDP, the nation's economic hero is a terminal cancer patient who is going through a costly divorce. The happiest event is an earthquake or a hurricane. The most desirable habitat is a multibillion-dollar Superfund site ... One begins to understand why politicians prefer to talk about growth rather than what it actually consists of ... Prozac alone adds more than $1.2 billion to the GDP. (1995, p.56)

The GDP affects our lives because politicians, business men and corporate boards the world over use it to make decisions. Since the GDP embraces the bad with the good, policies designed to increase it often spur harmful activities — including pollution, family decline and pillage of resources. Small wonder we have a hard time straightening ourselves out.

Yet, the GDP is most relevant because it serves as the keystone of a value system which begs self-destruction — namely, gluttonous consumption. This value system undermines most of the traditional values people hold dear including integrity, social justice, mutual support, and quality itself. People the world over despise this value system and it is clearly behind many a collapse. Yet, clockwork economists have so convinced themselves and policy makers that it is necessary to wellbeing, that people cling, aspire and are afraid to put this value system down ... even as they despise it.

To really understand our plight, therefore, we need to understand how economists evolved this system.

Gluttonous Consumption and Crumbling Values

> *A cynic is someone who knows the price of everything and the*
> *value of nothing.*   Oscar Wilde

The GDP evolved out of an attempt to track a nation's wealth so that administrators could manage it better. This seems fair. Today it is a key part the nation's accounting scheme, which means it affects all policy efforts aimed at making a prosperous society. Today this accounting scheme seems beyond question, but two-hundred years ago when clockwork economics was starting, the question of how one should measure a nation's wellbeing was a topic of hot debate.

How do you track a nation's wealth? In Adam Smith's day (1700s), most people lived in small villages and engaged in economic behaviors which were invisible to economists. Therefore, when early economists discussed 'the economy,' they were referring only to those activities which interested their employer, the king. Hence, following kingly concerns, most early economics focused on the flow of money (mostly gold) between nations. This innocent beginning laid the groundwork for three distortions which are still with us today.

- When economists discuss 'the economy' or 'the market,' they are not referring to the whole economic ecosystem, just a small, easily-measured portion.

- Because money is easy to measure, it — *not* people, work or wellbeing — is put at the center of economics.
- Because the rich pay the bills, economics is written largely from the perspective of those at the top.

Early on, debates over the hub of economic wellbeing also reflected national concerns. The Physiocrats of France, for example, saw agriculture as the core of economic wellbeing. Being from Britain, Adam Smith was much more interested in industry and trade. As the industrial revolution began to roll in the 1800s, Smith's views became dominant. Finance, trade, and investment became ever more pivotal concerns.

Focus on these three led to a more insidious shift. First, economists began to view paper transactions as a valid measure of significance. In laymen's terms this meant that one hundred dollars of lawyer fees was the same as one hundred dollars of potatoes. They also believed that market forces unerringly sorted wheat from chaff, forcing prices to their correct values. Therefore, the price of something always accurately reflected its 'value.'

It all seemed logical, but Oscar Wilde was beginning to be correct. *Worth was defined by price and the market was always correct.* This last thought became an economic law. One didn't have to discuss whether an activity added or subtracted from wellbeing. Social worth, moral value, long-term destruction: the market would handle these automatically.

Focus on paper also meant that everything that didn't have a price was left out. This included everything from raising children and serving on charity boards to barter and barn-raisings. The impression that these grass-roots socio-economic activities don't count began to seem scientific. Where earlier economists had merely overlooked these non-priced items, the new economics now suggested directly that they had exactly *zero value*. The logic was compelling. No price, no worth. High price, high worth. Modern thinking was being born.

The stage was now set for accounting schemes based solely on money exchange *regardless of its nature*. The market would do our thinking for us. As national accounting schemes became yoked to price, questions of benefit or detriment became unimportant. There remained but one last cornerstone of modern theory — rabid consumption and a measure that promoted it.

Confidence and Consumption

The Great Depression and the crash of 1929 naturally made governments wonder whether they knew how economies worked. In 1932 the American government hired Simon Kuznets to develop a new set of measures upon which to develop a new national accounting scheme. Kuznets developed the GNP (Gross National Product), the fore-runner of what we now call the GDP. He used neoclassical assumptions about price and value because they were the best of the time.

Kuznet's measure then linked up with a new theory. The Great Depression pushed the idea that government spending was a way to keep an economy moving. The American New Dealers who hired Kuznets, for example, had started with a view that government should prevent industrial concentration, because improper concentration seemed to be part of the 1929 crash. But by the mid-1930s the dustbowl was added to depression and a half million people left their land in search of work. The government was the only organization large enough to help and it moved in with work programs like the WPA and CCC and farming methods that conserved soil and restored grass and trees. The government spent its money to keep suffering down and to get the system moving. And government's efforts did help. John Maynard Keynes developed the theory which explained why government spending was good but, in fact, the pressure to spend existed before the explanation.

Keynes' theory and Kuznets' measure fit each other and the times perfectly. World War II made them both seem indisputable. Keynes and Kuznets were both heavily involved in war planning. The GNP and other aspects of Kuznet's accounting scheme helped American planners locate unused capacity and U.S. production levels soared, vastly exceeding what was previously thought possible. Kuznet eventually got a Nobel Prize and national accounting based on GNP began to look like true science.

The Keynesians got credit for helping win the war and they went giddy with confidence and power. They promoted their theory on the basis that mathematical precision would allow governments to control economies. Economics had become science à la Newton! With proper detailed knowledge of the GNP the dreaded 'business cycle' would be replaced by constant prosperity. In America, the Employment Act of 1946 turned the GNP into official policy and established the Council of Economic Advisers to apply it.

The keys to the economic kingdom had been discovered! Government spending, however, was only one small piece. The real Keynesian key was consumption. Keynesians saw consumption as *the* drive behind prosperity. For them the public — farmer, housewife, businessman, laborer, child and adult — all belonged to one class, *consumers.* Keynesians described spending as a solemn duty needed to ward off depression. Soon, shopping centers began to cover the landscape and Americans marched to them to help save the country.

The production frenzy that won the war, thus, became the model for peace as well. Going faster and consuming more is what allowed progress to continue. The concept of progress via consumption (at the highest possible rate) began to insinuate itself into the national mantra. No one asked what kind of progress this produced. Everyone knew they just wanted more!

We should recognize the concept of the consumer society. We may also recognize some of its destructive social results and the fact that America is now famous for both. Designed obsolescence? High-gaudiness/low quality? Buy whatever is new, newer, newest and throw away old things after the ash trays get full! Offensive, intrusive, degenerate, immoral — it doesn't matter as long as it is consumed. Buy addictively and don't worry about the effect on one's body, personal economy or soul. Being able to spend lavishly indicates power, value and being the best.

By 1962 Kuznets himself was struggling to warn economists that the GNP was not what they thought it was. He emphasized that GNP was just a first attempt and that the concept of growth should focus on 'growth *of what* and *for what.*' But economists were not eager to listen. Why not? We've been here before — the GDP had become the center of an institutionalized belief system. As Cobb says:

> the GDP serves deep institutional cravings, combining the
> appearance of empirical certitude and expert authority with a
> ready-made story line. It also serves the industries that thrive on
> the kind of policies it reinforces; those inclined to deplete and
> pollute are especially pleased with an accounting system that
> portrays these acts as economic progress.

It is not just America, of course. Both the accounting system and the belief system that go with GDP have been exported world wide. The effects have a similar cast everywhere — self-destructive frenzy. By GNP accounting, for example, Indonesia has been a phenomenal success story since the

1970s. But it achieved this status by clear cutting its forests, exhausting its soil with intensive farming and selling off precious non-renewable mineral wealth. In short, it sold off its future to pay for boom numbers, just as the economic establishment said it should.

In 1991 economists turned the GNP into the GDP. One major difference was that 'profit' was now attributed to the country in which a factory was located and not to where the owning multi-national corporation was headquartered. The profit still returns to the headquarters, but the remote country is listed as the beneficiary. As Cobb and his colleagues say, 'This accounting shift turned many struggling nations into statistical boomtowns ... Conveniently, it has hidden a basic fact: the nations of the North are walking off with the South's resources, and calling it a gain for the South.'

Measuring Genuine Progress

Have you ever wondered how 'knowing leads to doing' would play out in real life? In this case, a long, slow evolution of theory produced an economic belief system embodied in a measure, the GDP. This belief system urges people to engage in frenetic, destructive, addictive, offensive behaviors as a way of making their society prosper. Most economists and many lay people really believe this system is good. They have been taught to believe GDP measures prosperity no matter how awful that prosperity feels or how much it hurts everything from social fabric to the environment.

How do we stop this economic insanity? Cobb and others have been working on an alternative measure, the Genuine Progress Indicator (GPI), for many years. It is beginning to take root in a number of countries.[3] The GPI attempts to separate *real* progress from mere frenetic activity. Its first big step is to subtract the costs of various detrimental activities. For example, it subtracts the costs of crime and of defensive measures taken to deal with it such as burglar alarms, car theft devices, police and prisons. It subtracts the costs of resource depletion and environmental degradation, including, for example, the costs of water and air pollution on agriculture, health, and property (for example, beaches fouled by oil). Similarly, money spent on water filters, air purifiers, and so on, count as defensive measures brought on by wanton pollution.

The GPI also adjusts for extra work time, reasoning that people who work two jobs just to stay even are not making genuine progress. To measure national wellbeing as opposed to merely *élite* wellbeing, it also adjusts for income inequities which serve only the upper few percentiles. The GPI adjusts for other elements, but perhaps you get the idea.

As you might guess, the GPI paints a very different picture of the American economy, one much more in line with common experience. The GPI indicates that much of what the GDP calls 'growth' actually falls into one of three disguised categories: (1) fixing blunders and social decay from the past; (2) borrowing resources from the future; or (3) shifting functions from traditionally unpaid household and community activities to paid professionals. GPI also shows a very different picture of prosperity over the last fifty years. The GPI shows an upward curve from the 1950s to 1970 and a gradual decline of about 45% since then. The message: frenetic consumption has not generated much genuine progress. It has destroyed a lot of social fabric.

The GPI is embryonic, but it is the movement it represents that counts. Hence, Cobb and his fellows ask readers to imagine what a difference a more sane measure and more honest accounting would make:

> Imagine Peter Jennings reciting the latest Commerce Department figures, saying with polished gravity, 'The nation's output increased, but parents worked longer hours and so spent less time with their kids. Consumer spending was up sharply but much of the difference went for increased medical costs and repairing rubble left by hurricanes and floods. Utility companies made more money but resources declined sharply meaning that their increase was bought at the cost of our grandchildren's prosperity.' ...
>
> Perhaps such reports would break through the hermetic economy portrayed by economists and Wall Street analysts ... Politicians and reporters alike would have to confront the economy people *actually experience* ...
>
> Politicians could no longer get away with glib assurances that the nation can grow its way out of family breakdown and environmental decay, inequity and debt. Such assurances have become a kind of political perpetual motion machine. Newt Gingrich rhapsodizes about the ... economy and the 500 cable channels it will bring to the American living room. Think of the wonderful PROGRESS! He blames 'McGovernik liberals' for the breakdown in traditional family values. (1995, p.57)

We cannot grow our way out of social and environmental destruction using current measures. We must create more sane accounts in order to create more sane feedback loops. Small bits of progress are also being made in this last. For example, an economic action group called 'Getting the Signals Straight' is beginning to lobby for Green Taxes. In essence industries that pollute are taxed to pay for clean-ups or charged for the excess energy they use. Such taxes give correct signals by putting the costs back where they belong. In the Netherlands similar tax policies have radically reduced lake pollution. In the US, they could make way for as much as a 15% reduction in individual taxes which would no longer be needed to pay for environmental clean-up.

* * *

The one binding belief behind the seventeenth-century's scientific revolution was that mathematics made all things clear. What this century has made clear is that mathematical clarity can also be blinding. Assumptions may be innocent and destructive. Unfortunately, those who mistake their models for reality, often take many with them down a thorny primrose path.

Today's mathematical misperceptions also harken back to the same root cause: the clockwork view. Naturally, I am going to suggest that economies are better thought of as webs — and that webs do not work like simple machines. Yet, for these words to have meaning, we need a better sense of what intricacy looks like in economic life.

Web or Machine?

You will never solve a problem if you use the same thinking that created the problem in the first place.   Albert Einstein

Economists have always known that economies were webs. Yet, two-hundred years of using analytic tools, makes this terribly hard to see. Therefore, one usually has to look outside the mainstream for a deep understanding of why the web nature of economies makes a difference.

This brings me to Jane Jacobs, the economist/urban anthropologist who predicted the demise of the Soviet Union. Now in her eighties, Jacobs has been developing a web view of cities and economies in a series of excellent books spread over the last forty years. Her arguments are so lucid and well supported that she has been a favorite of those who seek a different way. This section looks at her view of how fine-grained, reciprocal economic relations create robust, synergetic and structurally-sound economic webs.*

Building an Integrated Web

> *Business is a system of organized human effort that produces*
> *power.*
>   Ben Cohen, Co-founder of Ben and Jerry's Ice Cream

Jacobs starts her explanation of how sound economic webs arise with a simple organic view of how our remote ancestors built economies by adding new work to old. Fishing, for example, started with hands, moved to spears and then someone invented a net. Nets not only helped people catch more fish, but they promoted the art of thread making, net making, and skills needed to do both. Each new technology was added logically and naturally to a specific bit of older work such that work diversified and expanded, yet also stayed integrated. Expertise also grew gradually and in many different arenas.

You will note that this kind of web involves a very intricate weave of human associations and expertise which co-evolved with tools and other means of production. Such organically expanding webs were thus more likely to be what we now call 'sustainable.' One element supported another and quality counted because people were still close. Children developed integrity and expertise on their way up. As a result, though change was sometimes relatively sudden, it was less likely to involve the booms and busts that often torment modern economies.

Today, of course, building-on-old seems quaint. Yet, it is not just an ancient phenomenon. Jacob uses the growth of the Japanese automobile industry as a more recent example. In the late 1800s Japan was dominated by cheap foreign imports, including bicycles. The Japanese could have slavishly imitated foreign bicycles or invited a foreign manufacturer to set up shop in Japan — but this would not have developed the expertise or related support systems that come from a more organic evolution. Instead

---

*   The followings sections are based on Jacobs' books, *Cities and the Wealth of Nations*. I
    refer readers to it because I cannot do justice to the logic and evidence she gives in this
    brief space. Omissions and over-simplifications are my fault, not hers.

they started by learning to repair bicycles and used the expertise they developed to build an entire manufacturing system as follows. A host of one-man repair shops sprang up in Tokyo. As their expertise grew, these repairmen began to make some of their own replacement parts. This stimulated growth in various support enterprises which provided needed materials and tools. Learning to make individual parts soon became a staging ground for the next level. Since many repairmen were making parts, every part was being made somewhere. Groups of shops began forming cooperatives which could assemble whole bicycles. Eventually motors were added and the home-grown bicycle industry broadened into the motorcycle industry and from there to automobile manufacturing.

What is most notable about this kind of development is that it builds integrated human and material relations which co-evolve from the bottom-up. Without anyone planning a grand outcome, many one-man efforts built an entire web of systems for obtaining raw materials, distributing, marketing, repairing, and all the support services that go with them. Far from being costly to develop, the whole system paid its way right through its development.

So, building-on-old is not merely an ancient form. Jacobs cites many examples, including Henry Ford's development of the Model T. She also points out that what the British call 'breakaway' systems create the same effect. Here individuals who learn their work in one organization breakaway to create a new organization that does a variant of the same. This tends to spawn innovation and create new niches. It also helps the network of related activities grow.

Of course, many home-grown industries grow into gigantic hierarchies following the usual dominator mode. These tend to replace millions of small intricate (and very human) connections with the streamlined command-and-control structure found in armies. Following machine thinking they also tend to replace local creativity and craftsmanship with prescribed, standardized tasks which require discipline, but no thought. Growing with the concept of 'scientific management' from the late 1800s on, this urge to control made factories much more efficient, while at the same time eliminating most initiative and creativity from work. Craftsmen became workers with little personal investment in their job.

According to our usual empire-building mentality, the growth of gigantic streamlined hierarchies is a good thing. Yet, from an intricacy point of view there are some real problems. Command-and-control tends to make people fall back into lizard mode. People stop caring and work suffers. If the system gets very big, the top is likely to become decoupled from the bottom.

If we are going to understand economics, therefore, we need to see why gigantic command-and-control structures are not the only way. It is quite possible to expand by staying small *and* well-connected (just like your body did). This too is an ancient economic pattern, though today it has a new name. Today economists call nests of small enterprises bound by invisible connective tissue, *flexible manufacturing networks*.

Flexible Networks

> *It is perfectly possible to imagine a company with an*
> *ambitious strategic intent being effortlessly out-performed*
> *by what appears to be a disorganized ... network of*
> *companies.*   Tom Lloyd, *Financial Times*, 9/8/95

Japan grew a fine-grained web of expertise and industries by learning to replace imported bicycles. Jacobs points out that many powerful webs get their start this way because replacing imports builds a foundation for versatility.

Successful replacing — be it in Japan or in cities such as Bologna and Venice in northern Italy or Boston and Chicago in the US — requires improvization and adaptation in design, materials, goods, services and methods of production. This happens best in small firms that are close to the problem and not hampered by bureaucracy and corporate norms. If, through some set of happenstances, lots of small enterprises fall into a natural pattern of cooperation and niche-building, then the economic pressure may not produce one or two lumbering giants, but a network of small, creative, high-quality firms. This is what people call a 'flexible manufacturing network.'

Charles Sabel provides a wonderful description of one such network built of 'innumerable small firms in a great cluster of small industrial cities between Bologna and Venice in north-eastern Italy.' 'Flexible' is the operative word since improvizations occur as an everyday matter. Thus, Sabel says:

> A small shop producing tractor transmissions for a large
> manufacturer modifies the design to suit the need of a small

manufacturer of high-quality seeders. In another little shop a
conventional automatic packing machine is redesigned to fit
the available space in a particular assembly line ... A
membrane pump used in automobiles is modified to suit
agricultural machinery. (Cited in Jacobs, 1984.)

Because they are small, cooperative, and still integrated, such enterprises tend to produce very sophisticated and high quality work.
Innovation is high because improvization is a central theme. Quality
is high because craftsmanship is still important. Craftsmanship is important because human ties still bind. Hence, here people pursue integrity, as well as profit.

Quality and creativity are also high because workers and ideas
circulate. Such circulation builds expertise, breadth of experience and
an invisible chain of valued human connections. Breakaway enterprises
spring up easily and often as workers from older enterprises move out
to start firms of their own. Such spin-offs often collaborate with the
older establishments because they share history and have related work.
In this way, people in the network establish their own 'coherent role
in the web of processes,' while members, information and expertise
cycle easily throughout. As a result, advances anywhere tend to
stimulate benefits everywhere. Members prosper in a synergetic, not
a zero-sum way.

Such networks achieve tremendous economies of scale not, as
conventionally assumed, within the framework of huge organizations,
but rather through large symbiotic collections of small enterprises.
Most have but five to fifty workers with a few more having one or two
hundred. Size is key. As Sabel says:

The innovative capacity of this type of firm depends on its
flexible use of technology; its close relations with other
similarly innovative firms in the same and adjacent sectors;
and above all on the close collaboration of workers with
different kinds of expertise. These firms practice boldly and
spontaneously the fusion of conception and execution, abstract
and practical knowledge, that only a few exceptional giant
firms have so far been able to achieve.

Synergetic Webs versus Traditional Theory

Now, these kinds of bubbling economic webs should be familiar. They fit the archetypal high-integrity way of making-a-living that many of us yearn for, even if we have not experienced it. Indeed, it is small enterprises in collaboration that set the tone for our cherished images of what capitalism can and should be. Quality, integrity and human contact all survive, somehow wrapped in a supportive network.

Unfortunately, these are not the only kinds of organizations that capitalism produces. Before going on, let me highlight some of the differences between synergetic economic webs and typical economic theory today:

- Synergetic webs are mutualist. They are based on what Jacobs calls, *reciprocal relationships*, ones in which 'I do something for you, and you do something for me.' When such relationships are relatively equal, they create fine-grained weave with intelligence spread throughout the web.
- Synergetic self-interest is pursued in conjunction with the wellbeing of the larger whole. There is an awareness that the health of the whole is important to everyone. Integrity is valued.
- Individuals join such webs because of the joy of being a unique and respected contributor to an honourable, larger whole. They are not wage-slaves. Freely given initiative joins with other such initiative to create a surge far beyond what any coercive measures can elicit.
- Competition takes the form of a game in which all strive to put forth their best. It is not war, empire-building or a zero-sum game. Rather, in synergetic webs, putting forth one's own genius contribution is likely to help others as well as oneself. In fact, spin-off enterprises are likely to be seen as potential cooperators, not as another mouth fighting for the last teat.
- Synergetic webs tend to increase everyone's wellbeing relatively equally. Instead of a few people getting massively wealthy, everyone in the system tends to go up and down together. (They are not funnels.)

The synergetic webs described here are a type of co-evolving mutualism. They are strong because human and materials systems are integrated. This also makes them faster, more creative, and more socially-responsible — much more so than an economy based on a stable of large corporations. They are not based on economic war or aimed at disproportional gain.

With this in mind, let me now tackle how clockwork thinking dangerously underestimates intricacy.

Web Thinking versus Machine Thinking

The way we see the world determines how we manage it.
W. Edwards Deming

Since synergetic networks are fast, flexible and high in quality, one might wonder why they aren't more common. One answer is that governments don't tend to support them. Having no concept of intricacy's role in sustaining civilization, governments often assume that the destruction of these fine-grained webs won't matter.

Because knowing leads to doing we get what our institutions believe. Because clockwork economics has little concept of intricacy, we often destroy our own best webs. Jacobs gives a detailed account of why clockwork thinking tends to exacerbate many economic problems precisely because it doesn't understand intricacy. The next sections lay out why a lot of well-intentioned and seemingly logical efforts don't work out as planned.

What Makes an Economy Surge?
Economies are webs, not machines! But surely, you say, a web view cannot be so different from the machine one! But it is, and Jacobs provides numerous examples.

The most basic difference can be seen in people's answer to what makes an economy surge. From a web perspective, of course, it is the back-and-forth stimulation of millions of little economic connections which makes an economy surge. Expertise evolves alongside tools and infrastructure. When such threads stimulate and build on each other, then an economic network may develop into what Jacobs calls a 'high-powered economic engine.' As companies grow, they add new jobs and accumulate capital. Support enterprises pop-up to serve growing needs. As people in the region flourish, they buy more. This, in turn, attracts more business. Successful companies then build offices and factories farther from home. (Jacobs calls these 'transplants.') In short, back-and-forth stimulation creates a surge of five outward-moving forces — jobs, capital, markets, technology, and transplants.

Now none of this is new. Synergy has created a surge. But, traditionally, economists focus on the other side of the equation. Hence, from a machine point of view, introducing any of five economic forces — jobs, capital, markets, technology, or transplants — should automatically create synergy and a sound economy. Unfortunately, this is often not true. Healthy webs create economic forces, but forces do not necessarily create healthy webs. The distinction is important.

Successful companies, for instance, often extend one or more of the forces into a remote region. But they often do so without creating any nests of symbiotic activities. In this situation, the remote region gets a line of influence, but not intricate development. A company may come in, build a plant and hire workers and then leave when labor is cheaper elsewhere. It is a common practice. Unless the transplant and the local economy have become symbiotically entwined such that *both sides* have a vested interest in the relationship, the remote region will be subject to outsider whims. The plant will have been a temporary windfall, not sustainable economic development.

There are many variations on this theme. High-powered economies may generate activity in regions that supply raw materials, cheap labor or scenic vacations for workers. Unfortunately, such activity is often a gossamer bubble that glimmers while it stands, but bursts as soon as the raw material runs out or the labor becomes cheaper elsewhere. Mayors and governors thus build convention centers and stadiums and entice companies to build plants and praise this as economic development. They assume this will automatically create robust webs, but the resulting local jobs are often menial and temporary. No local expertise is developed. No local ties bind. The common result of their assumption is shock when synergy fails to develop and the tendril of influence is pulled away.

Growing a Good Economy versus Buying One

> *In many cases, it is not lack of 'development' that has brought impoverishment, but 'development' itself, as when natural resources that provide a decent subsistence livelihood for large numbers of people are turned into industrial raw materials that benefit relatively few.*
>
> Paul Ekins, Economist, Birbeck College, England

If one sees an economy as a web, then development consists of human expertise, material infrastructure, and social patterns that have grown up together such that each supports the other. Development is served best when it spreads via small, flexible organizations as opposed to the big, bureaucratic, leviathans. Development serves the society best when people are joined to each other and the larger society in a commitment to common wellbeing. Here helping people grow is the most important need.

Economists armed with machine images do not see development this way. Human expertise and integrated relationships are rarely if ever added into the equation. From a machine point of view, money and material seem much more important. Hence clockwork thinkers assume that operators can stand outside and 'cause' development by applying economic forces.

Take the idea that money can produce a strong economy. From a machine perspective, it would seem that, if a nation has money, it can buy a plant or hire expertise and that a good economy will spontaneously arise from this. But, as logical as this sounds, it rarely works.

Uruguay's efforts in the 1950s are a good example. At the start of this century Uruguay was an unusually rich supply-region. It supplied meat, wool and leather mostly for cities in Europe. Settled by efficient self-reliant farmers and with no extremes of wealth or poverty, Uruguay prided itself on its accessible universal education. But in 1953 things began to go wrong. Ranchers in Australia and New Zealand began expanding their markets and European nations such as France became preoccupied with protecting their own meat and wool producers as part of their post-War recovery. Seeing the writing on the wall, Uruguay's government embarked upon a crash program of industrialization. Uruguay began building complete factories for producing such items as steel, textiles, shoes, and electrical equipment.

Uruguay's planners applied enlightened principles, but these didn't play out as hoped. They placed factories in places where work was most badly needed, but those places lacked the nests of services, goods, expertise, etc. that might have produced synergy. They brought in expertise and hoped employees would acquire it. The result was disastrous. When Uruguay's new factories produced at all, their products were vastly more expensive than comparable imports. Uruguay went bankrupt attempting to support its factories with imported parts, materials and expertise.

So, planner intentions were good, but their understanding of intricacy was poor. Sound development is an exquisitely human thing. It requires experience and understanding that is passed from hand to hand. It presumes a community mindset including a lot of tacit assumptions about how to work together, why one works, and who to trust. Not surprisingly, these kinds of human-material relationships need to be nurtured from the ground up. Machine-thinking sweeps by all this.

The Volta Dam in Ghana, one of the world's great hydroelectric projects, is another example of Jacobs' point. Machine thinking tends to assume that robust economies can be created by building factories, dams and other merely material means. The Volta Dam was thus built on the belief that cheap power would make factories who wanted cheap power appear. Yet, despite the extraordinary cheapness of the power, almost no power 'users' materialized. The only exception was the American-owned Kaiser aluminum refinery, whose promised participation was used to justify the dam in the first place.

In theory the dam was also supposed to promote irrigated case cropping. But this scheme proved so impractical that it was dropped. The 80,000 people whose traditional village economies were wiped out to make room for the dam were resettled on soil so poor that more than half found they could no longer feed themselves. These drifted away — most of them, it is believed, to become landless paupers.

Dams, factories, and other material means do not spontaneously produce development. Development, the web of human-material relations, must be cultivated. Material means are part of the process, but small ones are often better at stimulating true development because it moves from the bottom up. In the right hands, a plow, a water pump, or a grist mill is more likely to boost a local web than a Volta Dam.

Today's rampant cynicism about development is a direct result of not understanding human intricacy. Under the illusion that development would justify and cover the costs, backward countries have assumed vast unpayable debts. Interest charges then eat into poor countries' earnings such that, as Jacobs puts it, 'some desperately poor societies have been working, in effect, for virtually nothing except the honour of [being] promoted for a brief decade from "backward" to "developing".'

People in the so-called developing countries have become angry and disillusioned. Because their money begat failure, people in donor countries have become cynical about the worth of aiding others. But, the problem does not stop here. Having been cajoled into huge investments by confident economists, the international banking community now tries to shore up fragile debtor-nations in order to stave off an international banking collapse. Thus, in February of 1995 Mexico's near collapse brought loans from an international banking community which is now virtually unable to say no. What a fragile web we weave when we pour huge amounts of money into well-intentioned clockwork beliefs! Development does not become sound, nor is economic inequity cured — but the system must be held together at all costs.

These are not unusual cases. Mistaking money and material means for development has recurrent results. Jacobs cites examples, from Russia's Peter the Great attempting to buy industrialization in Moscow in the early eighteenth century to the Shah of Iran attempting to import helicopter factories in 1975. The problem in all these well-intentioned failures is that planners equated a robust economy with *one* of the economic forces — with jobs or technology or capital or training or facilities for production — not with the fine-grained human-material relationships that create them. Jacobs comments:

> Carried away by the power of money to finance great capital undertakings, many people seem to think of such investments as being development itself. Build the dam and you have development! But in real life, build the dam and unless you also have solvent city markets and transplanted industries, you have nothing. (1984, p.105)

Two Hundred Years of Seesaws

> *Macro-economics ... is the branch of learning entrusted with ... fostering national and international economies. It is a shambles. Its undoing was the good fortune of having been believed in and acted upon in a big way ... Never has a science, or supposed science been so generously indulged.*
> Jane Jacobs

This brings me to the center of the clockwork economic universe and why it is due for a Copernican shift. Thus, economists certainly know about fine-grained relations, they call it micro-economics. Nevertheless, by the time one gets to *macro*-economics (the wealth of whole nations) all this complexity is boiled down to the reliable ups and downs of a simple seesaw. In short, despite its sophistication, macro-economic theory still carries profound machine distortions.

Since macro-economics is used to set national economic policy, what macro-economists 'know' is of deep importance to the health of nations, not to mention our everyday lives. Let us see, then, why putting webs first, may make a difference.

The Nation

Let us start at the top. Macro-economic theory focuses on the wealth of the nation taken as a whole. Fine-grained economic webs are invariably centered in cities and regional economies and any nation is a potpourri of these. Many webs cross national boundaries. Some are so transnational that they are not really part of any one nation at all.

Individual webs can be strong when a national economy is weak (or weak when it is strong). One may be zooming, while ten others are wasting away. Yet economists who focus on the nation will miss all this. They average the robust and the stagnant and act primarily on an imaginary aggregate. In doing so they are ignoring vast differences in economic structure and the fact that what is good for one region is likely to be useless or bad for another. Lowering interest rates on a national scale, for example, does not help poor regions, say Appalachia in the U.S., because those regions have no producers that are seeking capital. On the other hand, lowering interest rates will help existing producers which means that whatever gap exists is likely to increase.

In short, traditional approaches tend to blur very real dynamic diversity into simplistic uniformity. This in turn creates a powerful urge toward simplistic, monolithic solutions which treat every web the same, regardless of its actual needs. Monolithic solutions treat a complex economy like a simple machine and not a real-life web. They also tend to increase funneling and destroy upstart growth because what registers most are the needs of big businesses.

Why use nation-centered measures that blur diversity? Focus on nations is largely an historical fluke that is sustained by political pressures. The mercantilists of the 1600s, for example, were concerned about the politics of national rivalries. Their theory of economic health focused on how a nation gold amassed because that was a central issue in buying arms and armies. In the 1700s Adam Smith added domestic trade and the concepts of capital and labor to the definition of wealth, but he continued the idea that nations were the best unit for understanding large-scale wealth. Others followed suit. The focus on nations has been handed down unchallenged across virtually all changes in economic theory for the last two-hundred years. Even Marx, who based his analysis on class struggles, nevertheless placed his faith in the nation as the suitable entity for analyzing economic life. Capitalists, communists, fascists and socialists are all alike in this.

Thus, the reason for the practice is simple. Economists have been taught to believe that a meaningful political entity, 'the nation' is a meaningful economic entity and this tends to obscure the real causes of wealth which actually lie in the dynamics of particular webs. Nation-centered efforts ignore diverse realities and so, fit into the category of not understanding complex systems.

The Seesaw of Supply and Demand

Focusing on blurred nations instead of specific webs is one way economists with good intentions may make matters worse. But the more clearly mechanistic core of macro-economic theory is the seesaw theory of supply and demand.

Thus, early economists watching prices and employment change pondered how the two might be connected. One early answer was that production (supply) and consumption (demand) were related by a simple seesaw dynamic — when one goes up, the other must surely go down. Price levels (supply) and unemployment (demand) also form a seesaw. Thus, during economic expansions, prices tend to rise and unemployment tends to fall. During recessions, prices tend to fall and unemployment tends to rise. We all know the story.

The seesaw idea started even before the mercantilists and generations of economists have elaborated it. It seems so well-established that it is now described as an inviolable economic law. It undergirds virtually every main-stream economic theory regardless of creed. It is so deeply assumed that for two-hundred years most macro-economic theories have amounted to increasingly elaborate explanations of how the seesaw works.

The only real question seems to have been which side of the seesaw drove the other. The answers have been many. In 1844 John Stuart Mill said that credit given to producers was the best way to create demand for labor because this stimulated production. Karl Marx, however, said it wasn't the producers who needed money to keep economic life expanding but the populace, consumers. Marx also reasoned that since owner's profits added to the price of goods, there was a gap between real cost and price. Marx said this unproductive gap led to cyclic crises of price collapse and unemployment and would eventually lead to the final inevitable collapse of capitalism. John Maynard Keynes used Marx's gap idea to provide an explanation of the Great Depression. He reasoned that the unproductive gap could be savings. When people save, they don't spend. Economies undergo periods when investment becomes flaccid and when this happens, savings don't stimulate production. As a result unemployment rises, demand falls, production falls, profits fall and bankruptcies, etc. ensue — in other words, you get the Great Depression. Governments, Keynes said, can stimulate the economy by spending, thus amplifying demand which would reduce unemployment and jump-start the economy.

Marxism, Keynesianism, supply-side, demand-side — a vast array of competing economic theories are all debates about which side of the seesaw is the *real* culprit. All assume that the seesaw underlies the whole economic problem. Hence, capitalists, communists, socialists, fascists etc. are all alike in this way. Even today most economic theories amount to increasingly elaborate descriptions of the causes and remedies of the seesaw.

What could be wrong with this? Let's take an example. In 1967 the American economy began experiencing stagflation, a situation in which prices and unemployment *both* rise. Nor is it just America, the Canadian economy, the British economy, the Chilean economy — most Eastern and Western European and North and South American economies have experienced stagflation some time in recent years.

In stagflation, the relationship between prices and unemployment *is not a seesaw*. Most mainstream economic theories handle stagflation as an aberration of the real driving force which they believe is the seesaw. Yet, stagflation is often a stable condition. One need only look at poor pockets in the U.S., such as Appalachia to realize that high prices and scant work have long been normal. Hence, in Appalachia stagflation is not a temporary aberration of a seesaw. It is the normal consequence of economic stagnation.

Stagflation is thus common in poor regions, be they in rich or poor nations. This has always been true but nation-centered math tends to make this fact invisible. For instance, Adam Smith used Scotland as an example of the problems high unemployment and noted in passing that Scotland was also subject to high prices. Scotland did not have a seesaw and this was normal for Scotland. England, however, did have high wages and low unemployment (the seesaw). Since both were part of the same nation, Scotland was averaged into the English condition and Scotland's problem became invisible — or at least, not a cause for theoretical alarm.

Examples such as Appalachia and Scotland suggest that stagflation is a standard condition of weak economic webs. But, if we say stagflation is caused by the state of a local web, then we are opening the door to a very big change. The implication is that economic webs can produce many patterns depending on their health. Stagflation is one pattern, the seesaw another. But if we see things this way, then the seesaw is not the *cause* of economic events, but merely one possible outcome of a particular economic web. This is all simple enough, but, if one sees the seesaw as an *effect* rather than a cause, then one turns economic theory on its head.

We have just reached another Copernican shift. Traditional macro-economic universe has been centered on nations and the seesaw. The goal of macro-economic theory was to control the economy by controlling the seesaw. The idea is simple — if you push one side of the seesaw down, the other will automatically come up! But, if webs are the real cause of wealth and these can produce many patterns depending on their state, then a nation's wealth depends more on encouraging synergy than it does on controlling the seesaw. The difference is subtle but important.

For instance, according to the seesaw theory, lowering interest rates should automatically stimulate growth. But, in destitute regions like Appalachia, low interest rates do not stimulate much growth because the people are too poor to qualify for loans and they may not have enough education or expertise to start a business. Seesaw predictions fail because economic forces play out differently depending on the state of real people in real socio-economic webs. Economists should be working with these.

Copernicus again

Economics is another great example of today's Copernican change. The supply-demand seesaw is cherished because it makes the economy seem like a controllable machine. By Keynes' time, the strategies for control began to seem quantitative, clear, and correct. The only question seemed to be about tactics — how the interest-rate and tax manipulations should be handled and how interventions were to be timed.

Yet, seesaw manipulations have few of the neat, controllable effects their advocates claim. This became clear with Keynesian deficit spending. Thus, in 1958, A.W.H. Philips, an engineer turned Keynesian economist, produced a curved graph that seemed to show that any given rate of wage increase was precisely associated with a given rate of unemployment. Keynesians said this curve meant that if a government wanted a given unemployment rate, it could arrange it by setting up a particular inflation rate which could be achieved by judicious adjustment of tax, interest rate and spending programs. But stagflation started in the early 1970s and by 1975 even leading Keynesians like Paul Samuelson abandoned the Phillips curve as unemployment in the U.S. reach 8.5% and inflation 9.1%. Sky-rocketing inflation in the 1980s created an about face. Today deficit spending is seen as the chief cause of economic woes.

Unfortunately, though Keynesian thinking was discredited, seesaw thinking continued. After the Keynesian programs began to fail, monetarists, lead by Milton Friedman in Chicago began to argue that the problem was undamped oscillations of the seesaw. They said unemployment came from insufficient investment. They recommended high interest rates for inflation and cuts in government spending. They produced the Laffer Curve that suggested that lower taxes could be counted on to stimulate production and employment. But, elegant monetarist ideas proved just as disastrous as the Keynesian prescriptions. Lower taxes did not create higher production or higher employment. So government revenues dropped and deficits increased. High interest rates made borrowing uneconomic and helped bankrupt many producers. Production shrank and unemployment soared. Monetarist theory undermined producers, the work force and the government all at the same time, yet all the while they held up their curve!

Ah, the power of pretty graphs! It is perfectly possible to describe economic outcomes via complicated epicycles of the seesaw, but when one does, the predictions don't turn out as neatly as hoped. Average believers are beginning to suspect that something is amiss. It is becoming quite obvious that a wide range of economic disasters — or more politely, 'anomalies' — come from using arguments that are contorted

because the center of the economic universe is misplaced. Most economists are not intentionally cooking the numbers, they are just following
tradition and what everyone in their cohort 'knows.'

We live in an incredibly tangled web of clockwork thinking, but it
is failing. A fundamental shift in economic perspective, from machine
to web, will eventually come about. The only question is how long it
will take and whether the change will be smooth or catastrophic.

How can I say something this radical? Because the gap between
economic theory and reality is of potentially catastrophic proportions.
It makes moon cycles pale. People care and the shortfall is blatant. The
incredible inertia of clockwork thinking will not be enough.

A more powerful perspective is also slowly taking form. Jacobs and
many others have already given us a more logically consistent way of
explaining why so many schemes have failed. Fine-grained, reciprocating webs are the real cause of prosperity and these can produce many
patterns depending on their state. Some webs are robust, some fragile,
some dependent and some stagnant. Facilitation is a bigger issue than
control and treating nations as undifferentiated aggregates is not a very
good idea. The question is not 'how does one control the seesaw?' but
'how does one grow a web?'

Jacobs' explanation of stagflation also gives us food for thought. Its
appearance in powerful European and American economies is disturbing because it indicates stagnation in the nation *taken as a whole*.
Jacobs writes:

> [Stagflation] is not just a problem of inflation to be gotten
> under control along with a problem of unemployment to be
> dealt with by mastering inflation, or vice versa. It is a
> condition in its own right, the condition of sliding into
> profound economic decline. (1984, p.27)

The economic body is going necrotic but most economists are still
wrangling about how tweaking interest rates will help. But they won't
wrangle forever because reality won't let them.

Our socio-economic health also faces a problem which is deeper
than any clockwork mistakes. This problem is the thread of dominator
beliefs woven insidiously into much of our world. I now turn to this
side of the puzzle.

Why We have a Crisis in Ideology

Socialism treats people as a cog in the machine of the state;
capitalism tends to treat people as commodities.

William Bennett

The Enlightenment Dream did not work out as planned. By the
beginning of this century, disgust with exploitative élites spawned the
great reactions of communism, socialism and fascism. Communism and
fascism blossomed into the two most horrific forms of despotism the
world has ever known. Socialism settled into inefficient, unresponsive
bureaucracy which tended to drain people's will, leaving its victims
feeling stultified, if fed. King Capitalism, seeing itself champion of the
field, is now giddily removing the last vestiges of corporate stewardship. We can have wealth! ... just at the cost of pollution, frenetic
depletion and exploitation of everyone below the upper class.

Today, the most notable fact of socio-economic life is the exhaustion
and/or despicability of all the major ideological forms. A few ideologues
believe they have the keys to the economic kingdom, but most people are
cynical. A handful of hopefuls believe they have the keys to a sane
civilization, but these are few and far between. For the most part, people
hold their nose and hope that the dark side of the choice they choose is
better than the malignancy they see lurking next door.

Let me give you a completely different view of this situation. Most
of today's 'isms' are facades for the same old plan. Hence, all of the
ism's listed above have failed or are failing in their own way, yet
paradoxically, all for the same reason. They all ended up reinventing
some aspect of the age-old dominator plan.

Clockwork thinking added elegance, but it didn't changed the
theme. Coercive hierarchies have been the basis of oppression for five
thousand years. Communists merely used scientific omnipotence to
justify their efforts to control economies, and people's lives.
Unfortunately, democratic and socialist bureaucracies have often been
controlling and disrespectful too. Politicians and experts often view
people as pawns. Then too, in capitalism people with money and
power often push governments to serve their interests *regardless* of
whether this serves the greater good or not.

Modern dominators also still use the image of war as the creator of all good things. Capitalists use war between individuals and Communists use war between classes. In both cases war is used to explain why people who reign are the unerring right choice. Superiority justifies the subsequent use of power, regardless of how many little people are ground under in the process.

The now mythic struggle between over-bearing states and untrammeled individualism is also misleading. We've had over-bearing states for five thousand years. We now have new privileged élites who use many of the same old techniques. Individualism was to be an alternative, but most people who cry for the untrammeled version are merely thugs with a new theory. Full laissez-faire makes it easy to pillage and exploit. Hence, both extremes tend to support the same plan — concentrated power used to maintain privilege for a few.

In the early days of each 'ism,' mutualist ideals like freedom and justice were held high, but somehow the struggle has been perverted. Now a host of apparently competing socio-economic theories — capitalism, socialism, communism and fascism — have all lapsed back into one dominator habit or another. Coercive hierarchies, gluttonous personal wealth and plans to control the world? Working people have ended up as cogs at one end of the continuum, commodities at the other, and cannon-fodder everywhere in between (see Table 9).

We have come back to the age old struggle for another round. The problem in most cases is not theory *per se*, but whether it is implemented as a mutualist or dominator plan. Capitalism is a good example. It can go either way. Therefore, let me take a moment to give a name to our pain.

Thug Capitalism

> *Nowadays there is only one economic orthodoxy, taught and*
> *proclaimed by almost all academic economists, happily*
> *celebrated by Wall Street and corporate managers, and fully*
> *accepted by Democrats and Republicans as well as the*
> *mainstream parties of Europe. This is the faith that 'turbo-*
> *charged capitalism' — accelerated change fueled by global*
> *free trade and domestic deregulation — is the only way to*
> *run an economy.*   Edward Luttwak

Movement	Theory	Practice
Laissez-faire Capitalism	In theory, unrestrained self-interest will make the whole society prosper.	In practice, unrestrained self-interest often produces ravenous exploitation of human and natural ecologies at home and abroad.
Socialism	In theory, government guarantees social welfare via a safety net.	In practice, money is funneled through bureaucracies which tend to become controlling, unresponsive, inefficient and disrespectful of their clients.
Communism	In theory, ownership by the people will end exploitation by those who own the means of production.	In practice, communism produced extreme élite control and planning (according to Newtonian principles). Working people were still enslaved.

Table 9. Theory versus practice.

Communism has collapsed and socialism has terrible bureaucratic woes. As a result, capitalist pundits now tout theirs as the one true economic religion, vindicated by the failure of the others.

There is a certain truth to this thought. But there is also a great deal of disturbing nonsense. The problem is that the word 'capitalism' covers a broad spectrum of behaviors some of which are more desirable than others. Does capitalism mean a small guy trying to benefit from his own talents and initiative? Or, does it mean a big guy who uses money, power and control of 'means' to extract disproportionate gain from the work of others? Does capitalism mean free individuals pursuing their own interest in ways that also serve the common good? Or does it mean ruthless individuals who pursue conquest and personal power regardless of the common good and often at its expense?

The first parts of these questions outline the capitalism which most people cherish. The second outlines the capitalism which most people despise. Unfortunately, we don't distinguish between the two. Today, it is the dark imperialist kind of capitalism which is growing, precisely at the expense of the cherished grassroots kind. This is one of the most disturbing aspects of our time.

If we are ever to understand our time, we need to distinguish between these two types of capitalism. I call the small-guy form, *synergetic capitalism*, in honour of its connection with the robust, synergetic networks seen in Northern Italy and elsewhere. Free, creative, realistic and honourable, most of us take pride in this form. I call the conquest type, *thug capitalism*, in honour of those calamitous fourteenth-century knights who destroyed the peasant economy and their society while pursuing personal gain regardless of common wellbeing.

We've seen a bit of the synergetic type of capitalism in the discussion of manufacturing networks. This type of capitalism is a boon. Unfortunately, it is thug capitalism that occupies center stage. It claims that uncurbed self-interest and competition automatically produce wellbeing — no matter how much destruction and social unrest ensues. You should recognize it, but let me take a moment to point out the kind of assumptions which get us into trouble.

Competition and Self-interest

Today American economic theorists teach that America is strong, not because of its soul forged in the struggle for a just society — but because Americans are very good at pursuing money regardless of its effects on anyone or anything else. These theorists often use Darwin to explain why self-interest and competition will make everything work out right. What could be wrong with this?

Competition, that poor abused word, is so devoutly worshipped by American business that few people dare point out that it is now taken to utterly absurd extremes. It has become a mantra, chanted long past sensibility. Let's take a simple example. The following quote from a *Wall Street Journal* article looks at how competition is helping the investment industry:

> ... climbing to the top quarter of the mutual fund rankings
> could yield a $150,000 bonus for the manager of a large,
> successful fund, on top of a base pay of $225,000 a year.
> Bottom-rung managers may get no bonus — or a pink slip. All

of which helps explain why the $2 trillion mutual-fund
industry is addicted to risk — and can't kick the habit even
though some funds are overdosing on derivatives.

In the name of getting the most from its employees, companies
create powerful incentives for competition and self-interest. In the
investment industry, these incentives promote risk taking behaviors that
are extremely dangerous to other people's money and the investment
system as a whole. This behavior continues because the incentive system is powerful and because the restraining social bonds are few. So,
here competition and self-interest are not producing an optimal
economic world, merely an over-heated, unstable one.

There are thousands of similar examples. Internal competition begs
people to undermine the person next door even when they are part of the
same endeavour. War-like competition encourages expedience — get rich
by hook or crook and don't think about quality or society. This kind of
competition is also bad for values. Lie, cheat, manipulate and make oneself
visible — that's how one gets ahead! All of this continues because true
believers have salted incentives for self-interest and competition
everywhere. We are now getting what they arranged for — a society in
which most people have to serve Number One *regardless* of its effect on
anyone else. Only a foolish few have time to worry about quality,
integrity, common wellbeing, and the long-term.

We have been trained to believe that competition and uncurbed self-
interest automatically produces the best of all possible worlds, but this
is absurd. Alternatively, some businessmen demur that it is the bottom-
line that forces them to pursue barbarous behaviors. Lean and mean,
ruthlessness is good for company and society. This is simply not true
and it is important to see why.

The Bottom-Line!

In May of 1996, Peter Senge, a professor at MIT and one of America's
premier organizational consultants, told an audience of other such
consultants that after thirty years it was now clear to him that most
American industry works, not toward the company's bottom line, but
primarily toward maintenance of power. If the issue was simply making
money, industry would have embraced the many methods of enhancing
creativity and initiative years ago. As it is, the only strategies that are
retained in most large companies are the ones which serve élite self-

interest — whether or not these actually add to long-term productivity.

Senge gave the story of the Ford Taurus as an example. After years of study, consultants now know how to create high-powered, innovative teams and the engineering group that had developed the Taurus station wagon for the Ford Motor Company was one of Senge's success stories. This creative, self-motivated group developed a station wagon touted by magazines and embraced by consumers which saved the company's dropping bottom line. Yet, within eighteen months of completion, almost all members of that team had left the company. Why? Because creative, empowered people don't make good cogs. They think. They care. They want to make a difference and they often have the audacity to speak their minds. In short, they threaten the command-and-control structure and anyone who believes their rank and privilege is going to be undermined.

Innovative, profit-making teams have been created over and over again, only to be demolished when placed back in corporate cultures which are still anchored in personal imperialism and command-and-control thinking. It is, therefore, naïve to believe that business automatically moves to what is best for the company or even the stock-holders. Thus, when theorists invoke the bottom line one has to ask *whose* bottom line. Theory says that it is the share-holders who are served. But the share-holders were served by the Taurus team and they left because of internal pressures. A more accurate description, is that most companies are designed to serve the bottom-line of an inner circle who run the company. Most companies are quite intentionally designed this way because their designers believe this is the way that quality is achieved. They too are victims of well-salted incentives and certain assumptions.

Theory begs us believe that this arrangement is best for the long-term. Yet it is quite obvious that such systems are suboptimal for most people. To take a large example, Americans are proud of being innovators and rightly so. But American industry is also known for suppressing innovations that threaten some influential system's monetary flow. Why haven't electric cars, mass transit, solar energy and health nutrition been better developed? The answer is — oil companies, automobile manufacturers, highway construction companies, power companies, drug companies and the American Medical Association. Because inner circles are often linked at the top, élites have a way of influencing what happens.

Stamping Out Synergy

Finally, there is thug capitalism's distressing tendency to dismiss humane practices and even stamp them out. There is a tremendous body of evidence showing that mutualist principles — equality, respect, social justice, fair play, camaraderie, freedom, etc. — actually promote efficiency and profits. Why aren't they used more? Because they don't fit the dominator image of callous, coercive, ruthlessness or the machine image of unthinking obedience.

Take the story of the Kellogg cereal company of Battle Creek, Michigan. The company's founding father, W.H. Kellogg, was an enlightened patriarch who believed that people were more productive if they were happy and healthy. He put this belief in action in the first part of this century by reducing the work week to six hours a day and encouraging employees to take an active interest in health, family and community life. His happy workers were soon producing as much in thirty hours a week as they had in forty hours and the community flourished along with the company and employees. After Kellogg died, family members continued his humane practices for a while, but eventually they hired professional managers as the industry became more complex. The professionals promptly restored competitiveness by returning workers to regular time and then overtime. Eventually, overworked, unhappy workers were producing as much in over-time as they had been in under-time.

Most managers don't treat employees like serfs, slaves, cogs, or commodities because that is the best way to make money. They do so because their world view says they should and because organizations are structured such that this behavior is best for their own self-interest. They take negative social effects in stride. They expect them. Everyone 'knows' that unhappiness, crumbling families and crumbling communities are a harsh fact of profit.

High-value and a Glimmer of Hope

The appearance of powerful thug capitalism is something to be feared, not cheered. It marks society-destroying behaviors rising to dominance in America and moving worldwide with no coherent force to oppose it. Like fourteenth-century knights, thugs tend to destroy the social root system while ravenously funneling more wealth to themselves. They invariably have a great explanation for why doing so is good. But, whatever the explanation, fragility and collapse is the usual result.

However, since I hate ending on a negative note, I am going to outline what may be a glimmer of hope. It seems that, after two hundred years of association with war and exploitation, the industrial side of capitalism may be finding another way. Here I explore Robert Reich's idea that one of the big hopes for our time is the shift from mass-production to customized goods and services. He calls this the shift from *high-volume* to *high-value*. It is rising alongside globalization. To explain its importance, however, I need to explain why mass-production has, of necessity, been linked to war.

Why High-volume Industrialism Destroys Itself

Perfect competition — the economist's Rosetta stone — eventually strips away all profits, causing even the best of businesses to fold.[4]

In theory, industrialism calls for free markets because superiority rises through competition. In practice, however, the only nations which actually argue for free markets are ones which greatly outstrip all others at the time. Britain, for instance, called for free markets when it was the industrial super-power in the mid-1800s and the United States called for them in the mid-to-late 1900s when it took this role. The obvious reason an industrial Goliath standing amidst a host little Davids would argue for free trade is that superiority already exists and can be used to advantage. Yet, there is also a more insidious reason called *over-supply* which is rarely mentioned because it has some nasty implications. It goes like this. When mass-production makes prices drop, it also makes wages drop which leaves people unable to buy products. Thus, if industrialism were practiced as preached, competition at home would be ruinous. The home market would be flooded with goods so cheap that profit could not be made. At the same time, workers would be so poor that they couldn't buy much.

Hence, underneath its well-polished image, competitive industrialism hides a dark flaw. Industrial Goliaths can only retain their well-being: first, by limiting competition at home, and second, by exploiting more backward economies. By the mid-1800s, for instance, it was clear that mass-producing giants needed backward economies that could be used as dumping grounds for their goods. These dumping-ground nations, euphemistically called, 'spheres of influence,' could not be allowed to grow their own industries lest these begin to compete with the Goliath. To ensure that their spheres remain backward, industrial giants shifted to military force if economic colonialism didn't work quietly. Hence, the term 'imperialism' was actually invented in the late-1800s in response to new rounds of conquest being driven by problems of supply and demand. It affected the history of India, China and Africa in particular.

Unfortunately, competition makes the over-supply problem impossible to contain. In the mid 1800s, for instance, the U.S. and Germany erected stiff tariffs which allowed their baby industries to grow to a place where they stood a fighting chance against the British Goliath of the time. Unfortunately, freer competition on a more level playing field lead to the problems of over-supply. Prices fell by almost forty percent in the 1870s and 1880s and both Europe and America were jolted with severe depressions in 1873 and again in 1893.

Crises like these intensified the sense that industrial nations were at war economically. The quest for domination then led to a new strategy. If competition kills, then one must limit competition at home, so as to better fight abroad. From 1870 on European ministers such as Otto von Bismarck, Georges Clemenceau and David Lloyd George began to consolidate and coordinate their nation's industrial juggernauts so as to better confront other nations doing the same. Hence, by the early twentieth century, most industrial nations were dominated by nationally-based syndicates, cartels, joint-stock banks, giant corporations, etc. which shared capital, jointly purchased raw materials and fixed prices at home and abroad. Governments supported their cartels at home by giving them public contracts and abroad with foreign policies which included bullying or invading countries with important resources.

This kind of economic war, however, produced many of the same problems seen in the demise of feudalism. Caught up with the moves of their rivals, industrial élites tried to get more and more from their workers, while giving back less and less. Since government support was assured, workers who objected were put down through force. Industrialists became dangerously powerful and quite unaccountable to their home populace. The resulting socio-economic unrest contributed heavily to fascism, socialism, communism and both World Wars.

World War II brought a distinctive shift for several reasons. First, social unrest caused by capitalist exploitation was now clearly an issue to be reckoned with. So too were boom-bust cycles which led to disastrous depressions. With communism and socialism taking root around the world, capitalists realized that, to avoid similar problems, a change had to be made. The direction of this change was also clear. World War II had had a strong element of mutualist soul. It had been about freedom and democracy fighting authoritarianism. It had been about saving people from bondage and horrendous abuse. It had been about working together to overcome a common foe. It was a first step in commitment to global wellbeing. This last was witnessed by the Marshall Plan. Instead of using its advantage selfishly, America, the only economy left in tact, used its wellbeing to help both friends and foes get back on their feet.

Surviving World War II thus renewed the idea that, to avoid similar problems, developed countries must implement the mutualist ideals that had saved them. By the 1950s this belief had produced a system which seemed to solve the problem of competitive industrialism. After the war company managers were urged to take a statesmanship role. They were to use their power to coordinate the needs of industry, workers and society for the benefit of all. They did this by coordinating prices, restricting competition at home and encouraging high consumption à la Keynes. Union leaders also cooperated. Instead of the old disruptive strikes, union specialists sat down with their corporate counterparts to compare numbers and haggle out equitable distribution of wages and profits. Soon the proletariat movement of the early part of the century began to settle into a well-oiled cog in the national industrial machine.

And for a while, it all seemed to be working. The middle-class blossomed. Fewer people lived in extremes of either want or wealth. CEO earnings were kept in line because making too much money was deemed unseemly. Besides, if the top seemed to be bilking the system, the unions would not keep their part of the bargain and strikes might return. In this way, cooperation and a firm belief in common cause, did indeed put most people in the same economic ship that rose together.[5]

The Return of Global Competition

Measured on any scale — as the portion of total national income going to shareholders and other business owners or as the rate of return on investment — profits declined or stagnated from the mid-1960s onward.

Unfortunately, as we have seen, this rising tide reached its peak sometime in the late 1960s. Ever since then, productivity, profits, and common wellbeing have been slowly going downhill. The question that now preoccupies economists is — why? The obvious answer is that competition has returned, now on an utterly global level.

The economies devastated by World War II are back along with many new players. Producers in third-world countries are particularly willing to under-cut prices because they have very cheap labor and few social or environmental restrictions. The downward spiral of shrinking wages and profits now looms large.

Economic élites have been struggling with the problem of shrinking wellbeing for almost thirty years now. They have tried three main strategies in this time.

- *Protectionism.* Starting in the late 1960s, industries attempted to keep out cheap foreign products by erecting tariffs, anti-dumping levies, voluntary restraint agreements, etc. This provided temporary relief, but it failed because manufacturers themselves wanted to buy cheaply in order to undercut their competitors.
- *Cutting to the Bone.* The second strategy was to slash costs to match the competition. Wage and benefits were rolled back starting in the 1970s. When this failed, companies began closing plants and laying off thousands of workers. When this failed, they began moving their factories abroad, usually to the very lands whose cheap production costs were cutting into their profits. Unfortunately, third-world producers often sold more cheaply even when industries

world producers often sold more cheaply even when industries moved to their countries.

- *Financial Dexterity (rearranging assets).* When the first two strategies failed, executives in many corporations tried to maintain their profits by paper-transactions and empire-building. They started by forming conglomerates of unrelated businesses, arguably for synergies, stimulants and other efficiencies these would bring. When it became clear that these mergers didn't actually help profitability, they switched to unfriendly take-overs and leveraged buyouts. These strategies served to enrich a few corporate executives, investment bankers and speculative marketeers while undermining thriving companies by saddling them with the debt of their own hostile take-over.

This last strategy still holds sway. It is responsible for the sense of broken contract between large companies and their societies. Vast economic power increases leverage and reduces social responsiveness. Cut loose from concern about community or unseemly behavior, senior executive wages, bonuses, golden parachutes and so on, have skyrocketed. Meanwhile, layoffs have become the strategy of choice even when a company is making money.

The concept of corporate stewardship has fallen apart and thug theory has taken its place. Competitive industrialism's tendency to ravenously enrich a few while undermining many now leaves us in a very strange and confusing world. But, like all turnings, this one can go two ways.

A New Word Hidden in High-Value

The standard of living of ... citizens of [all] nations, is coming to depend less on the success of the nation's core corporations ... than it is on the worldwide demand for their skills and insights. Robert Reich

On the surface developed economies are still a traditional high-volume industrial system, but underneath much is changing. The two forces driving this subterranean shift are, first, increasing global entwinement, and second, the shift from high-volume to what Reich calls *high-value*.

The first is easy to see. As a result of the last thirty years, most corporate headquarters are facades for a complex web of contractors, subcontractors, subsidiaries, allies, etc. which diffuses work all over the globe. Companies called German, French, British or American, are less and less so. Foreign parts fill assemblies, foreign workers constitute a large percentage of the work force and foreign companies own part or all of what are ostensibly national companies. Enmeshment goes both ways, however. Japanese, German, Indonesian, Thai — parts, work and ownership are so mixed that it is often hard to tell what the dominant nationality is.

It is the second, more invisible shift that is the most relevant, however. Slowly, through trial-and-error and often without awareness, the industries that are thriving are shifting from mass-production to serving the unique needs of particular customers. Whether the industry is old or high-tech, service or manufacturing, the pattern is similar. For instance, the most profitable part of steelmaking is no longer long runs of steel ingots, but in particular alloys with particular properties that serve particular needs. The fastest-growing truck, rail, and air freight businesses meet shipper's needs for specialized pickups and deliveries worldwide. The most profitable financial services tailor a custom blend of banking, investment, management, and information for specific types of people. The highest profits in software derive from customized services to particular businesses and individuals.

In this simple and growing trend, all things change. These businesses are lucrative because customers are willing to pay a premium for goods or services that exactly meet their needs. They thrive because high-quality, customized goods and services cannot easily be duplicated by cheap-labor competitors around the world. Thus, while competition around mass-produced goods tends to reduce prices, wages, quality and profits, high-value goes in exactly the opposite direction. Prices, profits, wages, and quality all stay sound together. Uniqueness helps open millions of niches in which quality and innovation are the biggest differentiators. As in nature, the economic eco-system stays strong by building quality within an endless array of specialty slots. Head-to-head competition over price, fades.

There is also another up-side. Armies of obedient workers and their coercive overseers cease to be central. In a high-value world, *human capital* — the knowledge and creative skills of individual people — is the key to prosperity. Conversely, many central tenets of traditional competitive industrial theory fall apart. For instance:

(1) *A high-value firm requires a very different kind of organizational*

structure. A high-value firm's prosperity lies in its ability to facilitate learning such that breakthroughs in different areas can be rearranged into wondrous new forms. Habits of bureaucracy, standard-procedures and coercive power run against these. Hence, creative links tend to emerge from frequent and informal exchanges between team members — formal meetings don't reveal them. Communal learning occurs fastest when problems and insights are shared at ease. Formal ranking and corporate pigeon-holing tends to stifle this. Finally, distributed intelligence and authority is crucial since speed and quality are of the essence. Sending ideas up a chain of command and waiting for instructions to come down is too slow for fast times.

Hence, if one wants synergy, creativity and collaboration, then management structures must be more facilitative than controlling, more horizontal than vertical, and more egalitarian than classist. But there is more.

(2) *Commitment and creativity come best from sharing power, risks, returns, and wellbeing.* High-value firms must embrace experimentation and change, but this only works in a group which is both diverse and committed to one another. Diversity increases creativity and heightens the chance of success. Commitment and stability are heightened by broadly shared risks and benefits. When risks are shared, the whole web sustains the failures and the whole web benefits from successes. When returns are shared too, then everyone has incentive for everyone else to succeed. Thus, in high-value firms, contributors are apt to opt for a piece of the profits instead of a fixed salary.

Power relationships also change. High-value goods and services are invariably collaborations. When one person attempts to own or control such creations, others are apt to jump ship to the detriment of all. Hence, power is more diffuse in these webs. Real power hinges on one's ability to positively aid the web, and not on formal authority or rank. Similarly, leadership is witnessed by the ability to help many others add value, not by the ability to manipulate or control. Hence, if you look closely, you'll see that high-value firms look a lot like the synergetic webs mentioned earlier. This leads to another important point.

(3) *Theories based on materialism do not hold for businesses based on human capital.* A high-value enterprise is a dynamic web of relationships between talented individuals whose combined skills give the

enterprise its value. Such an enterprise is not a commodity which can be acquired like a factory — a fact which has surprised many power-brokers who have attempted to make such acquisitions. Reich cites the experience of General Electric when it purchased the financial-services house of Kidder-Peabody in 1986. Kidder-Peabody was known for its quality and creativity, but talented people often leave when new owners try to restructure relationships along traditional lines. Hence, when GE tried to exert control over its new acquisition by imposing stricter reporting requirements and tighter accounting costs, many of Kidder-Peabody's most skilled people left for more agreeable surroundings. GE was left with little more than Kidder-Peabody's good, but fading name.

Similarly, where factories wear out and standard parts are easily re-placed, creative human capital grows with age and is not easily dupli-cated. Thus, people who are fortunate enough to have had an excellent education followed by on-the-job experience doing complex things can become steadily more valuable over time. Their country is apt to appreciate with them. This leads to another important shift.

(4) *In a high-value economy, a nation's wellbeing depends more on its people's skills than on the profitability of its core corporations.* Many corporations broke the contract with their society in order to remain profitable. Headquarters, factories, workers, resources, capital — all this is a floating game which brokers rearrange to suit themselves. Loyalty and commitment to any larger common good is frequently (even generally) absent. The simple implication here is that corporate profits are no longer a good measure of a nation's economic health.

Where else should we look? Reich points out the obvious. As eco-nomies convert from high-volume to high-value, the best measure of a nation's economic wellbeing will be the skills its people bring to the global economy. Skills and experience are what raise people's standard of living and the nation's as well. These are what allow a nation to compete world-wide. A country benefits most when *its citizens* acquire skills and experience and thus become more valuable.

Hence, the problem of shrinking wellbeing has less to do with corporate profits than it does with how people are educated and what kinds of experience they can acquire. This leads to a major need for the new age.

(5) *Traditional patterns of education won't work for the emerging world* because quality human capital cannot be stamped out by cookie-

cutter molds. In high-volume days, companies needed factory workers whose chief characteristics were the ability to read and follow directions. Traditional education did well by this need. It stuffed facts into young brains, taught discipline, conformity and the ability to work alone on isolated tasks. It also encouraged the competitiveness that was thought to make all things good. Yet, with the high-value age, all these needs are reversed. Teamwork is critical. So is originality and the ability to make connections across fields. Commitment to one another is often the saving virtue of a team and the chief virtue of a high-value leader is the knack of helping others be successful. Traditional education tends to stamp out all of these characteristics.

By the 1990s the sense of crisis in the schools was growing as test scores dropped. Yet, not understanding the nature of the high-value world, many reformers called for a stronger version of the old. More tests! More uniform curriculum! More discipline! More competition! As Reich says, 'The fact that standardized tests only reflect a student's ability to regurgitate facts — as opposed to think or collaborate — remained an unmentioned topic.' The fact that factory-like schools also make learning fragmented, meaningless and odious also goes unmentioned.

The yuppies who already dominate high-value jobs, however, don't want any of this for their own children. They pour their money and children into élite private schools and advance track programs where young minds are trained to be skeptical, curious, creative and collaborative. Here the curriculum is integrated, interactive and communal. Instead of regurgitating pre-packaged bits of history, math and biology, the focus is on learning to think and connect. Students learn to examine reality from many angles and to ask why some facts have been emphasized and how current interpretations might be contradicted. The best classrooms also make learning a group project. Students learn to listen to others, to seek help and to give credit. They learn to articulate the patterns they see and to clarify and restate for one another. Here the benefits are more profound, if less tangible. Students learn about the bonds that come from working together and the pride that comes from contributing to a committed whole.

The result is better learning, in more dimensions, for everyone. The result is actually a return to the concept of a society of mind. Human systems are most creative when they are collaborative. They are the most intelligent when they are integrative, inclusive and egalitarian.

Brain research tells us this, but now, on the edge of a global economy
the stakes are much higher. Since what a country's people can do
matters more than what its big capitalists own, developing human
capital is crucial to national wellbeing — for all nations.

Developing human capital will not be easy because it requires
profound social and educational reforms. Yet, the benefits would be
more profound. If high-value succeeds, synergetic capitalism might just
evolve into a world-wide web which supplants the thug capitalism
which currently dominates. Our children might find more hope and
more meaningful work. Because customization opens the door to
endless niches, quality and creativity might be more valued than
obedience, aggression or self-service. If we can figure out how to link
niches through cooperation, we might finally have a sustainable world.
The next chapter looks at some efforts already underway toward this
end.

PART IV

INTEGRAL SOCIETY

Imagine that the year is 1543 and you have just completed reading the newly published On the Revolution of the Heavenly Spheres *which has attempted to convince you that the daily experience of a stationary earth being illuminated periodically by the moving sun is an illusion. What do you think the chances are that you would have accepted the Copernican argument that violates your direct perceptions?*

Thomas Gentry, 1995

CHAPTER 9

SEEDS OF A NEW WAY

Small scale or large, the fundamental condition of peace is
federation for mutual advantage.   Ruth Benedict

So, how is world civilization doing? Do we think we are on the right track? Is progress being made?

Paradoxically, as world civilization grows ever more intertwined, social fabrics seem to grow ever more tattered. Life is fast, complicated and increasingly disjointed. Distance and speed keep us apart, even as communications appear to make us more connected. Relationships become more impermanent and, hence, more superficial and now social loyalty seems all but obsolete. Ideals have become icons which are manipulated at will. Many ideologies have become dubious, but ideologues grinding axes are still found a-plenty. Few people have time to think, to do things well or to worry about consequences — which we vaguely sense may be building.

Which way do we turn? One doesn't want to turn too far because nightmarish alternatives lie just over the hill. Petty, strutting chieftains who wreak their capricious wills are still plentiful and torture and genocide are still political tools of choice in many parts of the world. So, while Amnesty International does a land-office business, the rest of us try not to comprehend that such things could really be taking place.

What can we do? I don't think most people believe civilization is on the right track, but then, I think most of us are too bewildered and tired to feel like revolutionaries. The failure and/or despicability of the great ideological forms of the last two centuries has also left a strange absence of direction. We know the problems well, but the usual solutions are in question. The only people without doubts are those so wrapped in their ideological blankets that they have lost all touch with history and society as it is. The only ones who are certain are the ones who are mindless, unscrupulous or naïve.

Yet, underneath today's endless impassive whir, the seeds of great potential are being sown. The hive mind has been at work. All over the globe, small swirls are arising and some may ignite a change. People rethinking the conundrum in front of them — business, public policy and religion — are coming up with remarkably common insights. Some are beginning to rework old institutions so that they serve needed ends (instead of merely following usual modes).

Underneath a bewildering diversity of names a common social push is building. It doesn't have a name yet, but I believe Ruth Benedict defines the dream — 'the fundamental condition of peace is federation for mutual advantage.' It doesn't have a lot of pat formulas yet, and I think that is good. In light of recent history, most people concentrate first on staying small and building up, and then on staying grounded while keeping one's heart and humanity closely in tow. If we are lucky, the people of this great push will develop the seeds of a new civilization — a reinvention that will help us become more sane and humane as well as more prosperous.

Turbulent times bring an age of possibilities. Turnings can go either way but let us concentrate on the positive potential — beginning with Sorotkin's great lesson. All truly great traditions rise from an Integral soul born of compassion, forged in the search for social justice and anchored in a society which feels itself whole. Recurrently we find justice, freedom, equality and community. One for all, all for one. Do unto others as you would have them do unto you. Live in sympathy with the web. These ideas are ancient, but with each rediscovery we move one notch closer to realizing the dream.

Nowadays we can also refine ancient images with concepts from the new science. Let me therefore, recast the crisis in terms developed throughout this book.

The Challenge

Cultural Creatives have been at work all over the world for a very long time now. Despite the diversity of efforts, they are producing strong common themes. Their efforts are more populist than authoritarian, more collaborative than controlling, more concerned about community and good governance than about power and parochial interest. Though most do not know it, they also have a lot in common with the web view in science which is rising in the wings. This book is largely for them. Right now there is very little decent theory to support them. As a result they are disconnected and disorganized, a million voices crying in the wilderness. I think a decent synthesis of the new science may help ground Creatives' sense that they are part of one thrust. It might also help them build the new world more soundly. The last thing we need is another Utopian scheme.

Many Creatives intuit parts of the theory they need. The new science puts three issues at the center of human evolution: learning, collaboration, and intricacy. These are relevant to every aspect of civilization — economic to spiritual. They are all intertwined. I believe that intricacy is the most crucial, however, because it is the least understood and the most overlooked.

Hidden Crisis: the Exhaustion of Coercive Hierarchies

Imagine intricacy as fine-grained, interwoven connections that allow energy and information to flow robustly throughout. These are what allow an organization to thrive. Furthermore, since evolution is a matter of increasing intricacy, then human organizations too face the challenge of intricacy. How do you build it, how do you sustain it, what makes it blossom and what pulls it apart?

This challenge of intricacy is more specific than one might imagine. Intricacy is like a hidden obligation that rules all organizations. A society must work together to survive. As an organization grows, however, the forces holding it together get stretched. It eventually reaches a point where it splinters into smaller systems. This brings three possibilities (see Figure 41). If parts stay linked in a way that is mutually-supportive, the whole becomes more intricate and more powerful. If subsystems simply pull apart, the system begins to work at odds inside. We say it is fragmenting and on the road to collapse. The third possibility is that the organization shrinks or at least ceases to grow. It may then be able get by on existing patterns.

If the various theorists are right, then we are on the cusp of a very big turning. For five thousand years we have been ruled by coercive hierarchies, despots and conquest as a major way of making a living. For most of this time the mutualist urge has fought back creating a fractal landscape of brilliant bursts embedded in one overall push.

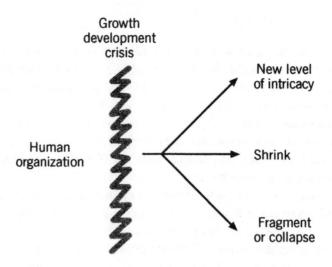

Figure 41. Growth Crises in Human Organizations — The Three Main Choices.

Today, this push is being aided by a crisis in intricacy. Thus, the structures born during the Age of War are now exhausted. We have reached the limits of coercive hierarchies. This exhaustion is creating pressure for change.

Ranking creates a stream-lined type of organization which is very good at war. This kind of organization, however, tends to stifle creativity. It tends to abuse lower levels and to move toward entrenchment and the creation of false Gods. It drains energy away from the grassroots and funnels it into ostentation and destruction. We use ranking for historical reasons and because it is very good at creating focused force. It is not, however, a great way to create a vibrant civilization. This is why we had the Enlightenment, among many other revolts.

We have mollified this combination, but the ideological essence is still there. Today's burgeoning complexity, however, is wreaking havoc with this ancient system. We all know the problems. The larger and more conventional the organization, the more information is lost on the long dissipating trip, up and down the chain. Bonds break vertically and the top becomes effectively disconnected from the bottom. Absurdity is common. So is disproportional gain and resentment.

Today's technology and global entwinement make the problem worse. Globalization means that everything affects everything else in a rapidly moving web that is ever-more comprehensively interdependent.

Technology means that local catastrophes can have massive and devastating effects — think of Chernobyl, Bhopal, global warming and the collapse of Asian markets. Economic entwining means that injustice and greed anywhere undermines justice and wellbeing elsewhere. Exploited workers in one part of the world are used as leverage against workers in others. And then there is gluttonous personal wealth which is used to promote self-interest regardless of others. Some personal fortunes exceed the wealth of entire nations. Political leaders find it necessary to keep alignment with such people. As a result, self-service now has the potential to create a domino effect of epic proportions.

The much touted globalization going on about us, thus, pushes an evolutionary juncture coming to international climax. We are at a complexity crisis like none that has ever existed. The exhaustion of coercive hierarchies *plus* the increasingly high cost of dominator pursuits leaves us hanging on the edge.

Today we can say that the meek must come to reinherit the earth because ranking and intimidation are too rigid and dangerous for a fast-paced world. Dominator structures now look like a product of primitive times which endanger our health. They only work below a certain size, speed and complexity and they are now floundering on all these dimensions.

What then shall we do? Lacking a theoretical basis, massive organizations do what they can. Governments and large corporations are struggling to rid themselves of bulk, usually in the form of middle-management and lower-echelon roots. In doing so they are acting like Carneiro's villages in Chapter 3. They have hit a complexity barrier, but, having no concept of how to increase intricacy, these organizations settle for shrinking instead.

Shrinking and breaking into smaller pieces is now rampant. Big companies remove mounds of people flesh, in a process the Wall Street Journal calls 'corporate anorexia.' Work piles up on ever more skeletal frames. At the national level, both the old Soviet Union and Yugoslavia have split into a profusion of smaller states which represent more ancient, closely-knit peoples. In the U.S., micro-businesses (those under fifty employees) now employ more people than the all the Fortune 500 companies combined. All of these events have a similar cast. They involve huge organizations stretched to their limits. They also involve huge organizations that rely heavily on coercive hierarchies and dominator traditions.

Shrinking and breaking up alone, however, are not enough to make a new way. Intricacy suggests that the problem is deeper and more paradoxical than this. Getting rid of middle managers or workers, for instance, does not help the organization work faster or better or with greater power. It merely delays the problem. Thus, getting smaller is not enough. The organization must also stay connected, committed and collaborative or descent will ensue.

So, today we straddle a razor's edge where big is no longer better and small has problems too. Our challenge, therefore, is to develop social systems that can support our needs in an Integral way. The only way to end the Age of War is to develop self-sustaining social, political, economics and spiritual systems which stay committed to common wellbeing world-wide.

Unfortunately, this goal is still a dream and new ways are obvious only after the fact. Meanwhile, when a human organization hits a complexity barrier, it hits a wall and everything begins to crumble. Patterns that used to work, no longer do and no one seems to know why. Fragmentation increases, as does insularity and working at odds. Breaking up leaves scattered, despairing people who are prone to the politics of resentment, including scapegoating, nativism and xenophobia. Charismatic tyrants leap in to fill power vacuums, playing little Hitlers to desperate people. This is now seen in the remnants of Yugoslavia and also parts of the U.S.

Then too there is another side to the problem. New Age romantics point out that linking creates stronger bonds. We did it once, we can do it again! Linking (also called partnership or mutualism) is our most creative form and it is still common world-wide. Because it is based on mutual advantage, distributed intelligence flourishes and is still oriented towards the common good. On the other hand, mutualism works best when people are close to each other and the land. It is easily disrupted by greed. It has a nasty tendency to turn into tribalism when times are bad. Hence, linking works when systems are small and mutual need is high, but we do not yet know how to extend concern for common-cause across a far-flung global community.

Hence, both older ways have problems. While dominator hierarchies are powerful compared to their primitive mutualist predecessors, they are simplistic when compared to the needs of the modern world. While mutualist organizations are noble, we must figure out how to keep them that way as they grow, pull apart, and attract the greedy and self-serving from inside and out.

An Integral Society, therefore, will have to be old and new at the same time. It will have to build local autonomy which is still committed to the common good. It will have to keep smallness well-connected and embraced in a sense of community. It will have to renew ancient ideals while building a socio-economic system which supports them. And so the goal is:

- more networked than hierarchical,
- more collaborative than coercive,
- more mutual than exploitative.

Can the top orchestrate such a switch? It seems unlikely because the view from 50,000 feet is not very acute. Can the bottom do it alone? This seems unlikely too because small mutualist webs are easily overwhelmed by dominators seeking advantage. In short, if self-organization is going to save us it is probably best thought of as *joint* organization — top, bottom and everything in-between. Whatever we do, we must do it together.

The meek must eventually reinherit the earth because linking builds better intricacy than ranking. The meek have a big challenge in front of them, however, because they need to develop a *networked* mutualist form, which does not yet exist. This is the greatest challenge of our time. It is a result of the rules of intricacy.

What is networked mutualism? For that matter, what is social intricacy and how does one develop it? I think we should start exploring these questions by looking at how intricacy has played out historically in real life societies. This will provide a sense of what helps and what hurts human intricacy.

This brings me back to Jane Jacobs. Though she didn't use the word intricacy, by 1961 Jacobs was already contemplating city life as a problem of subtle order arising from fine-grained flow. Her work provides some early insights into how intricacy helps sustain civilization and why traditional city planning has tended to destroy intricacy and with it natural flow. The following section is based on her book, *Death and Life of the Great American Cities.*

How Human Eco-systems Self-organize

Cities ... need all kinds of diversity, intricately mingled in
mutual support. We need this so city life can work decently
and constructively, and so the people of cities can sustain ...
their society and civilization.   Jane Jacobs

In 1939 North Boston was a slum. Its four- and five-storey tenements
had been built to house the flood of immigrants first from Ireland, then
Central and Eastern Europe. They were desperately over-crowded and
pushed up against heavy industry near the waterfront. Yet, by 1959, a
remarkable transformation had taken place. Dozens and dozens of
buildings had been rehabilitated and fresh paint and Venetian blinds
lined windows that had once been covered with mattresses. Families
had uncrowded themselves and now lived one or two to a building
instead of four or five. Homes mingled with splendid food stores, and
small carpentry, metal work, upholstery and food processing enterprises had sprung up near their owners' homes. The streets were alive
with children at play and people strolled, shopped and talked in an
atmosphere buoyant with friendliness and good health.

What had brought about this stunning revitalization? The money
hadn't come from the great American banking system because, as one
banker said, 'No sense lending money to the North End, it's a slum!'
It had windy streets. It had businesses intermingled with homes. It had
too many poor people and too little grass. It was near industry, the
waterfront and downtown! In short, it didn't fit the clockwork picture
of tidy suburban order tucked in separate, well-orchestrated bins. As
a result, the largest mortgage loan granted in twenty-five years was
$3000 with a few for $1000 or $2000 scattered in. For the most part,
money was simply not available to this district of 15,000 people
because of what all the bankers 'knew.'

Revitalization therefore had come, not from money-lenders or
experts, but from local people working together. Families had pooled
their resources to buy back foreclosed buildings. They had rehabilitated
these buildings using skilled work bartered among residents and bolstered by small amounts of money from local businesses and other
community groups.

This kind of working together had created a place that was alive and mutually supportive. It was also lively and safe. North Boston, for example, had virtually no crime. The reason for this is understandable. When people feel a vested interest each other and in the place they live and work, a natural network of self-policing evolves. Jacobs describes how such self-policing works using an example from a New York neighbourhood where she lived in 1961. Looking out her window one day, Jacobs noticed a man trying to cajole a young girl of eight or nine to come with him. The girl was backed up rigidly against the wall of a building while the man alternated between appeasing gestures and acting as if he was going to walk away. Concerned and trying to decide what to do, Jacobs then noticed that she was not alone in her vigil. The husband and wife who ran the butcher shop across the street had come to their door and two men from the local delicatessen had emerged with arms folded and stern looks. Several heads poked out of upper windows and the locksmith, the fruit man and the laundry proprietor all soon joined the watch. It was clear, as Jacobs says, that 'Nobody was going to allow a little girl to be dragged off, even if nobody knew who she was.'

Jacobs' story is American, but the image is international. We know these kinds of streets. Some of us know them only from stories, movies or books — because they are increasingly difficult to find. Yet, we know them just the same. Jacobs' neighbourhood was a community in the deep sense of that word. The people who lived there were involved with daily life of that space. As a result they *saw* what was going on and *cared* about what they saw. They also felt *safe* in taking action and responsibility. Theirs was not a faceless, sterile world owned by élites or operated by experts. People felt they had support and a say in what happened. For reasons we know too little about, their world had evolved an intricate web of mutually-supportive, binding relationships. That is what human intricacy is about.

This invisible intricacy, at once haphazard and tight, aided many aspects of community and civilization. People in such webs, for example, exchange ideas regularly and casually, which helps information flow and keep its quality. Businesses are more apt to deal fairly in such places because people know each other and word travels. Goods and services also propagate better because they are aided by fortuitous information about who has what, who needs what and who can do what. Political ideas are exchanged in the well-greased flow of the evening pub and timely intervention is also more likely. A fight brewing, a child or a family in distress? As local clergy, police, parents and teachers have long known, the way to get word of a problem before it gets too far is to have comfortable connections with people in the everyday web.

Safety and civilization also moves toward another generation. Most children who live in such places begin taking an active role in supporting that web at an early age. They learn about life, mutual support, caring and integrity by *doing*. Hence, if streets are safe and interesting, children will come out to play and learn about life at their own choosing. Stickball games existed before orchestrated little leagues and these self-organized games had unseen dimensions. They taught children how to live together and play fairly, and not just how to win. None of this is part of the modern view of learning which equates education with pumping facts into brains and games with learning to win. It is however, the traditional way of sustaining mutualist civilization.

Getting Intricacy to Grow

It is not how dense you make it, it is how you make it dense.
Alan Littlewood, architect

So North Boston and Jacobs' New York neighbourhood had intricacy, a maze of messy self-integrated relationships which played a huge role in the hidden-order side of life. This maze made information flow and civilization flourish. It made people feel connected and this reduced anxiety. People felt supported, in good times and bad.

Unfortunately, it is quite clear that social intricacy is failing today. People don't know their neighbours, they don't feel like they have a say and they don't have time to care. Life is too fast and the system too Byzantine. These kinds of feelings are common today and they contribute to the decline of liveliness, safety and civilization. Many people sense this, but most have no idea of what to do.

What could help restore intricacy? We tend to think of North Boston's wholesome vitality as a small town syndrome, which is one reason urban planners invented suburbia with lots of grass and tress. Wholesome vitality, however, happens in poor inner city pockets as well as rural settings. Indeed, this community condition had nothing to do with race, class, religion, intelligence, nationality, or population density. Wealth may make a difference, but not necessarily of the expected variety. Jacobs notes that no heads peered out of the high-rent apartments in her neighbourhood because most of those residents were so transient and disconnected with the daily life of the space that they neither saw nor cared. They had no idea who lived on their street or who kept it safe.

What supports wholesome vitality if not wealth and rural setting? In true web form, Jacobs argues that natural intermingling and flow helps build bonding and buoyancy. Take the issue of safety and crime. City safety, she says, depends on the number of eyes looking out; the sense of involvement with others and the place; and the feeling of support and power versus isolation and fear. But no one can *make* people watch, care or feel supported. These things emerge only for everyday self-organized reasons. Thus, in intermingled neighbourhoods, proprietors watch naturally because they are there and business hates crime. Residents watch naturally because they are there, they take out the trash, look out their windows and watch for their children. Many people watch and find reasons to go out because friendly bustling human activity is fun to watch and to join.

Natural reasons thus support natural flow which becomes a self-sustaining cycle. In North Boston, people walked about because they needed/wanted to go to its many sites — grocery stores, bakers, doctors, shoe-stores, pubs, and home. This created bubbly activity because these sites had a human face and a natural proximity. Thanks to intermingling, people came for the barber or butcher, but, since paths meandered, people wandered and discovered new things. Pleasant wandering created bubbly activity which itself brought more people and proprietors who wanted to be near the bustle. Thus, contrary to the usual clockwork streamlined dreams, buoyant flow and self-sustaining safety comes best from intermingling with a human feel. Remnants of old-time city centers the world over show how this works.

What Destroys Intricacy?

There is a quality even meaner than outright ugliness or disorder, and this meaner quality is the dishonest mask of pretend order, achieved by ignoring or suppressing the real order that is struggling to exist ...

We must now ask what causes such bubbly systems to go under. The first answer here is 'growth.' If a locale becomes too popular, the human connections which made it desirable will be swamped, lost to outsiders trying to make a fast buck regardless of the effect on the community.

The other big destroyer is belief systems. What powerful people 'know' profoundly affects how all of us live. Thus, Jacobs' story about self-organized intricacy in North Boston ends with an ominous warning. Paint and patchwork improvements go only so far. Deeper structural repairs required loans that no North Ender could get. Thus, though North Boston had a thriving atmosphere and great statistics — low death rate, low crime rate, low infectious disease rate, etc. — bankers and urban planners still 'knew' it was a slum. They had recently bulldozed a similarly self-revitalized area, the West End, to make way for one of those neatly parceled, if sterile and insular communities that planners have been taught are optimal. Without a stronger political voice and more financial backing, the North End's nest of self-organized happiness and would also be razed in favor of planned sterility — Big Brother with a grassy lawn.

Clockwork beliefs are hard on intricacy. The problem is clear. Expert planning often destroys self-organized intricacy because this warm, sticky stuff of life is not part of the clockwork scheme. Jacobs tells a story about a housing project in East Harlem, New York, that had a small conspicuous piece of grassy lawn which the project's tenants hated. Surprised at how often the lawn came up, one of the local social workers finally started asking why it created such resentment. One of the more articulate tenants said this:

> Nobody cared what we wanted when they built this place.
> They threw our houses down and pushed us here and pushed
> our friends somewhere else. We don't have a place around
> here to get a cup of coffee or a newspaper or to borrow fifty
> cents. Nobody cared what we needed. But the big men come
> and look at that grass and say, 'Isn't it wonderful! Now the
> poor have everything!' (1961, p.52)

Jacobs' simple story illustrates the classic conundrum of the clockwork world — it has been destructive of human happiness and wellbeing even though it is often well-intentioned. One need not invoke conspiracy, however; insularity and assumption work just as well. Jacobs comments:

> Planners ... are not consciously disdainful ... On the contrary,
> they have gone to great pains to learn what the saints and
> sages of ... orthodox planning have said about how cities *ought*
> to work. and what *ought* to be good for people and businesses
> in them. They take [these teachings] with such devotion that
> when contradictory reality intrudes, threatening to shatter their
> dearly won learning, they must shrug reality aside. (1961, p.8)

This brings us back to clockwork assumptions of separation and control. Traditional planning tends to run roughshod over self-organized intricacy for the usual reasons. First, clockwork experts are taught that they can (and should) plan and control everything. As in all machine-age Utopias, however, the right to have plans of any significance belong *only* to the planners in charge. Secondly, clockwork thinking tends to assume that everything works better when parceled neatly into separate bins.

In the case of urban planning, clockwork assumptions started early on, with Ebenezer Howard, a nineteenth-century English court reporter who became the first urban planning theorist. Having seen the squalor of late nineteenth-century London, Howard assumed that population density was *the* problem. His prescription was to repopulate the countryside, by creating self-sufficient small towns, really very nice towns, called Garden Cities. His solution was well-intentioned and romantic. Yet, Howard also set in motion a powerful set of intricacy-destroying ideas. He believed the way to deal with a city was to sort messiness into simple uses and then to arrange each of these uses in relative self-containment. He focused on getting material aspects like housing to have physical characteristics reminiscent of pastoral towns. He conceived of good planning as a series of static acts in which each plan must anticipate all that is needed. Finally, since each plan only worked if its pieces stayed as designed, plans had to be protected against any but the most minor subsequent changes.

Howard was a classic clockwork thinker, a man of his times. His plan had no place for human ties or self-organization. There was no concern about natural entwinment or about support-systems of friends and relatives. There was no place for unplanned detours, like the direct paths that forever form on college campuses. In short, Howard's plan — and most planning since — has focused on arranging things neatly, regardless of how the people involved felt about the whole thing.

Neat plans, however, did not work as hoped. Traditional planning oriented people for privacy and separate life/work bins. It then streamlined routes between those bins. Since Garden Cities were the ideal, planners put decorative grass and trees in promenades where people could stroll at leisure. It all sounded rational and wonderful! Unfortunately, planners left few everyday reasons to promenade. So, people didn't. The result was the reverse of North Boston. Lack of regular reasons, meant fewer people on the street. Fewer people with natural ties also meant less involvement and less concern. The result was city districts custom-made for crime.

Thus, well-meant, paternalistic plans often create what Jacobs calls 'The Great Blight of Dullness,' no natural flutter and a lot of natural crime. Few reasons means fewer regular encounters which means fewer bonds and little sense of ownership or empowerment. Decoupling and fear drives the good people off the streets and violence flows in behind. Prudent residents don't venture forth at certain times or in certain places. Police admonish residents not to loiter, go out after dark or open a door unless they know the caller. This happens in middle-income, tree-lined residential areas as well high-density slums.

Paternalistic plans also contribute to the frenetic pace of non-integrated life. In America, separate bins and suburban private-kingdoms (with grass) have led to increasing time spent transporting one's self, spouse and children to all the activities that used be part of the natural flow. Commuting time, the parent chauffeur, and finding time to do the shopping, leaves very little time to promenade as exhausted families collapse in their homes each night for a brief respite.

Exhausted families also have to decide how to approach life now that natural activity no longer supports either safety or civilization. Jacobs cites three main approaches to insecurity: (1) let danger hold sway, (2) take refuge in tight boxes of vehicles and home, (3) cultivate the 'institution of Turf.' We usually associate the word 'Turf' with gang wars, but the rich have used it to the greatest degree. The rich use barriers from cyclone fences to moats, enforcers from doormen to patrol cars, and an ever increasing array of technology to create little islands of safety in an increasingly unsafe world. Houses are grouped in colonies surrounded by barriers and exclusivity requirements. People who do not fit happily in such colonies eventually leave and the remainder tend toward homogeneity and pleasant social distance. Stockaded life becomes normal and even cherished for the rich, but it creates ever deeper rifts in the social fabric. Classism and racism flourish because stockaded people have no contact with any one outside their highly homogenized group.

Lack of natural intermingling, thus, has far-reaching effects. As everyday encounters disappear, natural public life evaporates and extended private life develops. People form 'life-style cohorts' of like-looking, like-thinking and like-employed people. Weak ties to the space mean less foundation for public interest. Fewer connections with the local web mean most people have no practice or ease in applying the most ordinary techniques of public life. Schools draw some parents into community problems, but very little else does.

Social disconnection and frenetic activity then begins an accelerating cycle. Fear of trouble outweighs the need for neighbourly help or friendship. The idea of putting out effort in an already strained life makes people shrink from others and people begin to feel threatened even by casual contact. Privacy becomes of utmost concern.

Jacobs described all of this in 1961. Today the problem is rampant. American intricacy, in particular, has been shattered in the last forty years. Fragmentation, isolation and a sense of saturation and insecurity have driven most Americans inside. A recent US General Social Survey found a drop of 25% to 33 % in the average American's involvement in community groups and other freely associative exchanges. The newspapers call it 'the strange death of Civic America,' but perhaps it is not so strange after all. America, the child of the Enlightenment dream, is the most clockwork country in the world.

Thus, Howard's plans don't work — as a parade of well-meant, but failed development schemes attests. In America well-planned grassy parks are now the preferred site of gang violence, even in suburban areas. Los Angeles, for example, is almost all suburban sprawl because planners believed spreading population thinly would encourage community. Yet, as early as 1959 Los Angeles supported one of the highest crime rates in the world. In the same period the North Boston area described earlier had had no cases of rape, mugging, or child molestation in twenty-eight years.

Nor is the problem solely an American one. Studies of English planned housing projects reveal a similar increase in suspicion of neighbours and ensuing aloofness and social withdrawal. Most of these débâcles can be attributed to a failure to understand intricacy which is the true source of safety, vitality and civilization.

The Elements of Human Intricacy

> *I think that the science of city planning ... must become the science and art of catalyzing and nourishing diverse, close-grained working relationships that support each other economically and socially.*

Human intricacy is an odd thing. It is so attractive and deeply familiar when somebody points it out, yet it is so often omitted in clockwork plans. Much has been destroyed. Unfortunately, when everyday intricacy goes away, so does safe, buoyant activity and the power of a community woven tight from everyday getting and giving to one another.

Before looking at what people are doing to restore intricacy today, let me take a moment to highlight some of its core elements:

Mutualism (Egalitarian Give and Take) — All societies, whether of cells or human beings, are built of millions of specialists who depend on one another. This means that each of us counts on our brethren to be committed to the common good. Intricate collaboration, therefore, assumes the dignity of all labor and the importance of everyone in the society. It depends on integrity and commitment to one another and the larger whole. Conversely, when individuals serve themselves *regardless* of others, then the very fabric of society is at risk.

Integration — What is most noticeable about Jacobs' stories is that lively, livable communities are integrated. Threads entwine and information flows back-and-forth in a way that makes the inhabitants not only feel connected, but also whole. We have a frenetic world precisely because our various needs are not integrated. Integration can emerge spontaneously, but it does not necessarily do so. It requires certain conditions, many of which clockwork-thinking has destroyed.

Distributed Intelligence — If one looks at places like North Boston, one is struck by how important distributed intelligence is. The reason safety and civilization are so strong in such places is that *everyone* makes it happen. Each person applies their energy and talents as best they can. This gives them greater pride and sense of purpose. Quality, resilience and belonging all increase.

Emotional Ties that Bind — Commitment and distributed intelligence require integrity and trust. These come only from emotional ties. Nature bred warm emotions such as caring, nurturing and mentoring into us as a way of binding us together. If we are ever to build intricacy, we need to realize that bonding emotions are vital to our ability to act like a intelligent society of mind.

Clockwork thinking tended to disdain bonding emotions, casting them off as either romantic tripe or epicycles of the *real* emotions which are cold and self-serving. One sees the effects of this perversion in the loneliness, fear and numbness in people's lives. Discounting the need for bonding is one of the great killers of society. In the end, it really is love which makes us sound and intelligent.

Values and Vision (Knowledge Web) — The way people look at the world profoundly affects the level of intricacy their civilization can sustain. Knowing leads to doing!

The clockwork thinking is bad for intricacy, but dominator thinking is much worse. What happens when people are rewarded by how well they put their own interests above those of others? What happens when people treat each other as objects to be manipulated or commodities to be acquired? What happens? We create a world filled with loneliness and mutual distrust, of course. People feel like they must look out for number one because nobody else will. Everyone knows, however, that at some point their market value will fall. One's spouse may find a younger, more attractive mate and one's company may find a younger, cheaper employee.

To approach people like commodities to be exploited for personal gain, is to create that same tendency in others. The process escalates and soon no one feels they can stop. No one feels OK. Knowing has led to doing and we have built a world in the image of what we believe — selfishness, ruthlessness and quality through war! Small wonder our world is fraught with dissension and defensiveness. We have built these into our culture.

* * *

Human intricacy is an odd thing. We know its elements in our bones, but most modern theory actively runs against it. Now, somewhere between overbearing states and untrammeled individualism we have to find a new way — one that promotes strong selves *and* strong bonds! How do we do this? Jacobs makes us think about how our schemes for structuring physical things, like roads, homes and factories, affect the kind of social reality we get. If we want intricacy, our schemes must take self-organization and human ties more seriously. These are what hold civilization together.

What else supports a robust human ecology? The way a society structures its human relations in work, play and home is of equal importance. Since this is the case, I thought we might learn something from how other cultures manage to promote collaboration. This will bring me back to Ruth Benedict in search of a more realistic framework for understanding why some societies are incite aggression among their member while others stimulate peace.

Searching for Synergy — and Peace

To understand aggressiveness ... persecution or mutual helpfulness, in any human social group, one must check the social order and its man-made institutions for their provisions for social synergy.   Ruth Benedict

Ruth Benedict is the anthropologist who pointed out the two main types of economic systems: siphons which circulate wealth and funnels which pull wealth to the top. She also spent a lot of time studying why some societies are peaceful and collaborative while others are fraught with anxiety and aggression. In 1941, she developed a framework for understanding why societies go one way or the other. This framework helps shed some light on our current quagmire.

Benedict first teaches us to look more closely at whether behaviors help or harm. She developed the concepts of 'social synergy' and the 'synergy gamut' as measures of such help or harm. Her ideas are clear, if non-traditional. Dominator culture teaches us to value zero-sum games. It says self-interest will automatically benefit all. But these ideas are naïve. One person's self-interest can obviously destroy the wellbeing of many more. Thug capitalism shows this handily with endless examples of pollution, shoddy products, exploitation and deceit. Synergy, on the other hand, refers to how actions combine to make something *more* than existed before. Still, there are actually three possibilities. First, some human acts cancel each other out — one person gains and another loses in kind. Other acts drain the society as a whole — one person gains and many suffer more. Some human acts, however, are mutually beneficial. These may combine into a system that benefits far more than those immediately involved.

Benedict suggests that a society is just as healthy as the sum of its people's positive, negative and zero-sum acts. The synergy gamut gives one a sense of where a society falls. At one end of the spectrum are societies where individuals almost always act to advantage themselves at the expense of others. At the other end, individuals almost always act in a way that serves self *and* the greater good. Aggression and anxiety marks the first, peace and security marks the second.

The question is: what makes a society prone to one side or the other. Benedict suggests a relatively simple reason. After studying many cultures, she came to the conclusion that societies get the social behavior they arrange for:

> Non-aggression occurs not because people are unselfish and
> put social obligations above personal desires, but because
> social arrangements make these two identical ... The problem
> is one of social engineering and depends upon how large the
> areas of mutual advantage are in any society. (Cited in Combs,
> 1994, p.65)

Today, we usually attribute the sorry state of the world to natural orders and warlike ways fixed in our selfish genes. Benedict's idea brings a welcome breeze of sanity. The way to create a powerful, peaceful society is to develop large areas of overlap between what is good for the individual and what is good for the larger whole. Productive societies, she writes, 'have a social order in which the individual by the same act and at the same time serves his own advantage and that of the group.'

This is something we might hope to arrange. Create incentives for mutual benefit! Make destructive acts costly! Arrange institutional practices to encourage involvement in common cause! Moving from a selfish society to a common-cause one might not be so impossible. A lot of people are already trying. This brings me to a description of efforts that are already underway.

Healing Human Ecologies

Synergism *(in Theology):*
— the doctrine that the human will cooperates with the divine spirit in the work of regeneration.

We hear a lot about preserving natural ecologies today, but problems in human ecologies are actually more pressing. When human ecologies grow frail, societies collapse. Today, people the world over are trying to heal human ecologies large and small. Whether they think in these terms or not, most are developing ways to build synergy.

Our world is a living laboratory with experiments bubbling throughout. Efforts are numerous. The list below is a sampling whose characteristics help illustrate central points.

The Jigsaw Solution

When Robert Shahan began as the Bishop of the Episcopal Archdiocese of Arizona in 1986, what he saw disturbed him. His diocese was fragmented culturally and geographically: rich-poor, brown-white, educated-illiterate, mountain, desert and city. Small groups within the Diocese competed with each other for funds and influence and most people were distrustful of the central authority.

Now the idea that people who are bound by a belief in love and compassion, should spend so much time squabbling seemed contradictory to Shahan. Most people blamed human nature and the way the world works, but Shahan believed that many of the Church's organizational practice unwittingly encouraged wrangling. Deep meaning was put on hold during the fray.

What to do? Shahan started by trying to see if his parishioners shared any common binding vision about how they would like the diocese to be. He asked parishioners: 'Tell me who you are and what your hopes are for yourself and the diocese.' He soon appointed a Vision Council whose job was to listen to as many people as possible and then meld what they heard into an articulation of the kind of community the people wanted to have.

After much listening, the council came up with the following statement: 'We are One.' Just as their religion said that, underneath endless diversity, God was One, so too the parishioners wanted to feel like they were One underneath all their diversity.

With this vision in hand, Shahan began to reorganize Church practices so that they encouraged diversity bound in unity (instead of squabbling separation). He started by building overlapping ownership. The diocesan professional staff usually administered projects which benefitted multiple regions, such as youth ministries at Universities. The Diocese assessed each local church 20% of its income to fund these common-cause efforts. Shahan, however, felt that giving money and control to central administration was one of the things that decreased local involvement and increased distrust of the central authority. What else could be done? Shahan challenged various regions to take over projects that had once been handled by the central authority. He also gave them a say in the diocesan budget and decreased local Church assessments.

Shahan's approach was particularly important because it got regional groups involved in efforts which *crossed* regional boundaries. As a result, separate groups became more involved in each other's wellbeing. Shahan also restructured the diocesan governing council to help make this stick. He had representatives elected from local parishes and not from the Diocese as a whole as in the past. Each locale thus had a representative and each representative was in charge of a mission that was important to all regions. One region, for example, was in charge of all university ministries, while another handled cross-cultural efforts and another outreach programs. Representatives then met to budget the monies required for everyone. Each representative acted as an advocate for their region's mission, but since all missions benefited everyone, negotiations became serious discussions of the best strategy for common good (and not a feud for more local monies).

Since everyone participated in budget decisions, assessments also began to feel more like a freely given commitment and less like a tax.

The effects of overlapping ownership and involvement in global wellbeing were thus striking. Where under central control the parishes were assessed 20% of their income and the Diocese had run a deficit, under distributed, overlapping control, the Churches were assessed 17% and the Diocese ran a surplus. Spending actually increased because contributions went up. Apparently when people feel they are truly 'in this together,' they willingly contribute more money.

The Arizona Archdiocese story is small, but instructive. It highlights the following elements of intricacy building:

■ *Institutional practices affect how we act.* We build institutions in the image of our assumptions and then our institutions shape us in kind. Many modern institutions are designed to encourage separation, control and competition. Member parishes, for instance, were organized like competing self-interest groups under a controlling hierarchy. No wonder people felt like separate warring pieces, instead of diverse facets of a unified whole. The system itself set the tone for how people behaved and this thwarted collaboration.

■ *Create overlapping ownership and common involvement in global wellbeing.* Why did mutualism thrive in early agricultural communities? Because people needed each other. Why did it thrive in small intermingled neighbourhoods? Because people felt a vested interest in each other and the space. Psychologists call this the Jigsaw Solution. If you want a community to stay peaceful and whole, help separate pieces overlap and need each other.

■ *Dialogue and deliberation build community better than does debate to win.* This story also touches on a form of information processing which is absolutely necessary to synergy — dialogue. The goal of any society of mind is to create better tapestries by pooling information from diverse perspectives and developing strategies for the common good. Complex problems can only be solved by deliberation among individuals who are committed to the common good. Win-lose debates encourage division, not resolution.

■ *Change works best when you start by identifying the cultural centerpiece you want to preserve and make stronger through change.* This is an important key to change which the Japanese have known forever. The way to change systematically is to figure out the core feelings or ideals that bind the group together and which they want to preserve. Holding on to the binding cause then allows the system to shed the limiting surface structure like a snake sheds its skin. In the Diocese's case, people wanted to feel like they were One. This desire created motivation. Articulating the vision also created a guide that helped everyone see if changes were having the desired effect.

Westerners tend to mistake current practice with the inarticulate core which holds a group together. As a result they tend to see change in terms of what they are going to lose. This confusion tends to keep people clinging to old practices long after they have failed. People fear change will destroy what they love instead of renewing it. In fact, clinging to practices which no longer work is the fastest way to kill a dream whether it is a religion or, say, democracy.

■ *The Diocese change worked because they implemented multiple changes which all reinforced one another.* Westerners also tend to focus on single causes and single solutions, but webs rarely work like this. Hence, if a group wants its dream to survive, it will probably need to change multiple systems in tandem. It must also continually re-examine how changes are working. This is the central message of a Jigsaw solution.

The Diocese story is small, however, and it presumes a community that is already committed. Let us therefore try something bigger and not already bound by common beliefs.

Fertilize the Grassroots

The aim which should motivate all ... is to create an economic entity providing justice and wellbeing.

Antoine Antoni

Muhammad Yunus had always wanted to help his people. Born in Bangladesh where poverty was often grinding, he chose business and economics as his avenue. He studied at great universities in the west, got degrees in economics and business administration and returned home as a professor of economics and a government advisor. When he began to apply his fine theoretical training, however, he found that most of it didn't help at all.

Depressed, he went on a walk one day to collect his thoughts. Wandering through a local market, he struck up a conversation with one of the street vendors who was also depressed. The vendor wanted to expand his business by buying a bicycle to transport his wares across town and open another stand. But he couldn't afford the bicycle and no bank would loan him money. At last! Yunus thought, at least he could affect this part of the economy. He rushed the vendor to a local bank and found the bank was willing to make the loan — as long as Yunus agreed to guarantee repayment by co-signing. Since Yunus would be taking the same risk whether the bank played middle-man or not, he decided to lend the vendor money himself.

He was rewarded for his efforts. Within a few months the vendor had set up a new stand and repaid the loan. He had also begun to employ several people who had been unemployed before. Yunus got his money back and he also got an idea. The vendor's story was common. There was a huge need for very small loans which no bank would touch. Yunus had found an avenue for helping his people and making a big difference. He founded the Grameen Bank for the purpose of making microloan.

The story of Muhammed Yunus and the Grameen Bank is true. For twenty years now the Grameen Bank has made loans to over two million people from the poorest levels of society. Yet, contrary to current theory, the economic benefits have been unprecedented. Though loans average less than $200, they have enabled 78% of the borrowers to raise themselves out of poverty. Furthermore, the bank's profits have been good through it all. To join the bank, borrowers must have no personal assets, yet 98% of the loans have been repaid with a fair interest rate — a record unmatched by any traditional bank with secured loans. More importantly, Yunus has made a difference. Village children don't starve to death anymore and houses keep out the monsoons. The women have more than one sari and some have started schools with their savings.

Getting Small Funds to Create Big Benefits

Mutuality without practicality does not work.   Jane Jacobs

If you want robust grassroots, you need to fertilize them, give them the resources they need to grow and empower themselves. Current banking practices are not designed to meet this need. What Yunus' story tells us, that the problem has nothing to do with whether microloans can be profitable or with whether they have an important effect. It actually has lot has to do with how one goes about organizing people.

There are now over 170 microloan projects found worldwide, from Malaysia to inner cities of the U.S. The Shorebank Corporation of Chicago is an example of the latter. Founded in 1972 'to foster permanent renewal in blighted neighbourhoods,' the key to the bank's success, as one of its officers says, 'is the creative tension between its social goals and the bottom line.' We find some recurring themes. By keeping the loans small and within the community, the bank stays integrated with the neighbourhood. The bank also acts as a networking agent among borrowers, helping them find and keep the support they need in various dimensions (information, expertise, services, finances). It is this combination of seed-capital and support services which helps the community 'self-organize.'

Why do microloan systems release local energies? There are two keys. First, microloan enterprises create support networks along with financing. Training courses and intensive group discussions take place before loan-giving begins and borrowers are generally organized into support groups. The support system helps borrowers find their way and weather ups and downs. This makes them more likely to succeed which means the loan is more likely to be repaid. One reason traditional banks don't do microloans is that, without borrower networks, small loans tend to become uneconomic.

Ethics and a commitment to human wellbeing are also important. The Grameen Bank, for instance, provides seeds and rehydration kits for infant diarrhea at cost. Borrower groups are also encouraged to accept a sixteen point program for social justice, group solidarity and women's emancipation. Grameen staff abide by this program too. Centering on solidarity and human wellbeing builds commitment which builds synergy and profits. Distributed intelligence and initiative are high. Grameen borrowers, thus, took over a failed fishery project originally funded by the UK Overseas Development Administration, and made it productive in only three months.

The microloan movement is much larger and its effects more profound than the Archdiocese story. The story also helps illustrate a number of important points:

- *Fertilize!* A very small amount of money can make a big difference when applied in the right place (usually the bottom). Money, however, is not enough. It isn't even really the center of the story.

- *Support networks are essential to grassroots development.* Individuality is extremely important to socio-economic health but, contrary to the teachings of rugged individualism, going it alone is neither efficient nor realistic. The best way to get people to thrive is by developing support systems.

- *Ethics are important too.* Self-service often undermines community wellbeing (as the modern world attests). Mutualist ethics help counteract the problem. Incentives which encourage benefit to both individual and community complete the package. If you want a socio-economic system that is peaceful and robust, you need a tight weave of ethics and incentives for common-cause.

- *Ownership aids empowerment and is an important way of countering abuse.* Another Grameen story is apropos. Yunus talks of a woman he met who made pennies a day making baskets. The baskets were so beautiful and of such high quality that he asked her why she earned so little. She explained that she gave her baskets to a local merchant who paid her wages and supplied her with materials. She couldn't break this relationship because she couldn't save enough to buy her own materials. He gave her so little that she stayed dependent. A ten dollar Grameen loan allowed her to buy her own supplies for the first time. Selling her own baskets made her income double. This allowed her to keep on buying her own materials and it also helped her family's health improve because of better nutrition. Within a few weeks she had also repaid the loan with interest.

- *Joint ownership opens the door to greater synergy.*
Ownership of one's own means helps stop exploitation but joint

ownership does even more. In the dawn of history, mutualism was supported by joint ownership of major means (from land to looms). Today, this possibility is being explored again Employee ownership (in various forms) has, thus, risen dramatically in the last fifteen to twenty years. Italy, for instance, has 11,203 worker cooperatives and France has 1,269. The trend has even been pushing into the US with examples such as United Airlines and the plywood firms of the Northwest.[1]

The reasons for this shift are obvious and of interest to anyone who loves capitalism in its synergetic form. Initiative, productivity and distributed intelligence are all higher when people feel they are working *for themselves*. Whenever people feel exploited all three go down. Joint ownership is the best way to encourage quality and commitment to the greater good at all levels.

Conversely, as long as ownership of means gives someone the right to benefit disporportionally from the labor of others, we will have a system prone to resentment, malaise, bubbles and collapse. This brings me to the last important message of the microloan projects.

■ *Emancipating the oppressed virtually always creates major gains in the whole society.* Helping people extract themselves from a system of exploitation (which, à la dominator thinking, is designed to disproportionately benefit someone else in the chain) is good for social health.

A story from the 1994 United Nations Population Conference in Cairo is apropos. The Cairo conference found that many dire predictions about third-world population explosions had not come to pass primarily because liberation movements in a number of underdeveloped countries had improved the plight of women. When women's oppression lessened, they were able to control how many children they had. They also improved the quality of life in the society as a whole. Education, nutrition, infrastructure and economic productivity all improved. As one study based on data from 89 countries said: 'When the status of women is low, the general quality of life for everybody suffers. When the status of women is higher, the quality of life for everybody rises.'

Here too, the key to building wellbeing often has a lot to do with building support networks. Newly emancipated people who can't sustain themselves economically generally fall victim to oppression again. Liberation without mutual support, therefore, is not necessarily a blessing.

To sum up, microloan systems show first, that ideals work best when supported in a variety of practical ways; and second, that well-fertilized roots give back more than is put in. Andrew Pring writes:

> Microcredit costs nothing once initial backing is given. Funds are constantly recycled, offering more and more opportunities. The small locally controlled enterprises are at the root of truly sustainable development. (1997, p.49)

The last example also touches on the that wonderful distinction between (a) justice and common wellbeing, and (b) funneling, that is, accumulation of wealth at the top. So let me take a moment to look at a less obvious implication, namely, how unexamined assumptions keep funneling alive.

Dominator Assumptions in Maintaining Inequity

The microloan story shows that fertilizing the grassroots can make a huge difference to individuals and to the society as a whole. Yet, it also shows the realities of economic life the world over. Small guys have a hard time getting financing regardless of their personal abilities or work ethic.

A classic American example demonstrates these same two facts. After World War II millions of ex-soldiers who would never have gone to college, got an education thanks to the GI-bill. Like their more distressed Bangledeshi counterparts, this brief financing allowed these men to move themselves and their children into the middle-class or higher and, hence, is one of the major causes of American prosperity and technology today. Yet, it is an exception not much contemplated today.

So, let us think. If fertilizing grassroots has such dramatic benefits, why then doesn't it happen more often? The Grameen story tells us that the reason does not have to do with profit *per se*. Rather the core issue has to do with assumptions about what makes a society run best. Indeed, much that is bad in our world is maintained by a vast web of assumptions abut how societies run best. Some of these assumptions run afoul innocently. Rugged individualists, for example, merely take all the support they got for granted and then assume that others should not need help. Most assumptions, however, are part and parcel of the dominator dream. These may be unwitting, but they are not innocent. Racism, sexism, classism: some people assume that societies run best when run by males, whites or members of important families. Social gate-keepers who believe this, end up creating a self-fulfilling prophesy in which those who start with advantages always get more.

The connection between gate-keeper beliefs and institutional practices means that the rich always have more opportunity to get richer than the poor do to get anywhere. This furthers the funneling system. For instance, most wealthy Americans attribute their success solely to hard work and brilliance. They do this regardless of how many mitigating factors — such as good education; insider connections from college or clan; timely acquisition of some kind of leverage in property or position also went into the brew. The catch is that bankers are also likely to believe that success is solely a result of merit. As a result, bankers are more likely to loan money to previously wealthy people who have lost millions, than they are to a poor person who works hard, has many abilities and has never lost any money.

Circular beliefs also further stereotypes. If gate-keepers believe, for example, that men from Oxford are always more intelligent, then they will give Oxford men more jobs. This means more Oxford men will be found in positions of power which means that Oxford men will appear to be more intelligent than others. These men will also become gate-keepers who are likely to hire people they know or who are like themselves. The circle of stereotypes, preferential treatment and retention of wealth will continue regardless of how many higher quality people are lost in the shuffle.

The down side of self-fulfilling beliefs also holds. Muhammed Yunus, for example, had a hard time getting regular banks to participate in microloan projects because, no matter how often he demonstrated the power of microloans, most bankers 'knew' that poor people were lazy, unintelligent, unimaginative people who had brought misfortune on themselves. The poor couldn't be trusted with money which is why secured loans were invented. Of course, as the Grameen story suggests, requiring security was exactly what kept the poor out of income and education, thus, reinforcing the banker's beliefs. The poor stay poor? Grassroots rarely get fertilized and beliefs are a major reason why.

Thus, despite their great ideals, democratic societies often still have economies which are designed to funnel wealth toward the top. Unfortunately, funnels create four social effects: anxiety, aggression, fragmentation and malaise. So, ask yourself, what is our economic aim? — justice and common wellbeing? Or accumulation of personal wealth? Western civilization at large is currently pursuing the latter under the misguided belief that it will automatically promote the former. This theory does not work because it fails to understand the importance of intricacy and common-cause commitment.

This brings me to the next story of intricacy-building which, not surprisingly, is being driven by the growth of a gluttonously wealthy few alongside a parallel dwindling of the middle class.

Rebuilding Community

> *A big political idea has to address a big fact, preferably the*
> *dominant fact of the age. Our big fact is globalization, both*
> *the wealth it can bring but also the fear that powerful world*
> *markets will turn us into thistledown people, blown about by*
> *forces beyond us — people without gravity, without a stake.*
> Andrew Marr, *The Independent,* March 1996

This opening quote came from a London newspaper article[2] announcing the arrival of what may be a new force in British politics — 'do-it-yourself democracy' or as it is sometimes called 'the voice of modern self-help.'

Regardless of what globalization could be, right now it seems to be a push toward oligarchy. A few extremely-wealthy people seem to be trying to establish world-wide economic domination. Thug theory tells us this will be good for all. But is it? Income is going down for most people and most jobs are becoming less secure. Small wonder many people feel like thistledown, tossed by swirling winds. Insecure and endangered, what roots people have grow thinner by the year. But what can everyday people do? The article continued:

> ... disillusioned with conventional politics, 'stakeholders' in
> local communities are organizing themselves; thistledown
> people are working class and strikingly idealistic.

The announcement was British, but the phenomenon is international. Centuries of clockwork thinking are reaching a climax. Liberal paternalism has failed and capitalist corporations serve themselves regardless of any common good. Technology moves us faster and now speed sends our lives careening ever more out of kilter. Exhausted, desperate and empty — today the message is clear. Our world is running toward ruin and those with power seem unable (or unwilling) to stop it. Clockwork amorality tends to benefit a few at the expense of many.

What can one do? One can put one's feet down and try to make a difference where one stands. Do so with others. Care about community and the common good. Try to rebuild communities such that they are enlivened by common cause and wound tight with everyday getting and giving.

There is a small eddy swirling silently in our world. Overlooked by the pundits and the powers that be, it appears to be the beginnings of a move to *self*-reorganize coming largely from the bottom up.

This eddy is very tiny now. Modern self-organizers usually implement their efforts through local social and political action. For example, the 'Merseyside Broad-Based Organization,' a group cited in the London article, persuaded a local supermarket chain, Kwik Save, to attend citizen meetings to discuss opening times, traffic patterns, play areas, etc.. Often located in inner cities, the supermarket's activities affected local residents acutely and often ran counter to their needs. This wasn't necessarily intentional. The company was a chain with a distant central office. Local stores following centralized commands, naturally lost touch with the communities in which they lived. Self-organizers helped raise corporate awareness of community needs and, in this case, the ending was happy. The company's marketing director felt that sensitivity would benefit the company too.

Other stories are not so smooth. Campaigns against homelessness, forcing local councils to clean-up illegal dumping sites — picketing companies and haranguing politicians are also part of the picture. Nevertheless, self-organizers are often buoyant. They are serving themselves, their community and their common humanity all at the same time. This service makes them feel good about themselves in a way that self-centeredness did not. Then too, the promises are different. As one East Londoner put it: 'Here, most people spend their money on the lottery as a way of trying to get out. What we are saying is that, if you put a bit into local civic organizations instead, you won't escape from east London, but you will change things around you.'

Self-organizers are a natural product of our times. Neighbourhoods,

Extreme Right	The poor are victims of their own indolence.
Moderate Right	The social safety net suffocates the poor. Faster economic growth is the only way to cure poverty. Lower taxes and less government spending will increase prosperity by freeing market forces.
Moderate Left	Economic systems are intrinsically inequitable and poverty is the tragic but inevitable result. One helps as best one can, traditionally by creating an enlightened government that aids the poor through paternalistic programs.
Extreme Left	The poor are poor because they are ravaged systematically by the rich.
The Intricacy Alternative	Both Right and Left underestimate intricacy and its role in creating sustainable civilization. The only way to get a healthy society for all classes is to build sustainable socio-economic intricacy which is self-organized and oriented towards the common good.

Table 10. Current Theories of Poverty and the Intricacy Alternative.

communities, cities and civilizations are splintering because of growth, speed and failed paternalistic plans. Gaps are growing along with in-security. Self-organizers represent the natural return-swing struggle to restore sanity and humanity to communities whose wellbeing is being battered from all sides.

This struggle is astoundingly old and startlingly new. It is new because it doesn't fit neatly into the ideologies advocated by either the Right or the Left. Because government doles have not panned out, people realize they have to help themselves. Because simple self-interest has not panned out either, they realize that they have to organize into groups. Because the whole system seems self-destructive, people realize that they must band together to promote common wellbeing and not just parochial interest. Solidarity is important because individuals *alone* can save neither society nor themselves. This blend of organizing for self-interest *and* community wellbeing is neither Right nor Left, but exactly a mid-ground between over-bearing states and untrammeled individualism (see Table 10).

Yet, the same self-organizing movement that defies current labels, bases itself on traditions that are as old as society. Self-organizers cite Quaker and Victorian friendly societies, early trade unions, and religious traditions that have championed social justice for centuries. They find inspiration in Enlightenment thinkers such as John Locke, John Stuart Mills and Henry Thoreau. They find support among institutions that still honour social justice and common-cause traditions. Britain's 'Citizen Organizing Foundation' is thus funded by the Church of England, local mosques and numerous enlightened corporations.

This small eddy of self-organizers is thus old and new. It is also a Jigsaw solution. The hope is to rebuild communities by developing overlapping ownership and common involvement in global wellbeing. In the UK, self-organizers are beginning to cross-connect, but so far most efforts are still local. One reason for this is lack of theory. Self-organizers know what they want to fix locally. Home issues are immediate and so is the motivation. However, the question of what, if anything, unites self-organizers all over the country is much harder to explain. What is the need? What is the goal? What binds the many local issues into a broader common cause? Some answers are beginning to bubble up on the other side of the ocean.

Efforts to rebuild communities for common wellbeing is also beginning to blossom in that most individualistic of all cultures, the United States. The U.S. makes a good case-study for theory because there the problems are profoundly national. A 1994 survey by the National Civic League, for example, found that a whooping 81% of the U.S. populace believes that citizens no longer have any voice in decision making. As a result, they feel little ownership in their world. The U.S. thus faces problems similar to those in the UK, but on a more advanced scale which embraces the entire country. Let us therefore look at a bit of what is bubbling up there.

Grassroots Democratic Reform

*An interconnected, good society is a vision not beyond the
reach of today. Yet for it to exist in 2020, we will need to
reach into the best of our traditions today and claim a lost
art — the ability to care for each other, at times putting
others first.*   Rick Smyre

America is the epitome of the pros and cons of the clockwork world.
More than anywhere else on earth, Americans build their institutions
around mechanism, materialism and Darwinian theory. Americans
believe so strongly that quality arises from self-interest and war, that
they tend to structure most policy-making venues as win-lose competi-
tions between crassly self-interested groups. The common-good is supposed to naturally pop out of this, but it rarely does. Americans believe
so strongly that untrammeled market forces produce an optimal world
that they turn their society over to self-interested competitors no matter
how openly hostile to the common good they are.

Democracy suffers horribly from this system. America begins to resemble the late Greeks. Leisured intellectuals gleefully compete, trying
to advance their own theories and to publicly annihilate their fellows.
Media campaigns thrive on negativity. This builds urgency by pander-
ing to bigotry and fear. Polarization grows, while intelligent discussion
dwindles to non-existence. Practices often don't serve, but theory
makes the status quo seem inevitable. America begins to look like the
late Roman Republic. Democratic facades cover up a system increasingly dominated by monied interests. Politicians, contractors and
nouveau riche trying to make personal wealth at the expense of the
whole? It has all been done before.

But the problems are becoming glaring. Nowadays, influence
peddling, mud-slinging, and shrinking intelligence make it clear that
democracy does not do well as a win-lose competition governed by
untrammeled market forces. The problem is particularly bad since the
binding ties of community have largely been broken. What then shall
we do?

There is a small eddy swirling silently in America too. Operating under
titles such as 'Citizen Forums,' 'Councils for the Common Good,'
'Communities of the Future,' and 'The Rebirth of Civil Society,' this

broad movement is built of numerous small efforts which are beginning to meld together. These reformers are particularly aware that two things need to happen. First, concern for common wellbeing must be renewed and given support in a way that works today. For instance, institutional practices which discourage community must be restructured to support it (like in the Arizona Archdiocese). Secondly, the grassroots levels of society need to be fertilized and rewoven so that change can move from the bottom up. The top can and hopefully will help because sane civilization is good for everyone. But intricacy and synergy has to be built from the bottom up. It is a fine-grained affair.

Building community isn't easy, of course. The terrible fragmentation and speed of life leaves most Americans feeling like they have little time for themselves, much less others. How does one build social networks when most of the populace is too tired and overwhelmed to be involved? How does one keep a network alive and practical so that people stay involved? Early Americans took their networks for granted because their world was still small and their common need still great. Today, building citizen networks is a nightmare because so much has fallen apart.

How does one get from twentieth century fragmentation to twenty-first century common-cause potential? Figure 42 outlines the system of change advocated by one community rebuilding group. You will note that it is an interlocking approach.

Rick Smyre, the author of Figure 42, says that twenty-first century transformation starts with three realizations:

- First, because all aspects of a society (social, political, economic, scientific and spiritual) are interwoven, efforts must be *integral*, not singular. Change must take place in parallel with interlocking effects.
- Second, the goal is *renewal* of the deep dream and motivating ideals which still beat at the heart of the American soul. Democracy, freedom, justice, integrity, equality, compassion — the ideals have not changed, the problem is 'practices' which often don't serve. Thus, twenty-first century transformation requires we keep our eyes on the prize — our cherished core ideals — while figuring out how to get our systems to support the society we want to become.
- Third, the current change must embrace the concept of *learning as a way of life*. We can no longer afford the myth of final solutions. We must realize that life is about learning and societies are about

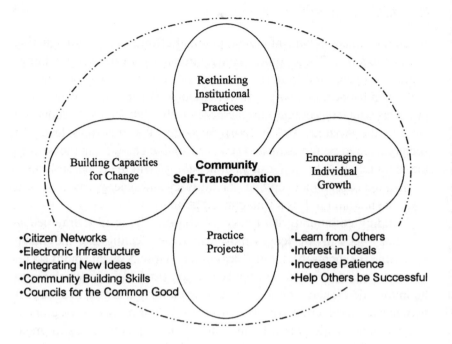

Figure 42. A System of 21st Century Transformation.
This figure outlines a multi-pronged approach now taking place in forty American communities in fifteen states.

ever-better approximations of cherished ideals. The only way to live in such a world is to embrace the concept of continual learning. The alternative to on-going evolutionary change, is regular and potentially disastrous revolution.

These three realizations set the context for the four lobes shown in Figure 42, namely:

Rethinking Institutional Practices
This lobe fits the Archdiocese story and Ruth Benedict's insight. If you want to figure out why an institution breeds squabbling self-interest instead of mutual helpfulness, look closely at how its practices encourage or discourage things like common involvement in global wellbeing. In short, look at how the institution helps or hinders synergy and true community.

Rethinking, however, should *not* be approached as a sudden, complete redesign. Such a response underestimates complexity and tends to invite new grandiose failures in place of old. This last thought brings us to the next lobe.

Implementing Process Projects
Two extremes threaten any social transformation: inaction and over-reaction. When a problem seems overwhelming (too large, too entrenched, too complex) people become paralyzed. When a problem goes unaddressed for too long, the eventual response may be explosive and/or Utopian (meaning, high on ideals but low on ability to deliver). This lobe, therefore, refers to the art of building know-how by doing.

Thus, the answer to inaction and over-reaction is to take small steps. Experiment. Revise and try again. Expand each time you do. Experiments build experience. Perceptible motion toward the ideal shows people that progress is being made. Openess to input helps keep the community committed. In this way grounded, gradual change helps build involvement and know-how while keeping cynicism and resent-ment at bay. Other supports must also be developed too.

Building Capacities for Change
For the most part, we don't have well-woven communities anymore. We certainly don't have a learning society yet. If we are ever going to have either, we must begin to develop the intellectual and social tools for the job. Smyre calls these 'capacities for change.' He suggests people start small.
■ *Learn Community-Building Skills* — People have been experimenting with how to build communities for years. This means that a lot of important skills have already been developed. A community seeking change can help itself by training community leaders, for example, in how be 'process facilitators' rather than command-and-control mana-gers. The skills are quite different and the more people with such skills a community has, the more its capacity for change.

To the extent that such techniques are successful, an interesting switch occurs. If people believe the system really is fair and oriented toward the best for all, then they become more willing to sacrifice their own immediate interest to support the larger cause. There is less back-biting and more sincere wrestling with developing good strategies for common wellbeing. As it was for the ancient Greek shop-keepers, so it is today. Fair, open dialogue in a system which people believe is

committed to the common good, is the best way to build community
and freely given effort toward a common cause.

■ *Establish Councils for the Common Good* — Another way to support
on-going change is to establish a council whose sole mission is to help
community rebuilding move forward. Councils can help in innumerable
ways. They can serve as a clearing house, cross-fertilizing and linking-
up existing efforts. They can initiate new efforts and help find funding.
They can establish information centers where people beginning an
effort can get training, expert advice or administrative aid.

■ *Integrate New Ideas* — The quality of twenty-first-century communities will depend on the quality, circulation and integration of twenty-
first-century ideas. As befits a creative age, there is no one right way
to circulate or refine ideas. Some communities bring in outside experts
to give seminars on twenty-first-century thinking or the new science.
Some integrate new ideas into the curricula of local schools or send
members to get hands-on experience from change efforts in another
community. The list of approaches is as long as a group's imagination.

■ *Build Citizen Networks* — This is crucial and we know too little. In
1859, John Stuart Mill wrote: 'the only government which can fully
satisfy all the necessities of the social state is one in which the whole
people participate.' Today, Americans are beginning to realize that personal freedom and 'one man, one vote' is not enough to create such
a government. The small guy needs the support of his fellows to have
any power at all. But people have to feel cared about before they are
going to care back. The small-town intricacy and backwoods mutualism which our forebears took for granted created an important backdrop for democracy which is now largely gone.

How does one create mutual support networks, now that we know
that even a high-tech world needs them and the ones we used to have
are gone with the wind. Smyre suggests one start simply by finding
ways to bring citizens together to work for a common cause — a
crime watch program, a beautification project, or a community event
that is fun and builds community at the same time.

The next step is to create *active networks* that allow citizens to
communicate their ideas and concerns to relevant governing bodies
such that both sides experience exchange (rather than uni-directional
flow). For example, in 1983 the North Carolina Citizens Forum began
developing an active network to address educational issues. The Forum
found volunteers from each neighbourhood who agreed to talk to each

family in their neighbourhood (5–10 families). These volunteers asked their neighbours what they wanted from the school system, what they thought the problems were and what they thought might be done. Volunteers from several neighbourhoods then met to distill the ideas they had gathered into a more coherent form (replete with statistics and suggestions). Representatives from these groups then met to build a picture of the entire town. Representatives from town groups then met to build a countywide picture.

The outcome of this effort was fascinating in three ways. First, the information gathered was amazingly rich and remarkably accurate — much more so than traditional polls. Secondly, access to rich, accurate input had a positive effect on school board officials. Like most modern people, school board members are often forced to rely on experts or their own small circles for input. Suddenly there was a clearer, more open channel of communication which made their job easier and which made them want to respond in kind. The third and most fascinating result then came from the families who had been queried. Many said that this was the first time anyone had ever asked for their thoughts. Being asked, made them feel both heard and respected in a community matter. This, in turn, made them more interested in the issue than ever before. As a result, both sides, lay and official, became closer and more involved.

Active networks help establish a sense of involvement in common wellbeing. If they go on for a while, they help reestablish a sense of community among neighbours who have withdrawn into separate shells. Getting them to work however requires human contact, human faces, and service to something beyond self-interest.

■ *Develop Electronic Infrastructure* — Community involvement can also be supported technologically. Electronic infrastructure allows direct feedback to officials, rapid circulation of information and a venue for on-going discussion. Many people hope that electronics will eventually allow a direct decision-making democracy in which small voices are heard and deliberation is done collaboratively in a forum visible to all.

Individual Growth
Computer connectivity is one of the great hopes for a networked society. But tools, no matter how sophisticated, do not automatically make societies better. Success depends on the values and attitudes with

which tools are used. This, in turn, depends on changes within in each of us. Therefore, if we want to create a better world, we have to start by examining ourselves.

Ah, the ancients are ever so prescient. All the technology in the world will not save us if we, as individuals, do not learn how to work with one another. Smyre suggests a short list of individual growth ideals:

1. Increase patience;
2. Learn to learn from others — for example, care about their point of view and listen;
3. Practice making other people successful;
4. Be open to new ideas;
5. Learn to think in terms of common wellbeing instead of winning.

*   *   *

The effort described above is but one of many. What unites these efforts most clearly is the idea that saving democracy must start with rebuilding communities and rethinking institutions such that they help us become the society we want to be. The dream of government by and for the people has not changed. We now know, however, that 'one man, one vote' is not enough to create such a government. The idea that common wellbeing will arise spontaneously through special interest advocacy and a kind of trial-by-combat is even worse.

These efforts also reflect a tacit understanding of intricacy. In the end, social intricacy is what allows a society to stay integrated, intelligent, active and whole. It does this by keeping intellectual and emotional energy cycling naturally and productively throughout. Fine-grained, human and committed to the greater good — it is not so hard to understand.

Rebuilding Business Too

> ... *a manager must let people grow within a community that is held together by clearly stated values. The manager ... must place commitment to people before assets, respect for innovation before devotion to policy, the messiness of learning before orderly procedures, and the perpetuation of the community before all other concerns.*
>
> Arie de Geus, *Harvard Business Review,* 1997

Variations on these thoughts are also rising in business. The opening quote comes from a study of business practices which have allowed some companies to stay vibrant for very long periods, say one-hundred to seven-hundred years. Stora, a Swedish company, makes a good example. Founded in the thirteenth century, Stora has survived the Middle Ages, the Reformation, the Industrial Revolution and this century's depressions and world wars. In that time it shifted from copper mining, to forestry, iron smelting, hydropower and eventually paper, wood pulp and chemical today.

How did they do it? Stora's managers encourage overlapping ownership and involvement in global wellbeing. (They discourage self-interest which is in any way separate from common wellbeing.) They keep their eyes on their core ideals, the ones which guide their common soul. They regularly rethink current practices to better serve their ideals. Most of all, they take great care to keep learning alive. They cherish eccentrics and ideas which come from the bottom up. They try to keep contact flowing between all levels. Finally, they avoid funnels and the antagonism they bring. They use commonly acquired monies to keep the whole body moving and growing. They use their concentrated wealth for the good of the whole, workers as well a stock-holders.

Arie de Geus, a member of the study group and author of the opening quote, found that most long-enduring companies had very similar cultures. These enduring cultures were centered on cherishing their people as their most important asset. Other key aspects were: a sense of community; awareness of their identity; tolerance of new ideas; and sensitivity to the world around them. These habits allow them to keep living and learning together. He called the result a *living company:*

> ... *living companies* have a personality that allows them to
> evolve harmoniously. They know who they are, understand
> how they fit in the world, value new ideas and new people,
> and husband their money in a way that allows them to govern
> their future.

This story is but one example of a larger change. Over the last twenty years management theory has been the scene of a simmering shift. The bubbles associated with this brew appear to be part of the same boiling pot I've described throughout this book. Living companies, learning organizations, teamwork, quality circles, distributed power, systems thinking, self-organization — the list of theories and concepts goes on and on.

Each of these theories connect to the larger change using now familiar themes. For instance, they advocate structures that are not of the dominator vintage. Power is to be more distributed, if nothing else, so that decisions can be made faster and more appropriately by lower levels. Flexibility, creativity and learning are emphasized. Relationships are to be more egalitarian and collaborative. Human capital counts more. Disproportional rewards and privileges are discouraged because these tend to undermine community and commitment. In short, lots of organizational thinkers realize that we can no longer afford coercive hierarchies because they tend toward rigidity and working at odds.

Some theorists are even struggling toward the concept of intricacy. Many know that small is good. Now the challenge is to figure out how to keep creative teams alive when they get put back into the larger system. This is a challenge of intricacy building. It involves rethinking institutional practices to support the society the organization wants to become. It requires reintegrating all parts, thoughtfully and continuously.

Networked Mutualism

> *Our destiny lies in our ability to both reach the stars and*
> *link our souls.*   Rick Smyre

A few silent eddies are swirling in this big wide world. Some of them are in politics. Some are in urban planning and some in community reclamation. Others are in business, education, medicine, religion and science They are all of a piece and some of them are beginning to link up.

The global problems caused by clockwork simplicity and dominator habits are mirrored in every community and every field of endeavour. Parallel efforts reveal parallel themes and a budding general theory. We have grossly underestimated the importance of staying connected. We have mistaken what we have, for what we need — a sane, humane, joyous and sustainable world. We have been pursuing false-idols. We had better begin rethinking and learn to learn, before it is too late. The question is: will rebuilding efforts work and will they work in time?

I have mentioned too few of the many efforts being pursued. For each of the ones I mentioned there are hundreds more with similar themes. Paul Ekins' 1992 book, *A New World Order: Grassroots Movements for Global Change*, lists some of these political, social and economic efforts. Beyond these are a vast number of smaller business, political and community reform efforts which are not on any list.

The efforts described above are utilitarian, not Utopian. They are successful real-life efforts that create noticeable benefits, often for large numbers of people. They enhance sanity, humanity and well-being. They also improve social fabric by:

- Making it more fine-grained,
- Making it more oriented towards the common good.
- Increasing the distribution of intelligence, initiative and wellbeing.

The ends pursued above are also in some sense deeply familiar. This is the ancient dream. A collaborative, supportive community. Liberation from an oppressive few. Justice, compassion and humanity. We know these things. Our forebears have been pursuing them all over the globe for over five thousand years.

Today, however, the dream will have to become networked if it is to become solid. Bubbly nests of self-organized happiness are often razed by some money-machine next door. Local self-organizations must, therefore, figure out how to connect and support each other. They need theory. They need methods. They also need money, infrastructure and protection. Hopefully, those who care about community and common-wellbeing at the top will help particularly with these last.

How do we develop a new way? It may not be so bad. The key in a learning universe is to *keep on asking the question*. Is the system in front of me furthering the cause of justice, freedom, compassion and common wellbeing? If not, we need to make some changes. After all, cherished images are often turned to other ends. Safety lies in common bonds and collective questioning — not in complacency, blind obedience or control.

CHAPTER 10

THE AWAKENING

We are at a tipping point in civilization. This means we
have to be ready to choose a good path.   Paul Ray

We of the modern world have longings and beliefs not answered by
clockwork philosophy. Clockwork thinking produced not only
alienation and anomie, but also rationales for arrogance, manipulation,
greed, self-centeredness and domination. This has been obvious for
decades, even centuries, but there has been no place to take it because
there has been no equally powerful, scientifically-substantial alternative. This last is changing.

The web view of how the world works creates a radically new
framework for thought. Over the next ten to fifty years you can expect
a flood of new philosophers outlining the social, spiritual, economic
and political implications of this view. I say this because that is exactly
what happened three hundred years ago after the first scientific revolution. They called that flurry of philosophers and their work, the
Enlightenment. My vote for this round of rethinking is, the Awakening, from what will have seemed like a long, dogmatic, mechanistic
slumber.

What new world is in the making? Let me illustrate the Integral
possibility, with its original theme. I started this book with a sociologi-
cal survey which had just counted 44 million Cultural Creatives in the
U.S. alone. These Creatives were trying to build an Integral Society
whose head, heart and soul were no longer at odds. We are now in a
position to see why their dream is not so unlikely. To understand it
fully, let me go back to today's Big Change to outline the major
cultural currents at play.

Past, Present, and Future Societies

Right now we are schismatic. Right now we assume that any rising new view will want to conquer and annihilate its predecessor. This, however, is not what Integral Society is about.

If we go through Big Change, then twenty-first century society will be as different from modernity as the modern world was from its medieval predecessor. What could be so different? I believe you can see the key difference in the name. In an Integral Society success must come from *integrating*, not from dominating. The only way to get an integral society is by synthesizing a new society out of what is best in the existing threads. Paul Ray, the sociologist who conducted the survey, helps us see what this might mean today.

Western civilization currently consists of three major cultural groups which Ray calls, Modernists, Heartlanders and Cultural Creatives (see Figure 43). These correspond roughly to present, past and future societies. Each has a core dream.

Modernists — the Present

> *Looking at the decline in incomes ... or at the perilous state*
> *of the environment around the planet ... it is not hard to see*
> *how a series of disasters superimposed on each other could*
> *lead to a decline in civilization ... Does that mean we're*
> *still looking through distorting eyeglasses supplied by our*
> *own ancien régime — eyeglasses that reflect anachronistic*
> *interests that are not necessarily our own? I think so.*

Modernism is what I have been calling the clockwork view. Its banners are science, technology, and industrial capitalism. It also has ties to modern nation-states because these were also born in the clockwork transition.

Modernity's original rallying cry was liberty, equality and fraternity. It started as the Enlightenment's child. It has brought us the wonders

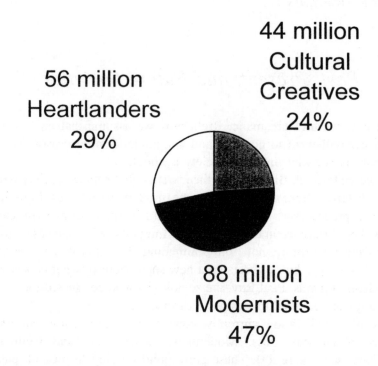

56 million
Heartlanders
29%

44 million
Cultural
Creatives
24%

88 million
Modernists
47%

Figure 43. What the Survey Shows (after Ray, 1996).

of science and the power of technology. It has also brought belief in universal education, humane treatment, religious freedom and tolerance of all kinds. It hopes that reason will build a sane and beautiful world. It also hopes that freedom will make economies prosper.

Unfortunately, though its early philosophers rose in opposition to abusive authority, by the mid-1800s clockwork establishments were already being decried for abuses of their own. Modernity, including science, capitalism and imperialist nation states, gained a reputation for uncaring efficiency and abusive use of power. Modernism is now enamored of monied interests and well bolstered by 'scientism,' the dogmatic form of science. It is noticeably low on heart and soul.

Heartlanders — the Past

> *Heartlanders believe in a nostalgic image of return to small town, religious America ... [and] what they believe are the good old 'traditional' American ways.*

Ray calls the second cultural group, Heartlanders. Most Heartlanders belong to an ancient mutualist stream. They want a return to the time when people cared about family, community and integrity, a time when commitment to something higher was strong. They center themselves on church and community because clockwork thinking provides no heart-resonating answers to the basic questions of human being.

Since Heartlanders find their solidity in church, community, and traditional values, they are often at odds with Modernists who tend to disregard these three. Ironically, however, Heartlander love of traditional Enlightenment values often make them better keepers of the Enlightenment hope than their Modernist counterparts. Heartlanders still cherish the original dream, a free people and a just society committed to serving a greater design. It is an Enlightenment dream on all counts.

Unfortunately, Heartlanders come in two forms. Extreme right-wing Traditionalists believe that the way to restore traditional values is via autocratic control, particularly in religion, but also in society at large. They reflect their late-stage medieval counterparts: the desire to burn anyone who dissents from the One Right Way which they define. Here reside the racists, bigots and fundamentalists who talk of a free people under God's design, but who are primarily dedicated to preserving remnants of the dominator design. They seek authoritarian control by an exclusive few over an oppressed many.

There are relatively few far-right Traditionalists. These have so insinuated themselves into crucial power junctions, however, that they tend to dominate people's perceptions of Heartlander beliefs. This is unfortunate. The two Heartland groups overlap, but at their core they are very different. One is mutualist, the other authoritarian.

Creatives — In Search of an Integral Whole

The new subculture includes people who perceive all too clearly the systemic problems of today, all the way from the local level to the nation and to the planetary. It also includes people who have higher standards for spirituality, personal development, authenticity, relationships, and toleration for the views of other people than the members of either Traditional or Modern cultures.

What is most notable about the Cultural Creatives is that they are *both* Heartlanders and Modernists. Hence, like Heartlanders, Creatives emphasize heart, soul, community and commitment. They too want to build a society where people care about family, integrity, community and commitment to something higher. They too have doubts about a world built solely on money and uncurbed self-interest.

Ray sees Creatives' spiritual roots as beginning with the revolutionary spirituality that started during the Renaissance and burst forth again in nineteenth-century Romantic and Transcendental movements. Yet, their wide-ranging spiritual interests — from Native American and Eastern to early Christian and Islamic roots — makes it clear that their concern is for the deep meaning that inspires all religion.

Creatives, however, also embrace modernity. They are often deeply involved with science, technology and industry, not to mention reason and critical thinking. For them, the problem is not science, technology and industry *per se*, but the way these are used. Thus, Creatives want the synergetic type of capitalism and a mutualist form of modernity. They believe that business and technology should be *tools* for the pursuit of prosperity, justice and common wellbeing. Dominator élites have corrupted the cause.

Thus, though Creatives are described as new, they are actually going back to very deep roots. They more nearly reflect the original thrust of both Modernist and Heartland tradition. This is why they try so hard to bring head, heart, soul and common wisdom back together. Bound together in a living world, Cultural Creatives believe that we must all learn the essential ecological truth, 'not separate, but together.'

Today, Creatives are closer to their dream than ever before. The main reason for this is the rise of a rigorous and increasingly well-synthesized web view in science. Our world view is about to change. This new view includes heavy doses of rediscovery and reconciliation. This will aid the Creatives' quest to integrate older currents.

Head, Heart and Soul

United we stand, divided we fall.

In the analytic world, one put one's head in one bin, one's heart in another and one's soul in a third. The pieces rarely conversed. Now, however, one can talk of a Creative Force which permeates the world and be perfectly scientific. One can also talk seriously about economics and advocate humane practices in business, quality education for all and developing collaborative skills in our children.

Thus, if you think about all that has been said, you may realize that a lot of old schisms have softened. This is particularly true of splits between scientific, spiritual, practical, and transformative endeavours. Slowly, humanity's four great spheres of knowing are beginning to discover similar truths. They are rediscovering the validity behind each other's domains. Paths for collaborating and keeping each other honest are also emerging. With luck these disparate pursuits may some day form an ecology of knowledge with connections and feedback cycles strewn throughout (see Figure 44).

We have built a world on separation, control, competition and either/or thinking, but an Integral Age is different. Let us start with how science and spirituality begin to connect.

When Scientists and Prophets See the Same World

The most sophisticated science that has ever existed is beginning to describe the cosmos as a Oneness which is creative, dynamic and permeated with order. Scientists now sound like poets, even preachers. We begin to understand that spiritual insight is based on apprehending something that is really there. This is a very big change.

We are used to science and spirituality being antithetical, even antagonistic, but our picture of the world is changing. The images coming from this science fit images central to spiritual beliefs which span the gamut of time and culture. For example, the Roman philosopher-king Marcus Aurelius gave this advice.

> Cease not to think of the Universe as one living Being,
> possessed of a single substance and a single soul ... and how
> all existing things are joint causes of all things that come into
> existence; and how intertwined in the fabric is the thread, and
> how closely woven the web ...

Christians, Buddhists, Muslims, Jews, Hindus, Taoists — 2000 BC and 2000 AD — there is no major spiritual tradition that has not called out a vision of the world much like that of Marcus Aurelius. My next statement, therefore, should come as no surprise. This match between the domain of science and the domain of spirit offers hope. Web science does not support everything that has been said by various religions, but at least one can tell that both great traditions are looking at the same world.

I have spent a lot of time mentioning various aspects that undergird the spiritual apprehension, past and possibly future. The Life Force of the great Goddess religions. The *Logos* of St John and early Christian thinkers. The numinous, the *mysterium tremendum,* the Harmonies and the Great Ordering Oneness of the Greeks and Romans. The Ineffable Reality and Sacred in all Things of the Hindus and Buddhists. The God of compassion and social justice of the Jews, Christians and Muslims. All of these are surely One.

I also believe that the new science goes a long way in confirming that there is a physical validity to these apprehensions. Hence, while the new science demystifies the world, it also helps us rediscover its profundity. We discover that an Ineffable Force did create us and is still at work. We discover that our mind is a reflection of a more Cosmic Mind, at play in the invisible weave. We discover that we are part of a great design which embraces and links all things great and small. We too find a world that is alive and imbued with purpose.

This reconciliation of physical and spiritual views also helps explain why there is an Eternal Truth at the heart of all authentic traditions. From a web perspective, great spiritual sages from across the globe and throughout the ages have regularly discovered this same Eternal Truth because they have been great observers in tune with a very real world.

Web thinkers are not the first to make this observation. The idea that there is a core agreement between the early forms of all great religions was first put to words twenty-five hundred years ago, at the time of the Axial Age. It was first mentioned in the west by

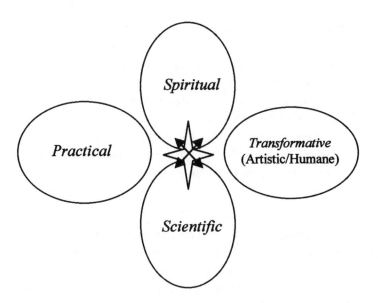

Figure 44. An Ecology of Knowledge: Reconnecting Humanity's Four Great Ways of Knowing. When human beings were first trying to understand the world, head, heart, soul and common sense were all enlisted in the task of understanding and improving. Then people began to specialize. Deep apprehension became the spiritual domain. Critical thinking tied to observation became the scientific domain. Daily conundrums created the practical domain. Charting a path and luring people along it became the transformative domain, the home of artists, poets, minstrels, writers, intellectuals, social activists and prophets too. After thousands of years, domains grew insular. Specialists pursuing their own concerns had little understanding of the others. An Integral view, however, is bringing us back to the beginning. Improved understanding may help restore connections between all four spheres.

Augustinius Steuchus in 1540. Leibniz made it famous in 1715. Apparently, science is now getting there too. Authentic traditions discover the same Eternal Truth because it is written in the world.

The reconciliation between science and spirit also helps explain why modernity failed to create the Utopia it planned. Clockwork thinkers disdained spirituality. They didn't believe in purpose or meaning, community or caring. This has been their greatest sin. Not only did analytic science supposedly do God in, but all the hard-won knowledge of the spiritual ages was relegated to the dust-bin of superstition with the snap of a materialistic hand. It is exactly this sin which is likely to end Modernity's reign.

Beyond Meaninglessness and Malaise

> *Among many academics it has been almost a rule of reason*
> *to believe that what people really care about is their own*
> *material wellbeing. Believing anything else is just some kind*
> *of populist romanticism ...*
>
> *What we learned was that many ... people hate living in*
> *a world governed by a money-oriented ethos, even as they*
> *simultaneously believe that it is impossible to change such a*
> *world.*   Michael Lerner

In 1976, a group of social theorists in Oakland, California began
exploring why middle-income Americans were moving to the political
Right. At first these theorists assumed that their subjects were motivated by material self-interest. But, discussions with actual people soon
revealed a very different situation. As facades fell away, a troubling
picture began to emerge. Corporate middle-managers, doctors, bus
drivers, teachers, scientists, government workers, auto workers and
electronic workers in Silicon Valley — all had lives filled with pain
and self-blame. The study's authors penned the opening quote. They
also came to the following conclusion:

> We found middle-income people were deeply unhappy because
> they hungered to serve the common good and to contribute
> something with their talents and energies, yet find that their
> actual work gives them little opportunity to do so. They often
> turn to demands for more money as a compensation for a life
> that otherwise feels frustrating and empty. (Lerner, 1996)

Even people who seemed withdrawn, hostile or very unconcerned
often ended up revealing a deep hunger for community, recognition
and a sense of higher purpose. Indeed, frustrated yearnings often
caused their hostility.

Westerners are taught that self-interest and self-gratification make
the world go around. Money is the only measure! Community and
humanity are romantic dreams. But, in this most money-conscious of
all societies, what middle-Americans hunger for most is a sense of
meaning and a sense of service to something higher than themselves.

How could this be? We have met the enemy and it is our theory of 'how the world works'! Westerners are caught in a knowledge web that makes them doubt that there is anything higher than material self-interest and looking out for Number One. That web is the materialist, reductionist, clockwork belief system — and it is killing us.

Emptiness drove many people to the Right because the religious Right spoke about the collapse of families, the absence of spirituality in people's lives and the difficulty of teaching good values to children. We have returned to Vaclav Havel's insight. People cling to their ancient beliefs because the clockwork vision gives no reason for being nor any honourable ways to proceed. It is empty and amoral.

Nor is this perception of clockwork sterility held only by Heartlanders. Many Modernists are abandoning this belief system for the similar reasons. No one wants to live in a selfish, pointless world. The last thirty years has made millions of people feel it is important to reject this vision regardless of whether it is scientific or not. Cultural Creatives are a good case in point. Most of them are Modernists who left because they found this vision repugnant. This response is now rampant. It is the unspoken impetus behind many of today's post-clockwork shifts, from holistic alternatives in medicine to belief in angels and interest in consciousness. The clockwork view is so barren and destructive that something must be wrong. It cannot be all that there is.

We begin to see what social exhaustion looks like in real life and why pressure is building. Today, even more than in 1976, the modern world is filled with frustrated people who want a more meaningful way, but who do not really believe one can emerge — at least not an intellectually valid one. One has to abandon one's head to follow one's heart.

Web science, however, belies clockwork beliefs. Hence, if Integral science and spirituality are done well, many Modernists will be happy to find them. If these are done well many Heartlanders may also feel reassured enough to relinquish the 'unquestioning' part of their religions for more free-flowing versions of the same. Hence, if Integral Age thinking is done well, it will tap a vast pool of pent-up energy, yearning for a more valid way. It will help integrate Modern and Heartland currents. Head, heart and soul will take one step closer.

Problems in the Everyday World Too

Make the heart of this people fat, and make their ears
heavy, and shut their eyes, lest they see with their eyes, and
hear with their ears and understand with their hearts, and
convert and be healed.

Then I said, Lord, how long? And he answered, Until the
cities be wasted without inhabitant, and the houses without
man, and the land be utterly desolate.   Isaiah (6:10f)

I've spent a lot of time arguing that we are on the cusp of a change
which includes all threads. Social, political, economic and ecological
dangers are real and world-wide. As a result, success is as crucial in
the Practical and Transformative domains as it is in Science and
Spirituality. Let us take an example.

In 1995 America's National Public Radio (NPR) aired a story on
a series of crises in Japan that seemed to be pushing fundamental
change. Major Japanese banks were trembling under nearly a trillion
dollars of bad debt and might need a bail out. The Japanese stock market had already crashed once and the economic dominance that had
seemed inevitable a decade before, was now a shrinking memory. The
conservative party which had ruled for nearly thirty years was being
rocked by a series of sex and money scandals. Yet, these political and
economic scandals obscured a more disturbing trend. Rates of suicide,
depression and early deaths from stress had skyrocketed in the last ten
years and everyday Japanese were beginning to question the materialism that had driven them to this state. Disenchantment was swelling.
All this and homelessness was a growing problem.

This story was told four years ago but the trend it represents world-
wide is still rolling forward. It was aired long before the economic
crisis in Indonesia erupted and then spread to Asia as a whole. It was
paralleled by the gruesome story in Korea. We now know that stresses
in Russia are even more profound. Today even the U.S. economy
seems ominously unstable, despite its bluster. These are only the best
publicized stories. In March 1996, the 24-member Organization for
Economic Cooperation and Development held its first meeting on
public management. Alice Rivlin, director of the U.S. Office of

Management and Budget, chaired the meeting. Her summary report explained the reason for the meeting. Most of the 24 governments were facing the same fundamental pressures for change, including a global economy, dissatisfied citizens, and fiscal crisis.

Social, political, economic, environmental and spiritual fragility? Archaeologists list the signs and historian Morris Berman gives us a few statistics which suggest that modern civilization too is moving toward a cusp.

> There have been other periods in human history when societies shook ... During such periods, the meaning of individual lives begins to surface as a disturbing problem ... the inability of the world view to explain the things that really matter, the loss of interest in work and the statistical rise in depression, anxiety and outright psychosis are all of a piece ... (1984, p.9)

The phenomenon we are in the midst of is quite world wide. Eerie similarity comes from completely natural causes. All industrial societies are riddled with modernity and modernity is failing — in large part because it reinvented dominator beliefs. Rationales for materialism and rapacious self-service run rampant. Their outcome is ever the same.

If the world seems distressing, you can take some solace in the fact that a great deal of work is already in progress. This turning was never just about science. Crisis begs effort. Reformers from across the spectrum of human endeavour have been attempting to meet the challenge for many years now. Thus, real people with real concerns are the ones who are actually leading this change. Most efforts did start as a result of someone facing a thorny problem — in public policy, in business, in education, in health, or in law.

The threads which support Big Change build because, after years of trying, thoughtful people in many fields have become convinced that no small tweak can fix things. The problems are systemic. They all reflect clockwork exhaustion. How do you hold a society together when the glorification of self-interest begins to pull it apart? How do you teach morality and community when God is dead and science suggests that manipulation is what works? More pragmatically, how do you run a business in a world gone wild with complexity and a feverish pace of change? What about a government? or a school? or a home?

The benefit of having science change too is that it helps clarify why we have gone wrong and what needs to be done. The basic insight is simple. Businesses, societies, economies and the biosphere all work more like webs than like machines. We've been using the wrong tools and the wrong images. Hence understanding how webs work has a lot of implications for the everyday side of life. Web themes (under many different names) are already bubbling in the society at large. Ecology is deep and wide. Similar rules apply up and down the line. We must learn to build sound ecologies — social, political, and economic ones. This is the only way to sustainable civilization.

Web insights also provide a new perspective on current beliefs. Today, for example, right-wing pundits blame socio-economic failure on Big Government, Big Bureaucracy, Big Spending and Big Deficits. Lord knows, there is reason for people's anger toward the first two and their fear of the second two. Yet, what web-thinking tells us is that, even if we were to get rid of all four completely, our problems would not be solved. Our problems would not be solved because getting rid of all four does nothing to build *socio-economic intricacy*. We will not learn any better, we will not collaborate any better and neither our economies nor our social fabric will be any stronger.

If we put human intricacy at the center of our view, an interesting thing happens. Not only do everyday people start to matter more, but so does social fabric. We also get a better sense of why many common solutions often go wrong. Current wisdoms are often riddled with assumptions which are anathema to intricacy. Jacobs helped us see the problem in urban planning. We streamlined our way out of community and caring (not to mention natural bonds). Welfare provides an example too. Welfare has been a disaster largely because it was designed like a placation of a discontented faction. Like all good placations it built dependency and stultification, not empowered citizens involved in an intricate social web. Hence, regardless of intent, welfare functioned like an opiate for the masses, not a way out.

The object of our time, therefore, is to figure out how to cultivate intricacy (not to give up on helping one another). We already have some clues. Intricacy is encouraged by education, empowerment, infrastructure, support networks, liberation and love. It grows best when fertilized and organized in circles with human faces and common-cause. It grows best when spurred by binding ideals, like liberty, equality, justice, compassion and serving a higher design. It requires

Maintain intricacy. A sound social fabric is like a lace tablecloth, filled with small and intricately entwined circles. Don't let it pull apart.

Encourage mutual benefit. Societies which stay well-linked do so because their everyday systems make it desirable to benefit self *and* others at the same time.

Encourage commitment to the common good. We depend on our brethren and on their integrity. We are going to have to develop ways to make integrity and concern for the greater good worthwhile for each and all.

Maintain a robust flow of resources and accurate information. A human society depends on a good flow of information and resources. People who swim a sea of lies lose their sense of direction. Gross inequities create instability. The only way to have a sustainable civilization is to build a mutual-benefit system with no great gaps.

Maintain ongoing learning. Collaborative learning is humankind's central strategy. Now that we know this, we have to teach our children and our institutions to be collaborative learners.

Table 11. Elements of sustainable structure.

lots of lessons about how to encourage collaboration, creativity and distributed concern.

Good intentions and noble visions are not enough to build a sound society. We have much to learn. Table 11 summarizes what I believe are the main lessons of the web view of human societies.

A Union of Dreams

Integral thinking is practical, transformative, scientific and spiritual. Therefore, if web science is done well, then I think Creatives will have the theory they need to forge an Integral Society out of what is best in existing dreams. They would still have a lot of practical and transformative problems, but at least the movement might take clearer form.

So, if I were a Cultural Creative (and presumably I am), I would use everything that Integral Science provides to bind every wound that I could.

I would tell Modernists that science, technology and industry are here. The twenty-first century will bring tools and concepts which are more appropriate to the world at large. Understanding interdependence and seeing its order is going to change scientific ideas across the map! Invest in this barely visible beginning because, at some point, the new methods and insights will take hold. You will want to be there. Change for practical reasons or for scientific ones! You have nothing to lose but your blinders.

I would tell Heartlanders of the rediscovery of community, integrity, and the roots of tradition and soul. An Integral Society too seeks service to the greater Design. It seeks a return to traditional values like justice, compassion and commitment — not to mention liberty, equality, democracy, civic duty, and political self-reform. This movement is not new, it is radically old. It is merely time to get our institutions into more workable forms.

I would tell the mutualist within us all that the pulse of our dreams is powerful. Today, as in all unstable times, we are again cringing in the darkness of a dominator night. But this time we need not imagine that this state is inevitable. Rather, history moves with us. For five thousand years the struggle has been met. Utopia eludes us, but each time we move a notch forward. Our ancestors have been here before and they faced much worse. They are the ones who died to bring us the Enlightenment dream — the democracy, the universal education, the belief in humane treatment — which, even today, is still becoming real. We stand on their shoulders and we are much stronger for it. Our chances are better than at any other time in history. There is no doubt that it is worth fighting another round.

I would also help arm other Creatives with the scientific substance that goes with their dreams. I would help them find each other, organize, learn and grow. I would help them see that what they are striving for can work.

I would also mention one last fact. The Integral Age asks us to save ourselves and the planet by returning to our original task — learning.

Integral consciousness
Networked mutualism
Synthesis of information and high-value synergetic capitalism
The Age of Wisdom

Table 12. Integral consciousness and its main socio-economic forms.

For thousands of years great insights have been converted into final truths which were then defended by zealous élites. Now, however, we find there are no final truths, only the collaborative quest for better ones. Learning to question, rearrange and connect is vastly more important than acquiring facts that you hope won't change. If we can just learn to learn continuously, we might just learn to evolve without catastrophe in between. That would be a joyous day indeed. It would also be a relevant one too, considering what we now face (see Table 12).

On the Edge

Changes from one kind of civilization to another do not
happen often in history: the invention of agriculture, the rise
and fall of conquest states ... and the coming of
industrialism. An earlier generation may have been justified
in discounting any further such radical changes. We cannot.
Most trends of the past are simply not sustainable ...

                                                              Paul Ray

We have not yet succeeded in reinventing civilization for a new round. The seeds taking root are still small. Integral science in all its diverse forms is still lost beneath mounds of jargon and hype. The substance which might save us, lies scattered and we remain dominated by usual ways. As with all great transitions, change proceeds in parallel with each little thrust feeling like a voice crying in the wilderness. The wilderness, however, is now filled with voices all murmuring similar themes. These voices do not belong just to scientists, they are rumbling in the society at large.

Integral science makes the picture clearer. Social evolution is not the inevitable progress envisioned by clockwork thinkers, but a punctuated pattern of growth and crisis. Societies go through regular growth trials in which they must learn or die, evolve or break. There even appear to be rules for when this happens. If we don't find ways of staying well-connected and commonly concerned, we too will fall apart.

Today, therefore, we face, not just change, but a developmental challenge of epic proportions. Can we change? How should we change? What theory there is makes our situation, if not solvable, at least clearer and more urgent. We of the great human web will either coalesce around a new design of social fabric, or the failures of the old will continue to build until their weight makes the system collapse upon itself.

Theory thus confirms what many suspect. We need to reinvent civilization. It helps to know that it has been done before. It helps us to know that our dreams can connect. Still, in the final analysis, I believe the experiment is still in progress and the outcome unclear. I spend much of my time nowadays working with reform groups, studying their approaches.

This brings me to the end of my story. I have but one more thing to add. If this were a clockwork book I would have claimed to have invented a theory that would stand as some final truth. I would probably claim to have answers to most problems at hand. But the world is too complex and the times too delicate to indulge such fantasies anymore. Besides, the truth is so much more intriguing.

We live in interesting times, the trick of which will be the weaving of a new way of being — socially, economically, politically, scientifically, spiritually. My goal, therefore, is not to conquer alternative perspectives, but to arm you as a fellow. The one truism which echoes throughout the entirety of the web view is that the world is a learning system. To fail to learn — and to fail to acknowledge that one needs to learn in conjunction with one's fellows — this is perhaps the one great sin. This book, therefore, is a call to arms. I want to paint a picture clear, concrete and understandable enough that you can help with the learning that we so desperately need. It is not so hard to understand. The call of the Awakening is simple:

Not separate, but together.

Appendix A
Copernicus Again!

*Sit down before fact like a little child, and be prepared to
give up every preconceived notion, follow humbly wherever
and to whatever abysses Nature leads, or you shall learn
nothing.*
                                                          T.H. Huxley

Here I would like to summarize how science's view is changing and why this
change is so shocking. Despite our sophistication we are facing Copernican
change now on many fronts. When you piece these fronts together, science's
picture of the world makes a rather large flip.

Still, it is not obvious why a big change in view should seem heretical. All
of the ideas described in the first two chapters of the book have scientific
substance. Many are quite old. The problem, of course, is that many also run
contrary to current wisdom and some range into areas that are considered
taboo. People who broach taboo topics are still treated like heretics, regardless
of the quality of their research. The concept of self-organization, is a case in
point. With the rise of the new science, the concept of self-organization is
becoming quite standard but it was not long ago that scientists who used such
words were in danger for their professional lives.

Self-organization theory says energy presses, diversity seeds and then the
process repeats! Why should this be controversial? The answer here is historical, not scientific. Traditional science had rejected all notions of spontaneous
organization for years, largely because this notion carried baggage from
medieval days when 'spontaneous' meant 'without cause.' Thus, early scientists fending off the mystical version of spontaneous organization, eventually
developed contempt for all forms of spontaneous organization. This left only
one way to explain order — through accident. Scientists eventually began to
claim that all organization on earth was the result of sheer unadulterated
accident. This is why today's theory of evolution rests on the famous image
of an army of monkeys at typewriters who would generate the works of
Shakespeare if kept busy long-enough. Today, we are told that life is a cosmic
accident and evolution as an entire process of accumulating accidents.

Now the idea that all organization is a result of accident doesn't make a
lot of common sense and many scientists have struggled against the notion for
years. Mathematicians, for example, realized long ago that there hasn't been
enough time for sheer accident to make life, which is why physicists such as
Fred Hoyle call the Shakespearean-monkey idea 'utter nonsense.' Yet,
conventional scientists viewed explanations other than complete accident with
extreme prejudice — as a heresy against true science. Early advocates of self-
organization were treated in kind.

Illya Prigogine's work in self-organization makes a nice example. His work
was rigorous enough, but it implied that life was not merely an accident. As

a result, Prigogine serves as one of the great Copernicans of our time. He made the term self-organization famous in the 1960s and in the process became infamous in establishment circles. He has not been alone. Zhabotinsky, the Russian scientist after whom the self-organizing chemical reaction is named, made his discovery in the 1950s but was not recognized for it until 1980. He died in 1970. As Brian Goodwin, a member of the new science movement in biology, says, "Ideas have their time, and if you happen to discover something before people are ready to recognize its significance, you might as well leave it in the bottom drawer until the climate is receptive."

History is a strange mistress. We too see the world through the lens of our latest beliefs and assume that our view will never become outmoded. This puffed up sense of correctness produces a tendency to righteousness. Establishment scientists regularly treat people who depart from the accepted view as heretics, even if these heretics use reason, observation, and math to make their point.

Times are changing, however. Self-organization is becoming less heretical as is the idea that life is a natural outcome of an intertwined world. What else is going to change? A lot more than most people expect.

The End of Materialism and Reductionism

> *Rather than discrete things and independent events, there*
> *are but ripples upon ripples...propagating in a seamless sea.*
> Ervin Laszlo

The central awareness which is about to sweep across civilization is that everything is connected or, more accurately, part of *one* thing — a unity from which all diversity emerges. How deep does the web go? All the way down. The things about us are but swirls in an ever-changing seamless sea. We may talk of separate bits, but these are illusion. You can derive this realization from energy, but quantum-level studies show it best.

This kind of thinking is a radical switch from clockwork tradition, which viewed separate, material bits as the basis of all solid knowledge. Paradoxically, it is getting down to the bottom-most bits that finally ends the age-old atomizing trend.

NO MORE SEPARATE BITS

Early Greeks hypothesized that the world was made up of atoms, but it wasn't until this century that scientists were able to see these atoms. The twentieth century, however, also brought relativity and quantum mechanics and these undermined the atomistic view which had just been confirmed. By the 1970s a new view was being bolstered by some startling experimental results. For instance, as researchers began to break atoms into smaller and smaller pieces, those pieces began to behave in extremely odd ways. Particles appeared to be composed of multiple copies of themselves. Splitting seemed to create more particles rather than reduce one particle to simpler components. This kind of logic-defying result precipitated a crisis. The late great physicist David Bohm began articulating the change early on:

> Relativity introduced a number of fundamentally new concepts regarding space, time and matter...The main point for our purposes here is that the notion of separate and independent particles as basic constituents of the universe had to be given up. The basic notion instead was the idea of the field that spread continuously through space. Out of this you had to construct the notion of a particle. I could illustrate these ideas in terms of the analogy of a vortex in a flow of fluid. Within this fluid there is a recurrent, stable pattern...'Vortex' is a convenient word to describe the pattern. But there is nothing but a flowing pattern of water. (1985, p.5)

Science has been equated with materialism for the last two hundred years or so. But materialism is about to end, demolished by the growing realization that there are no such things as separate material bits. Indeed, the concept of 'matter' itself becomes dubious.

ONLY ENERGY

The 'field' that Bohm mentions is a physicist's term for the fabric of forces that exist in a given region. Traditionally, one says a field is made up of all the matter and energy within that region. But, many physicists are beginning to argue that there is no such thing as matter. What we call 'mass' is an illusion of interacting forces and energy flows. As one recent article put it:

> The concept of mass may be neither fundamental nor necessary in physics. In the view we will present, Einstein's formula ($E=mc^2$) is even more significant than physicists have realized. It is actually a statement about how much energy is required to give the appearance of a certain amount of mass...If this view is correct, there is no such thing as mass—only electric charge and energy, which together create the illusion of mass. The physical universe is made up of massless electric charges immersed in a vast, energetic, all pervasive electromagnetic field. It is the interaction of those charges and the electromagnetic field that creates the appearance of mass. (*The Sciences*, Nov. 1994, p.26)

How times change. Once it was mystical to believe in anything beyond matter. Soon it may be mystical to believe that matter exists. Once it seemed obvious that separate pieces of matter were fundamental. Soon it may be obvious that there is nothing *but* interdependence and shifting patterns in an all-embracing sea.

FROM ROCK LOGIC TO WATER LOGIC

Now, at first blush, the end of materialism might seem overwhelming. How do we conceptualize a world in which matter is an illusion of energy in motion? Yet, we already know this world. A moment's thought reveals connections which every child knows. What does the end of materialism mean for everyday people? Systems thinker, Edward DeBono helps us see that very little changes except certain habits of mind. What is gained is a more appealing world.

DeBono points out that mechanism taught 'rock logic.' The world and everything in it was identified with its matter, usually envisioned as a fixed lump. The depressing statement, "you are nothing but a bunch of chemicals" is an example of rock logic. The new science, however, teaches what DeBono calls water logic. All things are like a whirlpool, a durable dynamic dance created by a web of forces.

For instance, what we call a whirlpool is an identifiable 'thing' distinct from its surrounds because of the patterned motion of molecules. But every school child knows that this 'thing' is not a fixed lump of matter. It is a whirlwind created by a web of forces. If we pause to think a moment, we realize that this set of statements is true of most things. A molecule is not a solid thing, it is a whirling dance of atoms — which are whirling dances of smaller particles still. A body, a society[1] and the thing we call life are similarly dynamic structures whose material bits circulate, never remaining the same.

When you think about it, water logic is not so strange. It is also much more appealing. So, ask yourself: are you "nothing but a bunch of chemicals" or are you an intricate web of dynamic dances woven into a world of similarly dancing sparks? If you like the first answer, you are a materialist and you believe rock logic. Matter is what makes the world and the patterns by which things move are less important than their parts. If you like the second answer, you are a dynamicist and you use water logic. What counts is the dance.

THE END OF REDUCTIONISM

Reductionism is also in jeopardy. To the extent that science was corrupted by materialism, it held that there was nothing but matter. Reductionism took this farther. If one could just get to the bottom-most bits, then one would know how everything worked! The parts are all you need!

Reductionists hate holism for obvious reasons. The dictionary defines holism as "the theory that *wholes*, which are more than the mere sum of their parts, are fundamental aspects of the *real*." Reductionists, of course, believed that only parts existed. The idea that wholes could be 'more,' seemed like nonsense. After all, the 'more' would have to be non-material and anything that wasn't material didn't exist.

In the new science, however, holism is not mystical nor is it nonsense. It is merely an observable fact. For example, water (H_2O) is more than the sum of hydrogen and oxygen taken separately. The properties of water are never found in its separate components. Why? Because when you put bodies together their dance produces new behaviors. This thought applies everywhere. Hence, a flock is more than the sum of its birds taken separately and a society is more than the sum of its people taken separately. It is the dynamic dance between bodies which gives wholes their substance and shape. Until pieces come together, there is no dance.

TOP-DOWN CAUSALITY

Reductionists objected to another aspect of holism even more strongly. Holism seemed to imply a kind of *top-down causality*, as if some invisible hand were ordering individual things to fit some larger scheme. Surely this is mysticism!

Yet, the new science rediscovers top-down causality too. Coupled cuckoo clocks, for example, knock themselves into synchronization 'as if' someone aligned them. Craig Reynolds' boids acted locally, but created an undulating mass movement which appeared to be bound together (but wasn't). Web dynamics often create global patterns of behavior which appear to have been orchestrated from outside or above. These actually arise out of binding forces and back and forth bumps.

Nor is global order merely an illusion. Once a dynamic pattern is established, its momentum often makes it an *active* participant. A treadmill is a simple example. You start it, but once it is going, you have to keep up the pace and may need to go faster to avoid falling down. You started it, but now it runs you. Similarly, once a whirlpool gets going it presses molecules in line. The momentum of the attractor pulls bodies in line. Belief systems, family systems, economic systems—self-reinforcing global dynamics are active in a very real sense. They press their parts to keep in step.

In retrospect, the holist-reductionist debate is a straw man, built around two extreme positions. Thus, reductionists once insisted that the bottom (the parts) were the only source of causation. Holists insisted equally vigorously that the top (the whole) was the real source. The new science finds the middle ground. It says that causality should be thought of as coming from *both* the top and the bottom — and also side-to-side (see Figure A-1). Descriptions from one side alone are likely to create misleading images. Like the chicken and the egg, most things are part of a cycle which is caused from many directions.

The Invisibly Structured World

The new science's view of bottom-up *and* top-down holds one more implication. All local events are embedded in a very *structured context*. This highly-ordered context creates pressures which shape how events unfold.

Let me provide an everyday example of this idea. A male friend of mine was recently confronted by an alarming study. The study looked at life decisions made by males born at a certain time, in a certain place and with a certain ethnic background. It showed that virtually every one else in his cohort ended up making the same decisions he had made—including the age

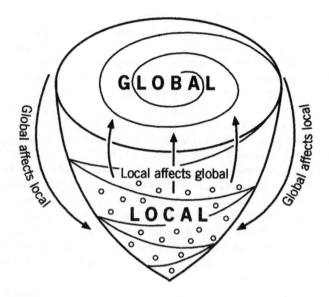

Figure A-1. Top-down and Bottom-up Causality, Ending the Reductionist-Holist Debate.
Local pulls and pushes create a global dynamic which then pushes back on the local dynamics in a very real way. As Crutchfield et. al. put it: "The interaction of components on one scale can lead to complex global behavior on a larger scale that in general cannot be deduced from knowledge of the individual components." (1986, p. 56) The bottom causes the top and the top causes the bottom.

of his first marriage, the number of children, level of education, type of profession, age of first divorce, etc. Innumerable decisions that he had made in response to his own unique life-struggle, were made by all these men. They seemed almost foregone conclusions. Unbeknownst to him he lived in an ordered context that exerted pressure.

In theory this should not be surprising. The history that brought his ethnic group to his place of birth, affected what his family taught. The way the society treated a child of his gender and ethnic background also had particular effects. I could go on, but the point is straightforward. We sit in a world whose swirling pressures are themselves intricately arranged. This idea is not even new. The terms *Zeitgeist* and *Weltanshauung* reflect the same notion. As each of us decides, the invisibly-ordered context pushes and shoves.

We now also find that ordered-contexts existed long before human beings. For instance, the biosphere too is an ordered-context which heavily shapes the evolution of all the things. The real culprit behind ordered contexts is energy and the seamless sea of forces which have been weaving right along.

THE ILLUSION OF RANDOMNESS

The concept of an intricately arranged world leads to another shocking possibility. Many thinkers now believe that randomness may be an illusion.

The worldview built around randomness is grim. It is a major contributor to the purposeless sense of the world. But, there appears to be no way to avoid this conclusion. When mathematicians say something is random, they are stating categorically that *there is no order*. They are also implying that the data before them is the result of *in*dependent happenings. No ties and no coherent process generated it. Yet, mathematicians tell us that their tests prove that many things are random.

The glimmer on the horizon is that the rigor of randomness is also misleading. To be sure, there are mathematical tests for randomness, but these are based on an infinite series of numbers — which no one ever has. This means that true randomness can never be proven. Furthermore, even radioactive decay, the most touted example of a random process, has indications of order at work. One can never tell when the next particle will decay, but half of them always decay in exactly the same amount of time. The implication is that the process undergirding decay is quite regular and coherent, if also unpredictable (like Chaos).

Discoveries such as Chaos and fractals are also creating new doubt about whether order might not exist within a system which looks disordered. Many mathematicians are beginning to wonder how one can tell *for sure* whether there is order or not. Skepticism is setting in as the following two quotes indicate:

> Could it be that in Nature there are no such 'genuine' random processes as we fancy them? (Chirikov, cited in Cvitanovic, 1984, p.933)

> We know that perfectly definite causal and *simple* rules can...generate numbers...[with] such a seeming lack of order that all statistical tests will confer upon the numbers a pedigree of randomness. Technically, the term 'pseudo random' is used to indicate this nature. One may now ask whether the various complex processes of nature themselves might not be merely pseudo random, with the full import of randomness, which is untestable, a historic but misleading concept. (Feigenbaum, 1980, p.50)

Several branches of mathematics are now trying to find better ways to judge whether something is ordered or not.[2] Perhaps something that looks messy actually has structure that we don't yet see? For example, the number: 0.42857142 doesn't seem to have any order until we realize that it is 3 divided by 7. It was generated by a simple underlying rule, a very coherent process!

Now whether randomness truly exists or not is beyond the scope of this book. But there is a very important reason for mentioning the growing doubt — namely, the reversal of image. Once upon a time we looked at the world through the lens of simple math and said, "No order here! Only randomness and accident!" This seemed to be the height of scientific rationality. Now, however, views are shifting. Scientists are beginning to realize that order is everywhere and it is often hard to see. Hidden within is a dramatic change of perspective. One can almost here the next stage — "No randomness here, only overlooked order."

The Question of Questions

> *If we ask whether the position of the electron remains the same, we must say 'No'; if we ask whether the electron's position changes with time, we must say 'No'; if we ask whether the electron is at rest, we must say 'No'; if we ask whether it is in motion, we must say 'No.'*
>
> Robert Oppenheimer

My last Copernican thought is about the way we ask questions. Simple causality begs us to look at problems in terms of one (and only one) thing causing another. As a result, clockwork thinking is dominated by either/or questions. The classic example is whether intelligence is determined by heredity *or* environment. This framing is not surprising as clockwork thinking is built around single causes, but it is extremely misleading. Most outcomes emerge from a blend of causes. One thing is rarely, if ever, the sole cause. Even simple chains of causality often split, intertwine and feedback in arcane ways. Interwoven causality requires one ask questions like 'which ones,' 'how much,' 'in what way,' and 'when' — but not either/or.

We are reaching a turning point in history. For hundreds (perhaps thousands) of years, people have argued that X was the cause of a situation, only to have someone else argue that Y was the real culprit. Groups would then square off and try to demolish each other. The idea that an event might be caused by both X and Y seemed impossible — at least until now. In a web world, one must avoid either/or questions because the usual answer is 'both.'

The new view is very clear here. If you want to understand why there is *no real conflict* in a host of seemingly irreconcilable positions, then you must resist the urge to force false dichotomies on the world. So, either/or questions seem logical, but the ensuing absurdities have been many. Hence, if you try to explore an interwoven world with either/or thinking, you are likely to get a double-bind answer. This creates both anger and confusion. The usual answer to an either/or question is 'Yes.' For example:

- □ Is intelligence determined by heredity *or* environment? Yes.
- □ Is poverty caused by social factors such as poor education and restricted opportunity *or* personal ones like lack of optimism or drive? Yes.
- □ Is the world caused from the bottom-up *or* the top-down? Yes.

So, heredity or environment? Yes. But what an inappropriate question. Much better to ask: how each contributes and how the two affect each other? One must also be prepared for contributions to vary. For example, the less food a child gets, the more environment contributes to the outcome. Starving to death is the obvious example. When a child starves to death, environment is the sole determiner of intelligence.

Either/or thinking is wasteful and painful. It begs academics and lay people alike to spend endless hours in divisive, destructive wrangling. It produces simplistic answers which then keep us from developing more sane midground routes. When you look at a complex system carefully, it is usually the both/and description which is most accurate. The trick in an interwoven world is to figure out how elements fit together. The trick is sound *integration* of 'when and how' elements.

Renaissance

> *The only solid piece of scientific truth about which I feel*
> *totally confident is that we are profoundly ignorant about*
> *nature. It is this sudden confrontation with the depth and*
> *scope of our ignorance that represents twentieth-century*
> *science's most significant contribution to the human*
> *intellect.*   Lewis Thomas, 1979

I started this book wondering how much our view of the world could change. Hopefully, you now have some sense of why interdependence makes a difference and how pervasive the resulting change is likely to be.

Interdependence affects how we see systems from dieting and ant paths, to planets and evolution. It ends materialism, reductionism and the fundamental myth. It says the world is subtly ordered and randomness is an illusion. It runs from classical mechanics to statistics and all points in between—and we haven't even gotten to the economics, sociology, biology and spirituality yet. In short, a little bit of interdependence is about to uproot, unravel and otherwise shake-up classical images all over science.

After four hundred years we have woven a clockwork web that is very broad and very tight. But new tools are emerging and with them comes a great retrospective. Science has been caught in a very small box that it mistook for the world. The moment one steps beyond the current limits of *non*-dependence, one finds chaos, complexity, fractals, attractors and a host of ideas that seem to fall totally out of the blue. A new generation of scientists has begun to decry classical images as illusion. Copernicus lives again!

Yet, for all the hue and cry, what we are witnessing is not an attack on science, but a rebirth and a reframing. The new science is 'new' because of its new tools and its new sense of how the world works. Yet, it also a rediscovery of older views all but lost in the arrogance of clockwork thinking. This new science is inevitable because it is based on including more of what we already know is there (connections). Yet, it is also a continuation of the old. It is an expansion of the same stalwart struggling-to-understand science that western civilization has come to rely on so heavily. Revolution? No, a Renaissance, a metamorphosis, a bifurcation.

Appendix B
Contrasts in Scientific and Cultural Visions

How much could possibly change? To help you see that there is an old and new, Tables B-1 to B-3 summarize some of the scientific differences we have covered. The last section summarizes some of the cultural differences between an clockwork and a web view.

Clockwork Perspective	*Dynamic Web Perspective*
Given the right equations and initial conditions, anything can be precisely predicted.	The same equation run on two different computers produces different end points, if there is chaos.
Emergence and attraction are mysticism.	Emergence and attraction can be seen physically and mathematically.
We can prove that some things are 'random,' meaning totally without order.	Order is often hidden in what looks like disorder. Randomness can never be fully proven and becomes dubious. The world may be ordered, but we may not know it.
The second law of thermodynamics means that order is improbable.	Organization is probable in certain conditions. Order and decay both fit an expanded view of the second law.
Reductionism and materialism are cornerstones of science, as is the analytic trilogy: control, isolate, breakdown.	Reductionism, materialism and analysis are simplistic. Reductionism underestimates interdependence's role in making the world. Materialism underestimates energy and the centrality of organization. Matter too is an illusion of energy patterns and dynamic dances.

Most systems in the world can be addressed by one of the two main methodological camps. Determinism or statistics. What we have is basically all we need.	For early science, simple models made absolute prediction seem inevitable but, at the beginning of this century, understanding of disordered-complexity advanced. Statistics became a major tool. Most systems are intricate, their parts interwoven in an orderly way. Understanding intricacy requires a new set of tools which leaves interdependence in and unveils its patterns. The ability to 'compute' faster is allowing more appropriate methods to emerge.

Table B-1. Differences in math, physics and general scientific beliefs.

Clockwork Perspective	*Dynamic Web Perspective*
Evolution is about genes and species. All evolution is explained by random mutations operating on genes, the source of heritable differences. Evolution is a gradual accumulation of productive accidents.	Evolution is about an energy, self-organization and increasing intricacy. Evolution is served by diversity and casting about but, these are part of an overall process which has both direction and structure. Evolution is punctuated and best thought of as an interwoven Great Ordering Oneness.
Life is an accident. Reproduction is the central miracle of life.	Life is an energy-flow event that brought together a host of simpler self-organizations into a truly astounding new system. For all its wonder, life was probable given the conditions. The central miracle of life is the *functional coupling* of its many parts.
Life is self-centered and separate. The object of evolution is adaptation to the environment.	Because life is made of energy, it is tightly tied up with chemical and energy flows everywhere. Because everything is fundamentally intertwined, the biosphere — life, land, oceans, atmosphere — co-evolve in a back and forth dance.

Natural selection equals survival of the fittest, competition, and nature red in tooth and claw. Nature is like a gladiator show. War is the true tester. Altruism can only be explained as a complex epicycle of selfish genes.	Natural selection starts before life and selects for speed, persistence and ability to play a role in the larger web. *Cooperation* is the central path of evolution. Nature generally avoids competition as war, though competition as diversity and freedom are important. Dominator culture is war's real proponent.
The miracle of life happened once. The origins only involved earth.	Living systems may have originated multiple times in multiple places. The origins of life involved comets and stars and energy from all over. The universe itself may be self-organizing.
Genes hold complete, inviolate blueprints. They are separate from the outside world. They change only by random mutation. If something is wrong genetically, the situation can only be cured by fixing the gene.	Genes are modifiers of form and function, not generators. Genes are interwoven with each other and the broader web of process. They are affected by conditions inside and outside the body. Genetic material cycles between forms of life, carried by viruses, etc. If something is wrong with a gene, there may be many other avenues of alleviating the resulting condition.
Selfish genes are the basis of innate superiority. Those who are on top of society are the 'best.' Eventually America will develop a hereditary upper class.	Nurture plays a tremendous role in ability. Success and power are just as likely to arise from leverage, prior money or abuse as they are from any kind of innate superiority. If America develops a hereditary upper class it will be for reasons of power, not genes.

Table B-2. Differences in evolution.

Clockwork Perspective	*Dynamic Web Perspective*
Human beings are basically selfish and competitive. Human behavior is largely fixed in our genes.	We are every bit as cooperative and playful as we are vicious, competitive and destructive. Human behavior is incredibly flexible (compared to other species) because it is shaped by higher levels of mind and culture.
Mind is mostly an epiphenomenon. If mind can be said to exist, it is separate from body.	Mind too is a natural part of evolution. It started slowly, long before there were brains. It is found fractally throughout the body. Mind and body are thus inextricably intertwined.
The evolution of societies is a sound and fury signifying nothing. It is not related to any larger evolutionary process.	Increasing complexity appears to be at work in non-living, living, and suprB-living systems such as societies. Humanity's survival strategy, for instance, is collaborative pattern-finding because our late evolution took place in a time which pressed for greater behavioral flexibility. Environmental pressure, therefore, do play a role in human social evolution.
Mind is singular, not communal. It is solely associated with brains.	Mind-like behaviors emerge from the intricate, coordinated action of parts. The higher up one goes, the more clearly those parts are seen as previously independent life forms. Human society itself is a kind of society of mind.
The only emotions that count in evolution are the ones involved in feeding, fighting, fleeing and reproduction. Everything else is romantic tripe.	Nature bred the warm bonding emotions into us as part of a later and very important evolutionary strategy – communal learning. You could say that love is crucial to human intelligence.
Consciousness is hard to talk about because it is so non-material.	Consciousness too is part of the process and it too evolves in punctuated bursts. Consciousness affects the way we experience the world and the kind of societies we build. The present stage of mental consciousness may be being exhausted. This may lead to the next stage – Integral consciousness and Integral Society.

Table B-3. Differences in mind, body and behavior.

A Contrast in Cultural Vision

According to professor Edward Schein of MIT, every society must answer certain basic questions about the world and the human condition. Tables B-4 through B-8 contrast the clockwork and web approach to each of these important questions. They include:

- *What is the nature of reality?* – How does the world work? What is it like?
- *What is humankind's relationship to the World?* – Are we above it? Are we of it?
- *What does it mean to be human?* – What is our nature? Our destiny?
- *What is the nature of human activity?* – What are we after? What do we tend to do?
- *What is the nature of human relationships?* – How do we relate to one another?

Clockwork/Dominator Perspective	*Dynamic Web Perspective*
Reality is separable, controllable, merely material.	Reality is dynamic, interdependent, co-evolving.
The world has no direction. It is largely purposeless, random and cruel.	The world is woven tight with design and it moves towards greater intricacy. Warmth and caring are important evolutionary principles.

Table B-4. The nature of reality? (How does the world work?)

Clockwork/Dominator Perspective	Dynamic Web Perspective
Man is the Master of the World. He conquers, controls, dominates, subjugates.	Humankind is a member of a community of Being. If we want to survive and prosper we had better learn how to live in harmony and to make things flow.
Life is about struggle and looking out for Number One.	Life is about learning, a process best done with ones fellows. The goal is strong bonds and strong selves.
The cosmos cares nothing for us. Why should we care about anything beyond ourselves?	The cosmos created us and we are part of a greater design. The farther we see, the more we realize that our own well-being is tied to everything up and down the line. Real intelligence lies in realizing that we must become stewards of ourselves and the world.

Table B-5. Humankind's relationship to the world

Clockwork/Dominator Perspective	Dynamic Web Perspective
Our nature is fixed in our genes.	Culture makes us the most flexible creatures on earth.
Human beings are basically selfish and competitive.	Human beings are as cooperative, playful, creative and loving as they are competitive, destructive and cruel. Culture makes most of the difference.
Life is about war because nature is about war. Everything else is an epi-cycle.	Life is about learning. Love is very important to this. Our over-interest in war is a result of our arrogant adolescence. Humanity is mostly about using our brains — but we have often botched the job.
Meaning is doubtful.	Meaning is necessary. Searching for it is fundamental to our nature.
We can control our affects.	We are arrogant and, so far, pretty ignorant and simplistic.

Humankind has only one innate culture. It is made of dominators, sycophants and conformists. Everyone else fits into loose groupings of mystics and Utopians.	We have two deep cultures. Mutualism produces our greatest creativity and integrity. Dominators tend to either yoke mutualists into service or wipe them out. Our third brain, is used to rationalize the latter and wonder about the former. We should reverse this order.

Table B-6. What does it mean to be human?

Clockwork/Dominator Perspective	Dynamic Web Perspective
Everyone is after money and power.	Some people are after money and power regardless of how it affects anyone or anything else. Lots of people simply want to find love, work, belonging and meaning.
Funneling wealth to the top is just the way things turn out in a competitive society. All those little mutual exchange activities which everyday people do, don't count.	Funneling wealth is a result of institutional practices and habits of mind. It creates anxiety and aggression which afflicts all classes. All those little mutual exchange activities which everyday people do, are mutualism. If such practices became the basis of economic systems, we might get powerful, creative, flexible, economic systems that still have integrity. A sustainable society might result.
Being 'realistic' means accepting that the world is ruthless. Humane practices and romantic images, however, are good for manipulating the masses.	Being 'realistic' means accepting that humane practices are powerful and ruthlessness and manipulation are destructive.
The current scientific view is essentially fact and all but done. Doubting this makes one a heretic — and someone who is probably incapable of critical thinking.	There are no final maps. On-going learning is more important that current beliefs because institutionalized beliefs often go astray leaving us worshipping false Gods. The only way to preserve our ideals is to keep on pursuing them.

Table B-7. What is the nature of human activity?

Clockwork/Dominator Perspective	*Dynamic Web Perspective*
Coercive hierarchies are nature's natural order. Some elements are meant to rule and others to be ruled. The goal is for superior people to rise to the top where they can guide/control society.	If you want a healthy society build 1) distributed intelligence, 2) distributed initiative and 3) lots of diversity and heretical thinking. Bind all these together with sincere concern for the common good which is felt top to bottom. Coercive hierarchies are a crude and often stifling system invented during the Age of War.
Might makes right; everything else is romanticism.	Pursuit of ideals is central to making a powerful society.
Societies run best when self-interest is king and people are set up to compete against each other.	Societies run best when people work together freely, creatively and with integrity. This seems to happen most often when everyone in the society feels committed to binding ideals and when the society orchestrates a great deal of overlap between individual and greater good
Trial-by-combat is the way to run science, politics, and economics. Coercion and control is the best way to run factories and schools.	Dialogue, collaboration, diversity and concern are the best way to run science, politics, economics, factories and schools. Loyalty, obedience, tradition and honor are a good way to run armies.
'Winners' can reasonably treat losers like cogs, commodities, serfs or slaves.	Treating people like cogs, commodities, serfs or slaves creates resentment that builds.
Societies run best on command-and-control plus conformity.	Social fabrics must be dynamic. Grassroots must be strong. Intelligence, compassion and resources must cycle robustly — or else intricacy fails.

Table B-8. What is the nature of human relationships?

Appendix C
Oneness and the Perennial Philosophy

Since the dawn of thought, human beings were aware of
being embedded in an ultimate mystery they were compelled
to understand and to use as moral guidance.

Gordon D. Kaufman

The birth of modernity and the end of the medieval world brought a rift between science and spirituality (religion) which has never really healed. Today, we stand a better chance of healing this wound than any time in the last four hundred years. The reason for this is Integral science and the now physically-substantiated perception of a Creative Force and a Oneness which permeates the entire fabric of the universe.

Web science thus allows us to view religion, spirituality and the ancients from a profoundly different perspective. The distinct post-modern possibility is that the great spiritual sages were great perceivers of currents in the real world. If this is so, then the reason so many great religions share a common philosophy at their core, is because their founders were responding to the same Reality.

The Axial Age was an amazing event. In the period from 800 to 200 BC, Taoism and Confucianism emerged in China and Hinduism and Buddhism in India. The Hebrew prophets evolved a new vision of monotheism and the Greeks gave birth to the philosophical God which led to rationalism in Europe. Christianity and Islam would come from the Judaic root much later, but they would share the same base vision. Indeed, all of these religions above share a common core perspective known as the *perennial philosophy*. This philosophy sees the world as undergirded by a Oneness (as shown in Table C-1 below). It argues for love, compassion, justice, equality and harmony. It believes that all creation carries a spark of the Divine because the Oneness which permeates everything is part of the creative force which created everything, including human beings.

Most modern people haven't the foggiest idea that the Axial Age existed much less that it was a world-wide phenomenon. We see spirituality through the lens of our own recent history. Thus, when most Western-trained people hear the word 'religion,' they think first of particular doctrines which tend to separate people. Most also assume that the ancient originators of these doctrines were trying to establish some theory about a God 'out there' who may look down, but is not of this world. This, however, is probably *not* what these sages were doing. Rather, this is our own cognitive map talking. If we are ever to rediscover the power of spirituality in a way that fits science, history and our times, we must rethink these kinds of assumptions. In particular,

I think we must return to the ancient concept of the Great Ordering Oneness.

So, let me paint a different picture. Early people were close to nature, embedded in it in ways we can no longer imagine. They often used different characters to represent the forces of nature. Yet, from what we know of similarly well-embedded people today, these different personalities were most likely seen against a backdrop of assumed unity. Thus, we usually attribute the idea that there is one encompassing God (monotheism) to the Jews and follow Christianity from there. Yet, the Oneness part of monotheism is quite old. Old Society spirituality, for instance, was essentially monistic. The Goddess *was* Reality, writ large. What words shall we use? The Life Force, the Mysterium Tremendum, Nature, the Wonder, the Power? Life and fertility were its witness and living close to nature early people felt enveloped in this reality. Even in the Bible, the original meaning of 'spirit' was a divine inspiring animating influence.

This ancient sense of spirituality is still alive today. In the South Seas Islands, for example, people call this mysterious force *mana* and many experience it as a power, like an electricity or radiance. People in many African tribes still worship what is best described as a Oneness with presence and power. Tribespeople believe this Oneness is watching and they yearn for it in nightly prayers. But it has no special cult, and its image is never seen in effigy. Indeed, the tribespeople say the Oneness is ineffable and cannot be described by the words of men. Attempts merely contaminate a deeper wonder.

Whatever words one does use, this sense of an embracing yet indescribable power or presence is basic to religion. As religious historian Karen Armstrong says, "It preceded any desire to explain the origin of the world or find a basis for ethical behavior." It is this indescribable power that the men of the Axial Age sought and, though it is often buried under centuries of interpretations, it is this that lies at the heart of all the world's great religions.

Today, it is possible to see this ineffable force as physically real.[1] Hence, the new science brings with it precisely a new appreciation of the *mysterium tremendum* now in the guise of a profound, pervasive, order-making process. Scientists have different words for it and have new ideas about how it works — but *that* it works is still left sitting there like the unmentioned elephant in the icebox.

This scientific understanding of the Great Ordering Oneness also matches many key spiritual insights. For instance, it is real and physical, but not material. It is omni-present and enveloping. It is powerful and paradoxical — in us, of us and more than us all at the same time. And though it gives us hope and reason to believe, it also sits in judgment. It is possible to go against the direction of this flow, a choice that would presumably lead to dire consequences in this very real world of ours. Finally, as the ancients said repeatedly, words cannot do it justice for each word lies incomplete and misleading, too limited to encompass that which is experienced. In the end, the new science provides but a more physical sense that the Ineffable Creative Force is real.

The perennial philosophy

More than twenty-five centuries have passed since that which has
been called the Perennial Philosophy was first committed to writing;
and in the course of those centuries it has found expression, now
partial, now complete, now in this form now in that, again and again.
In Vedanta and Hebrew prophecy, in the Tao Te Ching and the
Platonic dialogues, in the Gospel according to St John and Mahayana
theology, in Plotinus and the Areopagite, among the Persian Sufis
and the Christian mystics of the Middle Ages and the Renaissance —
the Perennial Philosophy has spoken almost all the languages of Asia
and Europe and has made use of the terminology and traditions of
every one of the higher religions. But under all this confusion of
tongues and myths, of local histories and particularist doctrines, there
remains a Highest Common Factor.

Aldous Huxley

All of the religions mentioned above and many not mentioned too, share the
same base vision of the world. Huxley wrote the above description of the
Perennial Philosophy in 1954, as part of an introduction to the *Bhagavad-
Gita,* one of India's great expressions of this philosophy. The Tao Te Ching,
the Kabalah, the Koran, and Christianity's Gnostic Gospels — Huxley suggests, there are many sources. Beneath the words, it begins to appear that
there was one common perception.

Huxley lists four core principles of the Perennial Philosophy. In the table
opposite, the left shows his description of those principles while the right
gives the Integral science similarity.

Huxley's Core Doctrines	*A New Science Similitude*
The phenomenal world of matter and of individualized consciousness — the world of things and animals and men and even gods — is the manifestation of a Divine Ground within which all partial realities have their being, and apart from which they would be nonexistent.	Integral science suggests that we are part of a single, unified unfolding evolutionary process that gives rise to all levels and types of Being. Individual beings arise and then recede in the ever-moving flow. Individualized consciousness is a temporary manifestation of the larger whole, a Great Ordering Oneness, a Divine Ground.
Man possesses a double nature, a phenomenal ego and an eternal Self, which is the inner man, the spirit, the spark of divinity within the soul.	Dual nature, eternal and ephemeral, can be understood from an evolutionary perspective. Energetically speaking, we are temporary manifestations brought forth in the evolution of a much larger whole. It is the whole field which is evolving. Each little swirl in it rises and subsides as part of a much larger quest.
It is possible for a man, if he so desires, to identify himself with the spirit and therefore with the Divine Ground, which is of the same or like nature with the spirit.	Because the Divine Ground gave rise to us, its essence is spread through every fiber of our being. The spark of divinity is within us. Because that Divine Ground also gave us relative autonomy, however, it is also quite possible to identify with our phenomenal selves and move against the larger flow. Presumably the eventual result would be 'selection,' also called extinction.
Human beings are capable not merely of knowing about the Divine Ground by inference; they can also realize its existence by direct intuition, superior to discursive reasoning. This immediate knowledge unites the knower with that which is known.	The human mind and no less the human body are inseparably interwoven with the greater whole. Furthermore, it seems quite reasonable that listening to the song that runs through our bodies might provide a more sensitive connection than our external five senses. The madmonkey of our intellectual mind is too distracted to be a good conduit of unitive connection.
Man's life on earth has only one end and purpose: to identify himself with his Eternal Self and so to come to unitive knowledge of the Divine Ground.	Identifying with our Eternal Self seems very much like Gebser's idea that, when we truly realize our inseparability from the larger whole, we will come to understand our true purpose and destiny — which appears to be stewardship, forming a Living Mind for the Living World.

Endnotes

Chapter 1

1. Since war was the mainstay of national expansion in these times, safeguarding the state's war-making potential was of great concern. Rulers and their advisors had developed Mercantilism as a theory of how to safeguard the state treasury by closely regulating the nation's economic life. According to the Mercantilists, the world's resources — its land, labor and raw materials — were all elements in a closed, finite system. Hence, if one state's share of resources increased, another's had to decrease. The implication was that each nation should direct its policies both toward guarding its share of the whole and acquiring more wherever possible. As a result states hoarded precious metals, prohibited skilled workers from emigrating, encouraged population growth, and tried to monopolize trade.

Chapter 2

1. From Kepler in 1617 onwards, virtually all mathematical techniques had been *analytic,* which means that they too involve 'breaking things down.' Kepler, for instance, had explained how to calculate the volume of a barrel by breaking the circumference into little triangles and then adding up the areas of these simple shapes. This is the same trick Newton used in calculus: break curves into small pieces and add up. In calculus, this process (called 'finding the limit') helps one find the equation that defines the exact path a body will follow, be it a planet or a bowling ball. This means that 'analysis,' *breaking things down,* is at the heart of classical mathematics as well as classical experiments. It is also why one finds the word 'analysis' cropping up everywhere from economics to anthropology.
2. The result was a type of motion which *could not* be handled by breaking it down into smaller pieces. What Poincaré showed was that the three-body problem could not be approximated by breaking the curve into smaller pieces. Though it is hard for the modern mind to grasp, breaking into simpler pieces didn't work because smaller pieces *were no less simple*!? It would take another seventy years and the arrival of computers, however, to understand what this meant. (It would turn out that the solution was a fractal, described later, but the concept of a fractal hadn't been invented back then.)
3. Chaos' real name is "sensitive dependence on initial conditions." This name makes sense because, in poised dynamic states, very small influences can lead to spectacularly new directions.

4. The term nonlinearity is itself a problem. It creates a harsh dichotomy between linearity and nonlinearity which clouds the real issue which is how interdependent dynamics work. Nonlinear has been used as a label because linear approximations dominated classical science because everything else was too hard to compute. In fact, virtually everything is nonlinear but linear approximations often work well. A simple example is the horizon which often looks like a straight line, but is actually a curve. Hence, as Stanislaw Ulam, put it: "to call the study of chaos, nonlinear science is like calling zoology the study of non-elephant animals."

5. See H.E. Huntley, *The Divine Proportion: A Study in Mathematical Beauty* 1970 (Dover Publications, New York).

6. Technically a fractal is any pattern with a "fractional" dimension, but that definition is a bit much for a book like this. We've seen that a fractal is a pattern that exhibits scaled self-similarity which means that if you keep blowing up pieces of the pattern you will find smaller and smaller versions of the same pattern. Fractals also have a number of bizarre mathematical characteristics. For example, a fractal coastline actually has infinite length but, because all measures are finite, the length an observer will record will depend on the length of the ruler he uses to measure. All of this makes fractals extremely non-traditional and very hard to understand.

7. This example comes from Rogowitz and Voss (1989).

8. Waldrop, *Complexity*, 1992, p.1.

Chapter 3

1. The BZ reaction is generated by a non-living mix of organic and inorganic chemicals ($[BrO3]$, $[HBrO2]$, $[Br]$, and $[2\ Ce4+]$). It is circular (or as chemists call it, "autocatalytic") because one reaction produces a bi-product which reacts to produce other bi-products which re-feed the first reaction. Circular chemical reactions make energy flow faster too.

2. Ascendancy is actually a precise concept based on energy principles. I refer interested readers to Ulanowicz's 1986 book.

3. An embryo starts as a single cell which gets bigger. There is a limit to how big a cell can get, however, because the forces holding it together get stretched. Nature's solution (seen in the embryo) is to divide into two smaller cells which then couple back together. The process then repeats. Each cell grows, reaches its limits, divides and recouples, first two then four, eight, sixteen, and so forth. After each round of dividing, the cells which make up the embryo are smaller which means that the forces holding each together are stronger. Because these smaller cells stay coupled, the embryo can get bigger without falling apart. As the embryo gets bigger still, these cells organize into subsystems, a whole fractal system of small within small. In the process the embryo becomes more intricate while also staying sturdy.

   Cells divide when the ratio of the surface being stretched and the volume being encompassed reach a certain value. The energy rule which leads to this precise break-point is called the surface/volume law. It holds throughout biology. Lungs, guts and blood vessels have all evolved lots of surface-increasing nooks and crannies because more surface means better exchange and flow. As the distinguished biologist, J.B.S. Haldane, once remarked: "comparative anatomy is largely the study of the struggle to increase surface in proportion to volume."

Chapter 4

1. The currently dominant form of Neo-Darwinism is called Synthetic theory. It blends Darwin and genetics. When I use the term 'Darwinian,' I am actually referring to Synthetic Theory. Even this is something of a straw man, however. Many different ideas are sold under the name of Darwinism and some are more likely to survive than others.
2. AMP is a nucleotide of RNA. Manfred Eigen (1981) has shown that under the right conditions nucleotide monomers similar to AMP spontaneously give rise to a nucleic acid polymer molecule.
3. Margulis' book, *Early Life* gives a detailed account of the process summarized here.
4. A summary of recent group selection studies can be found in the December 1994 issue of *Behavioral and Brain Sciences*. Gerald Edelman's 1987 book *Neural Darwinism* provides a summary of the reasoning in terms of brain evolution as well.
5. See Gould & Eldredge (1977) for a discussion of punctuated evolution in biology.
6. Normal human cells contain 46 chromosomes and Down's cells contain a 47th chromosome. The culprit chromosome 21 contains an estimated 700 to 2,000 genes and only some of these, the trisomic genes, are thought to be responsible for Down's. Trisomic genes affect at least four enzymes thought to be relevant in Down's. There are probably more effects but little is currently known about how genes affect enzymes.
7. A phrase from Tennyson which has been used to epitomize the Darwinian world.
8. In this game two prisoners are presented with a payoff scheme in which (1) one wins big if he betrays his colleague but his colleague does *not* betray back, (2) they both lose badly if *both* betray each other, and (3) they both receive a mildly negative outcomes if *neither* betrays the other. Cooperate or be out for oneself alone? Robert Axelrod's 1984 book, *The Evolution of Cooperation* provides an excellent summary of the computer theory.
9. For example, see Chaisson (1987), Fox (1989), Lotka (1922), Morowitz (1968), Odum (1953).
10. The concept of an expanded vision of the second law which encompasses order is too complicated to explain in detail here. I refer you to my earlier book, *Chaos and the Evolving Ecological Universe* for more detailed discussions. I also wish I could say the question of entropy and increasing complexity were completely resolved, but it is not.

Chapter 5

1. The reptilian brain consists of the midbrain and basal ganglia, plus a thin shell of cortex including the hippocampus. It is found in all animals with a brain. It is called the lizard brain because salamanders were the favorite subjects of early researchers trying to study this brain in its most basic form. The paleomammalian brain surrounds this core reptilian brain and is primarily associated with the limbic system (the part of the brain most associated with emotion). It is found from lower mammals up to human beings. The neomammalian brain, found only in higher primates, is the neo-cortex.

2. Paleontology is a rapidly changing field and estimates of the dates of this event vary wildly. I am using a rather mid-range estimate. More recent work puts the split between the *Homo* genus and its nearest relative *Pan*, the genus of chimpanzees, about 8 million years ago during a tectonic shift that left an East/West rift in the African continent with mountains in between.

3. And now championed most strongly by Elaine Morgan, see *The Aquatic Ape* (1982) and *The Scars of Evolution* (1990).

4. Riane Eisler is the most famous proponent of this theory. In her book, *The Chalice and The Blade*, she reports three main waves of barbarian attack, the first about 4300–4200 BC; the second about 3400–3200 BC; and the third about 3000–2800 BC. (1987, p.44).

Chapter 6

1. A special edition of *World Futures* (Vol. 35, November 1992) provides an excellent review of work on these two cultures. The following section is largely based on it.

Chapter 7

1. Large, empire-building industries often show the pattern too. The rise and fall of the American railroad industry in the nineteenth century is an example of this. See Pantzar (1991) for a good description of these railroads and Allen & McGlade (1987) for human habits which cause boom-bust cycles in fisheries.

2. All of the quotes in this section are from Ruth Benedict as cited in Combs, 1994, pp.63-65.

3. This section is based on Jacobs' book *Cities and the Wealth of Nations*, 1984.

4. All quotes in this section are taken from an early draft of William Bainbridge's textbook on the history of sociology. Bainbridge is with the U.S. National Science Foundation in Washington, DC.

5. The cycle is actually a fractal with smaller hundred year ups and downs fitting within larger waves. See Howe, *The Fourth Turning* (1996), for a tour of smaller cycles throughout history.

Chapter 8

1. From *Newsweek,* Aug. 15 1994.
2. In economic lingo, negative feedback is called "diminishing returns."
3. The problems with the GDP have not gone unnoticed. The French parliament, the Australian Treasury, the UN and the European Parliament have all called for new indicators of economic progress.
4. This section and all the quotes in it come from Reich's 1990 book, *The Work of Nations.*
5. It must be acknowledge that it was not *all* Americans, however. Negroes, for example, were still relegated to second-class citizenship and economic exploitation. Similarly, women were advantaged only as long as they were well married.

Chapter 9

1. One of the best known of such experiments is the Mondragon cooperative network in northern Spain. Starting in 1956 as a 23-person workshop for making stoves, by 1986 Mondragon become a network of over one hundred cooperatives and supporting organizations with 19,500 workers. And 'network' is the word. Education, manufacture and banking are all woven together. By the end of the 1970s there were seventy cooperative factories, a cooperative credit bank with 93 branches and 300,000 deposit accounts and an extensive system of basic and technical education. 'Robustness' is also a good word. In the forty years since its beginning 97% of the new cooperatives have survived over five years as opposed to the 20% of new businesses in the U.S. that last that long. And through it all, the Mondragon cooperatives have kept their democratic character. (Statistics from, *Making Mondragon*, W.F. & K.K. Whyte, 1991, Ithaca, NY: ILR Press.)
2. Article by Andrew Marr, then editor of *The Independent* newspaper, Copyright, Newspaper Publishing PLC. The Citizen Organizing Foundations he mentions can be contacted at 535 Manhattan Buildings, London E3 2UP.

Chapter 10

1. Ray's survey was done in America (and thus uses American examples) but the three cultural currents are found in similar proportions throughout the Western world.

Appendix A

1. Philosophers have spent thousands of words arguing about why people experience their society as an omni-present "they" which nevertheless can't be pinned down to any one or more particular individuals. (Society

made me do it!) Somehow 'society' has an effect despite the fact that it is not just a fixed set of people. Water logic helps us see why. Like a whirlpool, social momentum and mutual effect creates pressure which pushes people toward similar patterns of behavior. This pressure is largely a matter or momentum. There is a societal pattern, but it isn't just a fixed set of people.

2. Mathematicians are trying to develop new definitions of randomness and complexity that fit with the new discoveries. The pursuit of such definitions is the realm of *algorithmic complexity* theory. As with other parts of the new science, the discoveries in this area are fascinating and often counter intuitive. For example, there are proofs that a structure may have been generated by a simple rule but one will not be able to prove that fact in any timely sort of way.

Appendix C

1. Perhaps I should say that today it is possible to see *the physical paths by which the Ineffable Force works*. This phrasing side-steps the question of whether the Ineffable is the same as Nature and hence the question of whether a non-physical Transcendent exists. It is not my intent to address either of these questions. My point is simply that the physical understanding of the world is beginning to resemble the transcendent description in many key areas.

Acknowledgments

The author and publishers gratefully acknowledge permission to use the following copyright material: H. Peitgen and P. Richter for Figure 4 (p.100); John Wiley and Sons for Figure 7 (p.107); Michael Barnsley and Academic Press, Inc. for Figure 11 (p.122) and Figure 12 (p.123).

Bibliography

Abraham, R. & Shaw, C. (1982-87). *Dynamics: the Geometry of Behavior.* Vol. 1-4. Santa Cruz: Aerial Press.

—, & Shaw, C. (1987). Dynamics: A Visual Introduction. *In* Yates, F. (Ed.), *Self-Organizing Systems*, 543-97, New York: Plenum Publishing Corporation.

Adams, R.N. (1982). The Emergence of Hierarchical Social Structure: The Case of Late Victorian England. *In* W.C. Schieve and P.M. Allen (Eds.) *Self-Organization and Dissipative Structures: Applications in the Physical and Social Sciences.* Austin: University of Texas Press.

—, (1988). *The Eight Day of Evolution: Social Evolution as the Self-Organization of Energy.* Austin: University of Texas Press.

Allen, P.M. and McGlade, J.M. (1987). Modelling Complex Human Systems: A Fisheries Example. *European Journal of Operational Research* 30: 147-67. Armstrong, K. (1993). *A History of God.* New York: Ballantine Books.

Arthur, W.B. (1990). Positive Feedback in the Economy. *Scientific American*, February 1990, 92-99.

Augros, R. & Stanciu, G. (1988). The *New Biology: Discovering the Wisdom in Nature.* Boston: Shambhala Publications.

Axelrod, Robert. (1984). *The Evolution of Cooperation.* New York: Basic Books.

Baranger, M. (1990). Chaos A Primer. *In* C. Bottcher, M.R. Strayer, & J.B. Mcgrory (Eds.), *Proceedings from the Summer School of Computational Atomic and Nuclear Physics.* Singapore: World Scientific Publishing Co.

Barnsley, M. (1989). *Fractals Everywhere.* San Diego: Academic Press.

Bartley, W.W. (1987). The Philosophy of Biology Versus the Philosophy of Physics. *In* G. Radnitzky and W.W.Bartley, III. (Eds.), *Evolutionary Epistemology, Rationality and the Sociology of Knowledge.* La Salle, IL: Open Court, 7-40.

Basar, E.(Ed.) (1990). *Chaos in Brain Function.* Berlin: Springer-Verlag.

Belbruno, E. (1994). *Discover*, Sept 1994.

Benedict, R. (1941/1996). The Synergy Lectures. *In* Combs, A. (Ed.), *Cooperation: Beyond the Age of Competition.* Philadelphia: Gordon and Breach Science Publishers.

Berry, F.M. (1984). An Introduction To Stephen C. Pepper's Philosophical System Via World Hypotheses: A Study in Evidence. *Bulletin of the Psychonomic Society*, 22(5), 446-48.

Bohm, D. (1980). *Wholeness and the Implicate Order.* New York: Routledge and Kegan Paul Inc.

—, (1990). *On Dialogue.* P.O. Box 1452, Ojal, CA: David Bohm Seminars.

Bower, B. (1995). The Return of the Group. *Science News*, Vol. 148, No. 21, Nov. 18, Washington, DC: Sience Services Inc.

Briggs, J. & Peat, F.D. (1989). *Turbulent Mirror.* New York: Harper and Row.

Brinton, C. (1964). *Civilization in the West*. Englewood Cliffs: Prentice-Hall Inc.

Brooks, D. & Wiley, E. (1988). *Evolution As Entropy*. Chicago: The University of Chicago Press.

Bunyard, P. & Goldsmith, E. (Eds.), (1989). *Gaia and Evolution: Proceedings of the Second Annual Camelford Conference on the Implications of the Gaia Thesis*. Bodmin, UK: Abbey Press.

Burke, J. (1985). *The Day The Universe Changed*. Boston: Little, Brown.

Cairns-Smith, A.G. (1982). *Genetic Takeover and the Mineral Origins of Life*. New York: Cambridge University Press.

Calvin, William H. (1995). The *Ascent of Mind: Ice Age Climates and the Evoution of Intelligence*. New York: Bantam Books.

Carneiro, R. (1967). On the Relationship Between Size of Population and Complexity of Social Structure. *Southwestern Journal of Anthropology*, 23, 234-43.

—, (1970). A Theory of the Origin of the State. *Science*, 169, 733-38.

—, (1987). The Evolution of Complexity in Human Societies and its Mathematical Expression. *International Journal of Comparative Sociology*, 28, 111-28.

Chaisson, E. (1987). The *Life Era*. New York: Atlantic Monthly Press.

Chaitin, G. (1987). *Algorithmic Information Theory*. Cambridge, UK: Cambridge University Press.

Chance, M.R. (1992). Introduction: Socio-Mental Bimodality. *World Futures*, 35(1-3), 1-31.

Cobb, C., Halstead, T. & Rowe, J. (1995). If the GDP is Up, Why is American Down? *Atlantic Monthly*, 276(4), October, p. 51-58.

Combs, Allan. (1996). The *Radiance of Being: Complexity, Chaos and the Evolution of Consciousness*. Edinburgh, UK: Floris Books.

Corry, S. (1989). *Address in London on Receiving the Right Livelihood Award 1989*. London: Survival International.

Crutchfield, J.P., Doyne, F., Packard, N.H., & Shaw, R.S. (1986). Chaos. *Scientific American*, December, 46-57.

Csanyi, V. (1989). *Evolutionary Systems and Society: A General Theory of Life, Mind and Culture*. Durham, NC: Duke University Press.

Cvitanovic, P. (1984). *Introduction To Universality in Chaos*. Bristol, UK: Adam Hilger.

Dawkins, R. (1976). *The Selfish Gene*. New York: Oxford University Press.

—, (1987). The *Blind Watchmake: Why the Evidence of Evolution Revewal A Universe Without Design*. New York: W.W. Norton & Company.

Deneubourg, J.L., Pasteels, J.M. & Verhaeghe, J.C. (1983). Probabilistic Behaviour in Ants: A Strategy of Errors. *Journal of Theoretical Biology*, 105, 259-71.

Dyson, F. (1985). *Origins of Life*. Cambridge: Cambridge University Press.

Edelman, G.M. (1987). *Neural Darwinism: The Theory of Neuronal Group Selection*. New York: Basic Books.

Edelman, G.M. (1992). *Bright Air, Brilliant Fire*. New York: Basic Books.

Eigen, M., & Schuster, P. (1979). The *Hypercycle: A Principle of Natural Self-Organization.* Berlin: Springer-Verlag.

Eisler, R. (1988). *The Chalice and the Blade.* New York: Viking Press.

Ekins, P. (1992). *A New World Order: Grassroots Movements for Global Change.* London: Routledge.

Fox, R. (1988). *Energy and the Evolution of Life.* New York: W.H Freeman.

Freeman, W.J. (1991). The Physiology of Perception. *Scientific American,* Feb. 78-85

—, (1995). *Societies of Brains.* Hillsdale: Lawrence Erlbaum Associates.

Frost, A.J. & Prechter, R.R. (1990). *Elliott Wave Principle.* Gainesville: New Classics Library Inc.

Gay, P. (1966). *The Age of Enlightenment.* New York: Time-Life Books.

Gebser, J. (1949/1986) *The Ever-present Origin.* N. Barstad and A. Mickunas (Trans.). Athens: Ohio University Press.

Gentry, T. & Wakefield, J. (1990), Methods For Measuring Spatial Cognition. Paper presented to the NATO Advanced Study Institute on the Cognitive and Linguistic Aspects of Geographic Space. Reprints available through Cognitive Studies Program, California State University at Stanislaus, Turlock.

Ghyka M. (1977). *The Geometry of Art and Life.* New York: Dover Publications.

Gilder, G. (1996). *Harper's Magazine,* May 1996, 41.

Gleick, J. (1987). *Chaos, Making A New Science.* New York: Viking.

Goerner, S. (1994). *Chaos and the Evolving Ecological Universe.* Newark: Gordon and Breach Science Publishers.

Goertzel, B. (1992). Unpublished Manuscript.

Goodwin, Brian (1994). *How the Leopard changed its Spots: The Evolution of Complexity.* New York: Charles Scribner's and Sons.

Gould, S.J. & Eldredge, N. (1977). Punctuated Equilibria: The Tempo and Mode of Evolution Reconsidered. *Paleobiology,* 3, 115-51.

Haldane, J. (1954). On Being the right Size. *In* Harlow Shapely, S. Rapport, and H. Wright (Eds.), *A Treasury of Science.* New York: Harper & Bros.

Hale, J.R. (1965). *The Renaissance.* New York: Time-Life Books.

Havel, V. (1994) Speech, The New Measure of Man, at Philedelphia Freedom Hall, reprinted in the *New York Times* July 8, 1994.

Helleman R. H. (1984). Self-Generated Chaotic Behavior in Nonlinear Mechanics. *In* P. Cvitanovic (Ed.) *Universality in Chaos.* Bristol, UK: Adam Hilger.

Ho, M.W. & Saunders, P.T. (Eds.), (1984). *Beyond Neodarwinism: An Introduction to the New Evolutionary Paradigm.* London: Academic Press.

Hoyle, F. (1983). *The Intelligent Unvierse.* London: Michael Joseph.

Hubel, D. & Wiesel, T. (1962). Receptive Fields, Binocular Interaction, and Functional Architecture in the Cat's Visual Cortex. *Journal of Physiology,* 160, 106-54.

Huntley, H.E. (1970). *The Divine Proportion: A Study in Mathematical Beauty.* New York: Dover Publications.

Huxley, A. (1954). Introduction. *In* S. Prabhavananda & C. Isherwood (Trans.), *Bhagavad-Gita [The Song of God]* (p. 923). New York: New American Library.

Jacobs, J. (1961 & 1989). *The Death and Life of Great American Cities*. New York: Vintage Books, a Division of Random House.

—, (1969). *The Economy of Cities*. New York: Random House.

—, (1984). *Cities and the Wealth of Nations*. New York: Random House.

Jiayin, M. (1995). *The Chalice and the Blade in Chinese Culture*. Beijing: China Social Sciences Publishing House.

Krugman, P.A. (1996). *The Self-Organizing Economy*. Oxford, UK: Blackwell Publishers.

Kuhn, T. (1972). The *Structure of Scientific Revolutions*. New York: Houghton Mifflin.

Kukalová-Peck, Jarmila. (1995). Cited in 'When Life Exploded,' by J. Madeleine Nash, *Time*, Dec. 4, 67-74.

Laszlo, E. (1987). *Evolution: The Grand Synthesis*. Boston: Shambhala.

Laszlo, E., Artigiani, R., Combs, A., and Csanyi, V. (1996). *Changing Visions: Human Cognitive Maps Past Present and Future*. London: Adamatine Press Limited.

Lawton, B. & Connors, D. (1996). Unpublished Internal Document. The Progress and Freedom Foundation. Washington, DC. Lerner, M. (1996). *The Politics of Meaning*. Reading, MA: Addison Wesley Publishing Company.

Levinton, J. S. (1992). The Big Bang of Animal Evolution. *Scientific American*, November, 84-91.

Levy, Steven. (1992). *Artificial Life: The Quest For A New Creation*. New York: Pantheon Books.

Lewin, R. (1992). *Complexity: Life At the Edge of Chaos*. New York: Macmillan Publishing Company

Lotka, A.J. (1922). Contribution To the Energetics of Evolution. *Proceedings of the National Academy of Science*, 8, 147.

Lovelock, J. (1979). *Gaia: A New Look At Life On Earth*. Oxford, UK: Oxford University Press.

Mandelbrot, B. B. (1982). *The Fractal Geometry of Nature*. New York: W.H. Freeman and Co.

Margulis, L. (1981). *Symbiosis in Cell Evolution*. San Francisco: Freeman and Co.

—, (1982). *Early Life*. Boston: Science Books International.

Maturana, H. & Varela, F. (1987). *The Tree of Knowledge*. Boston: Shambhala.

Mizutani, H., and Wada, E. (1982). Material Cycles and Organic Evolution. *Origins of Life*, 12, 369-376.

Monastersky, R. (1988). The Whole-Earth Syndrome, *Science News*, June 11, 133, 378-80.

Moose, P. (1991). How Long is the Coastline of a Cognitive Map? Paper presented to the Annual Meeting of the Society of Chaos Theory in Psychology, San Francisco.

Morgan, E. (1982). *The Aquatic Ape.*

—, (1990). *The Scars of Evolution.*

—, (1995). The Rise and Fall of the Savannah Theory. *Revision: a Journal of Consciousness and Transformation,* Volume 18, No. 2, Fall 1995.

Morowitz, H.J. (1968). *Energy Flow in Biology: Biological Organization as a Problem in Thermal Physics.* New York: Academic Press.

Murray, C & Herrnstein, R. (1994) *The Bell Curve: Studies in Class and IQ in America.* New York: Free Press.

Nicholis, G. & Prigogine, I. (1989). *Exploring Complexity.* New York: W.H. Freeman & Co.

Oparin, A.I. (1957). *The Origin of Life on the Earth* (3rd Edition translated by Ann Synge). Edinburgh, UK: Oliver and Boyd.

Pantzar, M. (1991). *Economics and Replicative Evolution.* New York: Gordon and Breach.

Pattee, H.H. (1982). Cell Psychology: An Evolutionary Approach to the Symbol-Matter Problem. *Cognition and Brain Theory,* 5(4), 325-41.

Peitgen, H. & Richter, P. (1986). *The Beauty of Fractals.* Berlin: Springer-Verlag.

Pepper, S. (1946). *World Hypotheses: Prolegomena To Systematic Philosophy and A Complete Survey of Metaphysics.* Berkeley: Univ. of California Press.

Peters, E. (1991). *Chaos and Order in the Capitol Market.* New York: John Wiley & Sons.

Pettersson, M. (1978). Acceleration in Evolution, Before Human Times. *Journal of Social and Biological Structures,* 1, 201-206.

Potts, Richard. (1996). *Humanity's Descent.* New York: Morrow Publishers.

Prigogine, I. (1972). Thermodynamics of Evolution. *Physics Today,* December 1972.

—, & Stengers, E. (1984). *Order Out of Chaos.* New York: Bantam Books.

Pring, A. (1997). Credit Where Credit is Due. *Resurgence.* Vol. 4, No. 180, Bodmin, UK.

Putnam, R. (1993). *Making Democracy Work.* Princeton University Press.

Radnitzky, G., & Bartley, W.W.III. (1987). *Evolutionary Epistemology, Rationality and the Sociology of Knowledge.* La Salle, IL: Open Court.

Rapp, P.E. (1986). Oscillations and Chaos in Cellular Metabolism and Physiological Systems. *In* Holden, A.V. (1986) *Chaos.* Princeton: Princeton University Press.

—, (1987). Why Are So Many Biological Systems Periodic? *Progress in Neurobiology,* 29, 261-73.

—, Latta, R.A., & Mees, A.I., (1988). Parameter-Dependent Transitions and the Optimal Control of Dynamical Diseases. *Bulletin of Mathematical Biology,* 50, 227-53.

Ray, P. (1996). The Rise of Integral Culture. *Noetic Sciences Review.* Vol. 37, Spring 1996, Sausalito: The Institute of Noetic Sciences.

Redington, D.J., Reidbord, S.P. (1992). Chaotic Dynamics in Autonomic Nervous System Activity of a Patient during a Psychotherapy Session. *Biological Psychiatry,* 31, 993-1007

Reich, Robert. (1991). *The Work of Nations*. New York: Vintage Books.

Rogowitz, B.E., Voss, R. F. (1990). Shape Perception and Low-Dimension Fractal Boundary Contours. *In* Rogowitz, B.E., and J. Allebach (Eds.), *The Proceedings of the Conference on Human Vision: Nethods, Models, and Applications, SPIE/SPSE Symposium on Electronic Imaging*, 1249, Santa Clara, CA. (Or Contact: Rogowitz & Voss, IBM T.J.Watson Research Center, Yorktown Heights, New York, 10598)

Rucker, R. (1987). *Mind Tools: The Five Levels of Mathematical Reality*. Boston: Houghton Mifflin.

Sabelli, H.C., Carlson-Sabelli, L., Patel, M., Messert, J., and Walthall, K. (1994). Psychological Portraits and Psychocardiological Patterns in Phase Space. *In* Gilgen, A. and Abraham, F. (Eds.), *Chaos Theory in Psychology*. New York: Greenwood Publishers.

Sahtouris, E. (1989) The Gaia Controversy: The Case For A Living Earth. *In* Bunyard & Goldsmith (Eds.). *Gaia and Evolution*. (1989).

Schroeder, M. (1991). *Fractals, Chaos, Power Laws Minutes from an Infinite Paradise*. New York: W.H. Freeman and Company.

Schrodinger, E. (1944). *What Is Life?* The Physical Aspect of the Living Cell. Cambridge University Press.

Schuster, H. (1984). *Deterministic Chaos*. Weinheim: Physik-Verlag.

Simon, E. (1970). *The Reformation*. New York: Time-Life Books.

Skarda, C.A. & Freeman, W.J. (1987). How Brains Make Chaos in Order To Make Sense of the World. *Behavioral and Brain Sciences*, 10, 172.

—, & Freeman, W.J. (1989). Chaos and the New Science of the Brain. *Concepts in Neuroscience*, 1(2), 282.

Sorotkin, Pitirim A. (1937). *Social and Cultural Dynamics*. (4 vols.) New York: American Book Company.

Spencer, H. (1862). *First Principles*. London: Williams and Norgate.

Stewart, I. (1989). *Does God Play Dice? The Mathematics of Chaos*. New York: Basil Blackwell.

Swenson, R. (1988). Emergence and the Principle of Maximum Entropy Production: Multi-Level Systems Theory, Evolution and Nonequilibrium Thermodynamics. *Proceedings of the 32rd Annual Meeting of the International Society for the Systems Sciences*, St. Louis, MO, May, 1988, 32-43.

—, (1989a). Emergent Attractors and the Law of Maximum Entropy Production: Foundations To A Theory of General Evolution. *Systems Research*, 6(3), 187-97.

—, (1989b). Emergent Evolution and the Global Attractor: The Evolutionary Epistemology of Entropy Production. *Proceedings of the 33rd Annual Meeting of the International Society for the Systems Sciences*, 3, 46-53.

—, (1989c). The Earth As An Incommensurate Field At the Geo-Cosmic Interface: Fundamentals To A Theory of Emergent Evolution. *In* G.J.M. Tomassen, W. De Graff, A.A. Knoop, R. Hengeveld (Eds.), *Geo-Cosmic Relations: The Earth and Its Macro-Environment*. Wageningen, The Netherlands: PUDOC Science Publishers, 299-306.

—, (1989d). Engineering Initial Conditions in a Self-Producing Environment. *Proceedings of IEEE and SSIT Conference*, Oct. 20-21, 1989, California State University, Los Angeles.

Thompson, J. & Stewart, H. (1986). *Nonlinear Dynamics and Chaos*. New York: John Wiley and Sons.

Tierney, B. & Painter, S. (1983). *Western Europe in the Middle Ages: 1300-1475*. New York: Alfred A. Knopf.

Tuchman, B. (1978). *A Distant Mirror: The Calamitous 14th Century*. New York: Alfred A. Knopf.

Turkel, H. (1985). *Medical Treatment of Down Syndrome* and *Genetic Diseases*. Southfield, Michigan: UBIOTICA.

Ulanowicz, R. (1986). *Growth and Development: Ecosystems Phenomenology*. Berlin: Springer-Verlag.

Von Bertalanffy, L. (1968). *General Systems Theory*. New York: George Braziller.

Waldrop, M. M. (1992). *Complexity: The Emerging Science at the Edge of Order and Chaos*. New York: Simon and Schuster.

Weaver, W. (1958). Annual Report of the Rockefeller Foundation. Cited in Jacobs, 1989, *Death and Life of the Great American Cities*.

Weber, B., & Depew, D. (1985). *Evolution at a Crossroads: The New Biology and the New Philosophy of Science*. Cambridge, MA: MIT Press.

Wicken, J. (1987). *Evolution, Thermodynamics, and Information: Extending the Darwinian Program*. Oxford, UK: Oxford University Press.

Wilson, E.O. (1980). *Sociobiology*. Cambridge, Massachusetts: The Belknap Press of Harvard University Press.

Yoffee, N. and Cowgill, G.L. (1988). *The Collapse of Ancient States and Civilizations*. Tuscon: The University of Arizona Press.

Index